Gender & Sexuality

Gender & Sexuality

CRITICAL THEORIES, CRITICAL THINKERS

Chris Beasley

 SAGE Publications

London ● Thousand Oaks ● New Delhi

First published 2005

Reprinted 2006

SAGE Publications Ltd
1 Oliver's Yard
55 City Road
London EC1Y 1SP

SAGE Publications Inc.
2455 Teller Road
Thousand Oaks, California 91320

SAGE Publications India Pvt Ltd
B-42, Panchsheel Enclave
Post Box 4109
New Delhi 110 017

British Library Cataloguing in Publication data

A catalogue record for this book is available
from the British Library

ISBN 0 7619 6978 0
ISBN 0 7619 6979 9 (pbk)

Library of Congress Control Number: 2004099439

Typeset by C&M Digitals (P) Ltd., Chennai, India
Printed on paper from sustainable resources
Printed in Great Britain by TJ International Ltd, Padstow, Cornwall

To my colleagues in trying times, Carol Bacchi, Heather Brook, Jean Duruz, Carol Johnson, David Hollinsworth and Doug McEachern; to Peter Hall for his immensely generous provision of childcare and design input; and to my darling girl, Perry.

In memory of Paul Thewlis and James Falkenberg Thewlis. We remember you with love and laughter.

Contents

Introduction

What is this book about? What does it cover or do?

This book focuses on sex and power. In other words, it is about exploring and questioning every aspect of the organisation of our social life – from a kiss to the framing of states and international relations.[1] More specifically, this book is about the ways in which contemporary thinkers have understood the dynamics of power in current social arrangements regarding sex. In order to consider thinkers who attend to the socio-political analysis of sex, their field of analysis must be briefly clarified. What does the terrain of this field include? The term 'sex', throughout much of English-speaking history has covered both

- *sexed* regimes, identities and practices – which typically involve binary and hierarchical categories such as men and women, usually associated with an account of biology and reproductive function – as well as
- *sexual* regimes, identities and practices, which also commonly involve binary and hierarchical categories such as heterosexual and homosexual, usually linked to conceptions of biology and reproduction. (Edwards, 1989: 1–12)

Since this book is about critical theories dealing with sex – with sexed and/or sexual – you might expect that this would be the term of choice for the title. The word 'sex' is certainly still used in everyday language to refer to one's sexed identity (one's 'sex') as well as to the sexual. However, for the most part, its meaning within scholarship on the political construction of identities and self/other relations has increasingly narrowed. Sex has become more strictly a reference to sexual activity (Abelove et al., 1993: xv–xvi) or a language for the biological, for the material body.[2] Because of these developments in academic debate, it is now rarely used as a blanket term for the sexed and sexual. For this reason I have employed instead the most common shorthand terms currently used in scholarly analyses for sexed and sexual – that is, gender and sexuality respectively. These terms are employed in the three major subfields of Feminist, Masculinity and Sexuality Studies (Figure I.1).

Although (as I shall indicate in Chapter 1) use of the terms gender and sexuality may be the subject of some dispute, the content of this book can best be summarised as an analytical overview of contemporary critical socio-political theories and thinkers concerned with gender and/or sexuality. My concern is to provide a reasonably comprehensive account of theoretical directions in the ever-expanding field of gender/sexuality,

Figure I.1   The gender/sexuality field and subfields

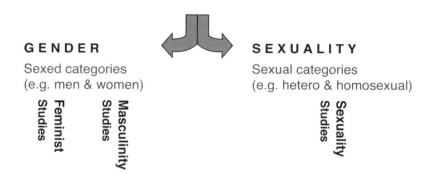

Sex and Power

GENDER

Sexed categories
(e.g. men & women)

Feminist
Studies

Masculinity
Studies

SEXUALITY

Sexual categories
(e.g. hetero & homosexual)

Sexuality
Studies

to offer a 'compendium' that is both accessible and not too lengthy. These somewhat competing aims mean that the book is focused in particular ways.

First, the theories and theorists I discuss foreground discussions concerning gender and/or sexuality, though a number of them see these terms as constructed through and within other relations of power such as class, 'race'/ethnicity or imperialism/colonialism. Secondly, because the scope of the book is already large, I have chosen to limit the content to critical theories and thinkers circulating in the English-speaking world. These theories and thinkers may nevertheless draw upon wide-ranging sources – for example, upon the work of continental European or Third World writers or hybrid perspectives that defy distinctions between English-speaking and non-English-speaking. Thirdly, the theories and thinkers covered are *critical* in two senses. They operate from a critical stance in which the organisation of sex (gender/sexuality) is not taken as given but seen as potentially problematic and associated with power,[3] and these theories/thinkers are also deemed to be critical in the sense of being influential. Fourthly, given my interest in keeping the book to a manageable length, I have been required to limit the number of major theories mentioned and to focus in more detail on a smaller number of writers whose works are taken as indicative of significant directions in these frameworks. The book attempts to balance comprehensive coverage (the demands of a compendium or survey overview) against the provision of analytical depth and contextual specificity by combining schematic discussion of theoretical frameworks with a closer reading of particular writers dealing with particular issues. There are of course methodological questions that can be raised regarding this mode of presentation, which I shall consider shortly.

The intention is to provide an *analytical overview* of critical frameworks in the field. I stress the analytical or constitutive nature of the enterprise here because, as you might expect, a book covering the sizeable field of gender/sexuality theory cannot be merely descriptive. Frameworks in this field deal with complex matters which are of intense interest to us all, are often sensitive, and may be passionately interpreted in sharply different ways. The project of providing an overview of such a fraught terrain therefore requires the development of an interrogatory approach regarding the nature of field and how to present it. I noted in an earlier book on Feminism that overview texts written in an environment of lively dispute demand both *argument* and *survey* (Beasley, 1999: xvi). This point is perhaps even more appropriate here, where the 'field' itself is not as self-evident, necessitates some explanation and is certainly a looser assemblage.

The analytical demands of an overview of the field of gender/sexuality theory are compounded by the fact that it is difficult to find texts that actually attend to the full range of major subfields of gender/sexuality theory – that is, Feminist, Masculinity, and Sexuality Studies. While theorising drawn from the gender/sexuality field is frequently deemed to be at the 'cutting edge' of contemporary social and political thought, publications about theory in this field are generally Feminist in focus and, more specifically, continue to be largely concerned with the position of women. Moreover, accounts that consider theoretical and practical interconnections between all of the main subfields within gender/sexuality theory remain undeveloped, despite the likelihood of these interconnections. In short, most publications concerned with theory in the gender/sexuality field explore only one of the subfields, while a smaller number refer perhaps to two but usually fleetingly. It is especially hard to find generalist[4] (rather than discipline-based) explanatory overview texts which offer even passing attention to two, let alone three, of the major subfields of Feminist, Sexuality and Masculinity Studies.[5] The effect is to place both the writer and readers of this book in the challenging position of negotiating and interpreting the landscape of the field in the absence of a ready-made and well-established view on the subject. Indeed, I would go so far as to say that, at the time of publication, the project of this book remains unique. Certainly, exploring and analysing gender/sexuality theory as a field remains a work in progress rather than a matter of reconsidering well-trodden ground.

Rationale for the book: why write or read it?

This book provides an explanatory overview of a highly significant field of thought. It is significant because it deals with thinking about two crucial elements in all areas of human life, sex and power. The book focuses upon the field of critical socio-political analysis of sex (gender/sexuality). This interdisciplinary field of gender/sexuality theory assumes that sex is ineluctably a matter of human organisation – that is, it is political, associated with social dominance and subordination, as well as capable of change. Theoretical frameworks and writers in this field are concerned with how power is constituted and perpetuated in the formation of sexed and sexual differences. Such theories and thinkers hence also offer a revaluation of 'mainstream' knowledges, which, by contrast, almost invariably marginalise the significance of sex in social relations while taking it for granted. Gender/sexuality in this setting is shorthand for the *politics* of gender/sexuality, and theories/thinkers in the gender/sexuality field are understood as engaged in theorising about this politics.

My central concern in writing this book is to enable readers who are interested in questions of sex and power to access a text attending to gender as well as to sexuality, and which outlines the range of main 'clusters' or subfields in this field – that is, Feminist, Sexuality and Masculinity Studies. Rather than offering a specialist focus on only one aspect of these questions or one subfield, my intention is to present in a condensed fashion the immense vitality and range of theoretical approaches in this arena in a deliberate attempt to work against insularity. It seems to me that there are considerable advantages in gaining a sense of the possible interconnections or even overlaps between theorising about gender and sexuality and their associated subfields, as well as a sense of their points of divergence. Hence, I endeavour to provide, within the evident limits of a single text, a comprehensive overview that takes as its starting point the notion of gender/sexuality theory as a field.

This field, I suggest, is marked by some recognisable elements (such as, a particular subject matter, a critical and change-oriented positioning). However, it must also be recognised that the field is neither self-evident nor accepted in any straightforward sense by all of the writers I have chosen to represent it. Some brief examples may illustrate the debate that arises in relation to my account. For instance, it was common for Feminist theorists in the 1960s and 1970s to argue or presume that sexual politics did indeed constitute a recognisable subject or field. Gender hierarchy (marked by systemic male privilege) was inextricably linked in these analyses to the organisation of sexuality and heteronormativity (systemic heterosexual privilege) such that it typically appeared that one followed from the other.[6] Michel Foucault, a writer who has strongly influenced the field of gender/sexuality theorising, uses the terms 'sex' and 'technologies' of power in ways that also make connections between gender and sexuality (Foucault, 1978: 141, 153). Micaela di Leonardo and Roger Lancaster, editors of *The Gender/Sexuality Reader* (1997), describe a broad field under the rubric of 'sexual embodiment' which attends to critical analyses of 'gender and sexual relations'. Furthermore, it can be argued that the vast majority of gender theorists (in Feminist and Masculinity Studies) continue to perceive gender and sexuality as strongly linked, historically if not intrinsically (Jackson, 1998b; Nielsen et al., 2000). On the other hand, some writers, most often though not exclusively those located in Sexuality Studies, are much more wary of this presumption. Queer theorists, in particular, dismiss any assertions that gender and sexuality are inevitably joined, and tend to ignore or reject gender (Martin, 1996; Hausman, 2001).

These disputes indicate that the gender/sexuality field is by no means a foregone conclusion. Indeed, Diane Richardson (2001) has suggested that the relationship between gender and sexuality has been theorised in at least five different ways, ranging from views that subsume one to the other or do not regard them as distinguishable, through to those that consider them as analytically separate.[7] All the same, I suggest that there are several important reasons for claiming it as a field *in process*. This province of theorising can be discovered in the continuing linkages which many writers, including those mentioned above, make between gender and sexuality. For example, Queer theorists – who dispute any *intrinsic* connection between the two terms – do so in the context of social practices that simply assume that normative gender and sexual categories naturally go together 'like a horse and carriage' to produce heterosexuals attracted to the 'opposite' gender. In the process of undertaking a critique of notions of an inevitable or ontological connection between the terms,

Queer Theory constantly invokes references to gender as well as sexuality. An example of this continuing interplay arises in Stephen Whittle's lively refutation of gender in 'Gender fucking or fucking gender?' which is found in a book entitled *Blending Genders* (Ekins and King, 1996).

The strong linkages between gender and sexuality, at least in existing social practices, are acknowledged even in approaches that develop an alternative politics based upon a disavowal of their intrinsic connection. However, such linkages do not exhaust their many interconnections. For example, Hausman (2001) argues that while transsexual/transgender issues are now often discussed in the terms of Queer Theory, these issues are also focal points of theorising within Gender Studies. Califia (1997: 245–80) notes that within Sexuality Studies many commentators on transsexuality, in particular, strongly reject Queer arguments on the issue of abandoning gender. Some writers attending to transgender issues in Masculinity Studies echo the point (see Halberstam, 1998). Moreover, Feminist and Masculinity scholars regularly draw upon the insights of Sexuality writers, including Queer theorists, in questioning heteronormativity.[8] More tellingly, certain schools of thought simply do not distinguish between gender and sexuality. Psychoanalytic theorists and those influenced by French theory often use the terms 'sexuality' or 'sex' to encompass what others would term 'gender' (Jackson, 1998b: 132). It would seem that the intimate and complex connections between gender and sexuality theorising are longstanding, productive – even in moments of disavowal – and materially sustained by ongoing conversations between and within the three subfields of Feminist, Sexuality and Masculinity Studies.

Finally, gender/sexuality theory may be deemed a field in process by examination of institutional forms such as tertiary teaching programmes. After researching these programmes in the United Kingdom, New Zealand, Canada, the United States and Australia, it is evident to me that gender and sexuality are almost invariably, albeit unevenly, linked. Departments or centres that focus on critical analyses of gender or sexuality offer some attention to both. Because these departments or centres mostly grew out of and indeed remain dominated by Feminist work and, in particular, theorising about women, they generally offer analyses which may be described as under the rubric of 'gender' but retain, and have thankfully often expanded upon, a longstanding tendency to attend to sexuality. Teaching programmes centrally focused on Masculinity under the rubric of Gender Studies also pay increasing attention to sexuality, while Sexuality Studies programmes discuss writers who, at the very least, debate gender matters. In this climate it would amount to a dismemberment of existing theoretical linkages and a significantly narrowed, more exclusionary political 'conversation' if Feminist, Sexuality or Masculinity Studies were *entirely* disengaged from one another. This compendium is intended to address their present engagement, as well as points of conflict between them.

Methodological approach and organisation[9]

The aim is to provide a comprehensive, yet concise and lively explanatory guide to the whole field of gender/sexuality theory through an analytical survey. The method I employ in undertaking this analysis involves using both the notion of a continuum along a theoretical range and a notion of major directions/trajectories. The account of a theoretical continuum and of significant directions is contextualised by reference to specific approaches, thinkers and debates. Sometimes this will involve a closer focus on individual texts and/or particular issues. I am guided in developing such a format by the twin demands of accessibility and a concern to enable readers to make their own judgements. Like Steven Seidman (1993: 135–7; 1998: 11), I consider that writings on gender/sexuality can contribute to scholarly and public intellectual life. Moreover, I share with Patrice McDermott (1998) an optimistic view of the potential of texts like this one, a view that conceives such texts as dynamic products which translate the tensions of theorising alternative social perspectives and which, far from settling issues, can enable broader collective reflection and debate. On these grounds I have employed a methodological approach and organisational structure that is strongly shaped by a concern not simply to inform but, more importantly, to assist you the reader in weighing up and assessing different directions in the gender/ sexuality field. I examine the critical agendas of theories and thinkers with the object of providing space for *your* critical reflections. For this reason I deliberately adopt an open-ended style, rather than an overly judgmental or directive mode which suggests prescribing what you should think. I will now briefly outline the three main methodological tools used in the book – that is, a continuum, major directions, and an interrogatory accessible style.

I employ the methodological device of a notion of continuum within gender/ sexuality theory, ranging from strongly Modernist to strongly Postmodern thinking, as a means of distinguishing between and yet simultaneously underlining connective relationships between different theoretical directions. The continuum is employed as a continuing theme, which provides a means of mapping out the terrain of this field. The usage of a continuum from Modernist to Postmodern approaches is similar to what many writers do when they signal major theoretical divides within large fields of thought.[10] My intention in using the notion of a continuum is similarly to distinguish large frames of reference, but hopefully to avoid or displace the sense that these broad distinguishing frames are necessarily neatly separated. The continuum also enables readers to perceive the ways in which the Feminist, Masculinity and Sexuality subfields draw upon a broadly similar terrain with similar main directions. In other words, it enables the depiction of an overview map of gender/sexuality theory upon which each subfield can be overlaid rather in the manner of three related colour transparencies.

In this book I have combined the continuum format with an account of major directions/trajectories which can be found in the three subfields, as well as giving some attention to more specific approaches and key authors/key texts. I outline five main directions that focus respectively on (1) The Human, (2) (Singular) Difference, (3) (Multiple) Differences, (4) Relational Social Power, and (5) Fluidity/Instability. These directions range from the firmly Modernist to the strongly Postmodern, and some include within them approaches that work across the border of the continuum. At the beginning of the sections of the book dealing with Feminist, Sexuality and Masculinity Studies, I indicate how approaches within the subfields take up these directions. In order to avoid overly repetitive analysis, I will not cover all of the possible five directions in each subfield, though I usually cover most of them. In order to flesh out the meaning of these directions and to indicate the unique detail of different points of view, specific approaches, authors, issues and texts will be examined and debated. This 'directions' methodology refuses any account of the field as a singular unity or as a set of incommensurable types of framework between which one must decide (see Young, 1997a: 17).

Relatedly, I have undertaken this analytical overview of gender/sexuality theory with an eye to examining *debates* between subfields, theories and theorists rather than merely describing different perspectives. Such debates show very clearly that there is no single answer or point of view available in the overall field. Given this complexity, it is all the more important that an overview of the field be presented in an accessible fashion. For this reason I have employed language intended to be understandable to those who are unfamiliar with the field as well as to specialists. I have also adopted an 'incremental' mode, such that complex approaches, concepts and labels are not introduced at only one point in the book. While the 'one-stop shop' method can provide a thoroughgoing account on the first occasion new elements are mentioned, this method tends to lead to the presentation of often overwhelming lumps of information. By contrast, the incremental mode builds up successive layers of analysis in order to make the information more digestible and context-specific. This means, for example, that a term like 'Postmodernism' may be discussed in many different places and contexts in the book, adding levels of complexity along the way. Those who also wish to access condensed definitions may turn to the Glossary and/or check the Index to find a shortcut to the several usages of names/terms. Glossary terms appear in bold the first time they appear in the main chapters.

The book attempts to balance and combine an emphasis upon interrogation of multiple perspectives with a focus on providing an informative, systematic and relatedly accessible overview. My aim is to draw attention to the usefulness of developing and maintaining a critical unease towards rather than a ready acceptance of all views, including my own characterisation of the field.

Conclusion

The content, rationale and methodology of this book, far from advancing a final answer, necessarily offer a selective window into the field of gender/sexuality theory. It is intended to be a window that enables a wide variety of perspectives to be visible and which does not preclude other windows. In *The Use of Pleasure*, Michel Foucault (1990: 8) comments that 'there are times in life when the question of knowing if one can think ... and perceive differently ... is absolutely necessary'. For me the field of gender/sexuality offers precisely the opportunity to think differently. I hope that this compendium conveys at least something of its vitality to you.

Notes

1. See Tickner (2001) on gender and international politics and Johnson (2000) on gendered and heteronormative features of national government leadership and policy.

2. Sex in this usage represents a distinction between nature and society, which may be taken as largely self-evident, or more commonly as indicating the site of boundaries of cultural

malleability, and/or a significant social distinction which some would argue should be displaced. See Stoller, 1968; Oakley, 1972; Keller, 1989; Phillips, 1992; Butler, 1990; Gatens, 1991; Andermahr et al., 2000.

3. My use of 'critical' is rather like that outlined by Evan Willis. He argues that the discipline of Sociology is characterised by a critical sensibility, but in this context the term 'critical' is 'used somewhat differently from its common meaning of being negative'. Rather the term is used to mean 'being reflexive or sceptical about the social world, and … being engaged in a critique of the existing social world' (Willis, 2004: 105).

4. While this book is generalist rather than discipline-based, it does not of course float free of knowledge typologies. The book reflects my training and interests in the Humanities and Social Sciences. My academic background consists of an undergraduate degree almost entirely devoted to Humanities subjects (English, Drama) and postgraduate studies largely within the Social Sciences, with some emphasis on Cultural Studies. I have taught in the disciplinary and interdisciplinary areas of Philosophy, Sociology, Politics, History, Aboriginal Studies, Women's Studies, Political Economy, Cultural/Media Studies and Education. While all writers have disciplinary/interdisciplinary limits, my research training and employment experience have been relatively broad. I suspect this breadth fuels my desire to write in ways that 'speak' across knowledge boundaries. Within the Humanities and Social Sciences I have taught gender/sexuality theory and politics/policy largely in relation to women for well over a decade, and in the last five years have focused more specifically on research and teaching in the area of Masculinity/Men's Studies.

5. *Genders*, by Kaplan and Glover (1998) is one of the few overview texts that attend to all three subfields, in this case within the disciplinary boundaries of the area of literary and cultural theory.

6. See the work of Adrienne Rich and Catherine MacKinnon in Chapter 4. See also Rich, 1980b; and MacKinnon, 1982.

7. Richardson (2001: 5491–3) describes five competing perspectives which variously depict gender as subsuming sexuality, sexuality as subsuming gender, their inherent co-dependence, the complex character of their interplay, and their analytical separation, citing the work of Stevi Jackson, Catherine MacKinnon, Tamsin Wilton, Judith Butler and Gayle Rubin respectively. See also Jackson, 1996a; MacKinnon, 1982; Wilton, 1996: 5491–3; Butler, 1997a; Rubin, 1984.

8. See Segal (1999) and Connell (2002) for examples of interplay between Gender and Sexuality theorising. For an account of 'heteronormativity', see Warner (1993b: xxi–xxv).

9. For a more detailed discussion of debates about methodology relevant to this book and, specifically, debates about the form of overview texts, see Appendix: Methodological Issues.

10. For instance, Karen Offen and Elizabeth Grosz have distinguished two major groupings or strands within the field of Feminist Studies. Offen (1988: 134–6) distinguished between 'relational' and 'individualist' feminisms, while Grosz (1988: 92–104) referred to 'equality' and 'difference' feminisms.

PART 1

Gender/Feminist Studies

1

Gender and Feminism: an Overview

In this chapter I initially discuss the term 'gender' in order to place Feminism as a subfield within the overall gender/sexuality field. This discussion also introduces some ongoing themes within that overall field which will be reiterated within the sections on Sexuality and Masculinity Studies. I then turn to an analysis of the first subfield, namely Feminism. Feminism is considered both in specific terms and also as a means to exemplify the methodological approach employed throughout the book. The analysis indicates in a preliminary way some of the features of the three subfields, as well as how I intend to characterise them. In particular, I undertake an account of Feminism that demonstrates how I will delineate the main directions in the gender/sexuality field.

Gender: the meaning of the term

Feminism is one of two subfields (along with Masculinity Studies) that arguably can be situated under the umbrella term 'gender'. For this reason, before we can examine Feminism, some brief account of this term is necessary. 'Gender' typically refers to the social process of dividing up people and social practices along the lines of *sexed identities*. The gendering process frequently involves creating hierarchies between the divisions it enacts. One or more categories of sexed identity are privileged or devalued. In modern Western societies[1] gender divides into two. This is not necessarily the case in other times, places and cultures (see Herdt, 1994). Gender in the modern West usually refers to two distinct and separate categories of human beings (the division into men and women) as well as to the division of social practices into two fields. The gendering of social practices may be found, for example in contemporary Western societies, in a strong association between men and public life and between women and domestic life, even though men and women occupy both spaces.

Gender in Western society refers to a **binary** division (into two categories) of human beings and social practices to the point of this division even being construed as oppositional. We see this at work in the phrase 'the opposite sex'. The two categories are not merely regarded as distinct and opposed, they are also put into a hierarchy in which one is typically cast as positive and the other negative. Cranny-Francis et al. (2003: 2) note in this setting that 'a buddy (a word derived from brother) is a good thing to have, but no one wants to be a sissy (derived from sister)'. Similarly, positive masculine categories such as 'bachelor' may be set against negative feminine equivalents like 'spinster'. While such categorical distinctions insistently divide, they also indicate connections. The binary nature of gender in Western society means that the features of one category exist in relation to its supposed opposite. To be a man is to be not-woman and vice versa.

Although the account I have provided so far indicates the usual contemporary meanings of gender in Feminist and Masculinity Studies, these meanings have altered over time and continue to be the subject of debate. Prior to the 1960s it was restricted 'primarily to what is coded in language as masculine or feminine' (Richardson, 2001: 5491–3). Many writers today describe gender comparatively narrowly in terms of social identities (men and women) (see Cranny-Francis, 2003: 1–4), while other commentators see it more in terms of social interactions and institutions that form between groups. The latter approach, which rather than locating gender *in* identities, conceives it as a structuring process, may be seen in Bob Connell's notion of 'gender relations' (Connell, 2002: 9; 2000: 23). Different understandings of the term are obviously evident in accounts of what it describes. In recent times it has, for example, been variously extended to denote personality attributes associated with men and women, social constructions broadly linked to the male/female distinction, the existence of social groups (men and women) produced in hierarchical relationship to one another, and social practices enacted through reiteration rather than derived from any natural distinction (Richardson, 2001: 14018). Although gender is commonly linked to social interpretation of reproductive biological distinctions, some analysts reject any suggestion that it is necessarily connected to notions of reproduction.[2] Attitudes towards gender and social change differ as well. Some writers advocate getting rid of gender and gender categories (Lorber, 2000: 1; Whittle, 1996), while others see such categories at the moment at least as a political starting point and indeed suggest that the premature abandonment of marginal group identities like 'women' may produce political paralysis (Young, 1997a; Bordo, 1990: 33–156).

However gender is understood or regarded by critical thinkers in the gender/sexuality field, in practice it covers or refers to two major subfields – that is, Feminist and Masculinity Studies. While Feminist studies talks largely about women, and Masculinity Studies largely about men, both increasingly discuss both. These subfields tend to focus on only two sexes,[3] but recently have begun to allow for more plural sexed identities. To the extent that gender encompasses these subfields, debates about the term itself reveal much about tensions in and between these subfields and provide signals regarding the current shape of the gender/sexuality field as a whole. Such debates about the term therefore offer a useful entry point to introduce the broader field and the discussion of the subfield, Feminism, which follows.

Debates about gender

Debate 1

The term 'gender' is now the dominant coverall one for analysis of sexed identities and practices – that is, for discussing social relations within and between groups identified as men and women (Kemp and Squires, 1997: 11). This dominance is comparatively recent; the shift from focusing on particular identities, such as occurs in Women's Studies, to a focus on Gender Studies has been disputed by many feminists on the grounds that this involves conveniently moving attention away from women's subordination. Such commentators suggest that the supposedly more neutral language of gender might well involve the imposition of a politically suspect agenda (Libertin, 1987; Evans, 1990: 457–62; Richardson and Robinson, 1994: 11–27; Serematakis, 1994). Gender is here associated with attempts to excise the radical critique of Women's Studies and with prescriptive demands that Women's Studies must be accompanied by a matched emphasis on men (Canaan and Griffen, 1990). By contrast, other writers have suggested that this scepticism is unwarranted. In this context, some note that analysis of gender still largely means a focus upon women, even though it should not (Carver, 1996).

It would seem that the term 'gender' as the 'proper' name for a combined field including Feminist and Masculinity agendas may be deemed problematic on several fronts.[4] While Masculinity Studies writers are generally more accepting of the terminology, they too often appear concerned about the potential for retreating from a focus on **power** relations between men and women. Moreover, some gay male writers are not convinced that their issues can be adequately addressed under the broad mantle of Gender Studies (Messner, 1997: 80–8; Brod, 1987a: 179–96; Dowsett, 1993; Clark, 1995: 241–55). Indeed a number of writers attending to sexuality see the term as not merely describing a particular socio-historical process of binary division into two sexed categories, but as *prescribing* such a division (Bornstein, 1994: 8, 114–15).

Ironically, it would seem that gender is disputed both on the grounds that it is associated with the diminution of a focus on particular sexed identities (such as 'women') and with the shoring up of such identities. Still others view gender's concern with sexed identities as precisely the means to undo these identities (Lorber, 2000). What this debate signals is an ongoing discussion central to the entire field of gender/sexuality theory regarding the question of whether focus on particular identity groups is politically helpful or harmful.[5] Discussion about the status of identity politics arises not only in Feminist but also in Sexuality and Masculinity Studies. Identity politics is also a question that highlights very clearly the array of different directions and frames of reference in the gender/sexuality field along a **Modernist–Postmodern** continuum. Indeed, the significance of this question and the way in which it reveals the diversity of thinking in the field is a crucial reason for my usage of the continuum in mapping out field characteristics.

Debate 2

The term 'gender' has also been criticised on the basis that it sets up too sharp a divide between social and natural/bodily. Gender has been used to indicate that nature (bodies) do not necessarily tell you much about human social organisation of sexed identities and practices. In short, a male body does not necessarily result in social masculinity, in a personal identity deemed 'masculine'. Gender in this setting was seen as a reference to 'social construction'. The word implied a radical critique of conservative views that asserted biological determinism. Gender, in other words, suggested a critique of the wide range of views that assumed that bodily 'sex' determines the self and that biological sex difference explains human social arrangements. Gender was a term that enabled a questioning of biologistic presumptions, such as that male bodies are naturally more aggressive, women are less mathematical thinkers, and so on.[6]

However, other thinkers asserted that setting up gender against (bodily) sex in this way recreates a Western tradition of presuming a sharp distinction between social/cultural and biological/natural distinction that cannot be upheld (Scott, 1999: 70–3; Moi, 2001; Young, 2002). This distinction is perceived as ignoring interactions between society and biology, and/or ignoring (bodily) 'sex' *per se* – as if 'the biological' were merely brute inert matter. Yet there is considerable evidence to indicate that notions of biology do change over time. Julia Epstein has noted, for example, that hermaphrodites were once seen as springing from the devil (Epstein, 1990). On this basis some writers (especially those employing **psychoanalytic** frameworks and/or attending to bodily materiality) prefer to use 'sex', 'sexuality' or 'sexual difference' as the coverall term rather than gender (Grosz, 1994a: 15–17; Mitchell, 1982; Braidotti, 1994b). Moreover, as Jackson points out, the term gender has a decidedly English-speaking heritage. Writers employing English but, for instance, influenced by French theorists like Foucault or Wittig may be less enamoured of the term. Even in the English-speaking world, gender did not become widespread in critical thinking on the topic until the 1970s (Jackson, 1998b: 132).

I have used gender in this book, not because I have any particularly strong commitment to it, but simply because it is the most common term today across the subfields of Feminist, Sexuality and Masculinity Studies. This pragmatic usage should not prevent recognition of the ways in which debates about the term gender reveal different understandings of the relationship between biology and the social ordering of sexed identities, as well as the historical/cultural specificity of theoretical names and traditions. The latter point raises another important problem.

Debate 3

Writers who justify the usage of the term 'gender' as against 'sex' or 'sexuality' do so as a means of indicating that the differentiation of men and women is not a simple direct expression of eternal nature. By contrast, those who dispute its usage reject the biological–social division this seems to imply and relatedly refuse to demarcate (bodily) sex, sexuality and gender. Biological (reproductive) sex differences, sexuality (erotic, sometimes reproductive) and gendered social arrangements (typically linked to sex differences and reproduction) are considered interconnected in this analysis. What we see here is also a debate about the *links* between what is described under the terms gender and sexuality. Commentators who reject gender entirely offer one example of theorising which asserts that gendered arrangements and sexuality are bound together, but they are not alone. Most writers in Feminist and Masculinity Studies (that is, in Gender Studies) view gender as intertwined with sexuality (Cranny-Francis et al., 2003: 7). Many go so far as to presume that gender (sexed identities and practices) is the foundation of sexual identities and practices. This approach asserts that gender comes first and that sexuality is subsequently shaped by gender (Jackson, 1995). Most Sexuality Studies writers are unconvinced. Gayle Rubin (1984), for instance, claims that sexuality should be treated separately from gender and is highly critical of analyses that reduce the former to the latter. Indeed, sexuality theorists in general are much more inclined – along with a relatively small number of Feminist and Masculinity writers – to assert that sexuality is prior to gender.[7]

These disputes, as I noted in the Introduction, indicate that the conception of a field of gender/sexuality theory is not straightforward but also demonstrates points of difference in orientation between the three subfields. Feminist and Masculinity Studies tend to line up together and focus on the significance of gender (sexed identities), while Sexuality Studies focus upon the organisation of desire (not on having or doing sex *per se*, but upon sexualities) and are increasingly somewhat antagonistic to gender approaches.

You can see by looking at the term 'gender' that there are ongoing and important debates about it, which also tell us something about other relevant terms. I have drawn attention to three of these debates:

1. The question of whether we should focus on particular (usually marginal) groups/ identities (for instance, focus on women rather than gender).
2. The question of the relationship between the social and biological/natural/bodily (which surfaces in considering gender, versus sex/sexuality/sexual difference, as coverall term for the field of study of sexed identities).
3. The question of the connection between sex, sexed and sexual, in particular between gender and sexuality.

These debates recur in various incarnations in all of the three subfields of gender/ sexuality theory – that is, Feminist, Masculinity and Sexuality Studies. I have drawn attention to them to show how such debates chart out the thematic terrain of the gender/sexuality field. They demonstrate the spread of the field across the continuum of Modernist–Postmodern frameworks, the character of its subfields and the significance of particular writers/writings within it, as well as indicating its simmering tensions. For this reason they also shape the format of this book. I will now show how the term 'gender' and debates related to it are played out in relation to the subfield, Feminism.

Introducing Feminism

Feminism is the first of the three subfields to be discussed under the overarching field of gender/sexuality (see Figure I.1 in Introduction). The short overview of this subfield that follows also provides an opportunity to show you *how* I intend to develop the whole book. Looking at Feminism gives me the space to model the format I use to characterise and differentiate between different directions/trajectories in the subfields of the field of gender/sexuality (G/S). In much the same way as I used the specific term 'gender' to show something of the broad 'terrain' of this field, I shall now employ Feminism as the initial specific exemplar which sets out in the way I intend to explore G/S theory and categorise its main directions.

Throughout the book I consider the G/S field in terms of *five main theoretical directions*, which are distinguished in relation to certain frames of reference and debates. In particular I use the Modernism–Postmodernism continuum of views on a range of debates (such as those around terms like gender mentioned earlier) as a means to highlight main directions. The overarching continuum and different views on specific debates are related to one another. Views on debates tend to be connected to weaker or stronger versions of Modernism and Postmodernism and hence to positions on the Modernist–Postmodern continuum. Each of the subfields of Feminist, Sexuality and Masculinity Studies have different emphases in relation to the continuum, the debates and the five main directions upon which I focus, but all three subfields may be usefully understood by reference to these elements.

Using Feminism as an exemplary model

Critical stance

Feminism, like the other two subfields of G/S theory, has a critical history. It starts from a critique of the mainstream, of 'the norm', of what is taken for granted. This subfield, along with Sexuality and Masculinity Studies, operates not as a mere description or analysis of 'what is' as given, but from the point of view of scepticism.[8] Such a form of thinking starts from the point of view of questioning whether 'the world *has* to be this way?', questioning even whether the world *is* as it is said to be. In the case of Feminism its *critical stance* takes the form of a critique of misogyny, the assumption of male superiority and centrality (Beasley, 1999: 4). As Bev Thiele says, feminists consider that 'social and political theory was, and for the most part still is, written by men, for men and about men' (Ibid.). Feminism is a critical theory that refuses what it describes as the masculine bias of mainstream Western thinking on the basis that this bias renders women invisible/marginal to understandings of humanity and distorts understandings of men. Feminist commentators offer a critique of the mainstream focus on men insofar as this focus and its limits are not recognised. They note that in Western thought to speak of men is taken as speaking universally (Ibid.: 14 and 8).

This falsely universalised MAN, who is supposed to represent us all, cannot acknowledge its gender specificity, its masculine particularity. As some feminists point out, this has meant that the masculine bias of mainstream thought is ironically sometimes dangerous to men. For example, feminist writers like Dorothy Broom (1996: 24–5) argue that without a focus precisely on the particularities of men's bodies it is difficult to develop appropriate health services for men. Clearly this orientation indicates that Feminism, as an instance of theorising in the G/S field, *starts* from a critical or questioning position in relation to social arrangements and takes as central the link between sex and power in society.

This means that Feminism is a critical stance that decentres the assumptions of the mainstream in terms of centre (men)–periphery (women). This is also a feature of Sexuality and Masculinity Studies, which similarly decentre notions of the norm in relation to sex and power. Feminism not only decentres the usual assumptions about what is central and what is at the margins, but also shifts the subject of the analysis, in that the notion of woman is placed centre stage (Beasley, 1999: 18–19). This occurs even when feminists question the validity of this sexed identity. Feminists focus, in short, on that which is deemed marginal/peripheral.

At this point there is some parting of the ways between the three subfields of the G/S field. Masculinity Studies offers a critical stance on sex and power but, rather than focusing on the marginalised, attends to those that are traditionally central to Western thinking – that is, men and masculinity. Indeed, while this subfield has become more attentive to diversity, it still primarily attends to white middle-class heterosexual men. By comparison, Sexuality Studies is mostly (like Feminism) concerned with marginalised identities and practices – that is, with LGBTI (lesbian, gay, bisexual, transgender, intersex) and/or 'Queer' sexualities. Nevertheless, more recently there has been a growing body of work in Sexuality Studies concerned with heterosexuality, with 'mainstream' sexuality.

What is important here is that even if the social positioning of the subject matter differs across the three subfields, the critical stance evident in Feminism remains. Critiques of the mainstream using a focus on the mainstream – such as critical analyses of masculinity by looking at the positioning of men – are becoming more common and a more accepted part of the G/S field. This movement towards reconsidering what is deemed the centre rather than the periphery parallels the ways in which Whiteness is now a more explicit subject in critical analyses, decentring the mainstream in relation to 'race'/ethnicity. All the same, the most usual technique of the G/S field has been, and remains, the decentring of mainstream assumptions regarding sex and power by focusing on the marginal. Why? Because the exclusion of the marginalised has been taken as clearly demonstrating the action of power in relation to sexed and sexual identities/practices.

Whether commentators in the G/S field focus upon the marginal or the mainstream, the intention in all these approaches is not just to be critical but to *challenge the normative hierarchy of sex (sexed and sexual)*. All of the subfields are characterised, in other words, by an inclination to challenge the notion of a proper, appropriate, natural 'norm' in relation to gender and sexuality. This central motivation to challenge the status quo has sometimes formed the grounds for disquiet, even rejection, regarding the status of certain writings. Masculinity theorists have been taken to task by feminist thinkers because they have been deemed insufficiently critical. Sexuality commentators have raised similar concerns in relation to Feminism. The existence of such disputes about 'adequacy' and 'belonging' suggest a shared sense that G/S theory and all of its subfields are committed to social reform, or at least social destabilisation. The subfields show a concern with some level of social change that resists the existing hierarchy of sex and power.

In order to show these critical, decentring and change-oriented characteristics at work, I shall now turn more specifically to the history and debates associated with Feminism as an example.

Content: frames of reference (the continuum of views) and main directions

The field of gender/sexuality theory (and its three subfields, Feminist, Sexuality and Masculinity Studies) may be described in terms of an array of five main theoretical directions spreading across the Modernist–Postmodern continuum (Figure 1.1).

Figure 1.1   Map of the gender/sexuality field: continuum and directions

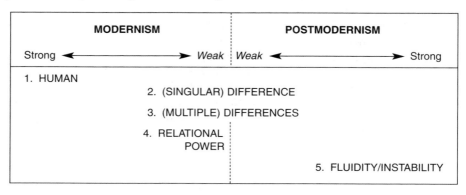

This general map of the G/S field, and the continuum of views within it,[9] can be contextualised and also clarified by outlining the specific forms these main directions take in Feminism. I will examine Feminism's main directions in brief to set the scene for the more detailed chapters that follow.

1   The Human: Modernist (Emancipatory/Liberationist) feminisms

The so-called 'first wave' of Feminism in the late eighteenth and nineteenth centuries was marked by its *critique* of dominant Western thinking of the time, that is, its critique of **Liberalism**. Liberalism during this period proposed a belief in the importance and 'freedom' of the individual, understood in terms of rights or claims to be free as far as possible from intervention by government. All individuals were to be 'free' to make their own way and their own wealth. The social and political rights of supposedly gender-neutral individuals were said to reside in their humanity, in what distinguished them as human, in their ability to **reason**. The ability to reason meant that individuals did not require the paternal hand of the father-figure state. Individuals – reasoning human beings – did not need the assistance of government. However, eighteenth- and nineteenth-century Liberalism, though using the gender-neutral language of 'humanity', 'individual' and 'reason', rested in practice upon a notional man and was indeed confined to men.

'First-wave' feminism noted that women were regarded as irrational creatures, were not permitted to vote, own property once married, and had little legal control over their children or their bodies. This form of Feminism advanced a critique of the supposed universality of Liberalism – of its conception of a universal human nature shared by all – by pointing out that women were excluded from this account. However, for the most part first-wave activists did not disagree with Liberalism's idea of a universal standard for social and political rights and selfhood. Instead they noted that the standard was male rather than universal. While some variants of first-wave feminism supported Marxist/Socialist refutations of Liberalism's individualist standard and of Liberal capitalist society, early Liberal feminists advocated the extension of this standard to women to enable women to have access to full adult citizenship within Liberal capitalist society (Tapper, 1986; Corrin, 1999: Chapter 2;

Tong, 1998: Chapter 1; Carver, 1998). Early Liberal feminists proposed women's inclusion in the Liberal universal conception of the *Human*.

By the 'second wave' of Feminism, which began in the 1960s and 1970s, there was stronger criticism of this universal standard. Several strands or 'types' of Feminism developed which included not only reworked versions of Liberal and Marxist/ Socialist feminism but additionally Radical feminism. There are many accounts of these several types of Feminism, which clarify how they have been characterised (Beasley, 1999: 51–64; Tong, 1998: 10–129; Bryson, 1992, 2003; Donovan, 2000). However, for the moment what is crucial is that all of these strands of Feminism, like first-wave feminism, had an 'emancipatory' orientation. They focused on a compensatory reversal in which masculine bias was exposed and women's theorising and activities were rescued from obscurity (A. Ferguson, 1994). The aim for the most part was to emancipate women from their past neglect and marginalisation, to make women part of the social landscape, to assimilate women into society, which would necessarily transform that society. While these second-wave commentators generally criticised the Liberal 'universal' standard more thoroughly than their eighteenth- and nineteenth-century sisters, they did not abandon all notions of a universal standard. In this sense these second-wave thinkers are seen as still offering an 'Emancipatory' or *Modernist* approach. It now becomes necessary to outline some features of a Modernist frame of reference in order to explain important aspects of feminist thinking, which will later be relevant to the consideration of Modernist themes in the Sexuality and Masculinity Studies subfields.

Second-wave feminists (like those of the first wave) may be seen as linked to a Modernist frame of reference on a number of grounds. First, all of them conceive of a universalisable truth or mode of analysis that can reveal the key mechanism(s) of all society/societies. This truth is about power and 'oppression'. In discovering the key mechanism/truth about power, the aim is to throw off macro (large-scale) structures of power that oppress women and other subordinated groups. Secondly, power in this model is understood in terms of suppression and dominance, as 'power over' rather than 'power to'. It acts downwards, in a negative fashion to constrict or restrict. Major analytical terms employed by second-wave feminism – like 'patriarchy' and 'compulsory heterosexuality' – indicate the negative nature of power, its quality of repression. Second-wave feminism, from the 1960s and 1970s to today, offers a theory about the truth of power, in particular men's systemic power as a group over women as a group (even if individual men and women might escape this social structuring). Power is owned by the dominant group, as an attribute or property. In short, men *have* power. Thirdly, the aim of this theory is to overthrow power, to overthrow men's authority. The fourth element of this Emancipatory/Modernist form of Feminism involves a particular notion of the self. Instead of accepting the mainstream Liberal universals of the 'individual', 'the human' and 'reason', second-wave feminists expanded and altered them. In Liberal feminism women are included in an extended account of the existing Liberal universal standard of human nature – that is, reason. In Marxist/Socialist and Radical feminisms an alternative, less individualist, less mind-oriented, more co-operative universal human nature, and one less firmly tied to a particular account of competitive masculinity, is generally propounded.

Most aspects of these several types of Emancipatory feminism are about assimilating women into an enhanced view of the social world, about developing a common political aim around a single theoretical platform. Their largely *assimilationist* stance is concerned with removing barriers to women's full social participation, enabling women to participate and be recognised in the social world as men are. With power peeled away, Emancipatory feminism suggests, women's true free selves will have an opportunity to flower.

Emancipatory feminism, whether of the first or second waves, is called Modernist because it presents several features associated with this term.

1. This form of feminism exhibits a faith in 'metanarratives' (Lyotard, 1984)[10] – that is, large-scale macro holistic explanatory accounts which offer notions of a singular central universal 'truth' about society, power and 'human nature'/human-ness.
2. It views power as domination downwards and as the property of the dominant, such that power can be thrown off and society can be made free of power.
3. It conceives the self as repressed/oppressed by social power but having an inner core (universal Human essence) beyond power, which can be emancipated or liberated.

There are equivalent frameworks of Modernist 'emancipatory' or **liberationist** thinking in Masculinity and Sexuality Studies. For this reason we will return to distinctions between Modernist and Postmodern frames of references on several occasions as they indicate ongoing differences between main directions in all of the subfields of the gender/sexuality field.

Nevertheless, it is important to recognise, even at this early stage of examining the G/S field, that such distinctions are by no means clear-cut. Some elements of Emancipatory feminism were rather less certain about Modernist general theories of power and society and less certain about a single path or key to social change. The universalist and assimilationist orientation I have outlined, which focused upon a common Human nature as well as a common political action agenda, was a feature of Liberal and Marxist feminisms of the first and second waves. However, this orientation was less straightforwardly embraced by Socialist and Radical feminisms. In the latter strands, general theories and universal conceptions of selfhood were sometimes upheld at the same time as a notion of particular *group identities*. Gender difference was increasingly promoted. In these accounts the focus was more upon *women's difference from men* (rather than a common humanity) and upon affirming women as a group, rather than upon enabling women to enter, participate in and assimilate into a man's world on equal terms. As Elaine Showalter (1985: 249, 260) puts it, feminist approaches evolved from an initial critique of the male-centred character of the universal Human standard towards an increasing celebration of '**gynocentrism**' or women-centred analyses, which emphasised gender difference. The concern with notions of difference led over time into an ever more thoroughgoing rethinking of Modernist general paradigms and a shift towards Postmodernism.[11]

2   Gender (singular) Difference: Identity Politics to 'Sexual Difference' feminisms

By the late 1970s and 1980s a focus on group difference, on a theorising and politics organised around a singular identity or category – that is, gender – had become the predominant tendency in Western Feminism. Such a focus identifies difference between the genders as *the* starting point for social analysis. Gender distinctions in this setting mean that women have or are identified with particular experiences at some distance from mainstream, supposedly universal presumptions about the world and what matters in it. Gender Difference feminists argue, like the Emancipatory feminists, that 'universal' presumptions are in fact not neutral but derived from men or notions of the masculine and constitute women as outsiders. However, the former theorists do not attempt to include/assimilate women in a gender-neutral universal Human standard in which men and women are 'the same'. Rather they speak for an alternative worldview which recognises and highlights difference, specifically gender difference. Some examples of gender difference (or sexual difference) writers include Mary Daly (Radical feminist), Nancy Chodorow (pychoanalytic Socialist feminist), Carol Gilligan (moral philosopher), and Luce Irigaray (psychoanalytic Postmodern 'French feminist'). It is evident from this short list that this singular focus on gender difference (rather than several differences) spans Modernist and Postmodern approaches. I employ the terms '**Identity Politics**' and '**Sexual Difference**' respectively to distinguish these frames of reference.

The aim of the Gender Difference framework in Feminism was, rather than attempting to locate the marginalised (women in this case) at the edges of existing society, to acknowledge difference positively. Such a concern involves reversing the traditional hierarchy of social privilege by revaluing the marginal. Indeed Difference theorising involves privileging the marginalised, at least strategically. In Feminism this has meant 'revaluing the Feminine' (A. Ferguson, 1994; see also Phoca, 2000). Rather than an all-embracing theory of social organisation and human nature, such thinking tends towards an at least bifurcated account of different social and cultural positionings. In the Modernist 'Identity Politics' versions of Gender Difference, this amounts to asserting differently constructed gender identities and experiences and mounting political platforms based upon the specific positioning of women. The 'women-centred' focus of this Identity Politics is seen as necessary given women's difference from men and as an antidote to the **androcentric** nature of existing society. Few feminists promoting this woman-centred Identity Politics argue that men and women are naturally intrinsically different, though sometimes the analysis runs close to this.

In the more Postmodern inflected versions of Gender Difference thinking – often termed 'Sexual Difference' thinking – there is a marked refusal of any particular content to gender identities like 'women'. 'Sexual Difference' theorists do not assume that women necessarily have any particular qualities that can be contrasted with those of men. Instead, Sexual Difference feminists revalue the Feminine as representing in cultural terms 'difference' from the (masculine) norm. The norm – what is deemed to be 'universal' rather than the merely particular – is associated with the Masculine. Gender (Feminine and Masculine) is here not so much about the actual characteristics of men and women as the exemplary symbolic register for power and hierarchy in society. It is the symbolic billboard for Western cultural insistence that differences between people must be conceived as expressing an intrinsically hierarchical order, that differences must be understood as normal/superior or abnormal/inferior and not as diversity. In revaluing the Feminine as having an autonomous potential and not merely as the other (lesser) half of the Masculine, in conceiving the Feminine as offering a vision beyond hierarchy, Sexual Difference theorists reinterpret it as the means to envisage plurality in society (Gross (now publishes as Grosz), 1986: 204). While Feminist Identity Politics and Sexual Difference approaches depart in their assessment of the meaning of the category women/feminine, they share certain features. They offer Modernist and Postmodern variants on the common theme of the incommensurability of the sexes and the importance of celebrating rather than suppressing difference in social life (Grosz, 1994a: 8–9).

This 'Difference' framework has equivalents in Sexuality and to a lesser extent Masculinity Studies. In the case of Sexuality theorising, for example, lesbian/gay studies strongly focus on marginal group identities and on the difference between homo and hetero sexualities. Difference theorists in the Sexuality subfield also offer an anti-assimilationist political agenda that refuses to accommodate to the assumptions of mainstream heterosexual society, and validates difference from that mainstream. Because commentators in the subfield of Masculinity Studies are committed to critical examination of dominant rather than marginal social identities, the typical stress in Gender Difference on revaluing different identities or social positionings has necessarily taken another path in Masculinity thinking from its deployment in Feminist and Sexuality theorising. While Masculinity writers have sometimes followed feminist Gender Difference models to stress women's particular world views or positioning, their agenda has largely disallowed any form of Identity Politics based on manhood or masculinity. These writers decidedly do not conceive their critical approaches as implicated in the validation of Masculinity's 'difference' – that is, its dominance.

Within Feminism the Gender Difference approach includes Radical, Socialist and Psychoanalytic feminisms. All of them contain some clearly Modernist universal elements regarding the aim of developing a singular macro account organised around a singular conception of 'difference' explaining the truth of power. Nevertheless, they do not all view power in Modernist terms as merely negative repression. Moreover, the account of the self or identity in Gender Difference feminism is not straightforwardly Modernist. Identity, in this analysis, is conceived as more than singular and not universally the same. It is marked by group difference (gender difference). Feminist Gender Difference writers are distinctly Modernist overall, but in some instances they can be seen as at the 'border' of the Modernist/Postmodern 'divide', situated on the Postmodern 'side' but drawing upon both paradigms. This border positioning is especially evident in the case of some psychoanalytic feminist work (Beasley, 1999: 74–7).

3   (Multiple) differences: 'race'/ethnicity/imperialism and feminism[12]

This theoretical framework provides one of the several feminist counter-arguments challenging Gender Difference. It is found right across the spectrum of the Modernist–Postmodern continuum. However, in recent times feminist writings which focus upon the arenas of 'race', ethnicity and imperialism (REI) typically cluster around the middle, on both sides of the dividing point of the continuum. For example, they have had a limited presence, though often an important one, in strongly Modernist Emancipatory feminisms. Their presence is most evident in the Marxist/Socialist tradition. Additionally, feminists dealing with race/ethnicity/imperialism are often suspicious of firmly Postmodern positions and, if they do adopt a Postmodern framework at all, tend to adopt modified versions. They often retain a more negative account of power usually associated with Modernism and are generally less inclined to disavow identity categories (like 'black woman') as a crucial site of political thinking.

Feminists attending to race/ethnicity/imperialism have a voice in both group Difference and '**Social Constructionist**' camps, sometimes simultaneously. Such feminists may wish to revalue and affirm group (racial/ethnic minority/'Third World') difference and identities. On the other hand, they also criticise *singular* group difference approaches that only emphasise gender/sexual difference. REI feminists assert that a focus on singular gender difference involves suppressing other differences and maintaining an **essentialist** account of men and women as unified groups without acknowledgement that 'racial'/ethnic/cultural location might sharply alter any generalised assumptions about the relative power of these groups. In short, the masculinity of Aboriginal Australian men is likely to be an overly narrow and partial descriptor of their social positioning. Categories of men and women cannot be seen, in this REI framework, as self-evident identities that are always the same and bear the same social consequences everywhere. This position has links with or overlaps with Social Constructionist criticisms of Gender Difference.

4   Relational Power: Feminist Social Constructionism

'Social Constructionist' or 'materialist' feminists strongly rejected the Gender Difference position that became significant in the 1980s. Social Constructionists argue that 'difference' does not adhere *in* the self/identity, is not an inherent essence, but is created by relations of power (Jackson and Scott, 1996: 11–12). They insist that the emphasis on gender or sexual difference is unhelpful and that people are not marginalised because they are different but made different by marginalisation. These feminists can be located on the Modernist 'side' of Modernist/Postmodern border on grounds similar to those used by the greater number of 'Difference' feminists. Social Constructionist approaches describe truth and power in universal macro terms and power is largely perceived as negative domination. On the other hand, this largely Modernist perspective is somewhat unsettled by an equivocal view of human essence. Social Constructionist theorists largely reject Modernism's humanist emphasis on a pre-existing inner core to the self. Rather, they assert, identities are made and made different by the social structuring effects of power.

Social Constructionism, along with Postmodernism, offers a critique of both Emancipatory and Gender Difference approaches in that both of the latter accounts stress relatively fixed notions of identity. Social constructionism criticises inherent or fixed notions of either 'the human' or group identities (for instance, lesbian, man) as 'essentialism', as supporting a notion of an original inner essence or core to the self. On the same basis, gay and lesbian 'difference' approaches within Feminist and Sexuality Studies are also criticised as developing overly narrow and romantic accounts of 'the lesbian' or 'the gay man'. On the other hand, Social Constructionism, with its emphasis on socially and historically concrete studies, continues to pay attention to identity categories. Unlike strongly Postmodern approaches, this theoretical direction acknowledges the potential stability of such categories over time and does not demand their disavowal. In Feminism, Social Constructionism draws for the most part upon Modernist Marxist/Socialist and Radical feminisms, but some writers within it show an increasing awareness of Postmodern theorising. This brief account of Social Constructionism is discussed in more detail in Chapters 8 and 12 (see also Burr, 1995: 1–16).

5   Fluidity/Instability: Postmodern feminism

Lastly, we come to Postmodern feminism. This is arguably the predominant feminist position in the 1990s and 2000s. Postmodern feminism offers, among other things, a multiplication of the notion of difference that appears in the group difference(s) approaches. In this theoretical trajectory there is an expansion of difference towards differences, towards a plurality that resists any set identities. Postmodern feminists do not aim to include women in the existing opportunities of a male world or broadening the male world into an expanded range of possibilities that can include women (the Emancipatory model). Nor do they wish to reverse the traditional hierarchy and focus on women/the feminine (the Gender/Sexual Difference model). Rather, Postmodern feminists intend to destabilise the very conception of identity (human or group) and the binary identities (such as men and women) upon which the two former strategies rest. Writers like Butler and Sedgwick question speaking as a woman, or for women, and instead emphasise differences between and within us all. The concern with Difference*s* that is characteristic of REI frameworks is here extended to the point where the issue is not multiple categories of difference but a movement beyond such categories of analysis which questions their very status. Some writers attending to REI may draw upon and be described as 'postmodern' thinkers (for example, **'post-colonial'** writers such as Gayatri Spivak). However, my use of the term Postmodern feminism is intended to convey a strong version of Postmodernism which disavows notions of identity in ways that are at odds with the commitments of REI theorising.

In similar fashion, Postmodern feminism in this usage represents a particularly thoroughgoing version of Social Constructionism. Where the Social Constructionist approach rejects overly fixed or inherent conceptions of identity in favour of a focus on the socio-historical constitution of identities, the emphasis of Postmodern feminism is to assert that there is no 'truth' behind identity. While Social Constructionism has not abandoned a conception of social humanity or an account of human agency which interacts with social requirements, Postmodern frameworks conceive humans as no more or less than a social product organised by power. Gender, for example, is an obligatory masquerade. There is nothing behind or before this 'mask'. Postmodern feminism is strongly anti-essentialist. In this form of feminist thinking there is no prior or authentic true self underneath power. Power creates multiple, fragmented selves and power itself is not a singular process. It is multiple, local (capillary) and productive in its operations. Such a viewpoint stands in contrast to Modernist conceptions of power as a monolithic macro and repressive action from above. Postmodern feminism, in short, is an anti-generalist, anti-humanist (antagonistic to the notion of a common core Human nature or agency) and strongly anti-essentialist position (Ahmed, 1996; Sullivan, 2003: 39–43; Milner and Browitt, 2002: 164–202; Beilharz, 1994: 7–22 and 2001: 173–87; Turner, 1997: 117–33; Best and Kellner, 1997; Rudel and Gerson, 1999).

While other feminist approaches may be regarded as postmodern or seen as influenced by postmodern theorising, I have deliberately chosen to capitalise Postmodern feminism to distinguish those writers who display an unequivocal Postmodern

Figure 1.2 Map of Modernism–Postmodernism continuum example: Feminism

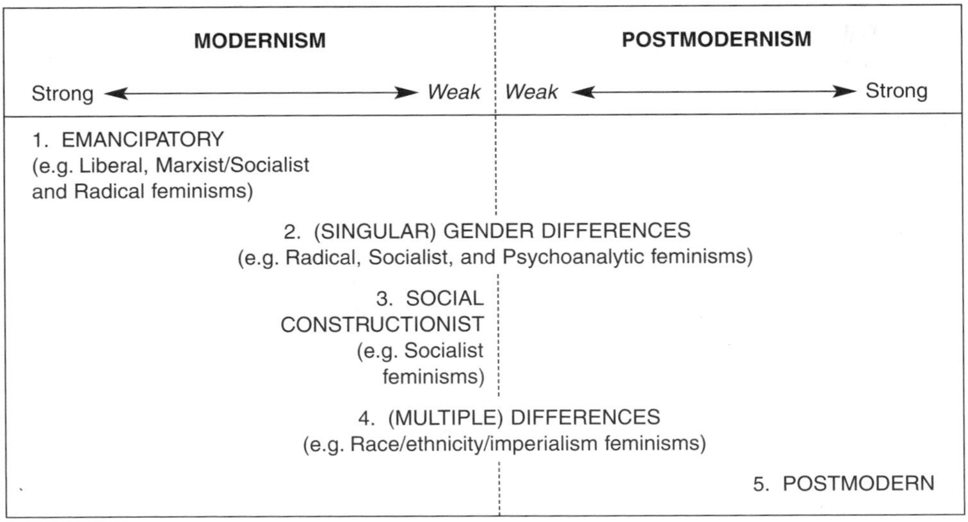

MODERNISM	POSTMODERNISM
Strong ⟵——————⟶ Weak	Weak ⟵——————⟶ Strong

1. EMANCIPATORY
(e.g. Liberal, Marxist/Socialist
and Radical feminisms)

2. (SINGULAR) GENDER DIFFERENCES
(e.g. Radical, Socialist, and Psychoanalytic feminisms)

3. SOCIAL
CONSTRUCTIONIST
(e.g. Socialist
feminisms)

4. (MULTIPLE) DIFFERENCES
(e.g. Race/ethnicity/imperialism feminisms)

5. POSTMODERN

stance and see this as *the* characteristic of their work. Such distinctly Postmodern views are even more strongly taken up in Sexuality Studies than in Feminism, but have so far had limited impact on Masculinity Studies. What I have delineated as Postmodernism might be labelled 'Poststructuralism' in other texts. The terms are often used interchangeably.[13]

It is important to note at this point that the distinction between Modernist and Postmodern frames of reference within Feminism, as well as in Masculinity and Sexuality Studies, is only broadly sketched out in this chapter. It will be further developed and contextualised in later chapters (for example, Chapter 5), especially in those which deal with individual theorists. As is often the case with such broad and complex terms, the range of their meanings is frequently better captured by considering their specific uses in particular writings. Moreover, since this is a book about the field of gender/sexuality theory and its writers, its scope precludes a lengthy, in-depth focus on the various interpretations of the terms Modernism and Postmodernism. Those readers who wish to consider the terms in greater detail can find many helpful sources in the notes for this and other chapters.[14]

Contextualising the G/S field by looking at Feminism

Having outlined the five main directions in Feminism we can now begin to contextualise the earlier schematic map of the whole gender/sexuality field. The five main directions outlined in relation to the broader field have specific forms when we look at the example of Feminism. These specific forms are similar to those found in the other two subfields of Masculinity and Sexuality Studies.

As I discuss the two other subfields, the maps of the Modernist–Postmodern continuum in the G/S field overall (Figure 1.1) and specifically in Feminism (Figure 1.2) will be reiterated in various ways. The debates related to this continuum will become increasingly clear as they are fleshed out in discussion of the work of different writers.

Notes

1. Many characterisations of the term 'gender' simply assume that the social setting is Western. Despite the limits of a label like 'the West', which does not acknowledge the permeability between Western and non-Western cultures as well as the non-homogeneous nature of the West, it seems to me that it remains important to acknowledge the specificity of the cultural assumptions in definitions. In a book that concentrates upon theorising in the English-speaking world, this appears all the more necessary.

2. See Connell's view of the reproductive character of gender in Connell (2002: 10) by contrast with Mary Hawkesworth's (1997a: 3) critique of this.

3. See for criticism of this limitation, Hawkesworth (1997b).

4. Some commentators have suggested that the term has problems beyond those I discuss in this chapter, and draw attention to what they see as its decided limits. Hawkesworth (1997a) argues that 'gender' has mistakenly been employed too broadly – for example as a means to explain rather than merely describe social phenomena – whereas Moi (2001) asserts that it has outworn its strategic usefulness. See also Scott (1999).

5. For an example of the continuing force of this debate, see interchanges in 'Beyond sex and gender: the future of women's studies', in *Feminist Theory*, 4:3, 2003 (contributors include M. Zaleswski, M. Lloyd, E. Rooney, M. Hill, P. Clough and W. Brown).

6. See, for example, Jackson (1996b: 62–73) on gender, Social Constructionism and female sexuality and Weeks's (1985: 108–20, 246–50) account of Social Constructionism as a means to offer a critique of *sociobiology*.

7. For an example of a Gender Studies viewpoint which posits sexuality as prior to gender, see MacKinnon (1982).

8. Meaghan Morris (1993: 300), for example, says that Feminism is 'minimally, a movement of discontent with the everyday and with wide-eyed definitions of the everyday as "the way things are"'.

9. I have employed an account of weak and stronger Modernist and Postmodern theories in the continuum. There are many other writers who discuss degrees of Modernism/Postmodernism (for example, Waugh, 1998).

10. Jean-François Lyotard (1984) associates Modernism with large-scale accounts of history and societal macro structures – that is, what he calls 'metanarratives'. Others use terms like 'master narratives' (see Milner and Browitt, 2002: 175–7; and Andermahr et al., 2000: 170–1, 207–11).

11. It should also be pointed out that the distinction between Modernist and Postmodern frames of reference is not as sharp as this preliminary account suggests. I have described them at this point as sharply differentiated to highlight general positionings. As you, the reader, move through the chapters, more contextual detail and related ambiguity is introduced that reveals the distinction as a complex continuum rather than a divide. (See also this chapter, note 9 and Chapter 2, note 6.)

12. The terminologies employed here will be clarified and discussed in Chapters 6 and 7.

13. Postmodernism is typically used as a more portmanteau and inclusive term, while Poststructuralism is perhaps more likely to be linked to a more specific intellectual field. For this reason I find the former is a better umbrella term for a general intellectual phenomenon. Some

commentators have been inclined to distinguish between Postmodern and Poststructuralist thinking and tend to view them as separate lines of analysis. For instance, Milner and Browitt – perhaps because of their central focus on culture – link the former with an attempt to define the new postmodern cultural condition of our times, while associating the latter with language, 'difference theory' and analysis of modernism's passing. I am less inclined to stress a divide between Postmodernism and Poststructuralism. Like Best and Kellner, among others, I emphasise interconnections between these terminologies in terms of social theorising. I would also reiterate that in the gender/sexuality field, and elsewhere, the actual usage of the terms as equivalents makes it difficult to maintain a notion of their separation. See Beasley, 1999: 81–96; Milner and Browitt, 2002: 170; Best and Kellner, 1991: 25–33.

14. There are numerous existing sources that may be useful for those wishing to understand the complexity of the terms Modernism and Postmodernism. You may find it useful to check the notes for Chapter 5 in particular, but in the meantime here are three references: Gibbins and Reimer, 1999; Natoli and Hutcheon, 1993, especially section 1; Milner, 1991.

2

Modernist Emancipatory Feminism: Liberal Feminism – Wollstonecraft to Wolf

I will begin consideration in this chapter of one of the main directions or trajectories within Feminism – that is, the Modernist Emancipatory perspective – and will attend to one of the types or strands of Feminism which take up this theoretical direction in order to provide an illustrative example. Liberal feminism offers a particularly useful instance of this Modernist positioning.

Characterising Modernist thinking

In the previous chapter I identified five main directions spanning over the Modernist–Postmodern continuum within the overarching gender/sexuality field and provided a preliminary outline of these directions within Feminism. The first of these feminist theoretical directions was Modernist Emancipatory feminism. I also outlined certain features of Modernist approaches.

- Modernist thinking, I suggested, is concerned with what is *universal* to human beings. Most importantly, a universal Human nature is envisaged. Modernism is for this reason typically associated with '**Humanism**' – that is, the notion that human beings intrinsically possess a foundational core (essence) which sets them apart from other animals and nature.
- Not surprisingly, given its focus on what marks out the universal Human as special, Modernism is preoccupied with what is universal about society and power relations within society. Modernist approaches conceive society and power as capable of being understood by a universal rule or law or 'truth'.
- This foundational and macro-explanatory 'truth' orientation in relations to humanity, society and power is linked to conceptions of power as negative and top-down.
- The human self upon whom power acts is also understood as having universal features, and as repressed/subordinated/oppressed by power. Hence a true, essential self (core human capacities) can be liberated/emancipated from power. It is possible to throw power off.

I would add to this list of features that Modernist thinking is optimistic about the opportunities for change. It assumes that over time society and the self will be liberated. History, in this approach, is progressive and linear. Everything gets better over time. Such a perspective may be contrasted with strongly Postmodern thinking. Postmodernists are sceptical about any universalising monolithic foundational account and wary of any notions of any founding explanatory centre that is eternal or fixed in human life. They declare there is NO foundational (essential) truth to the Human, society, power, the self or history. (The distinction between Modernist and Postmodern forms of thinking will be further elaborated in Chapter 4.)

Feminism's relationship to Modernist thinking

In Feminism, as in Masculinity and Sexuality Studies, there are frameworks along the whole continuum from strongly Modernist to strongly Postmodern. Feminism has a long tradition of Modernist or Emancipatory thinking and as you can see in Figure 1.2, there are several 'types' of this form of thinking in the feminist pantheon. The most strongly Modernist types are those which began in the eighteenth and nineteenth centuries (which continue to the present day) – that is, Liberal and Marxist feminisms, though even these may be said to have a differential attachment to Modernism.[1] Those types of Feminism that began in the 'second wave' of the 1960s and 1970s are distinctly more ambiguous in this respect and offer a weaker Modernism. I will concentrate initially on those feminist approaches which began before the twentieth century and in particular will attend to Liberal feminism because this instance remains a powerful and pervasive 'type' of feminist theory today, while avowedly Marxist variants are now significantly less common.[2] Indeed, as I have noted elsewhere, 'Liberal feminism … is often seen as synonymous with feminism *per se*' (Beasley, 1999: 51).

However, my reason for this choice is not just based upon Liberal feminism's ongoing established position. Marxist, Socialist and Radical feminisms all demonstrate, to different degrees, somewhat less clear-cut adherence to a Modernist frame of reference. Their more mixed relationship to Modernism may be clarified by a brief comment about the character of this frame of reference. Broadly speaking, Modernism in the West has involved two major traditions, which are more or less indebted to its universalist humanism (Martin, 1999: 159–62). These two traditions are the individualist tradition that may be traced through Hobbes, Locke, Kant, Mill and Wollstonecraft, and the collectivist tradition that may be linked to Rousseau, Hegel, Marx, Goldman, Kollontai and Said. While the former shaped Liberal political thinking and typically has become the mainstream 'ideology' of Western capitalist societies,[3] the latter has had its greatest impact in Socialist perspectives and has most often had an oppositional relationship to Western social systems. The oppositional stance of broadly Socialist inflected viewpoints, which includes Marxist, Socialist and Radical feminisms, has led to potentially more critical readings of mainstream (Liberal) Modernism. Such Socialist inflected feminisms are more inclined to question an unthinking assumption that a single viewpoint can give access to foundational Truth, because this may amount to little more than support for the status quo of Liberal capitalist society. While these feminisms remain indebted to Modernism and its concern with human agency, notions of the universal Human (that are so much a feature of the strong Modernism associated with Liberalism) are typically also undercut in Marxist, Socialist and Radical feminisms by recognition of specific social differences like class, 'race' and gender. Increasing recognition of such differences led to perspectives that began to question any foundation to the Human, to question Modernism itself. For this reason Liberal feminism appears as arguably the clearest, though not the sole candidate to illustrate Modernist perspectives within Feminism.

To make the strongest case for a Modernist Feminism I will give a broad outline of Liberal feminism in this chapter and briefly discuss the writer Naomi Wolf, and in the next I will focus in more detail on the work of Martha Nussbaum.

Liberalism and Liberal feminism

Liberal feminism is a response to and development of Liberalism. For this reason it is necessary to provide some background on Liberal thought. Mainstream Liberalism in the late eighteenth and nineteenth centuries, in whatever variant (Minow and Shanley, 1996; Beasley, 1999: 51–3), offered a form of thought in which 'the individual' (the full adult citizen) is a 'descendent of the Enlightenment concept of an autonomous rational being' (Gunew, 1990: 17; O'Neill, 1999) and political equality is associated with that ability to reason. The **Enlightenment** is a term describing a collection of ideas which emerged in the West in the seventeenth and eighteenth centuries. Such ideas opposed religious explanation (God as truth) and the divine right of kings in favour of secular rationalism.[4] According to Enlightenment thinking, all those who can reason are capable of independent thought and action and hence should be able to participate in society. In practice, however, all women and certain men (men of colonised countries and working-class men until they gained the vote) were excluded from these claims as less capable of reason. Mainstream Liberalism is a form of thought and a form of social regulation that has dominated Western societies since the emergence of the Enlightenment and draws strongly upon this two-fold legacy. Hence, in Western Liberal societies some groups of people are afforded full citizenship and others are not.[5]

In this context, Liberal feminism pointed out that Liberal, supposedly universal standards of humanity, equality and reason were not in fact universal because women were denied full social participation, public life and education. The seeming paradox at the heart of Liberalism, which asserted equality and liberty for all yet maintained a rigorous inequality in relation to certain groups, should be understood in terms of the particular meanings given these words. Equality and liberty (from intervention by government) refer to human beings capable of reason. Only they can be granted the status of belonging to the universal human. Only they are to be regarded as autonomous persons, as individuals, and therefore able to be granted public rights and freedoms. Those who are deemed outside reason – that is, the 'uncivilised' or those closer to nature and therefore more animal-like – are not quite Human, and thus not capable of receiving these rights and freedoms. They – the '**other**' – are instead to be controlled and cannot be 'free' within the private realm of the family (all women) and/or in public legal terms (all women and indigenous colonised men).

Liberal feminism from the late eighteenth century to the present day has pointed out that full social participation and public life has been denied women. Liberal feminism asserts that the universalist claims of the Enlightenment and its descendent, Liberalism, which strove to counter the fixed **social hierarchy** of medieval custom and to extend social status, did not extend so far as to include women. In excluding women, who constitute half of the populations of Western societies, mainstream Liberalism is revealed as less about justice than a narrowly Western masculine political project. While Liberal feminists continue to defend what they regard as the critical spirit associated with the Enlightenment reason,[6] they argue that mainstream Liberalism is a flawed descendent.

Liberalism's all-embracing pretensions are built upon the assumption that only Western men matter, that men's equality in the West is equivalent to equality for all fully human beings.

Liberal feminism: a broad grouping

Liberal feminists of the late eighteenth and nineteenth centuries, such as Mary Wollstonecraft (1759–97), argued for women to be included in this masculine project. Wollstonecraft's aim was for women to be given access to education, to the Liberal model of knowledge and rationality and to enter public life (Wollstonecraft, 1978 [1792]: 293–4; Gunew, 1990: 15). She wanted women to attain what men of a similar class had in terms of opportunities and access to public activities. Wollstonecraft, in common with other Liberal feminists of the eighteenth, nineteenth and early twentieth centuries,

> drew on the liberal tradition's value of equality and individual freedom to argue that, just as social status at birth was no longer a legitimate basis on which to discriminate among men as liberals argued, so also sex at birth was no longer a legitimate basis on which to discriminate against women. (Ackerly, 2001: 5499)

In other words, she did not question the model of a universal humanity based in rationality, or the universal notion of 'the individual' within mainstream Liberalism, but rather advocated women's simple inclusion/assimilation into its protocols.

By the second wave of Feminism in the 1960s and 1970s, most women in Western countries had gained basic social and political rights such as the vote after considerable social dispute. The new 'women's movement' gave rise to a new form of Liberal feminism. Activists like Betty Friedan and Gloria Steinem in the USA and Beatrice Faust in Australia exemplified this new Liberal feminism. They were crucially involved in the emergence of new reform-oriented women's organisations such as NOW (National Organisation of Women) in the USA and WEL (Women's Electoral Lobby) in Australia. They argued that despite most gaining formal rights, women remained confined to the domestic and were still subject to many legal and customary constraints which significantly hindered their ability to access public life and its opportunities as men did. The public worlds of politics, business and the professions still remained gendered. This view is supported by the ILO (International Labour Organisation, United Nations) which reported in 1993 that it 'will take nearly 1,000 years for women to gain the same economic and political clout as men if current trends continue' (*Advertiser*, 1993: 17). Relatedly, second-wave Liberal feminism asserted that women continued to be marked as lesser, because they were judged *as women* and only secondly as individual human beings, whereas men were still more likely to be judged individually. This meant that women continued to be discriminated against, not on the basis of merit but on the basis of their sex (Tuttle, 1986: 182). This viewpoint amounted to a development of first-wave arguments, like those of Wollstonecraft, supporting women's entry into the male world of public life.

Liberal feminism, from its earliest forms to now, may be understood as focusing upon the elimination of constraints facing women and gaining *equal civil rights* for women as public citizens. Today this focus remains an important aspect of the public face of Feminism. It is crucial to public campaigns regarding childcare, maternity leave and flexibility in waged working hours among others, which aim to make workplaces more 'family friendly', or perhaps more accurately more 'parent, relationship and community friendly'. Provisions like childcare are designed to assist women in juggling their continuing greater responsibilities for domestic and childcare labour with waged work in ways that lessen the impact of this 'double load' on women's public participation. The orientation of such political interventions is overall to assimilate women more comfortably into a basically masculine model of social life without much altering the discrepancies between the existing differential roles of men and women. Women are assisted in fitting into workplace priorities, rather than fundamentally confronting gender inequities in public and domestic life. This orientation towards assimilation rather than significant reform is also revealed in the Liberal feminist concern to reverse women's under-representation in various areas of public life, especially those associated with higher status, economic reward and authority.

Second-wave Liberal feminism has tended to extend the more 'welfarist' version of mainstream Liberalism and, as such, counters the marked **individualism** of most of its forms. This second-wave approach develops the welfarist strand within mainstream Liberalism in terms of advancing a sense of collective or social responsibility and a marked attention to social justice. The collective and social justice political programme of this form of Liberal feminism is evident in its focus upon overcoming discrimination against women as a class or group. It is also evident in the attention given to repealing or reforming social obstacles to women's public participation.

The emphasis on improving women's legal and political position as a group in second-wave Liberal feminism, while undercutting the individualism characteristic of mainstream Liberalism, nevertheless continued to be firmly oriented towards enabling women to become like men. Hence, even second-wave Liberal feminism's concern with collective politics, with women as a class/group, is strategic and temporary rather than long-term. Its political aim remains recognisably Liberal – that is, to enable women to achieve the status of autonomous 'individuals' in public life as equals of men and as equally capable of public participation.

More recently, a number of usually younger feminists have criticised this practical political **collectivism** with its focus on obstacles and discrimination/oppression against women. These '**third-wave**' Liberal feminists (sometimes called 'post-feminists') argue that the 1960s and 1970s women's movement and those which continue to adhere to its agenda are inclined to overestimate social obstacles and are disinclined to admit women's own responsibility for their lives and status (Gamble, 2000b: 44; Andermahr et al., 2000: 205). Third-wave Liberal feminists, some of whom are sometimes described as 'anti-feminist' (Modleski, 1991; Wilgman, 2001a), instead argue that women must take individual responsibility and not hide behind a group status as 'victims'. This amounts to a strong, indeed thoroughgoing, return to the individualism of mainstream Liberalism. Such writers may still be viewed as occupying a feminist position insofar as they still assume and advocate the equality of men and women[7] but their explanation for women's inequality resides more in individuals, and in particular in individual *women*, than in social discrimination. In the work of some third-wave writers like that of Katie Roiphe (1994) or Rene Denfeld (1995), this analysis amounts to women-blaming but in others like Naomi Wolf there remains a greater recognition of women as collectively subject to discrimination (see also Gamble, 2000b: 48–9; Lehrman, 1994).

Third-wave Liberal feminism: Naomi Wolf

In Wolf's books on beauty and motherhood, *The Beauty Myth* (1990) and *Misconceptions* (2001) respectively, she devotes considerable attention to the social obstacles women face and, in typical Liberal feminist style, she urges social reform of these obstacles. Nevertheless, like other third-wave Liberal feminists, she also focuses upon empowering individuals. Her political programme as well as her political aim is about individuals. She celebrates the autonomous individual in traditional Liberal terms and criticises what she calls 'victim feminism' (*Fire with Fire*, 1994) for saddling women with an 'identity of powerlessness' (Lehrman, 1994). Wolf suggests women should seize the power that is on offer (Hughes, 1997: 25). For Wolf this appears as a relatively simple matter (Gamble, 2000b: 49), perhaps as much as anything a question of attitude, a matter of will. She argues that seeing 'competition, ambition and aggression as male and somehow evil undermines women's quest for autonomy and self-determination' (Lehrman, 1994). Her 'power feminism' celebrates meritocratic social hierarchy, personal responsibility, public success and the individual. This paean to social mobility is also evident in more recent writings which return to the problem of obstacles for women but remain up-beat about women as individual subjects, as active agents of change – especially personal change. Personal individual change flows on to a collective result. In her rather traditional reiteration of Liberal conceptions of power and the self, empowered/emancipated individual women can alter power relations. There is virtually no reference to the state or other social institutions in the analysis, but rather a focus on the spreading impact of empowered individuals who take control of their lives. Hence, she says in *Misconceptions* (2001) that the 'greatest loss for many new mothers is the loss of self' (cited in *Weekend Australian*, 2001: 21).

Naomi Wolf specifically locates her 'power feminism' as an extension of the Liberal feminism of nineteenth-century thinkers like Mary Wollstonecraft. In common with Wollstonecraft and most Liberal feminists, she is little concerned with class or money or race, and appears primarily focused on the problems of women like herself – that is, white, educated, middle-class young women.[8] She encourages women, for example, to form 'power groups' to pool their resources in the way men do. Like all Liberal feminists, she seeks to incorporate women and Feminism into capitalism (a North American style of capitalism in her case). Her vision of 'power feminism' indeed appears itself to be a capitalist commodity: 'I propose specific strategies to make pro-woman action into something that is effective, populartist, inclusive, *easy, fun and even lucrative*' (Wolf, 1994: xix, emphasis added).

For Wolf this has not proved to be an outlandish claim. She has published very widely and regularly embarks on international lecture tours to packed houses. Wolf even seeks to develop a brand logo for Feminism to sell it all the better (Nemeth, 1993). This kind of approach, with its emphasis on self-improvement and marketing, has a peculiarly North American tinge which becomes perhaps most strongly evident when her notion of Feminism's future is linked to particularly North American conceptions of individual liberty. Wolf, for instance, celebrates 'gun ownership among women as a sign of progress beyond victimhood' (Lehrman, 1994). Nevertheless, the enthusiastic self-help and inspirational tone of her work, combined with its readability, has often been galvanising and highly effective in showing women in an increasingly conservative political climate what Feminism might mean to them individually. Wolf is indeed herself a highly marketable front-person for Feminism, a kind of celebrity feminist, in an age of celebrity worship. Perhaps this is a crucial Feminism for our times.

Conclusion

You can see from this brief and broad overview of Modernist feminism, and Liberal feminism within this, that there are many directions and debates to consider. Liberal feminism is an assimilationist and reformist (rather than revolutionary) approach. It aims to fit women into existing society and to remove obstacles to their public advancement. If Liberal feminism were a shirt, it would probably be pinstriped and have shoulder-pads. It dresses for success. However, its willingness to accommodate and indeed celebrate the virtues of mainstream capitalist democracies makes it a form of Feminism that is comparatively widely accepted and hence possibly the only popularist platform for feminist thinking today. In the next chapter I look in more detail at another Liberal feminist who provides a kind of scholarly version of Wolf's popularism.

Notes

1. Hartsock (1998a: 236) argues that Marx cannot simply be viewed as pro-Enlightenment. This point has implications for Marxist feminism.

2. A relatively limited number of feminist writers now espouse a scrupulously *Marxist* feminism. It is more common to find feminist theorists/writers who explicitly or implicitly repudiate a previous commitment to a Marxist or at least broadly Marxian approach. Michèle Barrett's movement from Marxism to Postmodern thinking provides an important example of this repudiation, which gained particular force during the 1990s. Nevertheless, aspects of Marxism remain a significant influence in the work of Socialist and Post-colonial feminist writers, like Nancy Hartsock and Gayatri Spivak respectively, as well in the work of feminists influenced by the Western Marxism of 'Critical Theory' and Jürgen Habermas. See Barrett, 1991, 1992; Milner and Browitt, 2002: 57–91; Benhabib, 1992a, 1994.

3. For short definitions of 'ideology', see Osborne (2001: 162) and Gamble (2000a: 252).

4. For an accessible and brief description, see Osborne (2001: 120–2); for another longer version, see Martin (1999: 156–67).

5. Jane Flax (1997 [1995]) has noted in this context that 'the freedom, homogeneity, autonomy and identity of the modern individual are produced and dependent on its marked other – the slave, the inferior races, the homosexual'. See also Flax, 1998; Carver, 1998; Hindess, 2001; Helliwell and Hindess, 2002; MacMillar, 1998.

6. See Nussbaum's defence of Reason in Chapter 3. This more sympathetic reading of the Enlightenment project is characteristic of Modernist approaches in Feminism and elsewhere. Nevertheless, the perception of a potentially useful critical attitude associated with the Enlightenment, despite its limits, is sometimes even expressed by strongly Postmodern thinkers whose positions are precisely supposed to be anti-Enlightenment. What this indicates

is that Modernist pro-Enlightenment theories are not always to be cast as the opposite of Postmodern perspectives. The continuum between Modernist and Postmodern frames of reference is precisely that, not a question of either/or but of shadings. See, for example, the embrace of the critical imperative in the Enlightenment in Michel Foucault's later work (Foucault, 1984b: 43–6).

7. Despite a strong attack on Feminism *per se*, Rene Denfeld (1995: 267) asserts that she is 'an equality feminist' who believes 'women should have the same opportunities and rights as men'.

8. See the debate with bell hooks et al. (panel discussion) in 'Let's get real about feminism: the backlash, the myths, the movement', *MS*, iv: 2, September–October 1993, p. 36.

3

Liberal Feminism: Nussbaum

In the previous chapter I noted certain distinctive features of Modernist feminisms and used Liberal feminist approaches as a clear example of a strongly Modernist Emancipatory trajectory in Feminism. While there are some elements that might be said to be common to Liberal feminism, these elements are not always precisely the same. Not all Liberal feminist positions are identical.[1] This point is worth keeping in mind in relation to the whole range of directions, frames of reference and types of thought we will discuss throughout the book. Emphases change over time and the thinking of individual writers does too. Commonalities or shared themes which enable us to consider categorising theoretical approaches under umbrella terms should not lead us to assume that within a particular feminist framework all writers will have exactly the same views on everything. The theoretical positions described in this compendium are inevitably 'broad-brush' accounts designed to assist you in understanding the general typology of the gender/sexuality map. They are not neat and entirely unified positions. In this context, Liberal feminism has some commonalities but is by no means homogeneous.

Liberal feminism as a 'broad church'

I have tried to indicate broad commonality at the same time as presenting some level of variation in the case of Liberal feminism by drawing your attention to differing emphases. To show such different emphases I have referred to the so-called first, second and third 'waves' of Liberal feminism,[2] even though the terminology of waves itself may be criticised as suggesting overly distinct groupings. As was indicated earlier, these emphases are not strictly chronological. For instance, both second and third waves coexist today. There are numerous overlaps and connections between them. Nevertheless, I have also noted a possible point of difference between third- and second-wave Liberal feminisms.

Third-wave Liberal feminists like Naomi Wolf focus strongly on individual self-development as the political means or *method*, as well as upon the political aim or *goal* of equality of rational autonomous individuals (in which the status of individual is extended to women). By comparison, second-wave feminists like Gloria Steinem and Beatrice Faust, who started writing in the 1960s and 1970s, outline a more collective political method to achieve the individualised goal of equality among individuals. Indeed, this is the grounds upon which many second-wave feminists discount third-wave/post-feminist writers. One example of this is Beatrice Faust's irritated dismissal of Wolf as narrowly individualistic and, in Faust's view, as providing an inferior model of political practice by comparison with Australian Liberal feminists because Wolf fails to attend to political and policy institutions like government (Faust, 1994).

Second-wave Liberal feminists are less focused upon individual self-realisation, self-expression and self-fulfilment as a means to alter social hierarchy. They are more likely to concentrate upon legal and political reforms, institutional reform, on lobbying governments and other organisations, as well as more likely to focus on a social justice agenda, as against Wolf's comparatively greater concern with enhancing individual women's competitive edge. However, both 'waves' can also be seen as drawing upon some pre-twentieth-century first-wave concerns.

I have noted already that Wolf specifically claims a debt to Mary Wollstonecraft (1759–97). The writer I am going to discuss now, Martha Nussbaum, has a socio-political agenda that identifies her own work more closely with second-wave Liberal feminism. Nonetheless, she also follows many of Wollstonecraft's concerns and talks specifically about the work of J.S. Mill (1806–73), who is often seen as the father of Liberal feminism. You can see here a very clear example of my earlier point that theoretical 'waves' are not confined to particular historical periods and are not strictly chronological given that they can co-exist today.

I will use the connections between Wollstonecraft's ideas and those of Martha Nussbaum to show you in a little more depth some of the features of contemporary Liberal feminism. This analysis provides an opportunity to outline some of the issues with which contemporary Liberal feminists are associated as well as a way to illustrate debates about and criticisms of this approach. In this context I will outline three of its key features: (1) the notion of Reason; (2) women as the 'test case' enabling assessment of a just society in Liberal terms – that is, assessment of its claims regarding equality and democracy; and (3) the focus on social reform.

1. Liberal feminism, Reason and the universal Human

Mary Wollstonecraft, in her work *A Vindication of the Rights of Women* (1978, originally published in 1792), argued for a particular version of Liberalism that highlighted women's position. This version rejected the divine right of kings, hereditary power, fixed social hierarchy and arbitrary rule over any being who possessed reason. In this Wollstonecraft was following and reinterpreting the kinds of classic Liberal argument developed by John Locke and Tom Paine (Corrin, 1999: 22). She did not ignore women's possible differences from men but asserted that these did not exclude them from reason or the rights that were attendant upon reason. On this basis, Wollstonecraft *includes* women in the notion of a universalised reasoning human being and rejects fixed/eternal rule over them.

Her writings led to social vilification. She was called a 'shameless wanton, a hyena in petticoats' among other names, and epigrams like this one were published to discredit her and her views:

For Mary verily would wear the breeches,
God help poor silly men from such usurping b ... ches. (Ibid.: 23)

The hostility Wollstonecraft faced is not of course a thing of the past. While men's achievement of civic and political rights continues to be celebrated to this day as the (universal) beginnings of modern democracy, women's rights continue to get a comparatively bad press and their past achievements are often presented in condescending terms as merely particular benefits for a few disgruntled harridans.[3] The now standard picture of 'the suffragette' is, for example, a figure of fun. This long history of hostility towards feminist ideas perhaps reveals even more clearly to us how remarkable Wollstonecraft's treatise must have seemed to a late eighteenth-century audience.

Wollstonecraft argued against the double standard applied to women in Enlightenment and Liberal thought. Instead, she applied Enlightenment ideas to women's situation, arguing that as men and women shared a universal human capability of reason, so women also deserved the same rights and opportunities as men. Valerie Bryson's analysis of core elements in Liberal feminism suggests that this orientation is characteristic of Liberal feminism *per se*. She says that Liberal feminism is

> based upon the belief that women are individuals possessed of reason, that as such they are entitled to full human rights, and that they should therefore be free to choose their role in life and explore their full potential in equal competition with men. (Bryson, 1992: 159; see also Kensinger, 1997)

Reason in this setting generates the capacity to be an individual, since it gives the freedom to *choose* rather than having to be told what to do. It enables freedom to compete with other choosing persons. Hence, reason becomes a universal Truth of Human-ness (a universal Human essence) which is linked to political equality – that is, the capacity for and right to public participation. Reason becomes the means to argue for entry into *the Human* and the means to rights, justice and social fairness. The argument goes, 'If I can think, I can make decisions, and thus there is no reason for my exclusion from public decision-making.' While the theme of a belief in a Human essence is characteristic of Modernism, the framing of this essence as individual reason is profoundly Liberal.

Nussbaum, Reason and the Human

Martha Nussbaum, an internationally regarded and highly influential academic from the USA, puts forward a Liberal feminist position in precisely these terms. She, like Wollstonecraft, is against convention (custom) and for reason. Reason, she says, overcomes the existing forms of power: 'convention and habit are women's enemies, and reason their ally' (1994). Reason in this approach enables us to see that what presently exists is not necessarily immutable or prescribed by nature. Reason overcomes the particular forms of social power because it is not part of the apparatus of power but outside it. An example of this thinking arises in her view that reason can persuade powerful people to act against their own interests, to give up power. In this sense, reason is an impartial, objective positioning from which to speak. Reasoning enables one to speak from a universal positioning beyond social power relations (social context) and beyond self-interest. Hence reason is not a male-biased term, not a term which expresses or is imbued with power. Nussbaum is also sure she speaks using reason, that she is on the side of objective, neutral truth beyond the particularities of her own social positioning. For this reason, although she comes from a highly privileged background (which she acknowledges), Nussbaum feels able to speak about and for women in poverty from other cultures. Indeed, prompted by six years of work as a research advisor at the United Nations University's World Institute for Development Economics Research, there is in Nussbaum's work a strong sense of responsibility to speak out on behalf of other women (Nussbaum, 1999b: 31; Charlesworth, 2000: 64–5). She believes that philosophers like herself should be 'lawyers for humanity' (Bjerklie, 2001). Perhaps you can already begin to see why her work has produced debate concerning both Liberal feminism and Nussbaum's account of it.

Nussbaum is particularly antagonistic to Postmodern feminisms because they refute any notion of any objective position outside a social context, outside social life, or which can escape power. This debate precisely differentiates Modernist (Emancipatory/ Liberationist) viewpoints from Postmodern ones. Modernist feminisms argue that underneath power lies the truth of freedom, a free self to be liberated. In keeping with this position, Nussbaum sees reason as the truth opposing convention and habit, in particular those conventions/habits which disempower or oppress us. Hence, reason enables us to throw off power, to throw off oppression.

Nussbaum defends reason against a range of other feminist views, but particularly castigates Postmodern feminists. The latter are perhaps the most sceptical of feminist theorists regarding the claims of reason, but Postmodern feminists are not alone in this. Although first-wave feminists had employed reason as a means to persuade men in power to grant women equal rights (Corrin, 1999: 23), by the second wave (beginning in the 1960s and 1970s) feminists began to argue that supposedly genderless universal standards like reason were not merely in practice only granted to men, but actually about men. The objective (non-emotional), autonomous (not connected to others) rational being who was therefore capable of making decisions at the centre of Liberalism was increasingly viewed as an account of existing social notions of unemotional, disconnected masculinity. Hence, rather than arguing, as first-wave feminists did, for *inclusion* in this supposedly disinterested universal standard for all, second-wave feminists increasingly drew attention to the status of reason as a thoroughly *social* term.

Second-wave feminists saw reason increasingly as a term not outside social context or history but as part of the social world and deeply imbued with its relations of power. And if reason was part of the social world, it might be *about* power. It could itself be complicit in power – that is, male biased. For many second-wave feminists from the 1960 and 1970s until today, 'reason' is seen more and more as a kind of legitimating device, a way of making one's argument seem knowing, of a higher order, and getting to the 'truth'. Hence, to claim one is speaking on the side of reason – in objective, neutral terms beyond self-interest and therefore from the realms of a higher knowledge or truth – is a potentially dangerous and arrogant point of view. Postmodern feminisms are even more sceptical. Indeed, ironically, Postmodern feminists were absolutely sure that claims to reason promoted universalist authoritarian absolutism – the belief that one is absolutely right. We see here competing claims regarding access to knowledge and truth.[4]

2. Liberal feminism and women as the 'test case' of a just society

Wollstonecraft argued that women's lack of rights – their dependence on the benevolence of men for their economic and social existence – was a domestic **tyranny**. She assessed the domestic authority of men *over* women as being destructive in the same way as was the royal tyranny of kings or slave ownership. Women, in this scenario, are a classic test case of a just society. Their social position provides a good litmus test of Liberalism's claims to advance equality and democracy. In short, Wollstonecraft suggested, if women are not free, then no one is. Modern Liberal society(ies) could then be judged illiberal. This assertion proposes that you can tell what a society's pronouncements mean and how to judge its claims to justice, by looking at the position of women.

Nussbaum and women as the test case

Similarly, Martha Nussbaum's books *Sex and Social Justice* (1999b, and especially Chapters 1 and 3) and *Women and Human Development* (2000) make the case for the position of women as exemplary in terms of 'global justice' (Quillen, 2001). She asserts that Feminism is a crucial part of this agenda. Her analysis is taken very seriously by a number of international agencies. She argues for global justice on the basis of a gender-oriented Liberal feminism (using a language focusing on women), as a means to enunciating the viewpoint of Liberal humanism. She asserts that the Liberal focus on the universal degendered 'Human' can be expanded, just as Wollstonecraft claimed, to *include* women on equal terms with men. By virtue of human-ness – the capacity for moral choice, the capacity to be 'choosers' – all human beings are not only worthy of equality but they compel us *to act* to achieve this equality (Nussbaum, 1999b: 9, 71, 57, 6). Reason, the ability to choose, is once again central to the universal Human, to the 'truly human'.

In both the books mentioned above Nussbaum argues that women's position – women's rights (or lack of them) – represent a case that must be answered *before* referring to cultural conventions/customs. In other words, gender equity must always come before (precede) the claims of **multiculturalism** (of cultural sensitivity and cultural integrity). Such a position is the result of her ongoing consultations in India – a place she describes as at the heart of her work (McLemee, 2001). There are, nevertheless, many examples of issues in which to prioritise a supposedly universal conception of (women's) human rights over cultural/religious protocols is highly controversial. Examples might include campaigns to eliminate selective abortion of female embryos, surgical practices such as hymen repair to recreate 'virginity' or to remove genital parts, and clothing customs such as the veil or burqa. Nussbaum's views enable support for a range of interventions (possibly even including armed interventions) on the basis of the human rights for women. These interventions involve a rejection of the inviolability of culture or nation-states (sovereignty) (Wylie, 2003: 220–1). While some feminists find the resolute certainty and grand scale of this approach practical and appealing, others perceive a return to the frankly imperialist tone of earlier Liberal thinkers, like Nussbaum's favourite, J.S. Mill.[5]

Relatedly, Nussbaum says in arguing for universal human norms as against cultural norms that, it is 'possible and necessary to work out a list of capabilities and rights any person should have to live a "truly" human life'. This truth of human life includes notions like, 'all people should have the right to form an individual life plan'. Such capabilities are, according to Nussbaum, not exclusively Western, even if they may sound like it.[6] Instead, they represent the universal requirement not to be 'pushed around', to throw off power (Wylie, 2003: 221). By contrast, she notes that some traditional cultural practices cause harm.

But what if people, including women, *choose* cultural norms that may seem oppressive to others – that is, choose to follow cultural convention as against an individual life plan? Nussbaum argues that while some things are universal and fundamental (she lists ten *core* human capabilities, ten essential requirements),[7] the ways to operationalise these fundamentals must be facilitative rather than imposed. She puts forward universal norms and criteria for judgement regarding their attainment, but acknowledges some need for cultural sensitivity and room for discussion regarding these 'universal' elements (Wylie, 2003: 221). Nevertheless, these caveats do not alter the fact that Nussbaum stands at some distance from a 'multiculturalist' stance, with its model of respect, tolerance and recognition for different cultures, including minority cultures (Saharso, 2003: 199). Her approach is one that ultimately disallows more than one cultural or ethical model. It does not place a high value on plurality nor stress differences between human beings, differences between cultures or between women. Human and women are universal categories (Nussbaum, 1994: 62, 1999b: 6–8; for a critique of this perspective, see Lazreg, 1988: 93, 96). Nussbaum adopts a classic Liberal feminist position when she asserts that there is a universal model for justice and 'the good', which can be put into practice globally. This is not a modest position but a typically '**grand theory**' approach, a '**metanarrative**' which offers to explain and solve global problems according to a singular conception of the truth. In short, it is a strongly Modernist perspective.

Indeed, Nussbaum argues that the goal is to become 'a **cosmopolitan**' – a citizen of the world – which means in effect to gain a universal point of view, a perspective that is objective, neutral, beyond power, beyond loyalties to any particular time or culture, including the West. Instead she supports a loyalty to a decontextualised Humanity. Nussbaum thus claims for herself that her commitment to certain norms is not limited by her culture, is not a reflection of her position as a Western woman. Moreover, Nussbaum is profoundly antagonistic to those who do not share her certainty, describing them as '**cultural relativists**' who see ethical values as merely relative and not right or wrong, who refuse judgement and who are therefore at a remove from necessary practical politics in which judgements must be made.[8] She accuses Postmodern writers like Jacques Derrida and Judith Butler of 'political quietism', of not being involved in the hard graft and real practicalities of genuine political reform. She asserts that Butler simply plays at abstract rebellious transgression, but in effect offers nothing to the poor and disadvantaged (Nussbaum, 1999a).

She is accused in turn of assuming she can speak for all, and as having a colonial mentality. Gayatri Spivak, an important Post-colonial writer who makes use of the work of Postmodernist Jacques Derrida, considers that Nussbaum is not only ungenerous in judging other points of view but writes as if she were on a 'civilising mission, instructing those in the developing world in what they want (cited in McLemee, 2001). Similarly, Ratna Kapur states that Nussbaum assumes that she can speak for India, Indian women and Indian feminists. In the process Nussbaum is said to misread political campaigns and reforms. As an example, Kapur cites Nussbaum's use of Indian sexual harrassment guidelines as demonstrating the priority of gender over culture. Kapur notes that in practice these have not been straightforwardly about gender equity but have sometimes been more concerned with the reaffirmation of cultural conventions in terms of regulating women's sexual behaviour. Women's complaints may only be taken seriously if the claimants have appeared sexually innocent. For Kapur this suggests some doubts about Nussbaum's large claims and indicates the limits of her positioning as a spokeswoman for Indian women (Kapur, 2001: 79–83).

3. Liberal feminism and reform

Wollstonecraft's work accepted the universal standard of reason and did not see it as implicated in male dominance. She argued that women's position of dependency diminished them as they were reduced to servility. This servility, or lack of rational choice, was bound to affect child-rearing. Women's dependency was hence having a negative impact upon the future training of all citizens, including boys and men. Instead she proposed that those responsible for this training (women) must be able to exercise reason (be able to make choices and given rights to enact those choices) in order to better train children and thus improve the whole of society. This argument accepted 'manly virtues' as the best standard for all and was calculated to show men that it was in *their* interests to give women rights (Corrin, 1999: 23). Liberal feminism as a whole has been characterised as seeking 'equality for women through *reforms* to existing institutional structures' (Felksi, 1992: 22, emphasis added). It is an approach associated with reform or modification of Liberal modern Western capitalist societies, rather than with support for significant **social transformation**. Liberal feminism may be seen as upholding most features of modern Liberal capitalist societies, even while preoccupied with improving women's place within them.

Nussbaum and reform

Many other feminists have argued that this **reformism** amounts to little more than improving opportunities for middle-class, white, educated women, rather than an interest in challenging social inequities at the heart of Western capitalist societies. Liberal feminists themselves claim to be politically pragmatic and realistic about what is achievable in terms of social change. This is also Nussbaum's position when attacking Postmodern feminism. Liberal feminists like Nussbaum make us consider the question of what *is* the best political strategy for social change, what will actually make a difference to women's lives. Is it the best strategy to support what is understandable in the world stage of human rights, to support large-scale universal reforms in order to draw attention to the appalling plight of great numbers of women, as Nussbaum insists we should (see Quiller, 1999 and Nussbaum, 2001 for Nussbaum's reply)? Or is this strategy fatally tied to national, institutional and international capitalist agendas

(Wiegman, 2001b)? Should we instead 'go for broke' and advocate revolutionary change (Hooks, 1984a)? Or perhaps the solution is Postmodern and more modest? Perhaps, contra Nussbaum, the most useful policy might be to advance many plural local changes, working out these changes contingently, with no certainties? Or something in-between these options?[9] The example of Nussbaum's work opens the door to many ongoing debates in the gender/sexuality field, but possibly none is more crucial than this last one concerning social reform versus transformation because it raises the issue of what the field has to offer to the future (see Wiegman, 2001b for a discussion of this).

Conclusion

Liberal feminism is a 'broad church', but it retains certain characteristic features with regard to reason as the foundation of the universal Human, a focus on women's status relative to men's as the measure of society, and the immediate importance of concrete practical social reform. The perspectives of Naomi Wolf and Martha Nussbaum, though different in a number of respects, provide instances of Liberal feminist thinking and the ways it can be employed in mainstream political discussions. They also provide instances of the ways in which Liberal feminism is often criticised on the grounds that it mobilises universalist claims. Critics assert that these universalist positions cannot and do not speak for and to all, but have particular investments. In the case of Wolf, critics suggest that her approach is in fact restricted to white, class-privileged North American women, and in the case of Nussbaum it is argued that her proposals are Eurocentric. It remains to be seen in later chapters whether these criticisms of Modernist frameworks are replaced by anything that is less flawed and more useful. Nussbaum remains profoundly unconvinced. Her passionate advocacy of a Liberal Modernist stance provides an excellent counterpoint to the work of most other contemporary feminists, who have taken up, more or less, aspects of the Postmodern critique.

Notes

1. See Kensinger's (1997) discussion of the difficulties of category 'types' like Liberal feminism.

2. See chapters by Sanders, Thornham and Gamble for a range of readings on these first, second and third (post) waves in Gamble (2000a).

3. This point was made to me in class by a former student, Stephen Woodlands.

4. For other examples of feminist writers discussing the value of an Enlightenment concept of reason, see Waugh, 1998: 177–81; Hekman, 1994.

5. J.S. Mill (1806–73) was a philosopher, economist, practical politician and policy-maker who is most widely known for his essay *On Liberty* (1859) in which he argued for the maximum individual liberty and only limited government intervention in an individual's life to prevent that person harming others. His association with Harriet Taylor led to the development of the classic Liberal argument for women's rights in an essay entitled, *The Subjection of Women* (1869). In this piece, he attacked the legal subordination of women to men and compared wives to slaves. Mill was also founder of the first women's suffrage society. His writings and political activism advocating the liberty of English citizens may be read alongside Mill's longstanding engagement

with authoritarian rule in India (see Zastoupil, 1994). For further discussion on the relation between Liberal and illiberal government within and across states see Chapter 2, note 5.

6. Charlesworth (2000) notes, despite her generally very sympathetic assessment of Nussbaum's capabilities approach, that the model tends to reflect the priorities and conditions of the West in its greater concern with civil/political liberties over economic/social equity, as well as its focus on individuals and upon 'legitimate' national citizens.

7. Nussbaum's listing of core human capabilities may be found in *Sex and Social Justice* (1999b: 41–2). Deveaux (2002) describes the listing in the following terms: 'among these capabilities are those of life; bodily health; bodily integrity; capabilities relating the senses, imagination, thought and to emotions and emotional attachments; and capabilities for practical reason, social affiliation and political engagement'. See also Kamtekar, 2002.

8. Indeed, one reading of Nussbaum's often vitriolic attacks upon Postmodern feminisms is precisely that it amounts to a recent version of an ongoing debate about the significance of (abstract) theory versus (practical) politics which has long haunted Feminism, in common with most other social movements. In contemporary times this debate is often simply transposed on to the Modernist/Postmodern division. Certainly Nussbaum, in common with Terry Eagleton, appears to adopt a sweeping view of Postmodernism as self-indulgent and politically compromised, but this view disallows any sense of Postmodernism's diversity. See Wiegman, 2001b: 515, n.2; Lodge, 2004: 39–43; Eagleton, 1985; Waugh, 1998: 181–92.

9. Examples of Postmodern and 'in-between' Modernist and Postmodern positions can be found in Charlesworth (2000). See also Cacoullos, 2001.

4

Gender Difference Feminism: 'Women-Centred' Identity Politics to Sexual Difference – Rich to Grosz

I noted in Chapter 1 on gender and Feminism that five main theoretical directions or trajectories may be discerned in the gender/sexuality field and within Feminism in particular. These trajectories were presented in the context of their spread over a Modernist–Postmodern continuum. I suggest that you may find it useful to turn back to Figures 1.1 and 1.2 at this point to remind yourself about this spread of viewpoints. The five trajectories spanning this continuum within Feminism are listed as follows:

1. Modernist Emancipatory
2. Gender Difference
3. Social Constructionist
4. (Multiple) Differences
5. Postmodern feminism.

In Chapters 2 and 3 I focused on the first main theoretical direction in Feminism – that is, the direction I have described as underwritten by a concern with the universal Human and with emancipation of humanity. This is a strongly Modernist version of Feminism. I used Liberal feminism as an illustrative example rather than Marxist, Socialist or Radical feminisms. Now I will move to the *second* main theoretical direction in Feminism, which cannot be described as only Modernist or Postmodern. It contains both frames of reference. I will initially outline this *Gender Difference* perspective overall, then discuss two variations within it that take up Modernism and Postmodernism in distinct ways, and finally delineate some general potential criticisms.

Challenging the universal Human: supporting (singular) 'Difference'

Gender Difference feminism in many ways developed from the 1980s onwards in response to the strongly universal and socially assimilationist claims of Liberal approaches in particular. The framework is somewhat more sympathetic to **Marxism** (the other major strongly Modernist viewpoint) and has continued to be influenced by Marxism. Nevertheless, Gender Difference feminists also challenged Marxism's universal (Modernist) claims regarding the one struggle, a singular political agenda based in a universal co-operative human nature. Marxism's conception of universal human nature as co-operative, its collectivist orientation, may be contrasted with Liberalism's conception of human nature as situated in competitive individuals 'whose interests converge on only a minimal set of shared principles' (Martin, 1999: 159). While Marxism is a socially criticial or oppositional perspective, concerned with overthrowing the mainstream politics of Liberal thinking, Gender Difference feminists suggested that Liberalism and Marxism in fact shared more than either was prepared to grant.

Gender Difference feminists argue that there is no *singular* universal human nature (either co-operative/Marxist or competitive/Liberal) that can form the basis of 'equality'. They assert that *equality feminists* (Liberal and Marxist feminists) in pursuing a notion of women becoming equal to men, assume a commonality between men and women which requires women to become *the same* as men. In other words, Gender Difference feminists argue that, in the strongly Modernist notion of a universal human nature proposed by Liberalism and Marxism, *equality* = *sameness*. What seems impartial or gender neutral is actually male-defined. Such a model of 'equality' cannot be just or fair and therefore cannot produce gender justice. The Gender 'Difference' feminists assert that the goal of equality takes for granted that ways of life associated with men and masculinity are desirable for all and thus amounts to yet another denigration of women and the feminine as less worthy, as something to escape from or overcome. They argue that the goal of universal equality (whether in the form of Liberal pro-capitalism or Marxist anti-capitalism) counters discrimination at the cost of presuming that women would be better off being like men, would want to be like men and would want to throw off the identity of womanhood. This, they say, is not necessarily the case and hence the goal of equality does not lead to justice but to the erasure of difference, to women's erasure (Raymond, 1986: 11–14).

By contrast, Gender Difference feminists *give value to women's group identity as women*, and try to avoid using men/'the masculine' as the standard of comparison. They suggest that women should be considered in their own terms (in autonomous terms). Hence, the focus is not on a universal human nature but upon positively re-valuing *group identities* like women/'the feminine'. Where the equality perspective associated with strongly Modernist accounts like Liberal and Marxist feminisms is inclined to argue that difference between men and women is either a myth or produced to perpetuate women's oppression and should be transcended, Gender Difference theorists 'accept and even celebrate' difference which they argue 'should not be read as inferiority' (Squires, 2001: 9). Showalter (1985: 249) describes this as a shift from a critique of androcentrism to a celebration of gynocentrism, centring on women/the feminine.

Nevertheless, it is important not to overstress the distinction between equality and difference feminisms. Equality and difference feminisms are typically associated with Liberal and Radical feminisms respectively but, as Squires (2001: 24) notes, many Liberal feminists 'invoke some elements of a difference perspective'. Similarly, some Radical feminist writers adopt the equality perspective's attack on androcentrism and advocacy of transcending gender difference.[1] As I have pointed out earlier, such distinctions between theoretical directions are 'broad brush' depictions and are intended to give an overview sense of *main* differences in theoretical trajectories. They should not blind us to the ever-present borrowings and movements across these differences. You, the reader, may indeed decide that you find combining several elements from a number of these trajectories is the most useful option.

Table 4.1   Gender Difference feminisms: Modernist 'women-centred' to Postmodern Gender/Sexual Difference approaches

Modernist	Postmodern
1. **'Category' 'Identity' politics termed 'Woman-centred'**	2. **Gender/'Sexual Difference' approaches**
(a) Women's difference from men	(a) The use of 'woman' as symbolising 'otherness' or difference from the 'norm' – woman as a social symbol of what escapes the norm
(b) Women's commonality with each other; shared experience of womanhood	(b) Actual women share only a symbolic location as the socially marginal
(c) The positive *content* of marginal identities, e.g. woman	(c) No particular content for identity of actual women is presumed
(d) 'Woman-centred' model	(d) Affirmation of the feminine and the female body as symbolising that which doesn't fit the (masculine) universal standard
(e) Includes Radical (Rich), Socialist (Hartsock) and Freudian psychoanalytic (Chodorow) feminisms	(e) Includes Postmodern-influenced versions of psychoanalytic feminism, e.g. Freudian (Flax) and Lacanian (Grosz)

In this context, what is most marked about the Gender Difference approach is the concern with re-valuing women/the feminine. However, it also has two main variants, which may be located in relation to the Modernist–Postmodern continuum. The Gender Difference grouping spreads *across* the divide. Table 4.1 offers a brief summary of critical features of the two main variants. The focus of this chapter is upon the Modernist version.

Modernist 'women-centred' feminism: broad features

The variant of Gender Difference feminism that may be described as on the Modernist side of the continuum is commonly termed 'women-centred' feminism. This variant was perhaps the predominant version of Western feminism in the 1980s but increasingly gave way to various Postmodern-inflected theories, including the Postmodern variant of Gender Difference thinking. Women-centred feminism rejects the stress on the universal Human of Liberalism/Marxism but remains committed to Modernist accounts of power and society.

Women-centred feminism arises out of some strands of Radical and Socialist feminisms which both foreground macro accounts of power and society using terms like 'patriarchy' (meaning systemic and trans-historical male domination over women). Patriarchy is a term that provides a Modernist account of social power 'analogous to Marx's ideas of systems of ... exploitation based on [class distinction] associated with private property' (A. Ferguson, 1994). In women-centred feminism the focus is on *women's difference from men.* The focus specifically is upon a system of oppression based upon sex/gender distinction, on women as a 'sex class' occupying a lower social status than men as a sex class. Women-centred Radical and Socialist feminists see patriarchy as the first form of social hierarchy upon which other forms then came to rest. These feminists concentrate upon the crucial significance of women as the first 'class' of subordinates. Their political project is therefore to undo the impact of patriarchy, in typically Modernist terms to throw off androcentric power. Dale Spender (1985: 142) sees this as the means to discover women's uncontaminated authentic difference: 'We can choose to dispense with male views and values and we can generate and make explicit our own: and we can make our own views and values authentic and real.'

In attending to women's difference from men there is a concomitant concern here with *women's commonality as a group*, rather than with Human commonality. Women-centred feminists assert the positive value of women's difference from men and commonality with each other. They highlight the value of what they perceive women share and in particular outline a specific positive *content* for the category 'woman'. However, in some women-centred analyses, as Spender's statement attests, women are also urged to throw off male-defined culture and access a 'true self', a true femininity. In Mary Daly's account, women can discover a pure essence of womanhood, the 'wild woman' within, that is free from social power relations: 'It is axiomatic … that all external/internalized influences, such as myths, names, ideologies, social structures, which cut off the flow of the Self's original movement should be pared away'. (Daly, 1978: 381; see also Gamble, 2000a: 213 for a short account of Daly's approach.)

This Modernist variant of Gender Difference feminism is often labelled 'category' or 'Identity politics' feminism because it claims to speak from and about the identity category of women. It advocates a politics that arises from that identity category. As a variant of gynocentric theory, this 'women-centred' approach perceives the world through the lens of a decisive division between male and female experience 'in order to critique the power of the former and valorise the alternative residing in the latter' (K. Ferguson, 1993: 3–4).

Women-centred Gender Difference writings

The overall spirit of Modernist 'women-centred' thinking has been to acknowledge and give credence to women's 'ways of knowing, being and valuing'. This central theme is taken up in various ways by different writers. Writers like Radical feminist Mary Daly are often depicted as providing archetypal examples of the 'women-centred' approach, but should instead be viewed as offering one representative viewpoint within this theoretical trajectory. Daly insists that women are intrinsically different from men. She specifically identifies women with the creative and life-affirming (A. Ferguson, 1994).

By contrast, '**standpoint**' theorists like Nancy Hartsock argue a position that is marked by its Socialist feminist commitments. In this account, women are not intrinsically (biologically) different from men, yet patriarchal power relations produce different experiences and senses of self. Because women are not powerful, they develop a different and useful 'take' on social life (like the working class in Marxist analyses).

This standpoint of oppression contains possibilities for social critique and alternative visions (Hartsock, 1998b: 228–30).[2] Hartsock's approach has some overlaps with the work of writers attending to race/ethnicity/imperialism Differen*ces* – such as bell hooks – who, as we shall see later, also advocate connections between a marginal social positioning and creative politics.[3] In similar fashion, feminists concerned with promoting a 'care ethic' in society (including writers such as Carol Gilligan, Sarah Ruddick and Virginia Held) argue that women's intimate interconnection with others, especially as experienced in their social responsibility for children, suggests a better model of self and of social relations than Liberal competitive individualism (Gilligan, 1982; Ruddick, 1990; Held, 2001).

Freudian feminists like Nancy Chodorow and Dorothy Dinnerstein outline a particular psychoanalytic version of 'standpoint' theory (Chodorow, 1978, 1992: 153–69; Dinnerstein, [1976] 1999). They propose that the organisation of the family within patriarchal society produces different kinds of self for men and women, and in particular induces women's nurturing qualities. Chodorow argues that such positive qualities could be used to reform society by spreading them to men. If family life were altered such that boys experienced fathers (men) as nurturing, men too could acquire these qualities. Like all women-centred writers, Chodorow asserts that the feminine, though produced in subjection, offers a better model for all people and for reforming society. As Hartsock (1998b: 236) puts it, women's social positioning provides political (that is, feminist) 'conditions of possibility for creating alternatives'. This is a kind of reversal of the traditional focus of social/political thinking upon valued masculinity. Indeed, if the Emancipatory feminism outlined in Chapter 2 is understood as a 'strategy of inclusion' or assimilation into existing society, Gender Difference feminism appears as a 'strategy of reversal', a positive reassessment of the socially marginal. (Squires, 2001: 9–10; A. Ferguson, 1994). It offers *a turning towards women and the feminine.* This positive re-valuation is usually couched in universal cross-cultural terms celebrating women's deep and specific sense of self (or sometimes it is described less concretely in terms of their subversive political potentiality[4]). Such an approach produces an increasing affirmation of women and of woman-to-woman relationships.

If men/masculinity is not to be inevitably valued, and women/femininity is to be acknowledged, even celebrated, then woman-to-woman relationships can no longer be viewed as of marginal significance against women's relationships with men. In a social context in which women are commonly characterised as 'engaged in a war among themselves over men' and 'incapable of sustained friendships with each other' (Cranny-Francis et al., 2003: 28), women-centred feminists typically promote a counter-strategy in which woman-to-woman relationships are given credit and encouraged.

This strategy is strongly at work in a crucial essay by Adrienne Rich, entitled 'Compulsory heterosexuality and lesbian existence' (1980b) (see also Yorke, 1997). The essay raises doubts about connections between lesbians and gay men on the basis that any coverall 'homosexual' label erases women's specificity. She sees lesbians as having more in common with other women than with men. Gender Difference is privileged over other axes of social differentiation and subordination. She also argues that heterosexuality is a socially compulsory regime, which conveniently masks women's existing and potential connections with each other and undermines their solidarity in the face of subordination. Instead, Rich outlines what she called a 'lesbian continuum', which suggests that the experiences of heterosexual women and lesbians are not as distinct as heterosexist and patriarchal society presumes. Rich describes a wide range of 'women-identified' or 'woman-to-woman' oriented experiences, which refuse stereotypical femininity and, against the grain of 'compulsory heterosexuality', involve support for other women. These experiences might or might not include sexual inter-actions. You can see in Rich's work the usual focus of women-centred approaches upon what is common to women, what is shared between women, and how this is different from men.

While the aim of this focus was to highlight the impact of gender hierarchy upon women and a political notion of sisterhood which could resist its impositions, the emphasis upon women's special shared qualities threatened to solidify into yet another prescriptive inflexible conception of womanhood. During the 1980s the 'woman-identified' woman increasingly became a controversial icon, more and more associated ironically (given Rich's stance) with demands for lesbian separatism and for feminists to separate from men (Radicallesbians, 1988). Women-centred models were increas-ingly read in terms of the narrower vanguard politics of 'cultural feminism', which advocated women-only communities often linked to goddess-worship and 'political lesbianism' that depicted even feminist heterosexuals of collaborating with patriarchy, colluding with men in women's oppression. Women-centred thinking became identi-fied with striving for an authentic identity, a pure womanhood, which was most suc-cessfully attained in removal from the contaminating influence of men (Echols, 1983b; Segal, 1987; Jackson, 1999: 10–19). Such a vision was closer to Mary Daly's approach and indeed rather at odds with the broad social reforms envisaged by other women-centred theorists like Hartsock or Chodorow. In this setting, Andrea Dworkin's link-age of heterosexual penetrative sex with what she perceived as patriarchy's rape culture, and pornography with the marketing strategy of this culture, appeared to offer a particularly intense account of a women-centred perspective. Indeed, critics of this perspective often cite Dworkin's work as showing in virulent form the dangers attached to its sharp division between men and women. Dworkin's passionate and confronting account of heterosex as the quintessential instance of social violence inflicted upon women is frequently regarded as the apogee of a holier-than-thou view of women's moral/political purity and of men's predatory inclinations.[5] Dworkin's analysis constructs men and women as unitary and distinct categories.

Dworkin's account of heterosex may also be viewed as related to 'Social Constructionism', an approach that rejects notions of identity difference in favour of a focus on the impact of power (Mackinnon, 1987a).[6] However, in her case the impact of power produces such marked and discrete gender groupings that this seems a par-ticularly categorical form of Social Constructionism barely distinguishable from 'polit-ical lesbianism'. Women appear to have a fixed, different and innocent way of being compared with men, even if Dworkin refuses Daly's inherent womanhood and sees this way of being as socially constructed. Dworkin's ambiguous location between Gender Difference and Social Constructionist frameworks also indicates the limits of terminologies like 'women-centred' and 'Difference' feminism (see Chapter 18). Some commentators might include writers like Dworkin in this chapter without question; others would not. My use of such terminologies, as I have noted before, is to outline broad assemblages and directions rather than to propound an account of highly defended distinctions.

Psychoanalysis and Difference feminism

Modernist women-centred writers employing psychoanalysis support the typical 'women-centred' notion that women have a different self/identity or way of being and a different relation to others. Furthermore, this particular kind of self – though subordinated – is valued positively as a source for social reform. Like all women-centred writers, women-centred psychoanalytic feminists see subordination as a source of insights, not simply as negative or lacking (that is, not simply lacking opportunities, not simply deficient).

Why do these writers turn to psychoanalysis for a women-centred approach? The move to psychoanalysis, and the work of its originator Sigmund Freud, among feminists and others in the gender/sexuality field arose out of a strong dissatisfaction with simple social learning or imitation models of the self – 'socialisation' models of gender and the self. Advocates of psychoanalysis and Freud's work argue that sexed (as men/women) and sexual identities are not simply the result of social imitation or modelling but are far more deeply internalised into the very structure of one's identity. Freud's view was that gender (or sexual) difference was *the basis* of the construction of identity itself. In this perspective, to become a self at all occurs through becoming man or woman. It is not surprising, in this setting, to find that Freud's work is seen as useful by feminists concentrating on gender difference. Psychoanalysis argues that gender (sexual) difference is what makes the self and indeed underpins social life.

Moreover, there is a more specific reason for feminists of difference to take an interest in Freudian modes of analysis. Most feminist interpreters of Freud's work consider that his model enables an understanding of the differential social power of men and women and its effect upon children's sense of self, but additionally offers a way of showing the positive and specific possibilities of the feminine. Gender Difference feminists stress the role of the Mother in the development of the self, in contrast to Freud himself who highlighted the Father/the masculine/the penis. However, whatever the emphasis, all psychoanalytic feminists suggest that Freud's analysis can be employed to support a positive re-valuation of women/femininity, despite its male focus and bias.

The inclination to stress the Mother over the Father in feminist readings of psychoanalysis is only one instance of the diverse interpretations of Freud's work. There is certainly more than one way to understand Freud's thinking and that of his followers. I will now consider briefly the relationship between Freudian analysis and that of Modernist, women-centred feminists, using Nancy Chodorow as the example. This discussion provides a means to introduce you to psychoanalysis and more recent reworkings of it, such as arise in the work of Jacques Lacan. This introduction is necessary since all Postmodern versions of Gender Difference feminism are psychoanalytic, and usually Lacanian in orientation. The Postmodern feminist contributions will be examined in more detail in the next chapter.

Freud's work and its uses for Feminism

Psychoanalysis has also been widely adopted by feminists because of its almost uniquely thorough account of the development of the self. While it is by no means the only option,[7] Freud's work on the constitution of personality was the first comprehensive theorisation of how infants come to be social human beings and has had the greatest impact on present-day understandings of this process. Moreover, all other approaches remain relatively 'fragmentary and undeveloped' (Jackson, 1996b: 65 and 1999: 23).

Freud is interested in how we become human, in how we develop a self. In Freud's essay entitled 'Femininity' ([1933] 1973: 145–69), he asks not what *is* a woman, but how is a woman *made*. Clearly this is very different from simply assuming, as is still usual today, that one is born a woman (on the basis of innate qualities, hormones, genes, and so on). Freud's work questions gendered and sexual identities/roles. Relatedly, he is concerned with the importance of our early years. Unlike much of Western thinking, Freud does not ignore children, nor see them as merely unformed adults. Freud sees children (and people with psychological problems) as offering us insights into what we are and how we came into being. Children become the key to understanding personality, social relationships and social organisation itself. In this setting, Freud focuses on how the self is constructed and does not see it as merely conscious or singular but multifaceted, full of tensions and fragmented. Where Marx sees struggle everywhere 'outside' the self in the social polity, Freud goes 'inside' and says our very selves are composed of struggle and uncertainty. Freud does not accept that we are fixed creatures. For example, in this scenario men are not simply unproblematically masculine.

Yet despite hopeful elements in this concern with struggle and tension, Freud's account also suggests serious problems in undertaking social change. According to Freud's account of the self we may consciously desire change but find our selves more deeply entwined with our gendered and sexual identities than the notion of just *deciding* to change suggests. For some feminists, Freud provides a useful combination of ideas. He can be seen as providing a space for change in gendered society in refusing simply biological and deterministic accounts of gender and yet insisting that the psychic construction of the gendered self is difficult to alter consciously. Psychoanalytic feminists assert that such an approach is helpful in considering how and why changing social assumptions about the centrality of men/the masculine is possible yet difficult.

Freud's account of the construction of the self and hence social organisation

Freud sees all very young children as possessing libido (a biologically based sexual or life energy) and as amorphously sexual/sensual in all directions, as 'shapeless' in the sense of having no distinct self or particular direction or desires. Very young children experience sensation or pleasure/desire through a range of bodily sites (mouth and anus, for example) but over time begin to concentrate this sensuality in the genitals: girls in the clitoris and boys in the penis. There is a gradual structuring of sensuality, a delimitation, an increasing fixing and prioritising, a 'shaping'. This period from birth in which children experience pleasure in an amorphous, unstructured way to beginning to focus on their genitalia, their body, their 'place', Freud called the *pre-Oedipal period*. He identified this early period with an unstructured relation to the Mother, a symbiotic period in which the child at first does not make distinctions but begins to become somewhat more defined in terms of self/body and 'other'. He asserts that gradually, however, children do begin to recognise themselves, to recognise themselves as distinct from the Mother.

They begin, in other words, to develop a more clearly defined bodily sense of self, a sexual identity, a sense of self which is separate from the Mother. Their symbiotic undifferentiated relation to her, their formlessness, begins to take a shape. Freud calls this second period in children's lives, the *Oedipal* period. The Oedipal period in boys and girls is marked by a movement away from the Mother. While both continue to see the Mother as desirable, they both begin to align with the Father, who represents what is separate, the notion of a separate self. Mothers and fathers in this setting are not just particular individuals, but represent women/femininity and men/masculinity in a more general sense for children. Hence, Freud's account is not just about actual specific biological parents. This may provide a rejoinder to those critics who discount Freud's work on the basis that today's families and non-Western cultures do not always consist of an intact nuclear family structure. For Freud, mother figures and father figures (usually the child's parents) are concrete particular instances that work as broad psychosocial symbols in the child's world. The Father is described as 'the third term', a representative male figure who symbolically steps in between Mother and Child. The Father is a figure who appears as different-from-Mother and who stands for separation – that is, he represents a distinct self, the one who is not symbiotically enmeshed with the Mother.

Distinct selfhood is thus symbolised by the one who bears a penis. Entry into society, into human culture, requires the development of a distinct human, a distinct 'I', rather than merely an unconscious animal self, in order to have the ability to function in society. To become human, according to Freud, hence also requires a degree of rejection of the Mother and alignment with the Father. All children must in some ways lose the Mother, must lose the sensuality and pleasures of connectedness, for the rewards of selfhood. To do so the Mother is psychically buried in the construction of the repressed Unconscious and the self is split into two. Despite the repression of the unconscious, it cannot be entirely denied and continues to affect conscious functioning. It escapes in dreams, slips of tongue and in the continuing impact of barely acknowledged desires. This construction of the split self, however, sets the scene for the ongoing social devaluation of women and the association of men with status and authority.

While all children are required to move towards the Father, because of the alignment of penis with separation/selfhood, this movement towards selfhood/Father is differentiated on the basis of biological sex characteristics. Boys note that they are like the Father and bear a penis. They observe that their symbiotic attachment is to the castrated figure of the Mother. Because they still wish to have the Mother all to themselves (to be with/be Mother), Mother begins to represent the danger of self-lessness, of lack of self, of a continuing primordial or infantile undifferentiated state. Boys therefore fear that they will lose the penis, fall back into castration (become women). They see their desire for the Mother as endangering their relationship to selfhood/ Father, and so, out of 'castration anxiety', must sharply reject Mother/woman. Girls go through a similar process but because of their physical similarity with the Mother figure, it is not the same. They discover that they are already castrated (lack a penis), continue to identify with Mother and thus eventually turn to Father in a more ambiguous way. Their selfhood remains less distinct; their escape from the undifferentiated self-lessness of union with Mother/others is less clear-cut. They continue, in other words, to have less marked boundaries between self and other and a weaker sense of individual selfhood.

Both boys and girls align with Father but in the case of boys this is attained through identification (a sense of sameness), while for girls alignment is established through desire (desire for the penis). However, the crucial point of Freud's analysis is that to become a self requires the adoption of a gendered positioning. *No self comes into being that is not gendered.* Freud does, however, note that not everyone follows these two paths precisely, and in any case the process is never absolute or completed. Tensions, confusions, ambiguities, borne of our attempts in childhood to achieve some form of self-resolution continue to mark our adult lives. Femininity, for example, is not a neat unified place of destination but a field of contestation.

Indeed, for Freud, girls' negotiation through this psycho-social maze is more difficult since they must change not only the orientation of their desire (from Mother to Father), but also shift from clitoral active sexuality associated with the Mother/female body to a sexuality which is associated with the Father/male body. Instead of having a penis they are required instead to try to gain one through heterosexual desire and heterosexual intercourse. Desire for the authoritative selfhood associated with the Father/penis (penis envy) and for escape from infantile symbiosis linked to the Mother, leads to a kind of displacement, into desire for a baby. Here baby comes to equal the penis, to symbolise girls' continuing attempts in the face of castration to annex the Father's power/love. Though girls have less anxiety regarding castration (that is, less fear of becoming woman) since they have no penis to lose and are already aligned with the castrated/less powerful category, they also have less to gain as they can never become (be like) the Father (have a penis). This means they experience less of a demand on them to move away from the Mother and establish a strong separation, a strong self. The psychic costs of these several struggles result in a weakened sense of self for girls/women.[8]

You may at this point be thinking what a load of speculative twaddle! However, it is useful to think about the psychological/social drama Freud is outlining. He says that girls discover early on that men are more powerful (men have got 'it'), while they are deemed as belonging to the category of lesser status (castrated) and can only aspire to achieve what men are willing to allow or give them (replacement penises/babies). Boys, by contrast, can go on having Mother/women (the object of infantile desire) with little psychological effort, without being cast as lesser, and at the same time gain the rewards of being associated with the powerful. Many feminists see this interpretation of gender and social power as showing how male dominance works and is reproduced over time at both a societal and psychological level. They also consider that Freud's work explained how both men and women might not simply be 'at home' in their gender and sexual positionings but might also resist them.

If you are still somewhat unclear about pyschoanalysis, I strongly recommend reading one or all of the very accessible accounts written by Stevi Jackson (1996b: 62–73), Jeffrey Weeks (1985: 127–81), Bob Connell (1994) and Sue Vice (1998: 162–76) (see also Grosz, 1994c: 57–61; Sullivan, 2003: 18).

Feminist reworkings of Freud: basic criticisms

Nevertheless, most feminists are critical of aspects of Freud's work. They criticise it initially on the grounds that it is biologistic (that is, psychoanalysis may be said to reduce social relations to effects of biology). Freud is said to demonstrate a psycho-social basis for gender identities and hierarchy which is undermined by equating gender with *anatomy*. The libido, for example, which underlies the development of the self in psychoanalysis, is presented in terms of a biological drive or force. The clitoris appears in his work as naturally inferior, while the penis seems naturally pre-eminent. This looks very much like a 'bigger is better' argument in which male power is naturally pre-ordained. Social relations then appear to flow from an innate biological sexual hierarchy.

Jacques Lacan, who will be discussed a little more in Chapter 5, is a contemporary interpreter of Freud's approach. His work precisely becomes important in Postmodern feminist psychoanalytic accounts because he replaces Freud's biological stance with a more thoroughly cultural perspective. Lacan sees gender difference as a psycho-social construction through positioning in language rather than responses to literal bodily forms.

Secondly, feminists criticise Freud on the grounds that he is not simply *describing* how male-dominated societies come into being, but is accepting and *prescribing* male dominance as the basis of all human culture and human selfhood. This penis or male-centredness is sometimes called phallocentrism. Most feminists consider Freud's work phallocentric insofar as the entire Oedipal story of the construction of the self is based around a male's response to his mother and to becoming a man. Moreover, this story is literally penis-centred. Finally, the libido is identified as male. Women and femininity appear as on the margins, as paler imitations of the male norm or as enigmatic and perplexing.

Women-centred (Modernist) Psychoanalytic feminists: Nancy Chodorow

A number of Modernist women-centred writers have employed these criticisms while continuing to make use of Freud's work. Nancy Chodorow extends the critique of Freud's focus on the penis. She points out that although Freud presents all children as initially polymorphously sexual, they are not. As Freud himself notes, the Mother is the primary love object for children. Chodorow is here suggesting that Freud's analyses illegitimately focuses on the Father, the penis and the Oedipal turning towards the Father to the extent of evading the prior significance of the Mother and woman-to-woman (mother to girl) relationships in social and psychic development. She asks in this context, 'Why is the mother's breast not at least *an* organising symbol in the development of young children and our gendered selves? Why is the penis so completely the focus of attention?'

Along these lines she rejects Freud's account of femininity as entailing a weaker sense of self. Where Freud asserts that girls do not experience the character-building effects of castration anxiety during the Oedipal period, Chodorow (along with most other psychoanalytic feminists) argues that women's supposedly negative identity as constituted by lack – lack of a penis – may be reassessed. In the first instance, Chodorow asserts that Freud underestimates the pre-Oedipal period and overestimates the Oedipal in conceiving the latter as enabling girls to leave the suffocating symbiosis of the former:

> Core gender identity for a girl is not problematic in the sense that it is for boys. It is built upon and does not contradict, her primary sense of oneness and identification with her mother. ... [I]it is not the existence of core gender identity, the unquestioning knowledge that one is female, that is problematic. Rather, it is the later-developed conflicts ... [which] arise from identification with a negatively valued gender category. ... [D]evelopmentally, the maternal identification represents and is experienced as generically human for children of both genders.
>
> But, because men have power and cultural hegemony in our society ... [they] have come to define maleness as that which [is] basically human, and to define women as not-men. ... Because Freud was not attentive to preoedipal development (and because of his sexism), he took this meaning and valuation as self-evident. (Chodorow, 1997: 16–17)

If women's negative constitution in Freud's work as 'lacking', as 'not-men', may be questioned, then the assessment of their supposedly weaker boundaries to the self might also be reconsidered. For Chodorow, girls' 'weak', less distinct self can be seen in another light. Because girls are not obliged to separate from the Mother in order to develop a (gendered) self, women can be viewed as not experiencing connection with others as at odds with or a threat to the self. Chodorow accuses Freud of assuming that proper selfhood depends only on separating from others (from the Mother). For her, rejection of connection and developing impermeable boundaries around the self is not inevitably a sign of psychological strength. Accordingly, in the context of women's more 'relational' self, men can be regarded as exhibiting negative characteristics. Men can also be seen as constituted by lack, by lack of relational qualities. They are shaped, says Chodorow, by a fear of being close.

Girls in Chodorow's story partially reject their Mothers not for a penis/Father (baby) but rather out of disappointed love for their Mothers. It is the Mother who is central to this story and who gives girls their strength rather than their frailty. Boys, because they must say a decided 'No' to Mother and must separate from their Mothers more completely, are in her account weakened by the psychic costs of separation from the primary/first love object. In other words, where Freud stresses boys and girls turning to Father in the Oedipal phase as they become gendered personalities, Chodorow locates the beginnings of significant personality formation in the pre-Oedipal period, in the sensory closeness of both boys and girls to their Mothers and the different ways they are obliged to give her up.

Chodorow, like Freud, argues that girls retain a longer connection in the pre-Oedipal period to Mothers than boys. However, for Chodorow, this does not mean that girls remain incomplete, and somewhat outside the order of human culture, but rather signals girls' greater 'relational potential'. This relational potential impels women to become mothers. They continue to desire the Mother, to be Mother, because they wish to re-create their infantile experience of connectedness. This reproduction of mothering behaviour continues to generate women's unequal responsibility for parenting. The gender imbalance in parenting, and hence in love objects for young children, unfortunately also continues the requirement for boys to develop conceptions of manhood which depend on rejection of women and distance from others – that is, patriarchal sensibilities. Women's mothering contributes to the perpetuation of their own oppression (Chodorow, 1992: 168). Chodorow recommends that men's greater involvement in parenting would disrupt this chain of effects.

Where Freud says the baby is a substitute, a bit of male power that, in a sense, enables women to be 'bought off' for their comparative lack of power, Chodorow says 'the desire to Mother' signals women's ongoing engagement with and nurturing of others, which offers a preferable social model of the self and society. In a period in which concern for others (think, for example, of the war in Iraq, asylum seekers and reconciliation issues between indigenous and non-indigenous peoples) has become a matter of some significance, Chodorow's views suggest that women can offer a model for reforming neo-liberal individualism and masculinity.

Debates about Modernist Gender Difference feminism

Rich and Chodorow provide two different examples of Modernist Gender Difference feminism. They focus on the deep significance of gender identities as the key to understanding patriarchal society. Such feminists highlight women's difference from men, the shared character of womanhood – that is, women's commonality with each other – and the specific and positive content of that commonality. Modernist Gender Difference (women-centred) accounts gained major influence in feminism in the 1980s and appear to have been widely accepted even in the mainstream cultures of Western societies. Popularist versions of this way of viewing gender are reflected in books like *Men are from Mars, Women are from Venus* (Gray, 1993), which discuss the age-old 'battle of the sexes' and their differences from each other. Even though these versions are usually more closely aligned to biologically fixed conceptions of gender, they certainly also reflect aspects of women-centred feminist thinking, indicating its widespread influence. We find such thinking in our everyday conversations in that probably all of us have at times complained ruefully about 'the opposite sex' as having 'no idea' (that is, not sharing our ideas) or being incomprehensible, and contributed to discussions which assumed that women as a group are more relational and caring. There are many criticisms of women-centred Gender Difference feminism precisely because it is viewed as reflecting back (albeit in inverted fashion) conservative popularist ideas about the immutable and unitary nature of men and women. The criticisms of this kind of Feminism tend to arise in relation to four major issues.[9]

1. In describing a universalised (and often trans-historical) content for womanhood, critics suggest that the Difference framework reinforces socially inscribed gender categories as if they were unchanging and self-evident rather than exactly what feminists should open up for debate. Gender Difference thinking is seen as confirming society's binary (two) and 'essentialist' categories, confirming that there are just two ways of being which amount to fixed core 'essences' associated with being a woman or a man.
2. The Gender Difference approach is also frequently challenged on the basis that it reaffirms a fixed content to an identity/self associated with being a woman or man. Social Constructionist and Postmodernist critics note that manhood and womanhood are not the same in every culture, and not all women are necessarily relational or nurturing. The so-called 'sex wars' in feminism during the 1980s and 1990s, which we will discuss in the section on Sexuality Studies, arose out of a dispute over women-centred accounts of womanhood. Sex radicals like Pat Califia (1996: 230–44) noted that while some women

might be nurturing, gentle and like 'vanilla' sex, other women might, for example, be interested in inflicting pain in S/M (sadomasochistic) sex.[10]
3. In addition, Social Constructionists in particular argued that focusing on 'difference' (on what men and women might be like) diverts from the critical issue of 'domination'. These theorists asserted that the point was not whether men and women are different or whether common positive features of womanhood may be discovered, but power. Difference is not the cause of social discrimination but rather arises from it.[11]
4. A wide range of commentators attending to Differences argue that the attempt to construct a 'monolithic' group, 'women', who share a common identity content, focuses exclusively on gendered power and ignores differences *between* women associated with other relations of power such as 'race' and class.[12]

Conclusion

What are we to make of the attempt by Gender Difference feminists, especially the Modernist women-centred ones so far discussed, to put a positive value on women/ femininity? Is it a dangerously repressive idea, putting forward in practice a respectable Angel-in-the-home WASP mother as a universal female norm,[13] or is it a practical and supportive notion which gives women a sense of political solidarity and direction? The criticisms of Gender Difference feminism largely revolve around a rejection of 'Identity politics' associated with Modernist women-centred accounts. Indeed, the first three of the criticisms outlined above actually contributed to the development of a Postmodern Gender/Sexual Difference approach, which reflected the broad move in gender/sexuality theory during the 1990s away from a stress on identity categories. However, the last of these criticisms, regarding the problematic construction of a monolithic category 'woman', continued to be an issue for the Postmodern variant. As I have noted earlier, the Postmodern turn in Gender Difference thinking was invariably psychoanalytic in orientation and continued to emphasise the significance of difference between the sexes. Nevertheless, writers like Jane Flax and Elizabeth Grosz refused Chodorow's macro claims regarding any particular content to identity categories. In the next chapter this emphasis on *sexual difference without determined content* within the Postmodern (and Psychoanalytic) variant will be outlined in more detail.

Notes

1. See for example, Kate Millett, (1971) and Shulamith Firestone (1970). Other Radical feminists are antagonistic to both equality and difference. Writers like Catherine MacKinnon (1987a: 51) assert that the point is not whether women and men are the same or different. Rather, she says, 'Gender … is a matter of dominance'.

2. For an early articulation of her position, see Hartsock (1983) and for her response to critics, Hartsock (1997).

3. Hartsock specifically notes connections between her feminist standpoint arguments and those of writers who argue for the usefulness of standpoints arising out of racial oppression (Hartsock, 1998b, 1997: 237–8, 241–5). For the take-up of this point, see hooks (1984a: ix).

4. Hartsock insists that she makes no claims about how existing women view the world. She distinguishes her work, from that of Radical and psychoanalytic accounts of gender difference

and women's selves, by arguing that she focuses on social positioning and not upon a universal gendered sense of self/identity (1998b: 236). However, most critical commentators on Gender Difference feminism suggest that Hartsock has employed and continues to operate with a similar macro understanding of women as positively different, as constituting a socially differential group identity that must claim self-definition to resist continuing subjugation. See Hartsock, 1987; Fraser and Nicholson, 1990: 31; Hekman, 1997.

5. Dworkin's approach is similar to that of another Radical feminist writer, Susan Griffin, who argues that ordinary heterosexuality is uncomfortably close to rape and about men's power rather than an egalitarian pleasure. I will return to this kind of approach in more detail in Chapter 18 on Masculinity Studies when discussing the work of John Stoltenberg. See Dworkin, 1981, 1987; Griffin, 1979.

6. See also this chapter, note 1 above.

7. Jackson argues that writers like Simon and Gagnon, as well as Michel Foucault, offer other perspectives on the psychosocial constitution of the self. See Jackson, 1996b: 64 and 1999: 24; see also Plummer, 1994.

8. For short and accessible accounts of Freud's views on women and femininity, see Vice, 1998: 162–76; Jackson, 1996b: 65–7; Ramsey, 2000: 168–71; Crowley and Himmelweit, 1992: 146–51.

9. For examples of these criticisms, see Segal, 1987; Fraser and Nicholson, 1990: 19–37 (especially on Chodorow); Gatens, 1994: 93–107 (on Daly and Chodorow); Young, 1997c: 21–37; Andermahr et al., 2000 (see characterisations of Identity and Identity Politics on pp. 124–6).

10. See also related discussions in the Sexuality and Masculinity Studies sections, Chapters 10 and 18.

11. See, for instance, discussion of Christine Delphy's views in Jackson, 1998b: 135–6. See also MacKinnon, 1987a; and Alcoff, 1988: 408–14.

12. See Audre Lorde's open letter to Mary Daly offering a critical assessment of the racial exclusivity of Daly's 'women-centred' approach (Lorde, 1981b, 1984). See also Omolade, Carby and hooks for similar concerns, and hooks and Hennessy regarding material social distinctions between women (Omolade, 1980: 247–57; Carby, 1982; hooks, 1990b; Hennessy, 1993).

13. WASP is an acronym for white Anglo-Saxon Protestant, but is frequently used more loosely to designate a staid and conformist mainstream social positioning.

5 Postmodern Psychoanalytic Feminism: Sexual Difference

In Chapter 4 on Gender Difference feminism I noted that this theoretical direction is concerned with 'more than one', with more than the universal Human. Gender Difference feminism stresses instead that gender makes a difference, that gender cuts across this singularity. This direction in Feminism announces that there are at least two conceptions of the Human. I also pointed out that Gender Difference feminism is spread across the Modernist–Postmodern continuum. Indeed, it consists of two variants: on the one hand, a Modernist, so-called 'women-centred', approach which is organised around an Identity Politics revaluing women and, on the other, a more Postmodern-influenced Psychoanalytic approach dominated by what is often called 'Sexual Difference' feminism (Figure 5.1).

The Modernist variant on the left-hand side of the continuum's divide contains several features. In the first instance, this variant displays a focus on a 'woman-centred' analysis which says that men and women have a different actual content to their different selves/personalities (or at least have a different way of being). Secondly, the women-centred approach asserts that women have a common identity, which is associated with a shared gendered oppression but is also usually seen as having positive features. Women are generally seen as more relational, more nurturing than men. This positive aspect of women's identity can be used in the reform of society. Finally, most 'women-centred' writers (with perhaps the exception of writers like Mary Daly) argue that women's common identity is not pre-given or natural, but socially constructed and hence men too can take on positive 'womanly' qualities and become more like women. This is almost the opposite of Emancipatory approaches like Liberal feminism

Figure 5.1   Gender Difference feminism across the Modernist–Postmodern continuum

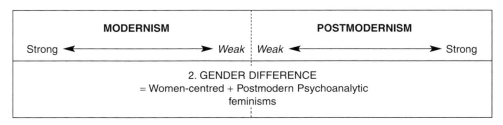

whose political aim is for women to take on what has been associated with men. While many critics of women-centred identity politics assert that such a framework associates women with a fixed essence (an essential self or mode of being), inasmuch as the framework asserts that men too can become 'womanly', the positive account of femininity is not necessarily specific or endemic to women. In this sense, a women-centred approach may not be as fixed in its account of gender and gender difference as is claimed by its critics.

The women-centred perspective has rather diminished in influence in scholarly work (precisely because of criticisms regarding its fixed characterisation of 'feminine' difference), but remains very significant in other social arenas. Indeed, probably the main forms of Feminism in everyday life and the popular media within Western societies are associated with either Emancipatory Liberal feminism or women-centred Gender Difference feminism. On the one hand, we tend to see in these societies Liberal feminist arguments about women attaining equal rights with men and entering the public sphere. On the other, we see broadly women-centred views expressed with regard to developing women's support networks, men 'getting in touch with their feminine side', and the overall importance of refusing selfish individualism and embracing social concepts of care and nurturance for others, nationally and internationally. In other words, Emancipatory and (Modernist) Gender Difference frameworks are by no means merely abstract theoretical trajectories, but rather very much part of ongoing socio-political debate.

When we move to the Postmodern variant (on the right-hand side of the divide) we find, by contrast, that this position has little popular influence and is typically expressed in highly abstract language.[1] Nevertheless, this Postmodern variant requires examination because it continues to be exceptionally significant within academic feminist scholarship, especially in the Humanities. It has many elements that require some explanation. For this reason I will not spend much time on individual instances, though I will briefly refer to the work of Jane Flax and Elizabeth Grosz.

Postmodern (Psychoanalytic) Gender Difference feminism

First, I will briefly return to a few summary points about Postmodernism, because this is our first encounter with a position which employs Postmodern thinking. Following this, I will provide a little more information about Freud and the psychoanalytic tradition, because *all* Postmodern Gender Difference approaches are psychoanalytic in orientation. This discussion enables consideration of the two main 'camps' of this Postmodern position – that is, those who follow Freud (for example, Jane Flax) and those who follow Lacan (for example, Elizabeth Grosz).

1. The Postmodern part

Postmodernism generally does not mean *anti*-modernism, but 'an extension of', 'after', Modernism (Best and Kellner, 1991: 29–30). This is especially the case for the 'weaker' versions of Postmodernism, in the 'borderlands', which is where Postmodern

Gender Difference approaches are located. These weaker versions may be distinguished from 'stronger', more thoroughly Postmodern feminisms precisely on the basis that the latter tend more towards an *anti*-Modernist stance. In other words, the Modernist–Postmodern 'divide' is not neat or absolute.[2] It is more a matter of emphasis. Some weaker Modernist feminists show certain Postmodern influences and some weaker Postmodern feminists show certain Modernist influences. The borderlands of the divide indicate these positions are not completely distinct or oppositional.

Nevertheless, I will at this point continue to talk about the distinction in rather decisive terms to clarify what it is about. Postmodernism in a broad sense does not accept that there can be any one, single explanation, account or 'truth' dealing with all of society, or power, or the self.[3] Postmodernism is at least wary of, or even (in strong versions) against, singular overarching conceptions of society, power, the self and history. It is sceptical about or antagonistic towards:

- **macro theories** ('metanarratives'/'grand theories') of everything and therefore forswears foundational universals – that is, it forswears views that say this or that is the absolute foundation of everything in society, power and the self;
- notions of power as *only* negative domination/oppression/repression and as 'out there' and external – that is, Postmodernism denies that power can be removed from the self and society;
- notions of the self that view it as having an essence/foundation, and one that is untouched by power – that is, Postmodernism refuses notions of a true self that can be liberated from power;
- notions of History as the story of the progressive liberation of the self, as a universal singular linear story of all societies in which human beings over time become free of power.

By contrast, Postmodernism is in favour of:

- multiple (plural and contextually specific), local (small-scale) and unstable theories;
- notions of power as everywhere and not all of a piece – that is, power is not just negative repression but is also constitutive/productive (including productive of the self);[4]
- notions of the self as unstable, not fixed, having no essence, and as made by power such that there is no place of absolute freedom from or beyond power;
- notions of History as unstable, having no essence or pre-ordained linear path.

In Postmodernism uncertainty, fragmentation, and multiplicity predominate. Not surprisingly, the term Postmodernism itself is associated with complex and multiple usages, developed by a range of disparate thinkers.[5] For this reason, it is helpful to compare the Postmodern frame of reference I have outlined with Nussbaum's strongly Modernist approach (Chapter 3), in order to gain some broad sense of the character of the distinction between the two.

2. The Psychoanalytic part

Now let us turn again to why 'Gender Difference' feminists as a grouping have often taken up Freud and psychoanalysis. We can then discuss why Postmodern as well as Modernist Gender Difference feminists employ psychoanalysis.

Gender Difference feminists (both Modernist and Postmodern) focus on difference, in particular the importance of difference between men and women. For this reason they are often drawn to Freud's work. Freud and his followers argue that the self comes into being through gender (sexed identity) – that is, the path to becoming a person is a gendered path. Selfhood *is* gender identity. Gender is what makes one a human rather than a creature outside complex human social life. Gender is that which places one in culture, beyond a merely physical being. In short, for Freud there is no such thing as a genderless *Human* being. Because he takes gender difference as crucial, as fundamental to all societies, to all social organisation and hence to all relations of power and forms of the self throughout History, it is not surprising to find Gender Difference approaches taking an interest in psychoanalysis. Psychoanalysis is after all the archetypal 'gender difference' theory. It is worth noting at this point that Freud's view of gender difference as fundamental sounds distinctly Modernist when you consider the elements of Modernism I have outlined above. For this reason it is no surprise at all to find some Modernist 'women-centred' Gender Difference writers influenced by psychoanalysis. In Chapter 4 I mentioned Nancy Chodorow's work as an instance. Her work does tend to assume that gendered personalities do have clear and different contents.

What is more difficult to grasp is that Postmodern Gender Difference thinkers are also interested in psychoanalysis. In this case their work has some Modernist and some Postmodern elements.[6] These Psychoanalytic *and* Postmodern Gender Difference writers, in common with women-centred Gender Difference thinkers, accept the fundamental significance of gender as the basis of the formation of the self. In other words, they accept some Modernist elements within Freud's approach (which makes them weak Postmoderns). Nevertheless, by comparison with 'women-centred' writers, they interpret Freud's work as also having some Postmodern aspects. While Freud's account of the key foundation of society, power, the self, and history as being found in the eternal gendered construction of the personality seems highly Modernist, other elements of his account of power and the self have been interpreted in Postmodern terms.

For example, Freud is one of the few social thinkers who does not offer a conception of power as largely 'out there' (in the state, government, the military, etc.) but sees power as creating the self. We are, in Freud's analysis, shaped *by* society's arrangements regarding what is valued and what is not. We *are*, in ourselves, living embodiments of social power. This kind of analysis of power and the self is associated with 'postmodern' thinking.

Secondly, Freud's account of the self may be interpreted in Postmodern terms. He sees the self as a socially constructed process. Moreover, his explanation of how the self is made postulates a split between the formless, unstructured pre-Oedipal infant repressed in the unconscious and the more structured regulation of a bounded (that is, gendered) self found in the post-Oedipal conscious. In other words, he postulates the self as not one singular essence but as necessarily uncertain, divided/split, and unstable. The self develops some form of resolution that is necessary for functional sanity, but this is never complete. The unconscious keeps leaking into the conscious such that you can never fully know yourself. Nor can the self ever be fully knowable, as the unconscious is largely lost to us, 'forgotten', repressed. What is Postmodern here is Freud's view that there is no set or fixed essence, no original 'true' self. For Freud, the biological body is not enough to explain, cannot explain our (gendered) identities. A male body, for example, does not necessarily lead to a masculine gender identity or to masculine heterosexuality. Nothing about the self is certain or fixed. This may be viewed as in keeping with a Postmodern approach, even if Freud himself did largely assume that failure to reach a gender identity resolution that is socially deemed as matching one's bodily sex was dysfunctional. In other words, although Freud noted the ambiguity and fluidity of the self, he took for granted that a body designated as female should become feminine and that failure to achieve femininity amounted to maladjustment and defective development.[7]

Distinguishing Modernist and Postmodern (Psychoanalytic) Gender Difference frameworks

On the grounds that Freud's work contains certain Postmodern insights, a number of Gender Difference feminist writers have pursued both a Postmodern and Psychoanalytic approach. For example, some of these writers, such as Jane Flax, have followed Freud's work while also employing the writings of key Postmodern thinkers like Michel Foucault. Postmodern Gender Difference writers like Flax (whether they employ Freud or other psychoanalytic approaches) are concerned with exploring the social impact of hierarchical binaries. They focus on the constitution of power relations. These writers use *gender* as the exemplary case and most often to the exclusion of discussion of any other social hierarchies. (Flax's work is atypical in this particular respect.[8]) Unlike their Modernist counterparts, they do not argue that men and women are actually necessarily different or that actual womanhood involves a common set of qualities or political potentialities.

Both Modernist and Postmodern variants of Gender Difference thinking argue that group (gender) differentiation is crucial – that is, they continue to make use of social categories/identities like gender and race – but also typically prioritise the former[9]. However, Postmodern Gender Difference feminists make no presumptions about the *content* of these differentiated gender identity groupings. Indeed, they criticise any assumption that women are a homogeneous group with common features as 'essentialism' – that is, they are critical of 'women-centred' writings (along with other Postmodern feminists).

The Postmodern Freud camp: Flax

Jane Flax's thinking provides a useful instance of the linkages and distinctions between Modernist and Postmodern Gender Difference thinking. Flax's approach in the early 1980s very much followed that of Nancy Chodorow, discussing the links between a male identity organised by repudiation of the Mother and the character of patriarchal social relations (for example, Flax, 1983). However, increasingly Flax became influenced by Postmodern criticisms of universalising macro theories and universalised unitary conceptions of gender identities. In 1987 she began to suggest that Feminism had a great affinity with Postmodern thinking, in that both forms of theorising are concerned to deconstruct supposedly neutral universalised singular explanations of the social world, in particular the Enlightenment concept of Reason as the singular truth of

Human nature and activity (Flax, 1987: 625; Hekman, 1997). Where Postmodernism proclaims the death of the notion of the Human essence (Humanism) in favour of analysis of contingent and variable practices, Feminism proclaims the death of central-ity of the Male Subject in favour of exposing the gendered character of such practices. The transcendental claims of Modernist Humanism are depicted as absolutist and actu-ally only about (privileged) Men.

By the late 1980s, Flax, like other Postmodern Gender Difference writers, was object-ing to what she saw as the fixed essentialism of the Modernist 'women-centred' model. She no longer accepted that there is something essential and common to woman-hood. Flax explicitly rejected the assumptions of 'standpoint theories' associated with Modernist Gender Difference thinking, exemplified by the work of Nancy Chodorow and Nancy Hartsock (Flax, 1987: 642).[10] The idea of a common sisterhood is viewed as a tendency to explain gender difference in universal and singular terms and, impor-tantly, resting upon the repression of differences between women (Fraser and Nicholson, 1990: 31). Furthermore, Flax asserted that the truth claims of standpoint theories (such theories assert their access to *the* Truth of social reality or at least to a more objective, Truer access to that reality[11]) also reveal a dangerous complicity in the impulse towards repression/domination (Majar, 2002). This is a crucial shift. The emphasis in Flax's approach is upon heterogeneous and multiple relations of power and partial vantage points, rather than upon the shared characteristics of subordinated groupings, their shared subversive political potentiality, or the greater access their marginal status affords them to a true/better understanding of reality.

Writers like Flax have become unabashedly Postmodern over time and increasingly may be seen as even moving away from or extending the boundaries of Gender Difference thinking and its singular focus on gender.

The Postmodern Lacan camp: Grosz

Other Postmodern Gender Difference theorists do not follow Freud so much as his more recent interpreter, Jacques Lacan. Those feminists who make use of Lacan's form of psychoanalysis, even if often very critically, do so precisely because Lacan attempts to move away from certain fixities (to do with the biological) he sees in Freud's approach and remakes it in cultural/linguistic, supposedly more thoroughly Postmodern terms. Those Postmodern feminist theorists who draw upon Lacan yet remain critical of aspects of his analysis, are labelled post-Lacanian and often describe their work as referring to 'sexual difference'. The writing of Elizabeth Grosz provides a useful example of the Sexual Difference framework. While I have described this post-Lacanian approach under the umbrella term of Postmodern Gender Difference theory, to indicate its links with and development from Modernist Gender Difference thinkers, writers following this approach in fact reject the usage of the term 'gender' for reasons I will explain shortly (Grosz, 1994a: 16).

Freud and Lacan: a short story

Having briefly established the parameters of Postmodern Gender Difference feminism and noted both Freudian (Flax) and broadly Lacanian (Grosz) interpretations, it is necessary to return to Freud and Lacan to show how the latter may be distinguished from the former.

Freud says that during the Oedipal stage, boys fear loss of the penis, becoming lesser – that is, penis-less (becoming girls). They fear they will be castrated by the Father because they want/desire the Mother. In other words, they are still drawn to the feminine. They want to be as one with the Mother, to be the feminine. Their anxieties lead them to psychologically reiterate continually that they are not Mother/woman/feminine. They must refuse femininity to become clearly separate beings, to gain something of the Father's power (masculinity). They must throw off the formless symbiotic relationship with the Mother that appears to have no clear separation. The boy builds a strong personality boundary by internalising the Father, the masculine. He develops a Father-in-the-Head, a strong (masculine) sense of self, and represses the pre-Oedipal self as the unconscious. Girls, by contrast, do not have to deal with the threat of castration as they are already apparently castrated, already the lesser. Consequently, when they sight the penis their motive for escaping the Oedipal (the self-structuring period) is less. Their motive for leaving the Mother is less. They are not obliged by fear of loss of the penis to strongly separate from the Mother, and are not going to gain the rewards of the full authority of masculine power. Hence, girls continue to have weaker self-boundaries and continuing symbiosis with the Mother. The pre-Oedipal is less clearly repressed and the woman in some sense remains 'stuck' with more infantile elements.

Lacan argues that this analysis is too literal and too biological. The process is not about a literal physical penis, but about a psycho-social principle he calls 'the Phallus' – that is, social power lined up with masculine authority. He notes like Freud, that the Father stands in at some point in a child's mind as a 'third term', a representation which cuts across the speechless, pre-cultural relationship between mother and child. The Father/phallus is a cultural representation of power, as the child takes on language. The Father/phallus represents the separate agent, selfhood, as the child learns the notion of 'I' and takes up 'the Law of the Father'. However, this representation is also of loss, loss of the Mother ('I' = separated stand-alone self) and loss of an associated sense of 'wholeness'. Neither boys or girls in this scenario have or get the phallus, but the entry into selfhood and language – that is, into the Symbolic human order rather than the experiential sensual pre-human – is represented by the Father's difference from the Mother (by the penis/masculine). This means that individuals line up according to their relation to the masculine. Femininity in this account is 'lack', incompleteness. Both boys and girls are constituted out of loss (of the Mother/of an imagined symbiosis) but the substitute benefit of entry into language and culture is not as complete for girls. They remain in some senses outside culture, outside the Father's Order. You can see here how Lacan recasts Freud's work, yet retains the basic story (Ragland, 1991; Grosz, 1990; Minsky, 1992). Contemporary Postmodern feminists have generally preferred to work with and reinterpret Lacan's linguistic and cultural turn rather than Freud's more literal engagement with the body.

Psychoanalysis as developed by Freud is understood by these feminist interpreters as an account of the ways in which male and female bodies are given meaning and placed within the context of a gender hierarchical society (Grosz, 1997). He outlines the psychological formation of subjects in the light of social projections concerning anatomical distinction. Such social projections mean that individual subjects cannot be immune or indifferent to the implications of specific (sexed) bodies, including their own. For Freud, the production of masculine and feminine subjects (the process by which male and female bodies become socially intelligible) involves their placement in relation to a valuing of the male body as complete and the female body as castrated, as lacking. Freud, though he recognised in certain respects the repression of women consequent upon this socially unequal valuation, saw few options to it. Lacan's analysis, while it shifts away from Freud's emphasis upon the implications of actual bodies towards their symbolic construction in language, is similarly disinclined to consider alternatives. Indeed, Lacan explicitly suggests that valuing of male body and the penis is a given, 'a fact' as he puts it, beyond culture and therefore presumably inevitable and unchangeable (Lacan, cited in Grosz, 1997: 307; Brennan, 1992).

Feminists who employ Lacan's work share his view that the acquisition of language is the means through which the feminine is constituted as lacking and women's subordinate social status is enforced but, just like feminists who use Freud, they reject his acceptance of gender hierarchy. Psychoanalysis is used by these feminist writers to question the notion that men and women *are* beings essentially different from the moment of birth and that gender identities are discrete and stable. Insofar as psychoanalysis outlines the somewhat uncertain and incomplete process by which subjects *become* masculine and women, feminists have found it a useful mode of thinking to consider how to uncover resistance to the process and possibilities for change. Like virtually all feminists employing psychoanalysis, and especially those employing psychoanalysis with a critical eye, feminists who make use of Lacan subvert the traditional focus in psychoanalysis upon the Oedipal period (in which children confront the social valuation of the masculine). Most feminist writers turn instead for signs of resistance and alternative possibilities to the pre-Oedipal period in which the Mother/feminine is still significant.

Figure 5.2 gives a brief outline of the various forms of Gender Difference Psychoanalytic feminisms.

Further considerations on the Postmodern Lacan camp: post-Lacanian feminists

Postmodern Psychoanalytic feminists generally suggest, unlike Modernist versions, that actual women do not have a common identity marked by a particular set content but rather 'the feminine' represents that which somewhat escapes cultural rules, which is 'other', and not the standard or norm. Indeed, 'woman', they argue, *is* difference. Female stands for difference *per se*. Woman in these Postmodern Psychoanalytical approaches is 'the marginalised', the symbol of what is left out of and different from the cultural order. Hence, the representation of woman/women can be redeployed for social change in that order (Beasley, 1999: 77–80).

The way this symbolic feminine is understood in contemporary feminist Postmodern Psychoanalytical approaches differs to some extent depending upon whether these approaches follow Freud or Lacan. Most are most strongly associated, not with Freud but with Lacan's camp. Writers in France, including Luce Irigaray and Julia Kristeva (see Marks and de Courtivron, 1981 for examples), and in Australia, such as Elizabeth

Figure 5.2   Psychoanalytic feminisms: an overview

MODERNIST VARIANTS	POSTMODERN VARIANTS
FREUD (Focus on the Father i.e. Oedipal)	

	LACAN
1. Freudian 'women-centred' e.g. Chodorow (focus on Mother and pre-Oedipal)	**2. Freudian 3. Lacanian 4. Post-Lacanian** **Postmodern** e.g. Flax e.g. Mitchell e.g. Irigaray and (pre-Oedipal) (Oedipal) Grosz (pre-Oedipal)
• Stress on actual women's identity and on their 'relational self' • Stress on identities	• Stress on 'the feminine' as representing marginality/the other, but having no specific content • Stress on the axis of Gender/Sexual Difference as constituting social hierarchy

Notes:
i   All feminist psychoanalytic approaches focus on mother–daughter relations
ii All except Lacanian feminists focus on the significance of the Mother/pre-Oedipal
    period – rather than primarily upon the Father – and re-evaluate women/feminine
    in positive terms

Grosz, have employed a critical reworking of Lacan. On this basis they are sometimes termed 'post-Lacanian'. I will now outline very briefly certain features of Grosz's post-Lacanian perspective in order to demonstrate features of the 'Sexual Difference' approach with which she has been associated.

Grosz, along with other post-Lacanian writers of 'Sexual Difference', focuses upon the problem of the masculine norm which equates difference with inferiority. Her work is intended to affirm the potentialities of women as *symbolising* difference (rather than as *being* different – that is, having certain set characteristics). She searches out the ways in which the female form (morphology) (Andermahr et al., 2000: 174) suggests that the ubiquity of the male norm may be questioned, not in order to reverse the masculine–centre/women–periphery dichotomy (as Modernist Gender Difference approaches are inclined to do), but to disaggregate such ordering. If the Modernist Gender Difference approach aims to 'put women in the centre', Grosz's Postmodern variant aims to 'deconstruct centres' (Squires, 2001: 12). While the dominant cultural code may present a monolingual disembodied masculinity that never was dependent on a woman and may present a 'phallocentric sameness' which denies and drowns out the voice of the Mother/feminine, Grosz's intention is to enable recognition of the materiality of sexual difference. To the extent that the feminine body is made present and brought to life, the limits of the centralised male norm and the costs of its maintenance may be explored (Grosz, 1994d: 32).

In this way Grosz advocates what she calls 'corporeal feminism' and, following 'French feminists' like Irigaray, is inclined to assert that that embodiment is specific and that there is not just one form of body/self but at least two (Grosz, 1994c: 22; Beasley, 1999: 78). The particular characteristics of the 'Sexual Difference' paradigm are revealed when Grosz's approach is compared with what I have described as the strong Postmodernism associated with the work of Judith Butler (Chapter 8).[12] Where Butler argues that 'natural' distinctions between male and female bodies are themselves an aspect of social prescription, Grosz notes the content of the body itself and suggests that the body cannot be reduced to the social. In simple terms, Butler's strong Postmodern feminism tends to describe bodies as *produced* by meaning, whereas Grosz's corporeal emphasis on 'sexual difference' insists that specific bodily forms are part of and *productive* of meaning. Corporeal feminism stresses that bodies have something to add to the analysis (Beasley and Bacchi, 2000; Grosz, 1987).

In Butler's analysis, feminine being is merely an effect of the normative cultural order, and for this reason cannot be appealed to by those who advance social change. By contrast, in Grosz's formulation, the feminine body is not simply a social construction which has nothing to offer, but precisely does actively contribute to what can be imagined and practised within the social. The sexually specific body is the material through which the social can come into being (Colebrook, 2000). Hence sexual difference can open up possibilities denied by the male norm. Excluded forms of embodiment raise opportunities for social rethinking.

For this reason Grosz champions the specificity and irreducibility of *sexual* difference. She rejects any neutral, sex or gender-free conceptions of the subject as a form of **universalism** masking a male norm. Sexual difference cannot be erased without concomitantly disavowing the marginalised, the feminine. Her intention is to incorporate the interrelationship between bodily and social in her analysis, rather than merely focusing on the social as the term 'gender' is inclined to do (Grosz 1994c: 19, 156; Milnes and Browitt, 2002: 137–8; Bray and Colebrook, 1998; Alcoff, 2000; Mason-Grant, 1997). Grosz opposes Butler's concern with the term gender as insufficiently attentive to the specific and embodied character of the sexually differentiated power. Moreover, she regards Butler's Queer feminist project of displacing or abolishing gender as problematic and calls instead for 'alternative strategies which acknowledge the ongoing complexities of differences between men and women' (Pringle, 1992: 95). When asked in an interview about her views of sexual difference in relation to coalition politics between gay men and lesbians, Grosz answered that:

> [i]t seems to me that the question of sexual is irreducible … there does seem to be an irreducible gulf between the two sexes. … It is possible to work together, however … we have very different stakes in the status of the 'phallus'. … [A]ll the various categories labelled under the title 'queer' are very different. … Whenever I see the word 'postmodernism' I ask which? … It is the celebration of difference that I want to record … an openness to what is really different. That difference means drawing a line in some places. (Grosz, 1994a: 9–10, 6–7)

On this basis, she defends 'difference feminism' and the political use of the category 'woman' so long as this usage is not tied to a particular content. Grosz asserts that speaking of sexual difference evokes a material reminder that women cannot be confined to the position of man's deficient 'other' and that the bodies of women contribute alternative possibilities (Diprose, 1994: 79). In keeping with all of the Gender Difference writers (whether Modernist or Postmodern Psychoanalytic), Grosz's work proposes that the category 'woman' can be used to marshal social criticism of the status quo and reform society.

Debates

There are a number of possible criticisms of the Postmodern and Psychoanalytic Gender Difference viewpoint. Its Psychoanalytic element, for example, may be criticised on the grounds that psychoanalysis does not allow any way out of gendered power/masculine authority since gaining selfhood in this perspective relies on incorporation into a gender hierarchy (Brennan, 1992; Segal, 1987: 126–34). Relatedly, lesbian and other sexuality critics dispute the '**heteronormative**' model of psychoanalysis. In the psychoanalytical story of gender development, girls learn to be attracted to men, not to identify with them. Lesbians are dysfunctional in the psychoanalytical account (Ryan, 1992). Thirdly, the focus of Psychoanalysis upon the ahistorical mechanisms of 'the family' as the mainstay of male dominance is regarded as overly narrow, ignoring the contributions of numerous other gendered institutions, including schools and media, and in any case insufficiently attentive to historically specific families (New, 1991: 18; Williams, 2001: 5512–13).

On the other hand, the Postmodern element in this Gender Difference thinking may be challenged. The move away from actual women to a focus upon women as symbol, as standing in for 'difference' *per se*, may be viewed as too abstract, too narrow and not about practical action. In particular, the approach can be seen as remaining largely limited to the social/cultural construction of subjects in relation to gender/sexual difference. Gender/sexual difference appears almost without exception as the only difference that matters (Bray, 2001: 315). This means a neglect of many aspects of the social space within which subjects operate such as race and class forms of power. Consequently, a less substantial account of the female body is reiterated (Lloyd, 1998: 124–34). The focus on the constitution of the gendered/sexed body largely in isolation from other differentiating interactions between bodies also diminishes the conceptions of sociality, power and the political in Gender/Sexual Difference writings.

Finally, there are critics who argue that this approach is not Postmodern enough (Fraser and Nicholson, 1990: 33–4). These commentators suggest that the Postmodern Psychoanalytic variant of Gender Difference still lines up the feminine/female body with a symbolic outsider status which is not that different from the essentialist unity the 'woman-centred' Modernist approach gives to women. The characteristics or content of the feminine outsider may not be spelt out in the former variant, but she retains a set identity which is given coherence through a conception of the specificity of the female body. This may return the analysis to a form of biological/bodily essentialism. The suggestion is that more attention to Postmodern concerns with diversity would overcome uncertainties about the focus on the female body and the unwarranted singular privileging of gender/sexual difference, enabling a more complex consideration of power.

Conclusion

Postmodern versions of Gender Difference thinking are also always psychoanalytical. They differ as a result from the strong, 'unadulterated' Postmodern feminist theorising we will consider in Chapters 8 and 9. The usage of psychoanalysis retains a degree of structural analysis in this Gender Difference perspective and thus moderates the emphasis upon destablising singular macro accounts of social life characteristic of Postmodern thinking. The perspective also retains a decided focus on gendered power and a determination to counter gendered power by celebrating difference associated with the marginalised feminine. This singular focus may, however, be precisely its limitation. Certainly the writers in the next chapter are inclined to think so.

Notes

1. Indeed, one advocate, Elizabeth Grosz, has strongly defended this uncompromisingly academic orientation by asserting that feminist activism is necessarily located in a wide variety of locations, including the realm of scholarship. In this context she says, 'struggle for the right to write, read and know differently is not merely a minor or secondary task within feminist politics' (Grosz, 1989: 234).

2. A number of commentators have noted the distinctions and overlaps between Modernist and Postmodern positions, which defy any conception of a clear break between them. There is also increasing evidence of feminist writers, among others, pursuing agendas that explicitly work across these positions. For this reason I have outlined a continuum with a highly permeable borderline. See Waugh, 1998; Best and Kellner, 1991: 1–75; Cacoullos, 2001; see also Chapter 1 of this book, notes 11 and 14.

3. The term Postmodernism can be variously attached to: a trend in poetic expression; an epoch; a reaction to Modernist aesthetics and architecture; a philosophical nihilism; a nihilistic view of the loss of meaning in the communicative signs employed in contemporary culture/society; a reworking of Marxist conceptions of late capitalism; the growth of a consumer culture; the development of new social movements and democratic politics; and an anti-foundational type of thought or view of the world typically associated with French poststructuralist thinkers. Since this book is concerned with critical theories and thinkers in the gender/sexuality field, I have particularly focused upon the last usage. Gender/sexuality theorists may draw upon many of the usages of the term 'Postmodernism' but are most clearly and strongly engaged with its employment to refer to anti-foundational thinking linked with French poststructuralism, as well as with political considerations related to this thinking. See Gibbins and Reimer, 1999: 12–15; Rose, 1991.

4. For example, women may be very attached to the identity of womanhood and this identity may produce pleasures and investments.

5. Gibbins and Reimer refer to Derrida, Lyotard and Rorty as exemplary contributors, while others commonly also mention Foucault, Deleuze and Guattari, and Lacan. A listing of influential contributors could also mention Irigaray, Kristeva, Bauman, Warner, Hassan, Nicholson, hooks and Spivak, among many others. Clearly there is not space in this book to provide detailed accounts of all these strands of Postmodernism, and indeed the purpose of the book is not focused upon enunciating the complexity of the Postmodern frame of reference, but rather its particular forms of development in the gender/sexuality field. See Gibbons and Reimer, 1999; Best and Kellner, 1991; examples of the work of Derrida, Lyotard, Bauman, Hassan and hooks can be found in Natoli and Hutcheon, 1993; Rorty, 1989;

Deleuze and Guattari, 1987; Lacan, 1977; Irigaray, 1985; Moi, 1986; Warner, 1993a; Nicholson, 1990; Spivàk, 1987a.

6. Elizabeth Grosz, for example, despite her commitment to an analysis associated with a range of Postmodern thinkers, makes use of psychoanalytic paradigms that she recognises as containing certain universalising Modernist tendencies. See Grosz, 1995; and Sullivan, 2003: 184.

7. See Freud ([1933] 1973: 145–69) and Chapter 4, note 8 for readings on Freud.

8. Flax has a strong interest in the interwoven connections between gender and race, and has increasingly developed a position that may now be said to sit between Postmodern Gender Difference and Post-colonial feminisms (see Chapter 6). In many ways she has moved away from the singular gender focus of Gender Difference in her growing concern with Differences. Nevertheless, she retains a rather distinct position from most writers on Differences. For example, her position continues to be attentive to psychoanalytic approaches which focus on the role of the Mother in gender identity (influenced by Melanie Klein and Dorothy Winnicott) and which are commonly used in the work of Gender Difference writers like Nancy Chodorow. Moreover, her concern with Differences, unlike that of Post-colonial writers, does not extend to class issues. See Flax, 2002, 2003.

9. In this regard Gender Difference thinkers, even those influenced by Postmodernism, remain at something of a distance from the more thoroughgoing assault on the status of such categories/identities undertaken by strongly Postmodern feminists. See Beasley, 1999: 83–4.

10. See also her more recent sympathetic, yet critical, assessment of the work of Dorothy Dinnerstein, whose analysis is frequently paired with that of Chodorow, in Flax (2002).

11. Early in the 1980s Hartsock and other standpoint theorists displayed little doubt that a singular perspective based in women's shared subordinate social positioning could claim privileged access to one true reality. By the late 1980s Hartsock, among others in this grouping such as Sandra Harding, had modified this assertion but only somewhat. In this later analysis, women's heterogeneous experiences of subordination were recognised but their subordination was still seen as derived from a unitary centre. Power continued to be seen as centralised and located in particular people. As in the earlier analysis, women are viewed as experiencing a common location at the end of this centralised power structure (even if their experiences differ), and they remain somehow imbued with a shared positive difference from this centre. Relatedly, women's marginalised perspectives are still regarded as offering, if not *the* Truth, at least something necessarily Truer than the view from the centre. In short, women's marginality in this analysis continues to yield a privileged vantage point. See Hartsock, 1987 and 1990; Harding, 1991; Hekman, 1997.

12. Grosz's analysis is by no means entirely distinct from that of Butler, however. See, for example, Grosz, 1996.

6

Differences: Feminism and 'Race'/Ethnicity/Imperialism (REI) – hooks to Spivak

In this chapter I will be discussing the fourth main direction in feminist thought which is concerned with (**multiple**) **Differences** between women/within the feminine and which points to intersections between gender and other axes of power. I concentrate on one major instance of this theoretical focus on Differences – that is, feminists attending to 'race'/ethnicity/imperialism or what I abbreviate to REI feminists. I refer here not to feminists who have occasionally discussed 'race'/ethnicity/imperialism but those who concentrate upon one or more of these related topics. I will first consider the terminologies employed in the chapter and provide a broad overview of the REI approach in terms of its key features. This will be followed by a brief account of its development over time, leading finally to a focus on contemporary feminist work in the area. In the process I will discuss a range of thinkers and attend more specifically to bell hooks in the next chapter.

Terms

Feminists working on REI have different views on terminology. In practice those working on 'race' generally tend to be discussing 'black' women/'women of colour' living in Western countries (that is, they have an intra-national focus).[1] Those working on ethnicity tend to discuss those not designated as 'black' but rather as ethnic minority women, including migrant women, in Western countries. Those writing on imperialism/colonialism tend to discuss 'Third World' women who have become resident in the West or women in 'developing' countries in the Third World. Some of these writers reject the term 'race' as inaccurately affirming the non-existent biological basis of 'races', while others do not reject the term but use it sociologically.[2] Similar uncertainties have arisen in relation to usage of associated terms like 'black'.[3] Still other writers question the use of 'ethnicity' (Roen, 2001). Furthermore, what such terms mean (even sociologically) differs from country to country and over time. For example, in the United Kingdom people of Lebanese origin may be included in the term 'black', but this would not be usual in Australia, and would certainly not be the language employed in the USA (see Kanneh, 1998: 86–7).

A number of feminist writers attending to REI also have misgivings about terms like 'Third World'.[4] Sangari (1990: 217) and Mohanty (1991b: 51, 74) both note the inclination of this indiscriminate label to lump together diverse women, cultures and places into a single monolithic grouping. Such a grouping is constituted in ways that may ironically replicate the vantage point of imperial definitions in presuming to name the vastly differentiated character of the supposedly 'non-Western' as singular and simply marginal/outsider. By contrast, writers like Gayatri Spivak attempt to shake up the heavy imperialist weight of the centre–periphery binary associated with apparently opposed terms like First World/Third World by reconfiguring the marginal as not simply offering an outsider positioning but simultaneously an integral vantage point (interview with Spivak in de Koch, 1992). These discussions clearly indicate some important terminological difficulties. However, following Mohanty, I find it helpful to continue to make use of the label, Third World women. She notes that, rather than referring to a commonality of colour or racial identification, the term is better employed to indicate a common context of struggle and resistance to 'sexist, racist and imperialistic structures' (Mohanty, 1991a: 7).

I have also, in referring to 'REI feminisms', linked race and ethnicity with the term 'imperialism' rather than 'colonialism' or 'post-colonialism'.[5] I employ the former to indicate that these feminist approaches attend to the broader issue of imperialism rather than the more specific one of colonialism. Imperialism refers to 'the formation of an empire', a process in which one nation gains dominion over other nations. Although this process did not become an articulated policy for gaining economic and other benefits until the late nineteenth century, imperialism in the sense of 'the practice, theory and attitudes of a dominating metropolitan centre ruling a distant territory' has a long history extending at least to ancient Roman times. Colonialism, the establishment of 'settlements on a distant territory' is only one aspect of imperialism (Said, 1993: 8; see also Ashcroft et al., 1998: 122–6). Imperialism may also refer to the continuation of economic, political and cultural dominance, which exists following the 'independence' of previously colonial societies. Its diffuse and largely negative associations are highlighted when it is sometimes employed as a pejorative adjective, to refer rather loosely to forms of cultural/national/personal self-aggrandisement, to the inclination to expand centres of power and authority.[6]

Despite the broad definitional distinctions outlined above between imperialism and (post)colonialism, feminist approaches attending to power relations between First World (typically Western) centres and marginalised Third World societies are likely to be designated 'post-colonial' thinkers. Post-colonial here describes a combination of Third World political orientation and Postmodern thinking regarding a rejection of universalist ways of conceiving the world. Such a combination leads specifically to a critique of dominant, white, European culture and its assumptions concerning its ability to speak universally. Post-colonial theory amounts to 'a revolt of the margin against the metropolis, the periphery against centre' (Milner and Browitt, 2002: 144). While the first writings to use the label 'post-colonial' focused specifically on *colonial* societies (Ashcroft et al., 1998: 186), recent Post-colonial feminist work attends to themes that are by no means confined to previous colonial empires. Moreover, according to Spivak – a key Post-colonial feminist theorist – all of us now live in a world of 'planetary capitalism', such that post-colonial thinking is no longer even especially about First World/Third World distinctions but about an all-embracing empire of global inequalities (Spivak, 1990: 94–5). In this context, I have used the more inclusive term 'imperialism' to describe *the subject matter* of Post-colonial feminist theory. This subject matter is concerned with previous and contemporary 'empires' and involves a rejection not only of the economic and political dominance of these empires but most particularly their (usually racialised) cultural dominance (Ashcroft et al., 1998: 127).

Finally, I use the cognate term 'race/ethnicity/imperialism' (REI) to signal overlaps in concerns between these subjects, while at the same time suggesting that these topics cannot be entirely dissolved into each other. There are clear linkages between racial and ethnic marginalisation in national settings, as well as between race/ethnicity questions and marginalisation in the international/global arena. For example, Milner and Browitt (2002: 143) note that the theorising of multiculturalism has, depending upon the national context under discussion, sometimes denoted 'ethnicity', as in the case of Sneja Gunew's work, and sometimes 'race', in the case of Stuart Hall's approach. Moreover, Hall has also increasingly linked multiculturalism to global matters (Hall, 2000). Relatedly, Indigenous peoples' experience of racism in a range of national settings is not necessarily idiosyncratic and discrete, but often connected by imperialist expansion. Nor can this experience be entirely divorced from the treatment of other culturally/racially marginalised groups. Paul Gilroy's work on race, class, nation and international hybridity is relevant here.

Gilroy discusses race within the context of English national identity and in developing notions of diasporic cultures which escape national sovereignty, in particular the 'stereophonic' form of 'the black Atlantic world'. He outlines not only the constructed meaning of 'blackness', but also its heterogeneity. This account refuses any racist diminution of black to the one-dimensional category of not-white. Like a number of other contemporary writers on race, Gilroy links notions of cultural/national belonging with racialised claims to uniformity and seeks to counter this 'race-thinking' with the strategic advantages of disasporic hybridity (Gilroy, 1992, 1993b; Gilroy et al., 2000). In similar fashion, Sandoval (1991) notes that 'US Third World feminist' perspectives necessarily partake of a political hybridity, weaving between feminist and civil rights movements such that an alternative fluid positioning may be identified (see also Mirza, 1997: 13). However, this post-colonial and/or postmodern inclination to stress hybridity and fluidity, a plurality at odds with settled belonging and identity, has not been accepted by all REI writers. Some suggest that such an approach precisely threatens a black identity which offers an oppositional voice against racist society, insufficiently recognises the distinctive contribution of a black perspective, or may even imitate racist refusal of the ongoing existence of black cultures and Indigenous claims to territorial belonging (hooks, 1990c; West, 1999d: 545; Parmar, 1989; Beasley, 1999: 103–6; Sabbioni et al., 1998; Hollinsworth, 1998).

These debates may not simply indicate different directions in REI feminist works, but indicate incommensurable elements associated with the terms 'race', 'ethnicity' and 'imperialism'. While the cognate label 'REI' asserts certain connections between them, these do not expunge the specificity of the terms. For instance, writings by immigrant ethnic minority or Third World women may not intersect with those of Indigenous women. Their perspectives may sometimes even be at odds (Mohanram, 1999: 92–6; Alice, 1991: 65).

The terrain of REI feminism

Feminists noted that the universal Human in mainstream theorising was predicated upon an unrecognised male model that ignored women's potentially different status and experience. However, most feminists then proceeded to inaugurate a conception of power as about men and women (gender/sexual difference) and a conception of women as a group experiencing a shared subordination.

The crucial first issue raised by all feminists dealing with REI is that *differences between women* point to the category of 'Woman' as bearing the same universalising dangers as the universal Human (Lorde, 1981b; Spelman, 1980–81; Mohanty, 2003a: 499–502). Just as the supposedly universal Human appears to be all-embracing but does not actually speak for all people, the universalised notion of Woman is not all-inclusive. REI feminists assert that the idea of a single 'woman's perspective' as against the dominant 'male perspective' in reality affirms the experiences of a privileged group of women – in particular, white, middle-class, Western women – and in effect excludes and silences those women whose experiences are dissimilar from this group (Collins, 1989: 747; Squires, 2001: 14).

REI feminists offer a positioning that is necessarily an alternative to and critique of those forms of Feminism which unthinkingly reflect white experiences by only focusing upon gendered power and viewing women as a homogeneous group. For REI feminists, if the notion of the essential Human – an over-arching neutral positioning which represents all – requires interrogation, then on similar grounds the conception of an essential Woman/Feminine must be questioned. This stance shifts analysis from exclusive attention to gender to a more complex account of power and an exploration of differences between women.

Such an approach leads to three further key features. First, the 'bifocal' view of gendered and REI forms of power offered by REI feminism leads to a stronger recognition of cross-gender commonalities forged by racism/ethnocentrism/imperialism. On this basis, REI feminists often note the strategic necessity for solidarity between men and women of culturally marginalised groups. The power divide is no longer simply located between the sexes. Rather, REI feminists highlight the divide between white (or Western) and non-white/minority (or non-Western) in this reappraisal of the position of men (hooks, 1984a: 67–8, 2003c; hooks et al., 1993: 37–8; Huggins, 1987: 78–9; Carbado, 1999c).

Secondly, this critical view of a simple commonality among women produces a refusal of any straightforward presumption of women's shared subordination. Feminists of REI pointedly note that the notion of women's commonality conveniently constructs all women as disadvantaged. The involvement of 'white' women or women of privileged ethnicity in the subordination of other women is thereby evaded.

Thirdly, feminists of REI note that the notion of commonality among women is not just complicit in power in that it enables comparatively privileged women to evade acknowledgement of their positioning, but also enables such women to speak for all, with impunity. Ironically, the unequivocal presumption of women's shared subordination actually permits privileged women to reiterate power relations associated with REI (hooks, 1984a: 1–15; King, 1988; Moreton-Robinson, 2002). Feminists focusing on REI have often, as a result of their attention to relations *between* women, been at the forefront of discussions about the meaning and practice of a feminist political solidarity in the light of women's diversity (see, for example, hooks, 1984b: 43–65; and Mohanty, 2003b).

History of REI feminism

Feminists of REI may be said (unlike all other feminist groupings) to be found across the entire Modernist–Postmodern continuum from the strongly Modernist to strongly Postmodern and in this sense offer the only *cross-spectrum* grouping within Feminism. This is often ignored in analyses of Feminism as a field of thought. Moreover, REI feminist analyses tend to be represented in an auxiliary function, as merely contributing an adjustment to (white) Feminism, rather than offering substantial new theoretical directions or being presented in relation to their connections with the broad grouping of REI perspectives (Trin, 1989: 80). As Sandoval (1991) suggests, ignoring these connections to theoretical and political movements beyond gender/sexuality – such as civil rights movements – results in a narrowed account of REI feminist approaches. For this reason it is worth considering aspects of the breadth of the grouping before turning to its present-day predominant forms.

Nineteenth-century first-wave 'white' feminism was largely dominated by a concern with 'rights', equality and notions of universal humanity. Feminists attending to REI also initially proceeded in this 'assimilationist' manner and contributed their voices to the first-wave agenda of including marginalised groups within the Liberal project of universal human emancipation. They provided an REI-focused contribution to Modernist emancipatory frameworks but, in so doing, also developed a perspective that could not be entirely subsumed within the Eurocentric cast of the universal and humanist claims associated with the Modernist agenda.

Just as white first-wave feminists like Wollstonecraft advocated women's inclusion in the Modernist project of universal emancipation, so African-American advocates like Sojourner Truth (1797–1883) claimed recognition and inclusion for those women marginalised by racial/ethnic hierarchy. Truth's speech at the second annual convention of the women's rights movement in Ackron, Ohio (USA) in 1852 demonstrated a viewpoint that does not, however, just proclaim inclusion into universal categories. She also announces during this speech that universal categories like 'woman' can silence other differences (Kensinger, 1997). In this way, as bell hooks (1981b) notes, Sojourner Truth prefigures contemporary critiques that cast doubt on such universal identities as 'human' and 'woman'.

At this point we can move to more recent Multiple Differences approaches in Feminism, which concentrate upon race/ethnicity/imperialism. As is the case for the Gender Difference feminism, Multiple Differences approaches that focus on REI include a variant that is Modernist and another that is Postmodern in orientation. Perhaps at this point it is worth returning to my earlier illustration of the five main directions in Feminism (see Figure 1.2) but in this case noting in bold the positioning of REI feminism (see Figure 6.1).

Figure 6.1   R/E/I feminism in the Modernism–Postmodernism continuum

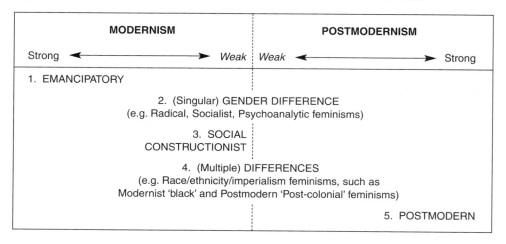

Predominant forms today

By the 1980s the Modernist Gender Difference framework which proffered a 'women-centred' model of identity politics was at its height. This (gender) identity-oriented model was anti-assimilationist (it did not assume that women wanted to be like men) and anti-universalist regarding conceptions of the Human. Feminists working on REI contributed to, disputed with and extended Gender Difference models, just as they had complexified nineteenth-century Emancipatory feminism. In the process, however, they also offered a specific theoretical direction.

REI feminists noted that if the 'women-centred' Gender Difference approach showed that the universalised category of the Human ignored gender difference, so universalised categories of Women ignored differences associated with race/ethnicity/imperialism. To place in doubt the universal Human must also place in doubt the universal Woman. This analysis nevertheless generated Modernist and Postmodern variants of REI feminisms.

Modernist variants: for example, black feminism

The Modernist variant of REI feminism typically remains focused upon Differences as differences in identity – that is, writings in this variant focus upon black/ethnic minority/ Third World women. They offer a challenge to Gender Difference identity politics by a focus on a proliferation of identity differences. The Modernist variant of REI feminist thinking in this sense offers a decidedly expanded version of the positive re-evaluation of women/feminine in the Gender Difference approach in that it offers a positive re-evaluation of black/ethnic minority/Third World women. Modernist versions of Gender Difference and REI feminists share a view of positive and independent identities associated with subordination.

There are indeed strong connections between women-centred 'standpoint theory' associated with Nancy Hartsock (see Chapter 4) and the largely Modernist 'black feminist' standpoint approaches of writers like Patricia Collins and bell hooks. Standpoint theory also has continuing resonance in the work of Chandra Mohanty, whose transnational feminist approach retains aspects of a macro Modernist concern with the universal and is distanced from Postmodernism (Hartsock, 1998a: 237; Collins, 1986: 15, 1990: 234–5; Grünell and Saharso, 1999: 210–11; Hekman, 1997; Mohanty, 2003b). Such connections arise in part at least because these feminist frameworks tend to give attention to class/economic issues. On the one hand, women-centred standpoint theories initially arose out of a reworking of Marx's concern with the positive political possibilities associated with the marginal class category, the working class. On the other hand, black and transnational feminisms often register black/ethnic minority/Third World identities in class terms. In addition, over time the Gender Difference and REI feminist accounts have become somewhat less distinct as the women-centred models acknowledged the limitations of a singular concern with gender difference and increasingly recognised the significance of differences like those associated with race/ethnicity (Hartsock, 1998a: 239).

Postmodern variants: for example, Post-colonial feminism

The initial challenge to the Gender Difference framework postulated that women were not all the same, not all women were 'victims', and disrupted the political innocence of the category women. This lead to a revitalised focus on REI Identity politics. The succeeding challenge to this Modernist REI approach to identity was a Postmodern, specifically a Post-colonial REI approach. Post-colonial feminism is a relatively recent development – from the 1990s onwards – and typically offers a more extensive refusal of overarching identity categories. If there can be no essential Human and no essential woman/feminine, then there can also be no essential black/ethnic minority/Third World women. The Post-colonial variant of REI feminism offers a postmodern-influenced critique of the homogenising and silencing effects of universalised identities by questioning any simple assumption of fixed cultural identity, or overly respectful view of cultural integrity. Such a viewpoint raises doubts about the innocence of conceptions of black/ethnic minority/Third World women, including doubts about whether these marginal identities are always positive. Modernist REI feminism initially displaces a singular emphasis on the notion of difference between men and women (gender difference) with a focus on differences between women (within the category of women). In the postmodern/post-colonial incarnation of REI feminism, this emphasis is also displaced by differences *between* black, ethnic minority and Third World women and *within* each of these categories. In Postmodern/Post-colonial REI feminism no simple identity-based politics or politics of cultural differences is pursued.

In keeping with Post-colonial theorising more generally, Post-colonial feminism is concerned with challenging arrogantly universal claims and homogenising tendencies in Western thought. This is seen as crucial because of the continuing legacy of European imperialism in the present day both in the West and elsewhere.[7] Despite the decolonisation of former European colonies, many parts of the world are viewed in this analysis as continuing to experience military, economic and political domination by Western powers and, importantly, the ongoing **hegemony** of Western ideas. Post-colonial theory asserts that the unsurpassed authority of Western thought is of concern because it remains imbued with an imperialist agenda (Ashcroft et al., 1998: 124–7). According to Edward Said – a thinker whose work is crucial to the development of Post-colonial thinking – European imperialist rhetoric endures in the continuing reiteration of the oppositional binary, the West versus 'other' (Said, 1978, 1993). The West is thereby cast as central and as the norm, while other cultures and peoples are represented as different and therefore inferior. This **'othering'** principle maintains hierarchical power relations between supposedly dichotomous, discrete, fixed and unitary identity groups and presumes that difference must be regarded negatively.[8]

Gender Difference and Modernist REI feminists have also been, in different ways, inclined to draw attention to the universalising tendencies of Western thinking which render inferior and marginal 'other' different voices. However, these feminists adopt a reversal strategy and put a positive value upon marginal voices by placing them centre stage. They valorise that which is different from norms of Western thought – women and black/Third World women respectively – in order to oppose it (Squires, 2001: 10–12; K. Ferguson, 1993: 3–4). In other words, Gender Difference and Modernist REI feminists accept and retain the dichotomous distinctions of mainstream Western thought, like Men/other and the West/other, but valorise that which is 'othered'. By contrast, post-colonial forms of analysis, including Post-colonial feminism, deconstruct such dichotomies and problematise their identity-based terms. Instead of questioning the centre–periphery distinction by reversing the terms of the distinction, Post-colonial feminism aims to destabilise any notion of a central focus or universal norm and relatedly deconstructs notions of discrete identities by acknowledging the hybrid heterogeneous character of cultures and peoples (Ashcroft, 1998: 118–21). Consequently, this form of REI feminism has given attention to the plural and fluid character of identity, as well as to the permeability of cultural borders, evident in writings on 'diaspora',[9] the possibilities of borderline/'impure' positionings and mixed cultural ancestry (Brah, 1996; Anzaldúa, 1990, 1993; Lugones, 1994; Ifekwunigwe, 1999).

Post-colonial feminism: at the borderlands of the Modernist–Postmodern continuum – Gayatri Spivak

Post-colonial versions of REI feminism disrupt identity categories as natural and distinct groupings, and are inclined to recommend considerable caution with regard to invoking such groupings as the basis for political activism (Gunew and Spivak, 1990: 59–66). Nevertheless, while these writers are inclined to treat identity distinctions like West/other, First/Third World and black/white as the subject of critical analysis and as unstable, they do not unreservedly advocate the disaggregation of identity to the degree advanced by Postmodern feminism. In Gayatri Spivak's terms, the Postmodern critique of the dangers of universalised group categories may not always be able to be relentlessly followed (Beasley, 1999: 101–3, 114–15; Winant, 1990). The problems attached to categories like Human, Woman or Black are acknowledged by Post-colonial feminists, but the political possibilities of claims made on behalf of marginalised groups are not dismissed. Rather, a coalition politics based upon a 'strategic' use of identity categories is advanced. At this point it is useful to turn to the example of Gayatri Spivak's work.

Spivak was born in Calcutta into a progressive, educated family and then moved to the USA as a graduate student. Her work offers an engagement with, and simultaneously a critique of, Western feminism's valorisation of 'women', post-colonial Indian studies rewriting imperialist histories from the viewpoint of the marginalised ('subaltern'), and Marxist analyses of the working class. Her critique of these approaches is based in a postmodern recognition that, despite their progressive politics, such approaches replicate the universalising and homogenising features of mainstream Western thought by advocating identities assumed to be widely representative that in practice are exclusionary. In this analysis, Western feminism's 'woman', supposedly capable of representing all women and their shared subordination, is once again revealed as Euro-centric and middle-class.

Spivak makes use of a particular kind of postmodern thinking derived from the work of Jacques Derrida, termed 'deconstruction'. **Deconstructionism** asserts that Western thought, including its progressive and politically resistant forms, is based upon the reiteration of hierarchically organised dichotomies – such as man/woman, black/white, good/bad, light/dark – which rely upon the exclusion of 'the other' lesser term. The task of deconstruction is not to reverse such dichotomies in an attempt to overcome this exclusion but rather to reveal the ways in which they work. Spivak puts a post-colonial spin on this task by noting the links between the dichotomous character of Western thinking and the practices of (gendered) imperialism. She rejects therefore any straightforward employment of categories like Third World or Women as a basis for political change and instead pursues a more pluralistic analysis intended to overcome the dangers of identity-oriented Self/Other, Us/Them distinctions. On these grounds, Spivak highlights the disparate, hybrid character of cultures and peoples, arguing that 'no rigorous definition of anything is ultimately possible'. For this reason she can only see herself resorting to identity categories in a provisional and polemical way: 'I construct my definition as a woman not in terms of a woman's putative essence but in terms of words currently in use' (Spivak, 1987b: 77).

However, Spivak – in common with other Post-colonial feminists – is by no means a committed advocate of Postmodernism and specifically states that 'Derrida is not my prophet'. For her, the usefulness of postmodern analysis is largely as an institutional discourse: 'deconstruction can only help in the big talk … in the academic arena' as a form of questioning. Those who are excluded (the subaltern) cannot be given voice through this method, rather such an approach 'makes you unlearn your privilege' and assume an ethical responsiveness which avoids romanticising them. At the level of practical politics Spivak suggests instead the notion of a 'strategic essentialism', in which concepts of group identity can be used provisionally, though with a constant sense of their limitations. While she notes that this seemingly paradoxical juggling of postmodern scepticism with a contingent usage of categories may seem to let homogenising categories back into play, nevertheless for her this nominal usage may be necessary in order to speak of power and marginalisation (Winant, 1990; Adamson, 1986; Landry and MacLean, 1996: Introduction and 269–70). Collective political struggle may require both the invocation of identity groupings – naming the direction of political activism – *and* a persistent critique of their essential status, thereby recognising the complexity of social life rather than upholding their self-evident authentic character. Spivak hence recommends, for example, that the group of South Asian scholars associated with Subaltern Studies remain committed to the sub-altern as 'the *subject* of history' (Spivak, 1987b: 209, emphasis added). In other words, she exhorts Post-colonial theorists and others concerned with political change to pro-ceed in certain circumstances – such as in resistance movements (Mills, 1998: 104) – as if the universal Human or other homogenising categories were still tenable, a strategic suspension of disbelief required because such labels remain the currency of existing politics in which we must intervene. As she notes,

> Essentialism is bad ... but only in its application. Essentialism is like dynamite ... it can be effective in dismantling unwanted structures or alleviating suffering; uncritically employed, however, it is destructive and addictive. (Darius and Jonsson, 1993)

Post-colonial writers like Gayatri Spivak and Sandoval (1991) stress that they are attempting to avoid set categorisations which reiterate imperialist and male-centred stereotyping, while enabling an 'oppositional consciousness' which is situated, is not neutral and must speak necessarily from somewhere. This point explains perhaps why even Post-colonial REI feminists tend not to be positioned at the strongly Postmodern end of the Modernist–Postmodern continuum within feminist theory. Where strongly Postmodern feminists challenge the status of categories like gender, class and race/ethnicity in a thorough-going fashion, Post-colonial REI feminists show a concern to question such categories but this typically does not extend to the point of resistance to any identity. Rather than a *singular* stress on the fluid nature of social differences, Post-colonial feminists offer a plural, even paradoxical emphasis on both fluidity and located identities.

Post-colonial feminists dispute – in common with strongly Postmodern writers – any set essence to identity. However, in order not to lose sight of those who are marginalised in the postmodern rhetoric about the general hybridity/fluidity of all categories, they are less inclined to jettison a positive advocacy of marginal group identities like 'black' or 'Third World' women entirely. They remain very conscious of pragmatic requirements regarding what they see as the ongoing political uses of these identity categories. Their consequent positioning on the borders of the Modernist–Postmodern divide can be regarded as a means to overcome the divide, a refusal to perceive these paradigms as incommensurable, or a form of creative eclecticism. However, some commentators sug-gest that this positioning is not integrative or intriguingly ambivalent, but rather incon-sistent to the point of incoherence. Milner and Browitt (2002: 148) assert that Spivak's work, for instance, does not hold together and is representative of the political failings of the postmodern critique: 'the *necessity* for this resort to strategic essentialism ... surely casts doubt on the wider anti-humanist enterprise. For what use is a theory that requires, for its effective application, that we pretend not to believe in it?'

Some transnational feminists who are concerned with imperialism echo this rejec-tion of the postmodern element in Post-colonial feminist work, and urge a return to Modernist universals (see, for example, Mohanty, 2003b).

Postmodern variants of Gender Difference and REI feminisms: the 'weak' Postmodernism of Sexual Difference and Post-colonial perspectives

Just as there are links between the Modernist variants of Gender Difference and REI feminism – between women-centred standpoint theory and black feminism, for example – there are also links between Postmodern variants. For instance, both Sexual Difference and Post-colonial feminisms highlight the deployment of power in the suppression of difference. Both invoke and deconstruct that which is cast as 'the other' in an effort to re-imagine symbolic and social arrangements (see Chapter 5). Indeed, many writers in these two frameworks share an interest in the Postmodern critique of fixed hierarchical binary identities derived largely from Foucault and Derrida, as well as in post-Lacanian psychoanalysis.[10] Moreover, the two frameworks both step back from a thorough-going engagement with Postmodernism, and retain some level of advocacy for marginalised groups rather than emphasising a resistance to any form of identity. Nevertheless, the frameworks part company in their point of focus. Where Postmodern Sexual Difference remains singularly attentive to the axis of sexual difference, Post-colonial feminist theorising of gender and race/ethnicity/imperialism is often another way of also thinking about global class distinctions/economic exploitation (Slemon, 1994: 16–17; Ahmad, 1992: 92–3).[11] Compare the work of Elizabeth Grosz and Gayatri Spivak in this context.

The range of REI feminism and related debates: from Modernist to Postmodern

REI feminist frameworks may be found across the spectrum of the Modernist–Postmodern continuum. (Table 6.1) However, in this range it is possible to see over time increasing doubt about identity categories and analyses based on the putative content of these categories. While the whole array of REI feminist frameworks is certainly spread over the Modernist–Postmodern continuum, the predominant ones today crowd around the borderlands rather than at its edges of the continuum (Table 6.2). These predominant frameworks may be best understood by comparing Gender Difference and REI Differences frameworks.

The debate at the borderlands between Modernist affirmations of identity (for example, affirmations of black women) and Postmodern scepticism about identities is perhaps particularly evident in a conversation between bell hooks and Nira Yuval-Davis published in 1999. Yuval-Davis argues that we should recognise but transcend identity categories to which hooks replies caustically, 'you cannot dismiss identity politics because … in everyday life people fall back on it again and again' (Grünell and Saharso, 1999).

Within REI feminism there is considerable criticism from Postmodern-influenced writers concerning Modernist identity politics but many, even most, REI feminists are uncertain about Postmodern/Post-colonial-inflected views. Boyce Davies (1994), for example, sees post-colonial theorising and its doubts about identity as itself a Western

Table 6.1   The range of race/ethnicity/imperialism feminism

Modernist Emancipatory	Modernist Differences e.g. 'Black feminism'	Postmodern/Post-colonial Differences	Postmodern
Critique of universal Human category	Critique of 'women' category	Critique of women and R/E/I categories	Critique of all categories
Positively include attention to gender and race/ethnicity group categories	Add race/ethnicity/imperialism category	Add multiple differences between groups and in them	Resistance to any identity

Table 6.2   Predominant forms of REI feminism

Frameworks	Group Difference approaches	
	Modernist versions	Postmodern versions
Gender Difference	• Stress on 'women' as identity	• Stress on feminine as marginal other • No specific content to actual women • Power expressed through gender hierarchy rather than located in identity
REI Differences	• Stress on black/of colour/Third World women as identity	• Stress 'others' of post-colonial/transnational world • No specific content to actual cultural/'racial' groups • Power expressed in process of post-colonial 'othering'

approach, which does not help to understand the specifics of Black and Third World women's locations. These debates in many ways provide an exemplary site for discussions that are critical to the current state of theorising within Feminism generally, in that they highlight the question of how to talk about social groups and collective political action in the absence of any 'essence' that unites such groups (Cacoullos, 2001).

Conclusion

REI feminist writers range across the Modernist–Postmodern continuum. While some (like Spivak) are decidedly cautious about employing REI identity categories (such as black or Third World) to speak for and mobilise 'racial'/cultural/ethnic minority communities, nevertheless these writers are disinclined at a pragmatic political level to dispense with these identities entirely. Hence, REI feminist work is typically located at the borderlands of the Modernist–Postmodern divide. This makes the work a particularly fertile site for recent discussions concerning the ways in which the divide may be disrupted and hybrid forms of thinking developed. Such discussions surface in critical re-evaluations of Postmodern and Queer thinking in Chapters 9, 15 and 21.

Notes

1. For a comparison of the uses of terms like 'black women' and 'women of colour/color', see Brah (2001: 5491–3) and Kanneh (1998).

2. See Beasley (1999: 103–6). For accounts of the long and convoluted history of the word 'race', see Banton (2002: 1–27) and Hollinsworth (1998).

3. One version of concerns regarding racial descriptors arises in exchanges between West (an African-American cultural theorist) and Klor de Alva (an anthropologist from a Chicano background). These commentators have debated whether the employment of terminologies, such as 'black', is affirming or deeply problematic. See West (1999c) and Klor de Alva (1997).

4. For a discussion concerning the development of and debates about the term 'Third World', see Buenor Hadjor (1993: 1–13).

5. I have followed Ashcroft et al. (1998: 187) and Spivak (1990) in employing the term 'post-colonial' rather than 'postcolonial', even though the distinction is by no means clear-cut.

6. For instance, 'Richard Nixon was dubbed an "imperial" president for seeking to take over powers that belonged to the US Congress' (Robertson, 1993: 237).

7. Post-colonial theory, including Post-colonial feminism, thus stands at odds with a range of approaches that regard considerations of imperialism/colonialism as no longer relevant since imperialism has been superseded. For an example of such approaches, see Becker et al. (1987).

8. For various accounts of 'other' and 'othering', see Ashcroft et al., 1998: 169–73; Gamble, 2000a: 289; Cranny-Francis et al., 2003: 14, 58–63, 65.

9. Diaspora is a term used to refer to the 'mobility of peoples, commodities, capital and cultures in the context of globalization and transnationalism' (Brah, 2001: 5494).

10. Spivak's use of Derridean deconstruction as well as Lacanian conceptions of the self in developing her notion of 'othering' provides one instance of such connections. See Winant, 1990; Aschroft et al., 1998: 171–2.

11. In this way, Post-colonial feminist thought may act as a counter to the diminishing concern with class in Feminism observed by some commentators. See Hennessy, 1995: 142–79.

7 REI Feminism: hooks

bell hooks (the name is not capitalised) has been described as 'the hardest working woman in academia' (Dauphin, 2002). She is the author of over 20 books for adult readers, starting with the ground-breaking *Ain't I a Woman: Black Women and Feminism* (1981a), written when she was only 19 years old, through to a myriad of works on feminist theory, masculinity, art, cinema, race, and more recently love and self-esteem. She has also managed to write children's books and to paint in-between times (Dauphin, 2002). hooks is a useful exemplar of feminisms attending to race/ ethnicity/imperialism (REI) because her work has ranged over time from a Modernist Differences focus on Identity towards more Postmodern-influenced concerns with diversity/multiplicity rather than overly unified and positive conceptions of identity. Her work therefore provides a particularly useful instance of the wide variety of perspectives in REI feminism, demonstrating both its cross-spectrum location as well as its tendency to congregate around the border of the Modernist–Postmodern divide.

Locating hooks in the Modernist–Postmodern continuum

What we see in hooks' early work is a Modernist, strongly identity-oriented approach, which stresses black/white differences in the context of the USA. This focus enables a critique of Feminism as largely a white feminism. In this early work there is little doubt regarding the benefits of Identity politics (in this case a black women's feminist politics). She also expresses a clear and certain sense of a singular macro political project. However, from the late 1980s onwards, hooks increasingly outlines a more broadly postmodern interest in acknowledging differences within 'race' (African-American) identity as well as within gender identities. This inclination can be seen in her discussion of heterosexism in the black community and her critique of black 'macho' men (hooks, 1989: 169, 1990a: 58–9, 1992a, 2003c). While hooks' work is still focused upon rendering visible marginal racialised identities, it is by no means uncritical. Increasingly, her more recent analyses deconstruct these racial/ethnic identities and are less inclined to configure them in unproblematically unitary ways than is evident in the early writings. This double action of invocation and deconstruction of identity, of stressing both race identity commonality as well as its diversity, is a characteristic move of REI feminisms today. Relatedly, her contemporary writings note 'racial' otherness at an international level, which further complicates any straightforward account of

Table 7.1   Predominant forms of REI feminism

Frameworks	Modernist Versions	Postmodern versions
REI Difference	• Stress on black/of colour/Third World women as identity	• Stress 'others' of post-colonial/transnational world • No specific content to actual cultural/'racial' groups • Power expressed in process of post-colonial 'othering'[1]

race/ethnic identity (Grünell and Saharso, 1999: 216–17). Nevertheless hooks maintains a strong focus on her African-American community, and its reformation, its sense of self, its identity.

On these grounds, hooks' body of work can be placed in both the Modernist and Postmodern camps. hooks both asserts and criticises identity-based politics at various points, thereby suggesting ways in which the divide between Modernist and Postmodern frames of reference may be seen as by no means impermeable (Ibid.: 208–9, 212). Her location at the borderlands of the Modernist/Postmodern debates on identity (albeit more strongly linked to Modernism) articulates an innovative direction that has implications for feminist thinking on both sides of the divide. For this reason it is perhaps useful to revisit one aspect of Table 6.2 presented in the last chapter, which outlines the predominant forms of REI feminisms (see Table 7.1).

Because hooks crosses over not only the Modernist–Postmodern divide but also to some extent the distinction between Black and Post-colonial feminism, her work offers the opportunity to rethink labels and characterisations. hooks is indeed a critical figure in Gender theorising (in Feminist and Masculinity thinking) in that her writings exemplify contemporary debates which place at odds those accounts which rest on set, clear-cut 'essentialist' identities and universal certain principles versus those which emphasise multiple fluid differences and less certain political projects. This positioning across supposedly opposed frames of reference also locates her work at the intersection of related debates regarding the significance of everyday accessible politics versus 'purist' theorising. Moreover, her location in terms of politics appears at the crossing of race/ethnicity and gender approaches. She claims a place in both 'homes' but also offers a critical perspective on both. While she has spent more time on developing a critical account of Feminism as unthinkingly offering a white perspective, the degree of criticism she directs at the black community in the USA is not always dissimilar. She sits, in other words, at the crossroads of a range of crucial dilemmas.

In this chapter I will discuss her earlier and more 'theoretical' work on Feminism and feminist politics. I will examine her critique of the singular privileging of gender difference and the 'women-centred' orientation of white feminism, her critique of white feminist accounts of men's positioning in Feminism, and her focus on 'revolutionary' politics. Secondly, I will outline later directions in hooks' work that offer *some* reworking of the earlier themes along rather more postmodern/post-colonial lines.

You can see here, as with other writers I have discussed and will yet consider, how theoretical approaches may not be set in concrete but rather still be in progress.

Thinkers of today are not only still alive but are still formulating and reassessing their views. Because this book is not about theories and thinkers of the past, it is necessarily a snapshot of the present. The book presents a frozen moment, which attempts to capture something in motion.

Early work

I started my analysis of REI feminism in the last chapter with Sojourner Truth's 1852 speech at the second annual convention of the women's rights movement in the USA. Sojourner Truth was born a slave and gained her freedom in 1827. She rejected her slave name and adopted a name intended to indicate that she saw herself as called by God to travel around testifying to the sins against her people. By the mid-nineteenth century she was well known in anti-slavery circles and had actively associated herself with women's rights. Truth was allowed on stage, despite some protestation, after a white male speaker had spoken against the idea of equal rights for women on the grounds that woman was innately physically inferior to man. She made a case for equal rights that sharply challenged this view:

> Well, children, whar dar is so much racket dar must be something out o'kilter. I tink dat' 'twixt de niggers of de Sout and de women at de Norf all a talking 'bout rights, de white men will be in a fix pretty soon. But what's all dis here talkin 'bout? Dat man ober dar say dat women needs to be helped into carriages, and lifted ober ditches, and to have de best places … and ain't I a woman? Look at me! Look at my arm! … I have plowed, and planted, and gathered into barns, and no man could head me – and ain't I a woman? I could work as much as any man (when I could get it), and bear de lash as well – and ain't I a woman? I have borne five children and I seen' 'em mos all sold off into slavery, and when I cried out with a mother's grief, none but Jesus hear – and ain't I a woman? (cited in hooks, 1981a: 159–60)

As hooks' notes, Truth is able to employ 'her own personal life experience' as evidence for her political claims (Ibid.: see also hooks, 1997a: 227). This perspective is one that also frames hooks' work. Indeed, her first book, *Ain't I a Woman: Black Women and Feminism* (1981a) employs Truth's famous phrase in its title. The books that followed in the 1980s – *Feminist Theory: From Margin to Centre* (1984a) and *Talking Back* (1989) – developed themes strongly influenced by this starting point (hooks, 1991: 27–8). She writes *as* a black (African-American) feminist. Her focus is on what she perceives as the central Western, particularly North American tradition of Feminism. Her *difference* from this tradition is a crucial starting point.

hooks' early works arise out of a so-called 'difference' approach, which became predominant in the 1980s in feminist and other progressive social-political movements – an approach I have described in Chapter 4. Importantly, however, her writings represent a challenge to the **singular difference** orientation I have described as Gender Difference feminism. In particular, hooks is highly critical of 'women-centred' accounts in which Feminism becomes a means to talk only of gender and hence to erase racialised difference (hooks, 1997b). Hence, her work may be located as attending to (multiple) Differences: in this case those associated with race and gender.

Because of this concern with differences, her thinking may also be linked with the broad field of theories associated in the West with analysis of race/ethnicity. Such race/ethnicity theorising includes consideration of indigenous peoples, immigrant populations and the diasporas created by slavery and forced labour – that is, populations which 'brought home' to the West the human spoils of its imperialist dominance of the world. Nevertheless, it is writers from the African diaspora which have so far particularly shaped this theorising. The effect has been to concentrate race/ethnicity analyses around certain terms of reference. As Stephen Howe (1998: 21) puts it, 'the central object has always been distinctions between black and white'. hooks' work represents a significant contribution to this focus, but it also offers an intervention in such theorising by criticising black men's sexism, as well as the overwhelming attention given to black men, within it. Her sense of the invisibility of black (African-American) women's experience, in both Feminism and writings on race/ethnicity, fuels a stance highly reminiscent of that of Sojourner Truth.

bell hooks (aka Gloria Watkins) begins her writings from her marginalised position, as a black woman. Truth's famous phrase 'Ain't I a woman' sums up precisely hooks' initial analysis of Western feminist theory and what she has to offer to it. Truth speaks and she/the Truth may be paraphrased as saying:

> I am black and I am also human and a woman. Human and woman are not one thing, not just white. They include me. I have suffered and I too deserve rights. I speak of my difference from you (my suffering as a black woman) and also of my commonality (human and woman). You cannot exclude me. I am the Truth. My identity is the Truth you cannot deny.

Sojourner Truth speaks a politics of identity, from an identity as universal human/ woman and as black woman. Her claim to be part of the universal Human sits side by side with a refusal to suppress her difference. This is an Identity politics that speaks through making her humanity/womanhood *and* her suffering, oppression and exclusion visible, in order to claim civil rights. hooks' early work in particular mounts a strong case for a similar enunciation of an authentic material identity as the grounds for a politics of social change.

I have described characteristics of Identity politics in the chapter on women-centred Gender Difference thinking, but it may be useful to revisit this briefly. Identity politics is based in the view that the most useful starting point for developing a politics concerned with changing the status quo arises out of one's own identity (experience of oppression).[2] This suggests the requirement to claim an identity (an experience of oppression) in order to develop political claims and that 'the character of the latter will be determined by the former' (Andermahr, 2000: 126). Barbara Smith, a black lesbian theorist, argues in this context that 'we have an identity and therefore a politics' (cited in Moraga, 1983: 131). hooks' approach in her early work and later bears many of the features of this way of thinking. In this context, she quotes approvingly from a student, Isabel Yrigoyei:

> We were not equally oppressed. ... We must speak from within us, our own experiences, our own oppressions. ... We should never speak for that which we have not felt.
> (cited in hooks, 1997b: 494–5)

hooks points out the ways in which black women in the USA are excluded and are oppressed. In *Feminist Theory: From Margin to Centre*, she inverts what she sees as white feminist claims to offer an authentic voice of oppression as women. She argues that the central tenet of feminist thought at this time, the notion that 'all women are oppressed', masks white women's monopoly over the movement. Moreover, hooks asserts that white women's claims to share in oppression are dubious and that black women's suffering is the real genuine article, indeed more 'true' (hooks, 1984a: 1–15). She establishes black women's authenticity, their right to speak in terms of suffering/oppression, initially by a rejection of the notion of a common bond between women – that is, a rejection of 'women-centred' feminism.[3] In *Ain't I a Woman*, hooks argues that race and class oppression creates differences between women that take precedence over the common experiences women might share. The suggestion here is that race- and class-based power relations are more oppressive than gender hierarchy. This emphasis tends to shift in her later work. However, in the early works she certainly argues that suffering/oppression is differential and that degrees of suffering can be identified. 'The motives of privileged white women', hooks asserts, must be questioned when they insist that 'suffering cannot be measured'. 'It is a statement that I have never heard a poor woman of any race make' (hooks, 1990d: 35). In the classic terms of Identity politics, hooks makes identity as an oppressed subject central to politics. hooks sets up here a dichotomy between privileged women and poor women and then goes on to link white feminists with privilege and black women with poverty.

In establishing this dichotomy, hooks is critical of the work of certain founding white feminists. She cites Betty Friedan's Liberal feminist classic, *The Feminine Mystique* (1965), which focuses on the oppression of women contained in their domestic 'housewife' roles, as an example of the limits of a white feminism that fails to attend to race or class. hooks says that it is a useful text, but nonetheless a book about a very specific (largely white) experience. The book can be seen 'from a different perspective … as a case study of narcissism, insensitivity, sentimentality, and self-indulgence' (hooks, 1990d: 33–4). Such feminist writing fails to note that most black women do not have the choice to be housewives.

In hooks' analysis black/poor women's oppression becomes more real, and more relevant to political thinking. In common with other Identity politics writings of the time, hooks suggests that those at the very bottom of the social hierarchy see more broadly the condition of society since they are not blinded by the rewards of that society and are consequently less committed to it. They are more in contact with the truth of society.

> I did not feel sympathetic to white peers who maintained that I could not expect them to have a knowledge of or understand the life experiences of black women. Despite my background (living in racially segregated communities) I knew about the lives of white women. (Ibid.: 37)

Such a perspective shares ground with the work of Nancy Hartsock, a theorist I discussed earlier in terms of 'standpoint theory' (Chapter 4). According to standpoint theory, you see differently depending on your standpoint in society and this has consequences for politics. Those who are oppressed are more able to observe the workings of social power than those who simply benefit from them. Despite hooks' overall antagonism to the 'women-centred' Gender Difference feminism associated with standpoint theory, she employs the logic of this theory to develop a view that black women can offer the most profound insights to a feminist politics since they experience the greatest levels of oppression (Ibid.: 39).[4] Hence, as the title *Feminist Theory: From Margin to Centre* suggests, hooks inserts black women at the core of Feminism. Using an Identity politics logic, hooks raises doubts about white feminism and makes a greater claim for the viewpoint of black women in terms of Feminism. Moreover, hooks questions whether feminists who are white and middle-class are truly oppressed as opposed to being merely 'discriminated against' (Ibid.: 35–6, 39; for a similar viewpoint, see also King, 1988).

hooks is putting forward, in precisely the same language as writers who developed Gender Difference Identity politics, a notion of true oppression and hence greater authority to speak in relation to progressive politics. In questioning the authenticity of white feminists' suffering/oppression, she raises doubt about the authenticity of their politics. Nevertheless, having made a broad-brush critique of white feminism, hooks also refines this critique. She echoes Socialist and Socialist feminist criticisms of Feminism as typically bourgeois, indulgent, self-interested and conservative. On this basis, hooks reserves her strongest criticisms for Liberal feminism and Gender Difference approaches, particularly the women-centred model associated with Radical feminist writers like Jill Johnson and Adrienne Rich (hooks, 1981a: 125, 1984a: 1–5).[5]

hooks derides the Liberal feminism of writers like Friedan on the grounds of their narcissistic and race/class privileged perspective, but in the case of Radical feminism focuses on their concern with the category of 'women'. Radical feminists, particularly in the 1970s and 1980s, were inclined to declare that 'any woman has more in common with any other woman' – regardless of other factors like race – than she has with any man (Sonia Johnson, cited in Rowland and Klein, 1990: 281). By contrast, hooks sees this supposedly politically radical conception of a common bond between women as an appropriation by conservative agendas. The notion of a common bond is seen not merely as insufficiently revolutionary but as a *tactic* of class/race interest not far removed from the approach of Liberal feminism. hooks suggests that the true feminist path has been hijacked. Upholding a common bond between women may appear to be an attack on gender hierarchy but actually it is heavily weighed down with class/race investments: 'The usurpation of feminism by bourgeois women to support their class interests has been to a very grave extent justified by feminist theory as it has so far been conceived. (For example, the ideology of "common oppression".)' (hooks, 1990d: 36).

hooks inverts what she sees as the condescension of white feminists who seem to believe they can provide black women with the correct thinking and strategy, by presenting black women as constructing a more genuinely resistant politics out of their greater, more real oppression. She suggests that a feminist politics is more likely to arise for black women necessarily and directly out of their experience than it is for white women: 'There are white women who had never considered resisting male dominance until the feminist movement created an awareness that they could and should. My awareness of feminist struggle was stimulated by *social circumstance*' (Ibid.).

hooks, like Sojourner Truth, converts invisibility into presence. Instead of being located at the margins of feminist thinking, black women are situated at its centre. In her early works, hooks says that black women have no institutionalised 'other' that they can exploit or oppress. They have no rewards from the status quo and hence a lesser attachment to it. By contrast, both black men and white women are oppressed and oppressors. Black women, therefore, possess 'the special vantage point our inequality gives us' (Ibid.: 39). For this reason they have a central role in feminist theory. They have a unique claim to expertise, to knowledge, to a truth based on their identity.

These views involve an archetypal Identity politics position, which is at the opposite pole from postmodern perspectives in the sense that hooks says that 'I (black woman) am Truth'. Black women are put forward as a gender/race identity that, because it is born of oppression, can be embraced as the means to political understanding. There is little emphasis here on the possible exclusions and stereotyping fixity that might be associated with this standpoint. On this basis she has been castigated by other REI feminists precisely for focusing too singularly on racism and on a common 'race' identity to the exclusion of noting gender. These commentators object to what they see as hooks' belligerent and sanctimonious shoring up of the notion of an impermeable authentic black voice which is made equivalent to her own and is beyond criticism. hooks has been seen, in other words, as imposing a falsely unified 'race essentialism' in place of the 'gender essentialism' she so effectively denounces (E.F. White, 2001; Suleri, 1992). This less than positive assessment arises in the context of a growing number of analyses by younger black feminists. Such analyses are engaged in reconsidering the inclination to focus on racism as indicating a disproportionate concern with legitimising black feminism in the eyes of black communities and with affirming race unity in such communities by upholding notions of a unified black sisterhood (Springer, 2002).[6]

Later work

hook's later works in the 1990s and 2000s on black representations and audiences in film and on black (African-American) masculinity in many ways continues the early concentration upon privileging or giving voice to a marginalised 'race' identity (hooks, 1992a, 2003c). These later works still focus on the political project of uniting black men and women in overthrowing oppression. Moreover, she retains an optimistic, unambiguous certainty regarding her political mission which may be said to be characteristic of a Modernist perspective. She assumes that she knows the true path to political change on the basis of her oppressed political identity.

In a 1999 debate with Yuval-Davis and in an article in 2003 she continues to refer to 'white' supremacist culture in ways that can be viewed as universalising from her own experience (Grünell and Saharso, 1999; hooks, 2003a). As Yuval-Davis notes, hooks' framework seems to give little space to the diverse forms of racism in that racism is not always 'white' versus 'black'. Moreover, it reveals a tendency to assume a global authority for her analysis of domestic American concerns. Similarly, her accounts of 'black' masculinity are often written in general terms, yet are decidedly North American-centric (see, for example, her chapter on black masculinity in hooks, 1990a). This may not necessarily be very useful in describing other 'black' male experiences in other countries.[7] Like Heidi Safia Mirza, hooks is inclined to employ terms like 'white' and 'black' in quite inclusive ways, in ways that appear to operate 'indistinctly across national and cultural boundaries' (Kanneh, 1998: 92). Mirza's usage of black to refer to non-white others is consciously intended to highlight connections between 'Third World' and British non-whites related to issues of migration. However, in the case of hooks' work, this inclusive usage seems less persuasive.[8] Rather, a certain degree of universalising from North American particulars appears to exist, even while she registers concern that white American women speak authoritatively about 'other' women in other parts of the world and fail to recognise their limits (hooks, 2000a; Parameswaran, 2002).

This inclination towards large claims and political certainty is also evident in her assessment of Feminism's direction. In 1993, in an exchange with Naomi Wolf (among others), she declares unambiguously against bourgeois feminists and asserts that Feminism is a revolutionary 'Left-wing' struggle which is not a 'women's movement' alone (hooks et al., 1993). Interestingly, while hooks does not entertain a separate women's political support base, she does note the need for African Americans to sometimes withdraw into separatist support activities as a sign of 'positive self-care' (hooks, 2003b).

She also remains certain about the 'true path' to political change as not only a radical/substantive political change orientation but as a singular movement. Women may be different (that is, 'race'/class differentiated) and all people (men and women) may be included in Feminism, but for her there is only one struggle: 'advancing the notion of many "feminisms" has served the ... political interests of women seeking status and privileged class power' (cited in Parameswaran, 2002). The concept of many feminisms, for hooks, enables us to opt out of serious social change and move towards narrow self-interest.

All of this sounds rather straightforwardly Modernist in most respects and still closely linked to ('race') Identity politics. Certainly her 1990 piece on 'Postmodern blackness' points out what she sees as the dangers of Postmodern perspectives (hooks, 1990c). While Postmodernism might seem to share her antagonism to the universalising claims of women-centred feminism as well as her concern to consider multiple differences, hooks sees these connections as limited. She sees in Postmodernism a different motivation or logic which, in aiming to deconstruct identities, displays a studied indifference to blackness and threatens to dismantle an oppositional voice to the realities of racism. She associates Postmodernism with 'white male intellectuals and/or academic elites' with little to offer black women (Ibid.: 24). In a similar fashion in an interview in 1995, hooks raises doubts about the benefits of Postmodern challenges to identity: 'If we say that there is no fixed sexual identity that we can call 'gay' or 'straight', then what becomes of the experiences and the understandings collectively that allow people to politically organise for gay rights?' (Smith and Petrarca, 1995)

However, alongside the firmly Modernist support for Identity politics in hooks' writings, there are other themes. Even in the early works hooks does engage in consistent identity critiques that deconstruct identity as unified commonality. In her 1984 book, *Feminist Theory: from Margin to Centre*, she calls on white feminists to break Feminism's white framing but also says that those at the margins (black people) are not immune from self-examination and must examine their exclusionary practices. She notes that she has experienced these practices herself (hooks, 2003a; E.F. White, 2003). Relatedly, in *Black Looks* (1992a) and *We Real Cool* (2003c) she discusses the dangers of a women-oppressive masculinity, dangers to both men and women. Furthermore, in her recent books on love (*All about Love* (2000b), *Salvation* (2001) and *Communion* (2002)), she castigates black men like Colin Powell as supporting white supremacy (Dauphin, 2002).

Furthermore, her apparent rejection of Postmodernism is not straightforward. While she claims that black and gay rights politics might be endangered by dismantling a sense of Identity politics, she is also at pains to suggest that she is struggling with identity because she is well aware of its limitations (Smith and Petrarca, 1995). She notes in 'Postmodern blackness', that the deconstruction of identity, including that of black women, 'allows us to affirm multiple black identities, varied black experience'. Representing blackness in a one-dimensional fashion reinforces racism (hooks, 1990c: 28).

Conclusion

hooks' focus, despite developments, has remained constant in certain crucial respects. The focus of her work is still, above all, on supporting and rendering visible a positive 'race' identity, and she still appears to assume that *she* has 'it together'. Tellingly, in an interview in 2002, when asked 'where did the feminist revolutionary bell hooks go?', she replied: 'When I wrote my theoretical books I assumed people had it together, that they were on the *same* journey as I was. Then I saw ... the collective hurt and trauma [among my people]' (Fleming, 2002, emphasis added).

The certainties which were most strongly evident in her earlier work have not disappeared, but have become somewhat less marked and less emphatically exclusionary. After all, her politics is also a celebration, an invitation to connect with others, some of whom are not like herself. She offers a call to solidarity. The core of her work is African American (socially located and specific) but it also summons a conscious political coalition, a coalition of difference across diverse experiences. Both Modernist identity and Postmodern plurality are in evidence.

The question remains, however, whether hooks' perspective is for the most part as universalist and exclusionary as the white feminism she criticises. Think, in this context, of Liberal feminists like Naomi Wolf and Martha Nussbaum or of Gender Difference feminists like Adrienne Rich and Elizabeth Grosz, who put gender centre stage. Does hooks in fact largely replicate the problematic character of this singular focus in her emphasis upon a unitary black identity? Or does her Identity politics, her refusal to jettison group identity, empower and open up practical political spaces for us all?

Notes

1. See Chapter 6 and/or the Glossary for more detail on this term.

2. For examples of an assertion of identity politics, see Combahee River Collective (US black lesbian group), [1977] 1982: 16; and Smith, [1977] 1985. See also for commentaries, Andermahr et al., 2000: 124–6; and Kanneh, 1998: 89–91.

3. Relatedly, in *Ain't I a Woman*, hooks questions claims that nineteenth-century white feminists sought common cause with black women. She asserts that such claims ignore evidence

of racist repudiation of any common sisterhood by white women and white women's rights activists (hooks, 1981a: 124–5). See also Davis, 1981: 53–4; and Andolsen, 1986: 78.

4. Such crossovers between supposedly antagonistic theoretical positions indicate once again the limits of labels I have developed in this book.

5. However, Rich has shown rather more awareness than most 'women-centred' thinkers of the issue of race. See, for example, Rich, [1978] 1980a; Lorde, 1981a.

6. Debates about the priority accorded race and the representation of black sisterhood raise, for example, long-standing issues regarding recognition of diverse sexualities. For an early instance of discussion about sexualities and black sisterhood, see Carmen et al. (1984).

hooks' own work was specifically at one stage criticised for ignoring homophobia and failing to acknowledge differences between black women associated with sexuality. However, this criticism highlights a common problem in black feminist writings which, as Evelynn Hammonds (1994) has noted, are – with few exceptions – 'relentlessly focused on heterosexuality'. See Clarke, 1981, 1983; hooks, 1989: 169.

7. For example, the sexualised construction of African-American men in the USA is not by any means the same as the construction of Indigenous men in Australia, even if there may be said to be some overlaps.

8. See Boyce Davies' critique of the tendency to homogenise notions of blackness associated with the privileged position of US writings (in Kanneh, 1998: 92).

Postmodern Feminism: Butler

In this chapter I will initially position strongly Postmodern feminism in relation to what we know so far and specifically in relation to identity politics and the issue of 'essentialism'. To contextualise this discussion I will then move on to begin analysis of a particular Postmodern feminist writer, Judith Butler (extended in the next chapter), and finally sum up in preliminary fashion some debates on Postmodern feminist approaches. After this schematic overview, hopefully you will be in a better position to assess whether Martha Nussbaum was right to dismiss Butler's Postmodern feminism or not (see Chapter 3).

Setting the scene: increasing problems with identity politics

I have previously distinguished two theoretical trajectories which particularly attend to questions of identity: the first involves a focus on singular Gender Difference while the second deals with (multiple) Differen*ces*, in particular intersections between race/ethnicity/imperialism (REI) and gender. I noted earlier that the Gender Difference framework may be described as containing a Modernist variant that aims to reclaim the content of the identity 'women', and a Postmodern – specifically psychoanalytic – variant that aims to reassess the gendered devaluing of the feminine as 'other', as 'lack'. The former deals with identity and women, while the latter deals with gendered ordering principles of power and the marginalised 'feminine'.

The (multiple) Differences framework complexifies the Gender Difference framework by examining not just gender difference but also differences between women that cut across the feminine. Here my example was feminist work highlighting race/ethnicity/imperialism as an instance of theorising involved in multiplying the axes of difference. I described this REI feminist framework, as I had the Gender Difference approach, in terms of two variants. The first has a Modernist orientation which reclaims the content of racialised/ethnic/Third World identities (for example, black women), and the second has a more Postmodern – specifically Post-colonial – orientation which aims to reassess the devaluing of 'the other woman' (for example, non-Western/'other' women). The former deals with identity and particular groups of non-white women, while the latter deals with the 'racial'/cultural ordering *principles* of power and the marginalised 'other' feminine.

Both singular and multiple Difference approaches (whether they emphasise gender, or race/ethnicity/imperialism and gender) reject the universal Human. The Modernist variants of Gender and REI Difference feminism concentrate upon group differences and *identity politics*. The Postmodern variants emphasise the *ordering* of groups in relation to one another along dichotomous (binary) and hierarchical lines.

These Group Difference approaches contain an increasing critique of identity politics. The critique develops *between* them (REI criticisms of Gender Difference) and *within* them (Postmodern criticisms of the Modernist variants challenge assumptions regarding the content of marginalised identity groupings). Over the 1980s and especially in the 1990s and 2000s, feminists became ever more wary of any set or fixed conception of social identities. All of these Group Difference approaches offer some level of critique of the strongly Modernist universal Human subject. However, in their Modernist variants at least, they reinstated identities. The Modernist variants put forward binary (two) group subjects: that is, men/women, black/white, First/Third World binaries. Postmodern influenced variants – that is, Psychoanalytic and Post-colonial feminisms – rejected this focus on the characteristics (content) of supposedly unified marginalised identities and instead attended to the binary ordering of groups. Nevertheless, these Postmodern variants concentrated upon the conception of 'difference/s', the construction of hierarchical difference between groups, which meant that they retained a politics concerned with reclaiming marginalised identity constructions as a starting point (even if this invocation was then deconstructed). In short, over time these Group Difference approaches do demonstrate a growing challenge to 'essentialism' – an increasing antagonism to fixed identities as the basis for politics – but do not entirely abandon a strategy of giving voice to the marginalised identities/positions in social binaries.

The Gender Difference framework and, within that, the Modernist, 'women-centred' model have been subject to the most severe criticism related to identity politics. Indeed, critical responses to the women-centred (women's common identity) model drive most of the developments in Feminism in the 1990s and 2000s, and fuel the increasing significance of Postmodernism in Feminism.

The critique of 'essentialism'/identity politics

The Modernist, women-centred model was the subject of criticism by a variety of writers who took up Postmodern doubts about universalised identity-based frameworks. Within the Gender Difference framework, Postmodern psychoanalytic writers like Jane Flax, and 'sexual difference' writers like Moira Gatens and Elizabeth Grosz, rejected notions of a set content for womanhood. The women-centred model was also attacked by all versions of REI feminism, noting its 'whiteness'. The primary criticism of 'women-centred' feminism was that it was 'essentialist'. In short, it presumed gender was the essential/fundamental core to power and presumed an essence to gender identity such that it proposed 'a fixed feminine way of being' with a definite list of characteristics attached to the category of 'women' (A. Fergusen, 1994).

The argument against 'essentialism' in relation to power, society and the self was that it amounted to re-asserting an exclusionary model of the subject of Feminism, a model of womanhood which was not a great deal better than the exclusions associated with the model of the universal Human. Just as the universal Human rested upon a 'norm' of the self which in theory and practice privileged a masculine model, so too the gender category 'women' places centre stage those women for whom race/ethnic/imperialism and class appear irrelevant and therefore privileges a norm of white Western middle/upper-class womanhood. If the essentialist notion of a universal Human self could be viewed as masking male power, then any simple usage of gender identity could also be seen as masking race/class and other axes of power.

However, this criticism of gender identity politics appeared to raise an immediate problem. Surely Feminism is about producing social change for women. Surely Feminism is precisely about a gender category. If to talk and theorise about a political struggle for 'women' and their interests was now open to question on the grounds of excluding numbers of women, what then?[1]

Responses to the charge of 'essentialism' and difficulties with the category 'women'

As I have noted in this and earlier chapters, writers in the Gender and REI Difference frameworks had certain responses which did not entirely jettison identity as a staging point for political struggle. The rejection of essentialism in terms of an overly specific or narrow conception of self does not necessarily entail a rejection of group categorisation or group commonalities *per se*. Despite their concerns about 'women-centred' feminist approaches, postmodern-influenced Gender Difference and REI Difference approaches usually offer some invocation of marginalised identity, which is then deconstructed to show its limits. In other words, the invocation of the feminine, of black women or Third World women remains. This critical and cautious usage of identity Gayatri Spivak terms a 'strategic essentialism' – that is, a use of group identities like women for certain political purposes – while also noting that it is impossible and dangerous to assume that one can speak from nowhere – that is, from a universal, objective position outside of power. (Spivak, 1985, 1987a; Winant, 1990; see also Fuss, 1989: 18). In this context, Spivak insists that Western feminists acknowledge their own privileged location. Her perspective may be placed against that of Nussbaum, who insists we can and must speak from a universal position based in objective reason (Chapter 3). Spivak's viewpoint suggests that, at least sometimes, it is worthwhile and perhaps even unavoidable to risk the dangers of essentialism in order to act politically, even though the limits and risks must always be acknowledged. This, as you will see, is a rather different emphasis from a more thoroughly Postmodern feminist position.

So far I have briefly summarised the analysis in the previous four chapters on the theoretical directions I have described as (singular) Gender Difference and (multiple) Differences. Now I will turn to some further responses to the charge of 'essentialism' and the critique of 'women-centred' feminism and consider the theoretical directions described under 3 (Social Constructionist) and 5 (Postmodern) in the condensed diagram (Figure 8.1) (see Figure 1.2 for a fuller version).

Social Constructionism

The Social Constructionist framework is one that I will only briefly mention in relation to Feminism, because the position is more usefully covered in the subfield of

Figure 8.1 Map of the Modernism–Postmodernism continuum – example: Feminism

MODERNISM	POSTMODERNISM
Strong ◄————————► Weak	Weak ◄————————► Strong
1. EMANCIPATORY	
2. (SINGULAR) GENDER DIFFERENCES	
3. SOCIAL CONSTRUCTIONIST	
4. (MULTIPLE) DIFFERENCES	
	5. POSTMODERN

Sexuality Studies and also receives an airing in Masculinity Studies. In short, the Social Constructionist framework takes as its central 'brief' a refusal of any naturalised set account of the self. It is particularly opposed to biological essentialism but also resists any social essentialism – that is, accounts of a socially fixed singular core identity. Rather than attending to what people *are*, Social Constructionism is concerned with what *people do together*, with the generation of social relations and processes in specific historical cultural settings. Hence, the focus on the terms 'social' and 'construction' (for a more detailed discussion of this form of thought, see Burr, 1995: 1–16).

Social Constructionist (SC) feminist writers (sometimes termed 'materialist feminists' (Jackson, 1998b: 134–7)) strongly reject gender difference models which in any sense talk about re-valuing women's difference from men or re-valuing the difference associated with 'the feminine'. SC writers consider this celebration of a subordinated position is an essentialist reassertion of a conservative model of woman/femininity and argue that the focus should be on relations of *dominance*, not upon 'difference'. They argue that we should focus not on identity categories but upon power.[2]

Social Constructionist feminist writers like Stevi Jackson (UK) (1996b), Catherine MacKinnon (USA) (1987a), Christine Delphy (France) (1984), and Denise Thompson (Australia) (1989, 2001) put forward this refusal of difference-oriented theories and focus on dominance. Their response to the dangers of essentialism in Gender Difference feminism is to expand and historically/materially contextualise the category of women as a complex 'class' of subordinates who do not share an identical content but do share a positioning in relation to power (Jackson, 1998b: 138). Women, as a group positioned in relation to power, are relevant to political struggle, but actual women are not all the same. They do not all have the same qualities. Moreover, 'women' is not simply a category of power but is a group capable of resistance, indeed a means to resisting power. It is necessary to mobilise around this positioning. In other words, Social Constructionist feminists do not jettison Feminism as a politics about women. As Judith Lorber (2000) puts it, Feminism involves 'using gender' – gendered identity categories – 'to undo gender'.

This is the point at which we finally get to the most thorough-going, most complete refusal of identity politics, of any essential core to the self as the basis of a politics.

What I describe simply as 'Postmodern feminism' without the addition of any other descriptors, refers to the 'unadulterated' or most unrelenting Postmodern theoretical trajectory in Feminism. While I have outlined in previous chapters two frameworks which show Postmodern influences, including Postmodern Gender Difference (Psychoanalytic) and Postmodern race/ethnicity/imperialism (Post-colonial) accounts, these retain a more ambiguous relationship with Modernist protocols, present more hybrid intellectual histories, and often assert quite critical views of Postmodern theorising.[3] In terms of emphasis, these Postmodern-inflected accounts – which in various ways undertake conjunctures with other frameworks and have more mixed or borderline agendas in terms of the Modernist–Postmodern continuum – may be contrasted with what I call 'Postmodern feminism'. The latter offers the most complete refusal in Feminism of women or gender as a ground for a movement of social change, as a place from which to speak or mobilise. Postmodern feminism represents the strongest and most strict employment of the postmodern trajectory in Feminism. It is a postmodern trajectory without hyphenated attachments or caveats. This more 'orthodox' Postmodernism has become more evident through the 1990s and is now arguably the predominant position in Feminism.[4] Before continuing, it may be useful to revisit those sections of Chapters 1 and 5 which provide accounts of the broad features of this position.

'Unmodified' Postmodern feminism: Butler

Postmodern feminism does not simply say that gender identity or any other identity cannot be viewed as fixed, or merely challenge the ongoing stability, unity and homogeneity of gender identity, as do some Gender Difference and all REI Difference and Social Constructionist approaches. By contrast, Postmodern feminists, following the work of major postmodern writer Michel Foucault, construe resistance to power as resistance to identity itself (Beasley, 1999: 95).

Postmodern feminists do not just offer a critique of identity as too fixed, too simple, too singular, but effectively disavow it as a basis for politics. Rather than a politics arising out of a reflection on women and their group status, seeking to empower women, this is a politics that says the point is that women do not exist as an inevitable identity. Postmodern feminism refuses the category women in a certain sense and indeed proposes to reject gender divisions. In common with Foucault and other Postmodern theorists such as Jacques Derrida, Postmodern feminists are concerned to displace identity categories (essences) and the dichotomous or binary thinking in which they are embedded (essential oppositions). Gender categories, as well as notions of binary gender difference and binary conceptions of gendered power dividing rulers from the ruled, are destabilised (Sullivan, 2003: 42, 50; Gamble, 2000a: 216–17; Andermahr et al., 2000: 61–3).

This is a very radicalised use of social constructionism. Everything in this analysis is a social construction, including the category women. Postmodern feminism does not simply challenge women's current social status but their status as a group. Women are not therefore the, or even a, means to resist power, but an effect of power, utterly *of* power and never outside it. Though the category may sometimes be a bare beginning for a politics, it is used with considerable reluctance and is emptied of content. Postmodern feminists like Judith Butler in some ways even go beyond Foucault in their refusal of any essential, immutable, pre-existent elements of identity.[5] This framework is a very thorough-going refusal of assumptions regarding the biological underpinnings of gender groupings to the far point of conceding no 'interior' or 'essential' foundation to the self. Gender does not 'express' a self, a way of being, or a bodily difference, but rather is a performance or enactment of power. One is a woman or man as an effect of power.

Postmodern feminists follow Foucault's 'genealogical'[6] work in espousing a typically Postmodern refusal of any macro or universalised explanatory claims about society, power or the self. In a rejection of Modernist claims to have the 'truth', the core foundation which enables an explanation of society, power and the self, Postmodern feminists, at least in principle, refuse any pre-given foundations. Power is not all of a piece, not simply negative oppression of a unitary core self. Rather, power is productive and multiple. It provides the dynamic shaping of the self.[7] On this basis, Foucault also questions Freud's model of gender and the self as based in 'repression' (Sullivan, 2003: 40). Indeed, he argues the productive (rather than repressive) nature of power can be seen at work in the Freudian account itself, in that this account supports the idea of an interiorised deep core to the self. The notion of a necessary deep self found in Freud is itself a mechanism of power, such that we learn to understand ourselves in Freudian terms as being the expression of a central core.

Foucault, despite his overall antagonism to Freud and psychoanalysis, offers a conception of interactions between body/bodily energies and 'regulatory practices of cultural coherence' that appears to retain some elements of Freud's account of a polymorphous libido or bodily sexual energy (cited in Butler, 1997c: 115). The body is granted some active status that exceeds culture and hence power relations. Postmodern feminists like Butler typically retain a less critical attitude than Foucault towards the psychoanalytic account of how gender identity comes into being, but tend to go further than Foucault with regard to a critical examination of notions of the body as a foundational element of identity/self (Butler, 1995a: 119, 122).

Butler insists that the body too is a thoroughly cultural product, such that bodily sex and anatomy itself can be seen in terms of cultural interpretations of gender difference. Gender (for example, distinctions between men and women) is typically interpreted as derived from the body. Bodily (anatomical) sex is seen as pre-dating culture, as eternal sex, the eternal male/female binary. However, in Butler's analysis, the body is also a gendered performance which is socially constituted as the essence of gender, as it's an intact, untouched foundation, and is all the more culturally powerful for this interpretation as being outside culture. Indeed, in her view, socially constituted gender creates anatomical sex, rather than the other way around, in the sense that the former makes the latter relevant in social practice.[8] And if gender does not follow automatically from anatomical sex, then it is not axiomatic that gender refer only to the two categories designated in the binary men/women distinction (for one discussion, see Jackson, 1998b).

To those who would exclaim that surely bodies *are* sexually different and this *is* the basis of gender, Butler retorts that (aside from arguments about the coherence of sexual/anatomical categorisation) such differences as exist need not be any more significant than the colour of one's eyes. While they are culturally registered as of overwhelming and all-embracing significance, this is not inevitable.[9] Butler exteriorises everything of the self/identity (including the body and the interior psyche) and deems it cultural, a social construction, as constituted by the particular socio-historical forms of power. Social power cannot be escaped, or overthrown, but it can be destabilised, de-massified.

The point, for Postmodern feminists like Butler, is not to return to identity as the basis of politics. Unlike Modernist 'humanist' conceptions of the self as an already existent site which is then subjected to power, this analysis constitutes identity as the house of power and as that which gives power strength. She says in *Gender Trouble* (1990) that 'the identity categories often presumed to be foundational in feminist politics ... simultaneously work to limit and constrain in advance the very cultural possibilities that feminism is supposed to open up' (Butler, 1997c: 126). In other words, categories like 'women' delimit rather than advance resistance to gender norms and hence can never form the basis of a feminist political movement (Butler, 1995a: 50).

Unlike the certainty of Nussbaum, who presumes she speaks from outside power, for the universal and objective, from the identity of 'the human', Butler works to displace all certainty and especially to displace norms of identity. She describes gender identity as 'performative' to stress that no interior essence, no 'real' self exists. Gender is performative because it has no 'real-ness' at all, no natural core. It is an effect of a 'decidedly public and social discourse' which requires the relentless reiteration of various gender acts/styles which make gender seem real/eternal/a deep truth of our lives, by repetition (Ibid.: 119, 122). Gender, she says, 'is a fabrication', a 'truth effect'. Here identity is a fantasy – that is, imagined and experienced as set in immutable concrete – which supports power. It is an effect of power and *not its means of escape*. Thus the task is not to enjoin a gender identity like women, which attends to a singular *difference* from men, or even to invoke multiple identities like lesbian, black women and 'Third World' women, which acknowledge *differences between* women. Moreover, such an approach does not stop at the psychoanalytic focus on *differences within* individuals (the splitting between conscious and unconscious that produces a self). Rather, the aim is to disrupt categories *per se*, to disrupt the fixity of identity, by showing up its non-natural incoherence. If gender (which seems so fundamental) is not an immutable fact of social life, then the whole of existing society can be questioned and can be viewed as potentially radically different. There is no core to which we must adhere. We can re-make our own rules.

The notion of the interior, real, natural truth status of gender can, Butler argues, be undercut by impersonations like drag, which mocks or parodies the notion of a true gender identity. These 'imitations' show up the artifice, the social fabrication that is the gendered self. Butler acknowledges the limits of these performances and calls for performances that compel a 'radical rethinking' of gender identity and sexuality. She says in 'Imitation and gender insubordination' (1991) that she is not intending to legislate against the use of identity terms like 'lesbian'. She notes that she will appear on 'political occasions' under the 'sign' of such an identity, but 'would like to have it permanently unclear what precisely that sign means' (Butler, 1993b: 309, 308). She proffers a disclaiming rather than a claiming strategy and prefers to use 'sexual crossing' like drag as a starting point. In *Bodies That Matter* (1993a), Butler makes it clear that she also does not think that undertaking such a strategy is simply a question of voluntarily and consciously deciding to do so. She stresses, by making more extensive use of Lacanian psychoanalysis, the unconscious and unknowable character of investments in identity.[10]

Conclusion

When Butler's views are compared with those of Nussbaum and hooks (in Chapters 3 and 7 respectively, it is possible to gain a clear sense of why Postmodern feminism might be the subject of intense dispute. The latter writers suggest in different ways that such a refusal of 'women', 'lesbian', of identity, is likely to become complicit in the erasure/denial/silencing of marginalised groups and in any case is impractical given that identity is where most people 'come from'.

Butler says we must sometimes use identities but is most reluctant. She sees the dangers of marginalisation/erasure associated with not using 'women' (disclaiming) on the whole as lesser than the dangers associated with claiming such identities. 'Should the risks of marginalisation dictate the terms of the political resistance to them?', she asks (Butler, 1993b: 311). Should feminists take their cue from conservative forces which see women as lesser beings? As for political practicalities, Butler says that the aim of rendering visible marginal identities is not seen as a sufficient strategy by those who argue for this 'pragmatism', since even they would wish to transform existing gender and sexuality identities. Butler refutes that she is assisting in the silencing of women/lesbians, but rather is making use of identities precisely to call them into question. She wants to ask from the beginning for openness rather than starting from closure hoping it will lead to openness later. In conclusion, Butler argues, 'There is a political necessity to use some sign now [like lesbian] and we do', but the question is 'how to use it in such a way that its futural significations are not *foreclosed*' (Ibid.: 311–12). For writers like Nussbaum and hooks, these are mere word games, mere critique and not activism.

In the next chapter the discussion of Butler's work will be extended by considering its contribution to 'queering' gender and to Queer feminist accounts.

Notes

1. See a brief account of the debate on essentialism in Feminism in Andermahr et al. (2002: 82–3). Compare this with a concise summary of its dimensions in the field of Sexuality Studies, in Sullivan (2003: 37–44).

2. For a short account of 'Social Constructionism' as a theoretical trajectory in Feminism, see Jackson and Scott, 1996: 11–12; Jackson, 1996b: 62–4; Andermahr et al., 2000: 248–9.

3. Such critical responses include Elizabeth Grosz's (1994c: 155–9) critique of Foucault and Spivak's critique of Derrida (Winant, 1990).

4. The notion of a more strict, orthodox or unmodified Postmodern perspective is somewhat paradoxical and even ironic, given that this perspective emphasises the unorthodox, the refusal of set positions. Nevertheless, as archetypal Postmodern writers Foucault and Butler indicate in their work, all theoretical discourses can and should be discussed in terms of their repetitions as well as their complexity. Burr's conception of 'family resemblance' as a means of describing such repetitions is a useful starting point here (Burr, 1995). While some writings display certain attributes of a Postmodern perspective – such as an antagonism to

essentialism – those developing a more 'orthodox' Postmodern approach show both a number of recurrent 'family' features and embrace these features in a decided rather than equivocal fashion. For example, they continually emphasise the fluidity of power and subjectivity (rather than drawing attention to the intransigence of their forms as REI feminists might do) and are inclined to challenge strongly uses of identity-based politics. See, for example, Butler, [1991] 1993b: 310.

5. Foucault can, for example, be read as a 'conflicted thinker', whose approach oscillates between a self/body constructed by social power and one which has pre-existing capabilities and pleasures, between annihilating the notion of the 'Human' capabilities of the self and resurrecting such capabilities. See Grosz, 1994c: 154–6; and Best and Kellner, 1991: 72–3.

6. This is the work that is particularly associated with Foucault's view of power as central to social analysis. Texts such as *Discipline and Punish* (1977) and *The History of Sexuality* (1978) are representative. The latter is the most commonly used text in feminist interpretations.

7. Some useful references here include: Ahmed, 1996; Sullivan, 2003: 39–43; Milner and Browitt, 2002: 164–202; Beilharz, 1994: 7–22 and 2001; 173–87; Turner, 1997: 117–33; Best and Kellner, 1997; and Rudel and Gerson, 1999.

8. For a different yet still Postmodern-inflected approach to the relationship between social and bodily, see Chapter 5 and the debate between Butler and Elizabeth Grosz.

9. As Jackson (1998b: 135–9) and Gunew (1990) argue, the Social Constructionist work of Christine Delphy offers a similar perspective on gender difference, though her work is arguably less thoroughly antagonistic to the active impact of biology/material bodies in the construction of the self.

10. While, as I have noted earlier in the chapter, Butler appears generally to offer a more thoroughly de-essentialising agenda than Foucault when it comes to notions of bodies/biology, in this later work she employs a reworked version of psychoanalysis which, she argues, evades Foucault's strong rejection of it. Psychoanalysis is used in *Bodies That Matter* (1993a: 22, 234) as the means to stress the socially determined, rather than voluntaristic, character of gender as performativity, but it may undermine Butler's de-essentialising project. It is a matter of debate as to whether psychoanalysis can be divested of its universalised foundational (essentialist) account of the self, yet its use within Postmodern feminism is almost ubiquitous. See Jackson (1999: 21–3) and Grosz (1995) for two views on this issue.

9 Queering Gender/Queer Feminism: Butler, Whittle

Identity has become very problematic in Feminism – in theory and political activism. Identity politics has been widely criticised, even sometimes vilified by a broad range of feminists. However, instead of disappearing, identity has 'become something of an obsession' within Feminism and indeed in the gender/sexuality field as a whole – that is, in Feminist, Masculinity and Sexuality Studies (Hekman, 2000: 289). Butler's work from the 1990s until today has been central to this stormy debate – a debate which in many ways articulates the Modernist–Postmodern divide that runs through virtually all contemporary socio-political and cultural theory and social activist movements.

Butler's work has been the subject of considerable dispute, but has had a 'profound effect' on Feminist and Sexuality Studies discussion (Ibid.). What is the central point of Butler's work? She replaces the notion of a fixed essential identity with a disclaimer, with a resistance to identity by revealing it to be a fiction (see Chapter 8). Why does this viewpoint come to be so important? Identity for a long time seemed to be the answer to women's problematic social positioning. First-wave nineteenth-century feminisms addressed this positioning by attempting to fit women into the universal 'Human'. Second-wave feminisms, starting from the 1960s and 1970s, generated a critique of the universal Human as inherently not just incidentally masculine. Yet this critique rested upon a categorisation of men and women, on gender difference, on a doubling of universal categories. The universal category 'woman', taken up so strongly in the 1980s, was then criticised in turn as inherently not just incidentally focused on white, upper/middle-class heterosexual women. Given this analysis, a greater focus on more specific identities seemed to be the solution, offering a plethora of identities from which women can choose.

Nevertheless, by the late 1980s and even more in the 1990s identity politics itself came under attack. Butler's work in particular draws attention to the ways in which identity is a product of power, not a means of overcoming it (no matter how many identity differences are embraced by identity politics). Identity positions do not offer a means of political resistance, says Butler, but continuing entrapment. On this basis Butler offers a critique of identity and identity politics, and an alternative strategy.

I spent some time in the last chapter discussing her particular critique of identity by positioning this Poststructuralist/Postmodern feminism against other critiques of identity and identity politics,[1] and by outlining her view of gender as **performative**, as a socially compulsory 'act'. I will now focus on the *alternative strategy* her work espouses, as this provides both a link to debates about the Postmodern contribution to the gender/sexuality field and to so-called '**Queer Theory**' (which will be further discussed and elaborated in the Sexuality Studies section). Because she provides what is seen as the most undiluted, the strongest case for Postmodernism, discussion of her work enables us to deal with a number of very important disputes within Feminism and throughout the gender/sexuality field as a whole.

Butler's strategy

Butler argues that the 'division' between Modernism and Postmodernism cannot be *simply* described as two opposing camps, the former defending universals and foundational claims and the latter repudiating these claims. The point, she asserts, is that these debates are both about authorising (making certain claims central/legitimate) and excluding. In this sense, both Modernism and Postmodernism have some foundational bases. The difference is that Postmodernism sees all knowledges, theories, viewpoints as being implicated in power (Butler, 1995a: 38; Cacoullos, 2001). Postmodernism, in other words, offers a questioning foundation. At least to this limited degree it does partake of universal and foundational claims. At this point I suggest a quick return to earlier characterisations of Postmodernism in Chapters 1 and 5 to consider how such an account may perhaps reconfigure these previous characterisations.

Butler's view is that Postmodernism is not so much free of **foundationalist** thinking, but is more averse to it – that is, employing such thinking only nominally and always in order to interrogate it. This questioning foundation, this sceptical critical mode, can be used to question the foundations of all viewpoints, including Postmodernism's own. For Butler the advantage of Postmodernism's founding ideas (as against those of Modernism) is that those of the former are self-reflexive and enable recognition of Postmodernism's own limits. Postmodernism's foundational claims can be used against itself, to interrogate Postmodernism's own investments in power. It is possible to ask, 'what does Postmodernism authorise (make central) and exclude (marginalise)? What are *its* political effects?' Postmodernism, according to Butler, refuses absolute objective knowledge (access to a singular Truth) to itself as well as all other positions.

On the basis of Postmodernism's questioning foundation Butler asks what is authorised and what is excluded by the use of Modernist 'universals', and notes problems associated with unacknowledged culturally specific assumptions. The excluded post-colonial/Third World subject reveals, she suggests, a privileged status for Western culture concealed in Modernism's supposed 'universalism' (Butler, 1995a: 39–41). Modernist universals have difficulty in coming to grips with the non-Western and thus are implicated in a veiled ethnocentrism.

Nussbaum interprets Butler's postmodern questioning of all perspectives as complicit in power relations as meaning that Butler offers a primarily negative critique in which we are forever trapped (see Chapter 3). However, Butler herself suggests that this scepticism enables us to override the dangerous temptation to believe that our own pet agendas/approaches are somehow innocent, on the side of Right and True, and without political consequences in terms of exclusions. In other words, such scepticism requires us to think about possible problems in our own position and stops us from assuming that it is utterly faultless and/or limitless. We cannot assume our position is God-like and speaks for all. As Jane Flax (1992: 446) puts it, some find Postmodernism threatening because it 'radically calls into question the belief (or hope) that there is some form of innocent knowledge to be had'.

Butler is accused by the strongly Modernist Nussbaum, as well as many others, of not offering much of a political guide about what to do (Hekman, 1995: 156, 2000; Benhabib, 1992b, 1992c; Webster, 2000; Young, 1997b: 12–37; Bordo, 1990: 142, 149). Butler does, however, offer some indications. A commitment to identity politics is detrimental to Feminism, according to Butler, because a politics invoking 'women' (gender identity) conceals the politically constructed non-natural, mutable character of gender and thus reasserts precisely that which Feminism seeks to question. She *is* clear, in other words, that identity politics is politically problematic. But, what then? What form of resistance to identity is appropriate? How do we create, in her terms, 'gender trouble'? How do we engage in a critical analysis of Feminism's traditional terms of reference – that is, gender and women – in order to advance Feminism's vision of 'a more fully democratic and participatory political life' (Butler, 1995b: 129)? Again she seems to give a degree of guidance at least. Rather than employing terms like Feminism, gender or women to represent a stable subject – that is, an identifiable group or group concerns – these terms become the means to demonstrate *how* socially constituted processes (power relations) generate forms of supposedly natural belonging and what they silence (Butler, 1993a: 221–2, 1995a: 50, 1995b: 128). Revealing how what is supposedly definitive/natural is produced, also indicates that it is capable of social change. Focusing upon the instability of identity categories, far from paralysing political action, produces political efficacy (Webster, 2000).

Gender trouble is hence 'created by not "doing" gender as it is supposed to be done' (Hekman, 2000: 292). In Butler's book, *Gender Trouble* (1990), this looks like what she calls 'pastiche' – that is, an imitation which involves a medley of identity forms and hence mocks any notion of an inner truth or original core self. Butler distinguishes pastiche from parody of identities like woman. Because parody involves caricaturing a supposed original, it tends, unlike the subversive potential of pastiche, to have the effect of reinstituting the identity norm. However, she sees elements of this 'pastiche' resistance to fixed identity in drag, in which a 'man' presents as a woman such that his manhood is also suspect, with the implication that all gendered positions are a form of impersonation. Behind the mask lies merely yet another mask (Butler, 1990: 36–7, 138, 147, [1991] 1993b: 312–13).

By 1993 in *Bodies that Matter* she more specifically notes that resistance to identity cannot mean just taking up marginal categories in relation to the social norm – that is, women, black, homosexual – and highlights more visibly both the power of the normative and the uncertainties of resistance (Butler, 1993a: 106–13, 116–17). While identity category terms like gender and women may still be used, they need to be opened up. The non-natural, non-eternal character of the social norm is shown by displacing its categories, its terms of reference, rather than employing and hence re-affirming them. Indeed, subversion of such categories is by no means a straightforward matter, nor is it likely to be complete or predictable (Ibid.: 193, 1997b: 402; Meijer and Prins, 1998: 279; Lloyd, 1998: 131). By mixing up categories of bodily sex (male/female), gender (feminine/masculine) and sexuality (homosexual/heterosexual), she suggests that we can generate a medley that is a specifically 'queer' politics. 'Queer' politics authorises, has as its 'identity', a refusal of set identity. It 'resists calculation' and revels in unpredictability (Butler, 1993c: 29).

Butler and Queer feminism

Butler's identity displacement strategy is explicitly linked to the term 'Queer'. Butler's work in this way provides an important contemporary linchpin between Feminism/Gender Studies and Sexuality Studies. At this point I will provide only a brief and schematic introduction to Queer theorising. The introductory comments that follow are discussed at greater length in later chapters and in relation to specific writers (especially in Chapters 10 and 15). This more contextualised coverage is necessary because there are many different accounts of the history of the term 'Queer Theory'. Whittle (1996), Jackson (1998c), Seidman (1993) and Jagose (1996), for example, provide accounts with somewhat differing starting points and emphases.

In short, Queer Theory arises out of same-sex Sexuality politics (gay and lesbian politics), as well as to some extent out of Feminist politics (though this is less often recognised). It develops as a specific articulated viewpoint in the 1990s and focuses upon the plethora of possible combinations of self-formation. Eve Sedgwick (1985: x) describes the 'explicit basis' of Queer thinking as 'criss-crossing' the lines of identification (self-identity) and desire (sexuality) among genders, sexualities, and other social categories, such that traditional demarcations are disrupted. In other words, Queer theorising is concerned with 'mixing up' traditional assumptions regarding supposedly inevitable combinations of attributes of the self (such as masculine gender is inevitably associated with men, male anatomical sex, desire for 'the opposite sex', and desire for the feminine gender). Queer Theory's invocation of category permeability and speculative open-ness marked it as a new development in relation to most forms of Gay/Lesbian Sexuality and Feminist politics of the 1980s, given their strong emphasis on the distinctive and separate character of identity groupings (see Chapters 5, 10 and 15).

Moreover, instead of framing marginal sexualities as an issue of minority group politics and minority rights, Queer Theory involves a refusal of this centre/marginal distinction such that normative assumptions are 'twisted' (Sedgwick, 1993: xii; Berlant and Warner, 1995: 345). As Steven Seidman (1997: 105–6) puts it, 'Let's declare war against the center, against all centers, all authorities in the name of difference'. In this way Queer Theory's focus on multiple, intertwined and porous differences (rather than on distinct minority status groupings) is presented as enabling it to offer a radical agenda for society generally (rather than a more limited agenda recommending mainstream tolerance/acceptance of minorities) (Epstein, 1999: 271; Sediman, 1993: 131; Probyn, 1995: 7). Queer Theory's concern with disrupting identity, as well as assumptions about what is central or foundational within society, signals its links to a Postmodern agenda. Nevertheless, Queer thinking cannot be merely subsumed under the Postmodernist label in that its directions may be the subject of sympathetic criticism by avowedly Postmodern writers (Seidman, 1993: 130–7, and note 58 in his article), and it has been associated with a particular emphasis within Postmodernism.

Queer Theory is most obviously linked to the Poststructuralist/Postmodern work of Michel Foucault (see also Chapter 15), and often particularly to the emphasis of his later work on remaking the self (for one exemplary instance of this link, see Blasius, 1994). Foucault, in common with other Postmodern writers, is at pains to describe human subjects in terms of their social construction by power relations and hence as having no foundational essence or core. Nevertheless, he notes that these subjects are 'vehicles of power' as well as its 'effects' and are capable of resistance (Foucault, 1972: 16, 47–8, 1980: 94, 98, 1982: 221). Indeed, he declares that 'it is not power, but the subject, which is the general theme of my research', and endorses the political project of remaking the self 'as a work of art' in ways which resist the forms of individuality 'imposed upon us for several centuries' (Foucault, 1982: 209, 216, 1986: 351). Such an aesthetic politics is not undertaken to reveal the self's hidden 'real' basis, but in order to reassemble the socially formed components in myriad ways. (Foucault, 1986: 362, 365).[2] Human subjects do not resist existing social norms by imagining they can go outside power or overthrow it, in Foucault's approach, but by creative reconstruction of these existing elements in the remaking of our selves. Such an emphasis has been criticised as ironically continuing the identity obsession of 1980s identity politics, albeit, in the case of Queer Theory, taking the form of a relentless attack upon identity. To the extent that Queer Theory appears 'driven by its centering on a politics of identity subversion', this can be viewed as an overly self-referential framework, dislocating its politics from a broader socio-political analysis which might locate identities in relation to institutional contexts (Seidman, 1993: 132–4; Litsan, 2004).[3]

Butler's elaboration of a politics of subversion linked to an antagonism to identity politics has provided a significant contribution to Queer Theory. Her analysis of gender and sexual identity as non-natural, as 'performative', as artifice, and her view of gender as central to 'heteronormativity' (heterosexuality as compulsory norm and non-heterosexuality as deviant) provides connecting links between Feminism (which focuses upon gender) and Sexuality Studies (which focuses upon the heteronorm) (Jackson, 1998c: 68–9). When we get to Queer Theory in Sexuality Studies (Chapter 15) we shall see that though Butler is often deemed as a crucial contributor to Queer, her typically feminist account of interconnection between gender and sexuality is largely discounted. Gender and Feminism are frequently viewed as passé (old-fashioned), as identity-bound. Gender and Feminism are indeed usually subjected to strong criticism and/or abandoned. By contrast, what we see in Butler's writings and in Stephen Whittle's work ('Gender fucking or fucking gender?', 1996) is a strategy which is relentlessly directed towards displacing gender while continuing to note its persistence and its links to sexuality. But if gender is still in play in these Queer *and* Feminist writers, how precisely is it recommended that we displace gender? What is a Queer *feminist* politics?

For Butler, the displacement of gender and sexuality categories of identity arises in emphasising 'sexual crossing', mixing up multiple or at least more than one identity pathway, and by doing so refusing the set identities laid out for us. Instead of taking for granted, for example, that a body deemed male automatically produces masculinity which automatically leads to heterosexual masculinity, Butler's conception of a politics of sexual crossing stresses the non-natural constructedness of these elements. Butler's alternative strategy focuses on hybridity or ambiguity, on body, gender and sexuality crossings. The positions of resistance recommended are thus those that are involved in 'queering' identity, in preference to merely promoting oppositional cate-gories like 'lesbian' (Butler, 1993a: 116–17).

Hence, it would appear that, as Butler herself has noted regarding the foundations of the Postmodernist questioning mode, there are some authorised positions and some exclusions in Postmodern/Queer feminism, just as there are in Modernist feminisms. There are, it would seem, some political moves in Postmodern/Queer feminism that are deemed enabling (resistant) and some which are not (Hekman, 2000: 293).

Nussbaum interprets Butler to be merely endorsing 'transgression' and notes that transgression may or may not be politically useful or progressive (see Chapter 3). Similarly, other rather more sympathetic critics, like Susan Hekman, suggest that 'we are never given particularly specific guidelines by which we can distinguish resis-tance from that which is not' (Ibid.). Butler herself recognises the 'uncertainty' of her strategy and says that Postmodern feminism has 'no *necessary* political consequences'. Nevertheless, its questioning stance, she asserts, is at the heart of the 'democratic' impulse to contest politics, an impulse that she describes as critical to any movement for social change (Butler, 1995a: 41, emphasis added, 1995b: 140).[4]

Despite her own caution, there is some further specificity in her queer strategy. Butler concentrates upon bodies that 'do not matter' in the gender and heteronor-mative. She focuses upon those bodies that are in some senses 'both/neither' (rather than either/or), that *cannot* or *will not* fit as the one or 'the other' in the gender and sexuality binaries. These are what Whittle (1996: 210), drawing upon the work of Kate Bornstein (1994), describes as 'gender outlaws'. Some of the ambiguous bodies that are authorised by this Queer feminism include drag queens/kings, transgenders and highly muscular women involved in body-building.[5]

Debates

As soon as we consider some of these more specific examples of queer resistance, certain debates arise regarding the political usefulness of 'resistance' via 'gender outlaw' positionings. For example, while transgender and transsexual individuals appear to qualify as gender outlaws who might provide concrete instances of Butler's alterna-tive political strategy regarding identity crossings, such individuals can also be viewed as restating gender identities rather than displacing gender. Transgendered people, for example, 'often seek out' what Queer renounces – that is, a gender 'home' (Prosser, 1998: 81–2) – and may not therefore be easily subsumed within Butler's thorough critique of gender as social domestication.

Moreover, the account of gender subversion in Butler's Queer feminism has been criticised on the grounds that it is narrowly focused. Queer feminism appears, iron-ically – even more perhaps than the rest of Feminism – to be an identity-obsessed perspective (Hausman, 2001: 484–6). Butler's approach has been seen as 'unhing[ing] identity from other material relations that shape it' and as fetishising the fluidity of terms (words) as against concrete social conditions and embodied social individuals (Hennessy, 1995: 153; Benhabib, 1995: 108; Fraser, 1995: 163). Queer feminism is thus criticised as fixated on identity often in isolation from the broader social context. This narrow fixation is then seen as having some political problems. For example, the destabilised, fluid identities encouraged by Butler are considered to be very difficult to deploy in actual social/political settings such as courts of law (Hekman, 2000: 297).

Apart from problems deemed to arise *within* the analytical framework of Queer feminism, critics have also raised a number of doubts regarding whether Butler's work actually does what she says she is doing in terms of identity displacement. Her interest in displacing identity and encouraging hybridity may be viewed as in fact authorising a romanticised 'queer identity', which is itself insufficiently questioned in terms of its investments in power. This queer identity has been argued to homogenise a range of differences (Seidman, 1993: 133), and even to erase lesbians/women under a sign of supposed sexual multiplicity. Some writers argue from different points of view that queer may actually be gay men's experience under another name (for example, Sheila Jeffreys (1994b) and Elizabeth Grosz (1994b: 6–10)) – and hence limited in its ability to pay attention to forms of men's/masculine privilege which may continue even among so-called 'gender outlaws'. Insofar as Queer Theory displaces the categories men and masculine and relatedly the question of dominance/subordination, the issue of power relations within queer culture may be excluded and not authorised.

Additionally, the romanticised outlaw positioning advanced in the name of Queer Theory may only be available to some people – that is, those who cannot or will not 'pass' as 'normal'/acceptable according to gender/sexuality norms. To the extent that Queer is a vanguard political position that foregrounds or requires a certain degree of confrontational exhibitionism, it may be less available to some than others (Weeks, 1995: 116). For example, individuals caring for dependents may need to pass in mainstream society to support these dependents. Queer thinking may well be politically exclusionary in ways that are highly problematic.

This point is extended by critics who consider that the romanticisation of outlaw positions in Queer Theory reveals a logic that prohibits its own claims. Hekman argues that Butler, despite refusing binary oppositional categories like 'lesbian', institutes another binary opposition of categories. Hekman states that Butler proposes an opposition of the Modernist universal singular subject versus the queer hybrid. By Butler's own reckoning (given her antagonism to binary thinking) this looks like a 'flawed strategy'. According to Hekman, Butler's presentation of Modernist accounts of core real identities versus their Postmodern apparently polar opposite (fictional, ironic, playful, fantasy identities) seems still oddly mired in what Butler herself identifies as Modernist thinking. Butler seems to assume, argues Hekman, a false antithesis in which one is faced with the dilemma of either upholding essentialist identity categories or a total refusal of categorisation, as if there were no 'middle ground'. And yet this is precisely the absolutist logic that Butler explicitly rejects (Hekman, 2000: 292–4).

Hekman's critique raises a further difficulty. Insofar as Queer thinking is obsessed with identity and romanticises outlaw positions, does it displace the Modernist truth of identity or merely reinstate other forms of Modernist universalism? Butler has often been interpreted as suggesting a strategy that amounts to a mere proliferation of 'choices'. While Butler has explicitly attempted to refute this reading of her work (see Butler, 1993a: 106–13, 116–17), such interpretations are common in Queer Theory writings. The tendency to promote a proliferation of styles or identities in

Queer Theory is inclined to reiterate a voluntarist and consumerist **libertarianism** in which we all get to 'choose' from a supermarket of identities, rather than displacing set identities (see, for example, Hausman's analysis of queer Transgender theorising in Hausman, 2000). In such accounts, rather than undoing identity, identity appears to undergo a rebirth, to be endlessly reproduced and endlessly available.

This libertarian outlaw individualism is, not surprisingly, often accompanied by the return of other Modernist ideas. The emphasis upon destabilisation of gender constructions – that is, the shift away from *group-based* identification as men/ women/gay/lesbian – is then viewed as the means to being simply human, or to simply being 'me' (just being an individual). In other words, Queer theorising frequently suggests choosing in a 'pick and mix' fashion from a range of identity attributes in order to assemble a customised, supposedly authentic selfhood beyond socially imposed categories, a stripped-to-the bone fundamental selfhood at the level of mere humanity/individuality. Whittle, for example, argues that the gender outlaws of Queer Theory view

> [g]ender ... as a means of oppression and a means of expression ... The human is first, the gender is an addition ... [They] take [their] human form and [impose] gender signi- fiers upon it. ... However, they choose not to gender blend, they do not claim the posi- tion of a third sex (meaning gender), rather they claim to be unique in their diversity and, most importantly, *themselves*. (1996: 212–14, emphasis added)

The return of 'the human' and 'the individual' sounds strangely like a return to Modernist liberal/libertarian universalism in some respects.

Queer theorising may not only involve the resuscitation of the universalised human/individual, but relatedly is often a means to place non-normative sexualities centre stage such that these become a new universalised norm for social change (Jagose, 1996: 97–8; see also Bornstein, 1994). While Queer Theory may be explic- itly associated with destabilising all gender/sexual identities, including heterosexu- ality, nevertheless heterosexuality is typically installed as inherently normative, as a position of conformity such that Queer is paradigmatically constituted in opposition to it. Hence, a queer heterosexuality is, with few exceptions, seen as an oxymoron. Heterosexuality is equated with heteronormativity (the institutional privileging of heterosexuality).[6] This hardly seems to break down gender/sexuality norms. In some versions of Queer Theory at least, one's identity (in this case the identity of a non- normative queer outlaw) is seen as producing a politics. Here queer identity gives rise to a politics, even though Queer theorising supposedly rejects identity as the basis of politics.

Finally, there is the question of whether Butler's Queer strategy is workable. The political strategy of asserting that we should reject any fixing of identity may be utopian or even dangerous. More fundamentally, its critics ask, 'can it be done?' While Butler notes in passing that some core self is necessary to psychic health, she never- theless invariably assumes that the dangers of fixity are greater than those of non- fixity. In sharp contrast, James Glass (1993) and Lynne Layton (1998) put the brakes on what they see as 'a facile celebration of performativity', the dangerous romantici- sation of identity instability. They note instead the extreme pain of 'the dissociative effects of gender fragmentation' (Malone, 2001; Hekman, 2000: 298–300). The distinction between an enabling fluidity and a paralysing disaggregation associated with mental illness remains unremarked in Butler's work.

Conclusion

'Many feminists have now argued on several grounds that Butler's theory of identity goes *too far* in destablizing identity' (Hekman, 2000: 290). Nevertheless, Butler's incisive criticism of identity politics is now widely accepted. Given this, it might be difficult simply to return to some model of identity as a basis for Feminist politics. However, if her theory can be viewed as going 'too far', what do we do with gender? What do we use instead of her notion of fluid instability? Is there a 'middle ground' between identity and fluidity, between the competing claims attached to Modernist 'essentialism' and Postmodern instability? Such questions continue to plague not only Feminism and Gender Studies, but also Sexuality Studies.

Notes

1. Butler (1993a: 22) explicitly links her work with Poststructuralism, in particular noting the influence of Michel Foucault. However, as indicated elsewhere in the book, I have employed the label Postmodernism as the coverall name under which I include Poststructuralist influences in the gender/sexuality field. See Chapter 1, note 13 and Chapter 5, note 5.

2. This analysis draws upon discussions with and the ongoing research of Belinda Sanders.

3. See also Chapter 14, note 6 and Chapter 15 for further discussions concerning how Foucault is connected with, and interpreted by, Queer thinkers.

4. Butler's allegiance to such a democratic politics is further outlined in Butler (2000).

5. Jagose (1996: 3) suggests in similar fashion that queer includes topics like 'cross-dressing, hermaphroditism, gender ambiguity and gender-corrective surgery'. For examples of links between particular bodies/topics and queer strategies, see Heywood, 1998; and Jagodzinski, 2003; as well as references in Chapter 21.

6. For an account of Queer Theory which does not conflate heterosexuality with heteronormativity, see Sullivan, 2003: 119–35; see also Wilson, 1997: 369.

PART 2

Sexuality Studies

10 | Sexuality Studies: an Overview

We now move away from our focus of the last nine chapters on gender and the subfield of Feminism, to the axis of sexuality and Sexuality Studies. As I did in the case of Feminism, I will initially provide a broad overview of the main theoretical directions. These directions in Sexuality Studies are not entirely different from those we encountered in our consideration of Feminism. As a result you will find much that is familiar in the terminologies, debates and content of this second subfield of gender/sexuality. Nevertheless, there are some new elements and a somewhat different set of dilemmas in Sexuality Studies from those associated with Feminism. A comparison of these two major subfields provides a useful way of introducing Sexuality Studies.

Focus/subject

Sexuality Studies here refers to *critical* analyses of the existing organisation and social meaning of sexuality and sexual identities, rather than merely descriptive accounts of doing sex. In Sexuality Studies, as against Feminist analyses, the focus is upon sexualities – that is, upon sexual object choice and desire – rather than upon sexed identities – that is, gender (Cranny-Francis et al., 2003: 7–9, 17–33; Richardson, 2001: 14018). Feminist approaches typically focus on gender and usually highlight women's positioning, even though many also discuss sexuality in tandem with this focus. By comparison, Sexuality Studies in general have produced a much greater volume of attention to men and their sexualities, specifically to gay men's sexual positioning. If the main subject of Gender Studies to this day remains women (see Carver, 1996: 4–5), then the central subject of Sexuality Studies has been gay men. This focus occurred partly because of a residual traditional privileging of men's perspectives and partly because lesbians have sometimes seen themselves, and have been seen, in relation to women's experiences. In other words, lesbians have often been located under the umbrella of Feminist perspectives rather than as primarily described in relation to (homo)sexuality (Jackson, 1998c: 68–9; Altman, 2001e: 5896–7). However, while Gender Studies continues to be more dominated by discussion of women's marginality, Sexuality Studies has become, at least comparatively, more balanced in its analyses of both gay and lesbian agendas, as well as **trans** (including, for instance, transsexual, transvestite and transgender) and intersex issues.[1]

Orientation towards central terms

There are a number of further differences that distinguish the history and content of Feminism from that of Sexuality Studies. Feminism has been obsessed with debating the problem of how gender identity and women themselves might be implicated in prescriptive and subordinating power relations. Sexuality Studies have debated in various ways over time how sexuality and sexual identities might be complicit in power (along similar lines to Feminism's discussion of sexed identities). However, Sexuality writers have also considered how sexuality might be the means to overcoming power or at least a means of deploying power for disruptive and pleasurable purposes. In other words, a marked distinction between Feminist and Sexuality Studies arises in the more evidently critical reading feminists have of gender than Sexuality Studies writers typically have of sexuality. Feminists (whether they take gender as a given or not) share serious doubts about gender as a social institution and set of activities. They tend to see much that is negative in it, especially for those deemed lesser within gender regimes. Womanhood may be re-valued positively by some feminists or at least its devaluation is questioned but gender, as a whole, is not re-valued in positive terms. By contrast, Sexuality writers see existing sexual regimes as problematic but frequently view not just marginalised sexual identities but sexuality as a whole in quite a positive way. Sexuality writers often remain attached, even if implicitly, to naturalistic biological assumptions regarding sexual desire or 'drive' and its association with various sexualities. For example, Libertarian arguments regarding the positive benefits of the power of sexuality run through many forms of Sexuality Studies. These elements stand in sharp contrast to the more circumspect, wary relationship which Feminism generally adopts towards forms of social organisation.

Power

Sexuality Studies writers are overall less alienated from power and its uses. Rather the subfield is shaped precisely by debates over whether sexuality can positively disrupt/deploy power or is in the grip of oppressive power relations. Feminist contributors to Sexuality Studies have generally tended to side with a view of sexuality as 'in the grip of power' – having a more circumspect view of sexuality (as well as gender) – but in more recent times feminist writers have adopted a more positive view of sexuality. In other words, feminist contributors have increasingly adopted the more positive orientation towards sexuality and power that is characteristic of, or at least widespread within the Sexuality Studies subfield.

History/politics

Sexuality Studies tends to start from a rather different beginning from that of Feminism. Where Feminism has a long and strong association with Liberalism stretching back at least into the nineteenth century, Sexuality Studies – as a fully articulated socially critical stance concerned with theorising/political action in order to promote social change – has had a more limited association with Liberalism. Sexuality Studies gathers steam later than Feminism – that is, in the 1960s and 1970s, though certain limited beginnings are evident earlier than this (Rubin, 1984: 302) – and draws much more strongly on Marxist-inspired radicalism (Phelan, 2000). By comparison, Feminism has an earlier development, a lengthier flowering and rather more mixed beginnings.

Sexuality Studies and its main theoretical directions

While the above comments provide some initial guidelines to understanding the critical theorising characteristic of Sexuality Studies, it is also useful to consider a range of 'histories' of this subfield of the gender/sexuality field. Such histories or overview accounts offer different stories of developments and hence theoretical directions, which in part depend on their 'starting point' (Seidman, 1993: 110). Three overviews that I have found especially useful are Stephen Whittle's transgender account (1996), Stevi Jackson's heterosexual feminist version (1999: 10–28), and Steven Seidman's focus on gay theorising (1993).

The characteristics of the subfield of Sexuality Studies may be further contextualised by returning to the overall picture of the gender/sexuality (G/S) field outlined in Chapter 1 (see Figure 1.1). In that figure I identified five main theoretical trajectories in terms of their central themes. It is useful to revisit this illustration (Figure 10.1).

These directions in the overall field of G/S theory take a particular form in Sexuality Studies. The five main trajectories outlined in Figure 10.2 in some ways parallel those in Feminism, but also show certain specific features. The first two may be termed (1) Emancipatory and (2) Sexuality Difference (singular identity politics) frameworks. The remaining three all offer critiques of singular difference and may be described as frameworks which focus on (3) (Multiple) Differences – for example, race/ethnicity/imperialism (REI) approaches, (4) Social Constructionism and (5) Postmodernism – that is, Queer Theory.

Figure 10.1 Map of the gender/sexuality field: continuum and directions

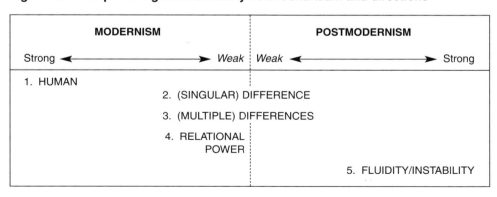

Figure 10.2   Map of Sexuality Studies: continuum and directions

MODERNISM	POSTMODERNISM
Strong ◄─────────────► *Weak*	*Weak* ◄─────────────► Strong

1. EMANCIPATORY
    (e.g.

- Liberal 'human rights'
  (anti-discrimination)
- Liberationist & Libertarian:
  i.e. 'Gay Liberation'-gay/lesbian coalition
- Liberationist Feminist:
  i.e. Women's Liberation movement

**2. SEXUALITY
DIFFERENCE**
(gay & lesbian separatism)
e.g.

- Libertarian Gay
- Women-centred
  Lesbian

3. (MULTIPLE) DIFFERENCES
e.g.

- Lesbian 'sex radicals'
- Sexuality crossings including
  bisexual and transgender
- 'Race'/ethnicity/imperialism sexualities

**4. SOCIAL
CONSTRUCTIONIST**

5. POSTMODERN

I provided in Chapter 1 a brief overview of the main directions in Feminist Studies and then elaborated in following chapters more detailed accounts of these directions and particular authors/texts. In the same way in this initial chapter introducing Sexuality Studies I will provide a short account of the main directions and in following chapters discuss them in more detail.

1   The Human: Modernist Emancipatory/Liberationist

Under this broad heading within Sexuality Studies there are a number of different substreams.

1(a) Liberal human rights

These approaches existed, in limited form, prior to the development of a fully formed critical Sexuality Studies approach. Such approaches were not necessarily pro-homosexuality, but were anti-discrimination and supported homosexuals as members of the universal 'Human'. Anti-discrimination sentiments can be found in late nineteenth- and early twentieth-century sympathetic medical, legal, psychological and sexological discussions of sexual pathologies/deviance (usually undertaken by sympathetic heterosexuals) and in organisations like the 'homophile movement', which advocated homosexual *assimilation* into full citizenship.[2] Liberal assimilationism is still pursued in popularist heterosexual attempts to support homosexual 'rights' and indeed arguably continues to be the public face of same-sex politics,[3] even if this vantage point is not so well accepted among most Sexuality Studies writers. Perhaps such a liberal 'rights' focus in the public arena is no surprise given that homosexuals remain, after all, the only group in modern Western democracies which is still formally unequal before the law (Whittle, 1996; Johnson, 2002; Phelan, 2001). (Other groups may still experience substantial informal discrimination but do have equal status as citizens before the law.)

1(b) Liberationist and libertarian: Gay Liberation

By the 1960s and early 1970s, the generally ineffective assimilationist model that had existed prior to this time was largely overrun by a much more radical same-sex position. This approach offered a liberationist *and* libertarian stance under the banner of **'Gay Liberation'** and notions of 'sexual revolution'. It viewed the history of critical Sexuality Studies as beginning 'after Stonewall', after a riot protesting against a police raid on a gay men's meeting place called Stonewall Inn became a broader rebellion against socially legitimated attacks on the homosexual community. The rebellion was described in terms of liberation for all, and to some extent drew on African-American 'Black Power' models of political struggle. 'Gay Liberation' (then describing a coalition between gays and lesbians) was a movement for *human sexual liberation* (Seidman, 1993: 114–15). Insofar as sexual liberation was seen as the struggle against romanticised, marital, genital and singularly male penetrative desires as the prescriptive norm of sexuality, 'Gay Liberation' was viewed as the vanguard of the revolution. Its intention was to throw off repression and assert an innate polymorphous sexuality – that is, throw off the oppressive strictures of social conditioning and revel in a foundational formless sexuality that does not demarcate or prohibit desires and pleasures. Gay Liberation combined Modernist liberationism and Modernist libertarianism, synthesising notions of throwing off power with conceptions of a natural, currently repressed sexuality as the source of the true self and the true society. Writers like Dennis Altman (see Chapter 11) exemplified this now largely disavowed viewpoint in Sexuality Studies, a viewpoint that may be summarised as *sexuality overthrowing power*.

1(c) Women's Liberation

A third element of Modernist Emancipatory Sexuality Studies may be found in the contribution of 'second-wave' feminists (see Chapter 1 and Glossary for accounts of second-wave feminism). Many commentators describe the beginnings of Sexuality

Studies in terms of same-sex analyses – that is, as arising out of writings from the homosexual/gay male movement – and as starting from Stonewall. However, theorists like Stevi Jackson (who writes from a heterosexual feminist perspective) and to some extent Stephen Whittle (writing from the perspective of transgender issues), note the work of Liberationist feminists in the 1960s and 1970s who developed a critique of heterosexuality.

Unlike Gay Liberation thinkers, these Liberationist feminists perceived sexuality as intimately tied to normative power. **Women's Liberation** developed a critique of existing heterosexuality as about a male model of sexuality in which penetrative sex *is* sex, and everything else is 'foreplay' – that is, just the preliminaries before 'the real thing'. Such a critical analysis of the problematic character of the social framing of heterosexuality also encouraged the development of discussions about other forms of sexuality such as masturbation and celibacy, topics that tended to disappear in discussions of women's sexuality after this time. Women's Liberation writers also noted links between (hetero)sexuality and violence, directing attention to a range of related issues, including rape, child abuse and harassment, as well as generally raising questions about conventional assumptions concerning sexual practice. Notions of men's sexuality as helplessly driven plumbing and of sexuality itself as driven by men's supposedly innate 'needs' were the subject of caustic, sometimes witty debate (see, for example, Koedt, 1972). In the process, (hetero)sexuality was taken from the realm of the simply natural and entirely personal and re-examined in terms of the political, in terms of the dynamics of power.

Over time Women's Liberation became divided over whether heterosexuality was inevitably problematic for women and therefore irredeemable, or not. Increasingly, heterosexual and lesbian women came to be at odds on this point, although the debate was not simply drawn along these group lines (Jackson, 1999: 13–15). The Women's Liberation position can be summarised overall as drawing attention to power within sexuality, conceiving *sexuality as a form of power, and not as having an innocent or 'natural' beneficent status*.

The dual themes of celebratory libertarian Gay Liberation (sometimes described as 'pro-sex') and wary Women's Liberation approaches, were in many ways to be reworked over and over again in Sexuality Studies for the next thirty years or more. In this context, it is also useful to distinguish somewhat between Sexuality Studies and sexuality *politics*. While Radical political agendas like Gay Liberation have been a feature of Sexuality Studies, assimilationist liberalism has never been a strong element in this form of theorising. However, reformist agendas like assimilationist liberalism have tended to remain significant within same-sex *activism* (see Glossary for the term **Reformism**).

2   Sexuality (singular) Difference: Modernist Identity politics (Gay and Lesbian Studies)

The second major theoretical direction in Sexuality Studies parallels developments in *Identity politics* in other social movements, including Feminism. By the late 1970s and 1980s the unstable coalition in 'Gay Liberation' between gays and lesbians was replaced by separatist identity-based approaches. Such approaches may be seen as drawing upon an 'ethnic minority' model of homosexuality. Rather than homosexuality being conceived as a diffuse possibility available to all, it was increasingly associated with particular easily identifiable characteristics, 'types' of people, and distinct communities (Ehrenreich, 1983; see also Altman, 2001: 5896; Seidman, 1993: 117–26). As the ethnic minority model gathered force, many lesbians became less convinced that their experiences were recognised under the supposedly inclusive banner of homosexual identity. Instead, they aligned themselves with women's concerns and left Gay Liberation for the Women's Liberation Movement.[4] The separate gay men's movement which arose from this split spawned a 'gay studies' approach which remained strongly Libertarian regarding sexuality, while lesbian analyses tended to become more strongly bonded with Women's Liberation and developed in this context along the lines of a 'woman-centred' approach (see Chapter 4). In such an approach lesbians and heterosexual women were seen as sharing a common female identity and experience. Sexuality, as a critical point of difference, tended to be downgraded or de-emphasised in 'women-centred' thinking. Nevertheless, in the woman-centred model, lesbians were cast as valorising woman-to-woman connections and thus they were granted a kind of vanguard status as the most woman-centred of all women, the most womanly in a politics based on identity as women. Heterosexual women increasingly faded from view in Sexuality Studies at this time, as they were seen in the women-centred model as both committed to a sexual practice that was mired in conformity to power and invested in men – that is, less committed to women (Jackson, 1999: 13–15; Marotta, 1980; Richardson, 1993a: 83–93; Phelan, 1989; Blasius and Phelan, 1997).

3 Multiple Differences: including sexual minority and 'race'/ethnicity/ imperialism theorising

By the late 1980s and 1990s these separate categories of sexual identity politics began to be questioned in Sexuality Studies, as they also were in Feminism. Many gays and lesbians expressed frustration with the divisiveness of identity politics (Smyth, 1997: 362–4). Relatedly, the limitations of the supposedly all embracing sexual identities, 'gay' and 'lesbian', became the subject of increasing concern.

These identities were questioned on the grounds of Identity Differen*ces* within sexual categories, which disrupted the neat homogeneity assumed by gay and lesbian identity politics. I outline below several examples of the kinds of questioning which clearly disrupted the gay/lesbian binary of separatist politics, and even began to raise new doubts concerning the heterosexual/homosexual binary.

First, lesbian 'sex radicals', who supported the more libertarian 'sexuality as pleasure' position associated with gay men's politics, began to mount a rejection of Women's Liberationist thinking. They refuted the negative account of sexuality as a mechanism of oppressive power associated with such thinking and developed a rejection of its emphatic insistence on non-penetrative, non-aggressive 'vanilla' sex. These lesbian 'sex radicals' turned their backs upon the notion of a shared womanhood which should be placed centre stage and, instead of following a Women's Liberationist 'women-centred' approach, began to promote a new gay/lesbian coalition. Following Gayle Rubin (1984, 1994), they suggested that the women-centred model revolved around a prescriptive conception of 'the good woman', of authentic womanhood, which was 'so heavily prohibitive as to make feminism resemble a sexual temperance movement'

(Wiegman, 2001a: 370; see also Chapter 12, note 2 and brief discussion in Chapter 18). By contrast, lesbian sex radicals actively supported SM (consensual sadomasochist) sexuality, butch-femme lesbian identities and the beneficial uses of pornography. Moreover, contrary to women-centred approaches, they insisted that such practices were not simply an imitation of the heterosexual prescriptive norm or of patriarchal relations of dominance and subordination. Gayle Rubin's (1994: 78) position is indicative: 'I looked at sex deviants and frankly they didn't strike me as the apotheosis of patriarchy' (see also Califia, 1980, 1996; Wechsler, 1981; for a related overview of the 'sex war' debates, see Echols, 1983a).

This advocacy of minority and marginalised sexual identities was in many ways anathema to women-centred lesbian feminists, who stressed overthrowing power relations in sexuality.[5] For these lesbian feminists a *feminist* sexuality involved rethinking the assumptions of women's normative positioning in heterosexuality such that it was necessarily about egalitarian and loving relationships (rather than about women's sexual domination, objectification and reduction to mere sexual usage). Hence, a feminist sexuality could not include the invocation of dominant/subordinate roles and the use of pain that are the stuff of SM sexual play.

Debates over the relationship between power and sexuality in the so-called 'sex wars' of the 1980s placed in doubt the self-evident unity of the category 'lesbian' (and their place in the feminist category of 'women') but largely did not involve heterosexual women or analysis of the homosexual/heterosexual binary. This was a dispute for the most part about lesbianism and lesbian sexuality (Jackson, 1999: 15). It also increasingly had some links with other sexual minority issues, such as transsexual/transgender/ intersex issues (Califia, 1983a, 1983b; for the counter-view in the sex wars regarding 'trans' issues, see Raymond, 1979).

Further examples of the growing critique of notions of homogeneous gay and lesbian sexual identities arose not only from other sexual minorities, but also from those drawing attention to race/ethnicity/imperialism identities. Gays and lesbians from minority *cultures* stressed the ways in which their experiences were largely excluded from 'mainstream' sexuality politics and noted, for example, ways in which race/ ethnicity/imperialism and class issues might be more crucial for them than sexual identity (Gomez, 1999; Goldman, 1996; Roen, 2001). Such approaches, like those from bisexual and transgendered persons, indicated how the positioning of minorities represented a disruption of gay/lesbian identities (Rust, 1995; Sturgis, 1996). Moreover, bisexual and transgender identities also disrupted the homosexual/heterosexual and gender distinctions upon which the categories gay and lesbian rest. For example, if a female-to-male (FTM) transgendered person is attracted to women, does this sexual identity register as heterosexual and/or as lesbian? If sexuality is seen as following gender identity, then perhaps this FTM person is heterosexual, but if sexuality is seen as following biological/anatomical sex perhaps this person is lesbian. If sexuality is viewed as having no particular relationship to either gender or supposedly self-evident sex, then this sexuality could be described not as heterosexual or lesbian but instead as both/neither. However the position of transgendered individuals is understood, it calls into question gay and lesbian identity politics.

Finally, certain practical political moments in the early 1990s raised serious difficulties regarding the coherence of gay and lesbian identities, as well as the coherence of the identity homosexual in the homo/hetero binary. These political moments involved the public rejection and expulsion of certain groups from gay and lesbian organisations, clearly indicating the precarious meaning of identity 'membership' and raising uncertainties regarding the grounds for an identity-based sexuality politics. Two instances are relevant here. The North American Man/Boy Love Association (NAMBLA) was expelled in 1994 from ILGA (a worldwide confederation of lesbian and gay organisations founded in 1978) after a decade of involvement in the latter confederation. This occurred in the wake of ILGA gaining consultative status to the UN Economic and Social Council in 1993. NAMBLA was ultimately positioned during this controversy as not belonging within homosexual collective politics and, in particular, as outside (legitimate) gay male politics. In a parallel move, the producers of the nineteenth Michigan Womyn's Music Festival (MWMF) – a women-only event in the USA initiated in 1976 – were faced with enforcing a 1991 policy which limited attendance to 'womyn-born women', thus excluding transsexual and intersex persons identifying as women. The ILGA and MWMF instances involve policing notions of legitimate/authentic collective identities invoked within sexuality identity politics, but also the difficulties attached to doing so (Gamson, 1997).

All of the examples outlined above disrupted any simple notion of gay, lesbian and homosexual identity political groupings. Growing concern about these discrete categories gave rise to greater stress on plural identities and increasing fragmentation.

4   Relational Power: Social Constructionism

The separate categories of gay and lesbian in (singular) Sexuality Difference frameworks were not only subjected to criticism by a range of thinkers discussing (multiple) Differences. Social Constructionists also mounted a challenge to sexual identity politics (see Chapters 12 and 13). The Social Constructionist framework did not necessarily disrupt identity categories completely – indeed Social Constructionist writers typically continue to validate the categories – but rather rejected 'essentialist' tendencies in them. This framework, rather than assuming that sexual identity categories have a set essence or character, outlined the changing historical forms of sexual identities and their links to wider social and 'material' processes. Both gay and feminist contributors to Social Constructionism also expressed significant doubts concerning libertarian accounts of an essential foundational sexuality, and noted – in keeping with Feminism's overall emphasis – that sexuality is implicated in and part of the negative, oppressive operations of power.

5   Fluidity/Instability: Postmodern Sexuality Studies (Queer Theory)

By the 1990s doubts regarding identity politics which had developed in the 1980s had been reworked into a more thorough-going refusal. The growing stress on multiple identities that had been associated with the increasing disavowal led into a critique of identity categorisation *per se*. However, the strands of the critique that stressed (libertarian) sexuality as pleasure and plural identities were taken up, while the Social Constructionist concern with sexuality as part of systemic material power relations was relatively de-emphasised. In the 1990s Postmodern positions influenced by interpretations of the work of Michel Foucault were strongly advanced. Such positions resisted Identity terms like gay and lesbian in favour of perspective-oriented analyses described as poststructuralist, postmodern or Queer (Seidman, 1993: 127–35). They included both those analyses which continued to link gender and sexuality analysis (for example, Queer feminists like Judith Butler, whose work is outlined in Chapters 8 and 9) and those which refused any connection between gender and sexuality (arguably many, if not most, Queer theorists).

In these Postmodern approaches there is a strong awareness of sexuality as a part of power but power relations in plural sexualities become themselves a source for self-fashioning and pleasure rather than simply negative and subordinating. In this sense, power is seen in positive productive terms as a means of subverting the singularity of normative power/sexuality by de-massifying and fragmenting it. If sexuality is no longer confined to one heterosexual path defined by a gendered binary opposition of men and women, then sexualised power can be produced in many places and can disrupt any simple 'othering' of marginalised sexual groups. The Postmodern/Queer and 'pro-sex' approach is now the predominant position within Sexuality Studies, even though gay and lesbian identity-oriented activism remains a major popularist point of reference.

Conclusion

In studying the subfield of Sexuality Studies we must come to grips not only with Modernist–Postmodern disputes over identity, as we did in Feminism, but also with debates concerning sexual desire and pleasure. These debates occur for example in relation to libertarianism and the 'sex wars' about notions of women's pleasure mentioned earlier. The debates place at odds those who affirm the positive possibilities of sexuality and those who insist we must consider the problems and dangers of sexuality and pleasure. Desire itself, it seems, can be questioned. Feminism asks us to wonder about *who* we are. Now we also begin to wonder about what we *feel/want/desire* in our most intimate moments.

Notes

1. For a brief account of terms associated with 'trans' and 'intersexual', see Valentine and Kulick, 2001: 15888–93; for a detailed discussion see Chapters 14 and 21.

2. For an analysis of late nineteenth- and early twentieth-century anti-discrimination views, see Weeks, 1985: Chapter 4. For analysis of homophile organisations, see Seidman, 1993: 111; Cranny-Francis et al., 2003: 30–1; Martin and Lyon, 1972; D'Emilio, 1983; Weeks, [1977] 1990; Adam, 1995; Segal, 1997: section 1; Shepard, 2001; and Altman, 2001: 5895–6.

3. See for example, A. Sullivan, 1996; Shepard, 2001. Responses to Sullivan include Warner, 1999; Vaid, 1995; Phelan, 2000.

4. Gender conflicts arose in many Western countries as lesbians increasingly criticised the failure of the often male-dominated homosexual political movement to consider women's issues. See Adam et al., 1999.

5. This position is put forward most explicitly by writers like Sheila Jeffreys (1990, 1994a), Kathleen Barry (1982) and Janice Raymond (1979; Linden et al., 1982).

11 Modernist Liberationism: Altman

When discussing the Modernist beginnings of Feminism, I focused on Liberal feminism as an example, and put to one side the more politically radical forms of Modernist feminism – that is, Liberationist feminisms such as Marxist/Socialist and Radical feminisms. While I suggested several different sources on these feminisms, I did not discuss them – largely because they have already been the subject of extended analysis within feminist texts. In my examination of Modernist accounts within Sexuality Studies, however, I intend to rectify this omission and consider the more radical versions of Modernism. I will adopt this kind of strategy throughout the book. Approaches or issues that are mentioned only in passing in relation to one subfield of gender/sexuality theory will be picked up in another. The aim here is to be reasonably comprehensive without being overly repetitive.

In this context, I introduce the first writer to be discussed under the umbrella of Sexuality Studies, Dennis Altman. Altman's work provides a clear instance of radical Liberationist Modernism. Dennis Altman is an Australian academic and activist. He wrote one of the most influential early texts in the area of Sexuality Studies. His analysis is interesting to consider because he has observed and contributed to Sexuality Studies over a long period: from its associations with the youthful exuberance of the activist 1960s and 1970s, followed by its difficult days in the politically conservative 1980s with the advent of the AIDS virus in the West, and of late its connections with both Queer Theory and with materialist consumerism. (Schneider, 1999: 4). Altman's comments on the tensions in current LGBTI (lesbian/bisexual/gay/trans/intersex) politics – for example, on the tensions between advocates of assimilation into the capitalist status quo and the anti-assimilationism typically associated with Queer – are informed by his own extensive experience in this movement.

The significance of his work in Sexuality Studies lies in the fact that it provides the archetypal theoretical expression of 'Gay Liberation' which, as he notes, was an inclusive term in the 1960s/70s (Altman, 1999: 27). In its aims at least, 'Gay Liberation' included both gay men and lesbians. Altman initially developed a 'Gay Liberation' theoretical model, a Modernist Liberationist mode of theorising, in his 1971 publication, *Homosexual: Oppression and Liberation* (see also [1971] 1996). The title concisely sums up the approach. It is a theoretical model that is macro in scope and sees power as oppression/repression (as negative). Power is viewed here as something you can throw off, to reveal a self liberated from power, a self that is free. As you will now be aware, this is classic Modernist territory.

However, unlike the more mixed and attenuated Modernist beginnings of Feminism as a mode of political theorising and action, the Modernist beginnings of Sexuality Studies were somewhat less entwined with Liberal reformist Modernism.

The importance of Dennis Altman's work is indicative of the rather more radical overall character of Modernist writings in Sexuality Studies. Sexuality Studies does, of course, contain a tradition of assimilationist reformist approaches (for instance, the pre-1960s 'homophile movement' which basically asked for little more than tolerance),[1] but it has drawn more crucially upon the 1960s and 1970s radicalism of both 'Gay Liberation' and aspects of 'Women's Liberation'.

Dennis Altman was a critical spokesperson for 'Gay Liberation'. His work exemplifies its tensions as well as the character of its continuing impact on each successive wave of theorising in the Sexuality Studies subfield over the last thirty years or so. In other words, Altman is not merely an established scholar in this subfield, about whom we should all learn as a matter of antiquarian interest. Though some writers, like Shane Phelan (2000), suggest that the 'liberationist' stance with which Altman is associated is 'now virtually unknown and/or discredited', there are several reasons why his work remains critical to Sexuality Studies.

First, Altman has continued to write. Throughout the 1970s, 1980s, 1990s and 2000s he has continued to contribute ideas on a wide range of issues. This work has offered a radical political position, an unapologetically 'Left wing' approach. Therefore, his work provides an important and continuing counterpoint to many other theorists in the field of Sexuality Studies. In short, his work offers an ongoing, not just historically interesting, position in the subfield.

Secondly, Altman's early work remains relevant to this ongoing position. As Altman himself notes, he has not abandoned his early 'Gay Liberation' views that were first expressed in *Homosexual: Oppression and Liberation* (Altman, 1999). Indeed, Altman asserts that 'Gay Liberation' thinking set the agenda for most of the significant questions we are still dealing with today, as well as playing an important role in shaping the political activism of AIDS groups (Altman, 1994, 1999, 2001e). For this reason it is clearly worth going back to the early material.

Moreover, his work can indeed be said to contain elements or strands which remain significant in newer forms of theorising. In other words, we need to consider 'Gay Liberation' as both an *influence* upon, and also perhaps as having direct *linkage* with, these newer forms of thinking. For example, Altman himself suggests links between Gay Liberation and Queer theorising. Why is it useful to attend to such influences and/or links? To the degree that newer forms of thinking reflect earlier ones, it becomes useful to examine the earlier positions to help us understand more about what is being argued today. Just as looking at nineteenth-century Liberal feminists like Mary Wollstonecraft and Sojourner Truth helps us to understand a whole range of present-day feminist views, just as looking at the early work of Mary Daly helps us to understand that of Judith Butler, the same may be said in this instance regarding Sexuality Studies.

These points also indicate that we cannot simply ignore or dismiss viewpoints on the basis that they were developed at an earlier point than those emerging today. Prior development does not necessarily mean that it is outmoded. It is indeed, as many contemporary theorists insist, a mistake to assume that history moves in a seamless line towards ever more enlightened thinking such that present-day thought is always better than that which is older. The difference between newer and more longstanding positions may simply be one of political stance, rather than simply of age. In short, debates between newer and older positions are political, not merely a matter of history moving along. They are just as political as debates between theorists of newer positions.

Having outlined *why* we might look at Altman as an example of a Radical (rather than Liberal assimilationist) Modernist – as an example of Liberationist Modernism – I will now turn to the plan for the chapter. I intend initially to place his early work in its political, historical context and then to clarify the liberationist and libertarian elements in his works, including some tensions between these elements. Finally, I will briefly discuss how these elements are picked up in more recent sexuality thinking and how they tell us something about ongoing tension/debates in the field.

Context

In the late 1960s Altman was in the USA. He apparently thrived in a heady atmosphere of social transformation. At this time the civil rights, anti-Vietnam War and New Left movements were on the rise, and the Women's Movement was reborn (see also Chapter 10 for a brief discussion of this period). This atmosphere of high hopes and burgeoning claims to just treatment produced perhaps the pivotal moment for Sexuality Studies in the West, the Stonewall riots of June 1969. The Stonewall Inn was a New York gay meeting place and subject to routine police raids in this period of criminalised male homosexuality. However, in June 1969 a police raid was the last straw and led to several days of rioting. 'Gay' people, gay men in particular, had had enough. In the same year the GLF (Gay Liberation Front) was formed (Teal, 1971; Bronski, 1998; Weeks [1977] 1990). Its name was intended to suggest an analogous political struggle to that undertaken by Marxian Liberation Fronts in the developing world. Fairly quickly after this, a group calling itself the GAA (Gay Activist Alliance) split off from the GLF to focus on legislative reform and decriminalising homosexuality. The GAA had a very specific focus on reforms related to homosexuals only – that is, it was a Liberal organisation concerned with attaining rights for homosexuals within the existing social system (Shepard, 2001). The GLF accused the GAA of being white, sexist and politically timid. More recently, writers describe the difference in approach towards assimilation as 'the suits' versus 'the sluts' (Ibid.). In other words, a similar political division is still evident today.

Altman's 1971 book *Homosexual: Oppression and Liberation* was written in the aftermath of Stonewall. It charted the development of GLF thinking, a Liberationist approach that was not always accepted by the 'mainstream' Left and was always under attack by the Christian and political Right in the USA. Perhaps for this reason it took until 1979, ten years after Stonewall, before the first national gay and lesbian march was held in the USA (Ibid.). This brief period of lively and optimistic political activism between the late 1960s and 1970s was soon to be almost swallowed up (Altman, 1999; Katz, 1983).[2] The political climate for 'gay' activism was increasingly constrained by a Right-wing political swing in the early 1980s which led to Ronald Reagan's election as President of the USA, Margaret Thatcher's election as the British Prime Minister, and the broad emergence of a 'neo-conservative' agenda in the West.[3] This political context coalesced with the rise of the AIDS epidemic in the West which threatened the very existence of gay communities, whatever their politics (Altman, 2001e: 5897; Shepard, 1997; Dalton, 1999a). No wonder these communities hunkered down in a defensive Identity politics which stressed internal unity/homogeneity, while at the same time refusing to become invisible (Altman, 1979, 1982a, 1982b; Seidman, 1993: 116–17).

We can see from this brief historical background that Altman's famous book *Homosexual* arises during a period between the predominance of largely ineffectual reformist concerns in the 1950s and the gay and lesbian separatist and activist community orientation of the 1980s. Importantly, the 'Gay Liberation' moment was not unique to the USA (Khan, 1999: 26–7; Altman, 2001e: 5896). Radical Liberationist Modernism was a feature of same-sex movements in Western capitalist countries around the world.

Content

What is the content of 'Gay Liberation', of Modernist Liberationist approaches in Sexuality Studies? 'Gay Liberation' theory was a synthesis of two main traditions: a Libertarian approach to sexuality which offers a 'pro-sex' individualism or humanism, and a Liberationist approach which stresses group/collective identity in revolutionary struggle for social justice. These two tendencies are not always at ease with one another, as Altman's own work shows (Ashbolt, 1998: 54). Later developments in Sexuality Studies often involved separating them out and revealed their potentially different trajectories. However, in 'Gay Liberation', Libertarianism and Liberationism were brought together. In this form of thinking, freeing up sexuality was the means to freedom (liberation) from the repressive status quo.

Gay Liberation Theory grew out of Marxism, but in particular out of the work of Herbert Marcuse (1955, 1969) (Phelan, 2000; Crozier, 1991: 90–8; Robertson, 1993: 301–2; Ambercrombie et al., 1988: 145; Held, 1980: Chapters 4 and 8). Marcuse made use of the writings of both Karl Marx and Sigmund Freud.[4] From Marx, Marcuse takes a Liberationist stance and from Freud an understanding of sexual repression that informs his Libertarianism. In Marcuse's book *Eros and Civilisation* (1955) he integrated themes of group/collective struggle and of sexual freedom. Altman drew heavily upon this text. Along with many others in the 1970s (for related works of the same period, see Mieli, 1977; and Hocquenghem, 1978); Altman asserted (following Marcuse) that the disciplinary strictures of capitalist society demanded 'guilt and renunciation'. However, without capitalist society's insistence upon the obedient, docile, money and time-controlled worker, 'we would all be polymorphously perverse, free to experience pleasure with a variety of different partners' and in a variety of different ways (Phelan, 2000).

What is the basis of Altman's integration of Marx and Freud via Marcuse? In the first instance, the Liberationist element of Altman's version of 'Gay Liberation' thinking drew upon Marxism. Karl Marx is a social theorist of revolution. In the 1960s and 1970s he was *the* theorist of revolutionary politics. As Craig Johnston (1999), an Australian gay activist, noted of the period, everybody who was anybody was a Marxist.

Marx argued that conflict was at the heart of class-divided (hierarchical) societies. Injustice bred conflict. For Marx the crucial conflict was broadly between those who have and those who don't. Those property owners who own or control the 'means' by which we produce things (tools, food, and so on), necessarily gain a privileged position over those who do not. The 'means' include owning or controlling people, money or technology/machinery. Marx outlined an inequitable divide between owners/controllers of the 'means of production' over those who do not own/control production but instead are themselves owned (slaves) or controlled (for example, workers).

This divide, he argued, fuels conflict until there is a revolutionary break in the existing social order. Just as the rising capitalist class overthrew the feudal aristocracy, so too, Marx hypothesised, would the power and privileges of the capitalist class be threatened in turn by the workers and their supporters. He postulated that the divide between the rich and poor would grow ever greater over time, exacerbating conflict and injustice, leading finally to a revolt and the revolutionary development of a new kind of society in which all would be treated justly at last.

Marcuse is described as a neo-Marxist because, among others in the so-called 'Frankfurt School', he developed a revised version of Marxism which de-emphasised economic divisions in favour of a more socio-cultural analysis and he saw revolution in broader terms than working-class struggle. You can see here why Altman and others in Gay Liberation might have found Marx and Marcuse's interpretation of Marxism congenial reading. In the period of 1960s and 1970s Gay Liberation, male homosexuality was still a criminal act and homosexuality was seen at best as a psychiatric illness or at worst as deviant, degenerate and/or sinful. The Marcusian Liberationist notion of homosexuals as an underclass, who exemplified the marginalised and their struggle for justice, cast homosexuals as capitalist society's natural enemies and put them in the position that Marx had placed the working class. Homosexuals' sufferings and rejection could now be reinterpreted, not as an error in the natural order or as an individual sin or disability, but in *political* terms and as part of a broader alternative struggle for a better society.

Secondly, Altman's approach linked this Marxian Liberationist model with sexuality (rather than economics) via Marcuse's use of Freud. Marcuse, like others in the Frankfurt School, was a German who escaped from Nazism to the USA in the 1930s. His work linked Nazism, totalitarianism and capitalism with sexual repression. This linkage was further developed in Altman's 'Gay Liberation' thinking. Altman took from Marcuse's reading of Freud the conception of a *polymorphous libido*, a natural sexual energy or life force conceived as a *biological* drive – a primordial innate force emanating from the individual – which is then repressed by social requirements and reshaped into an acceptably normative self. Altman made use of the Freudian notion of the sexual as an innate *universal Human* attribute that determines the self and is at odds with social order. However, against Freud's overall endorsement of the social order which 'civilises' polymorphous sexuality, Altman uses Marx to argue for a liberation of the sexual as producing a more natural, healthy social life. The liberation of sexuality is seen by Altman, in his early work, as necessarily producing social transformation and undermining capitalism. In an article published in 1999, Altman looks back on this early viewpoint and argues that 'Gay Liberation' did not foresee how capitalism could make use of a proliferation of sexual choices. His recent work extends this analysis. However, despite his reassessment of the political benefits of proliferating sexual choices, especially in terms of his concern with countering capitalism, Altman's work continues to express a Libertarian stance, as we shall shortly see.

Gay Liberation, along with some elements of Women's Liberation, created a 'pro-sex' vision of *sexuality as the means to cultural revolution*. For Altman, 'gay was a revolutionary identity capable of disarming institutions which pathologized sexuality', including institutions like education, the police force, psychiatry, among others. The Gay Liberation Front was a movement for social justice and not just for homosexuals.

This political movement 'would free us all from the shame, guilt and sin that attached to sexual activity and would expose the rigidities of gender' as well (Ashbolt, 1998: 54). As David Pattent, an AIDS activist, puts it, 'Gay Liberation was about more than just coming out. … It was about allowing all people to come out as *who they are* (emphasis added)' (Ibid.). Similarly, a former GLF member, Jack Nichols says: 'I began hoping … for a final melting of gay/straight divisions and the creating of a sexually integrated society in which everybody would be free to love and make love without self identifying through specialized sexual labels' (Ibid.).

There is in this comment an idea of a 'liberated uncategorized sexuality' shared by all and of the 'abolishing of sexual categories', as Altman puts it (Ibid.; Altman, 1999). Perhaps you can already begin to see why Altman directly connects Gay Liberation with Postmodern/Queer Theory.

Tensions/debates

Despite these possible connections, Gay Liberation offered a strongly Modernist approach. The Marxian *Liberationist* element within Gay Liberation involves overthrowing power to reveal a 'true' shared and universal humanity that can be free of power. This can be achieved through group/collective struggle to release a common human nature repressed by power. The *Libertarian* element of the analysis is equally Modernist, in that the universal natural foundation that is to be liberated by political struggle is sexual. While Liberationism and Libertarianism are both Modernist in orientation and both contribute to Gay Liberation, they indicate potentially different political trajectories in Modernist thought.

Libertarianism politically sits somewhat uneasily alongside a Liberationist orientation. Libertarianism holds that all people have certain inalienable rights which can never be taken away in the name or interests of the collective. Gay Liberation Libertarianism asserts sexual rights as inalienable and not to be removed by the social and collective body politic. In other words, society, governments, social institutions or agents have no right to intervene in sexuality. This deep distrust of social intervention and government is grounded in a strongly individualist, extreme or zealous liberalism. The rights of individuals, in this case sexual rights, are paramount.

Some versions of Libertarianism are not surprisingly highly conservative. For example, in the 1980s neo-liberal political leaders like Margaret Thatcher and Ronald Reagan pursued an economic Libertarianism that refused notions of collective good or social responsibility and on this basis cut back on public services, welfare and publicly funded education in the name of the unfettered individual and individual responsibility. Such forms of (economic) Libertarian individualism also remain popular in Australia's current conservative government. The Libertarian individualist, anti-'social' stance sits awkwardly with a Socialist or broadly Left-wing emphasis on group/collective struggle to overthrow capitalism. Yet Gay Liberation and Altman's work straddles precisely this conundrum.

On the one hand, Altman proposes a strongly collectivist, anti-capitalist revolution and is dismissive of 'do what you like, be what you want to be' forms of politics (Willett, 1999: 55), as party to Liberal consumer capitalism. In *Global Sex* (2001a), for example, Altman outlines the relationship between the commodification and export of Western sexual culture/sexual identities and an essentially American globalising capitalism (Altman, 2001b, 2002). He notes, in other words, that the globalisation of Western sexual permissiveness can support the spreading grip of capitalist agendas. Furthermore, as noted earlier, he has pointed out in recent times that he failed to foresee in the 1960s and 1970s that capitalism and the repressive sexual order of the West are not necessarily one and the same thing (Altman, 1999). The overthrow of sexual repression does not, he now argues, necessarily result in an overthrow of capitalism. Moreover, in his far-reaching analysis of non-Western countries in *Global Sex*, he suggests that capitalism and increased sexual freedom can happily co-exist and indeed support one another. In this analysis sexual freedom is not an unproblematic good. Altman's commitment to a Left politics seems at times to override or at least raise doubts about his Libertarian goals.

Similarly, in his article 'On not speaking' (2001d: 13), he very carefully suggests that progressive politics requires more than simply 'doing your own thing'. He notes his own waverings between a strongly essentialist identity politics, in which only those from the marginalised group under discussion may speak, and a scepticism about strict sexual or ethnic identities which draws upon contributions to understanding homosexuality from beyond the identity community. There is no question here in this discussion about the Identity politics of a Libertarian 'do as you will' approach. Altman displays a deep concern with developing a balanced political programme, rather than pursuing a politics of individual voices. Individualism in this example is clearly sacrificed to collective interest, to a collective good achieved in political action. On much the same grounds, he insists that mainstream political theorists should pay attention to the collective character of the gay community and is understandably piqued by Putnam's generalised view that American society is becoming increasingly less communal. Altman's assertion that such an analysis simply ignores the remarkably strong same-sex sense of community, as demonstrated during the AIDS crisis, is clearly not motivated by an individualist politics (Altman, 2001c; see also Altman, 1995).

On the other hand, he continues to speak from the 1970s to the present day in identifiably Libertarian terms. In *Defying Gravity: A Political Life* (1997) (see Ashbolt, 1998) he mentions an earlier 1982 article in which he passionately defended gay bathhouses. He continues to support the basic argument of this earlier piece of writing, insisting on sexual freedom, including his view that not all sex between children and adults is inherently exploitative. His definition of 'children', though critical to assessments of his argument, is unfortunately somewhat vague. It may include young teenagers, though not pre-pubescents. He also defends casual sex even with those one hates. Desire, even for the politically antithetical, is never questioned. It remains an unproblematised good. Despite concerns about racism and sexism, his pro-sex agenda does not allow him to be critical of Gay Liberation. He continues to wax nostalgic about those heady 1970s days, even when many like Jewelle Gomez note that Gay Liberation's celebratory style was much less available to African Americans who had commitments to their ethnic communities/families and could not always place sexuality first (Schneider, 1999).

Despite some worries about misogyny (woman-hating) in gay culture and the fact that his own work contains an acknowledged debt to feminist thinking (Ashbolt, 1998; Altman, 1999), there is little recognition in Altman's approach that Gay Liberation's pro-sex agenda was a major political problem for lesbians and feminists generally (Shepard, 2001; Khan, 1999).[5] Altman remains largely uncritical of the ways in which this pro-sex agenda might have been exclusionary. Indeed, Gay Liberation, for all of its radicalism, may be seen as remaining focused upon the experience of gay, white middle- and upper-class men who privileged sexuality precisely because they faced no other areas of marginalisation. Gay Liberation may be viewed, like Women's Liberation, as offering a much more limited form of political struggle than it was prepared to acknowledge.

Conclusion: Altman and contemporary theorising

Altman's combination of Liberationist and Libertarian politics raises some questions about its seeming polar opposite, Queer Theory. As noted earlier, Altman has asserted some points of influence and even direct links. For example, the Libertarian strand may be regarded as taken up by some promoting a consumerist, lifestyle-oriented Queer agenda that focuses on fashioning an individualist, sexualised identity, while the Liberationist strand remains evident in anti-capitalist, social justice-oriented Queer approaches (see, for example, Seidman, 1993). Yet, despite these potential connections, Altman himself is unpersuaded by Queer (Altman, 1999). Perhaps this is because he seems nowadays to be rather more ambiguous about his own Libertarian agenda and largely remains an advocate of Liberationist Identity politics. Altman affirms either a human identity or gay and lesbian communal identities. This places him at some distance from Queer objections to these identities. He does not go so far in his criticisms of Queer as some other Gay Liberationists like Craig Johnston, who declares, 'when I hear Queer I reach for my kalishnikov!' (Willett, 1999). Nevertheless, Altman's irritation with Queer Theory in terms of its lack of recognition of earlier forms of struggle concerned with abolishing sexual categories, and his antagonism to Queer Theory's rejection of any form of stable identity, are quite as decisive. For Altman, Sexuality Studies is still about defending the Gay community, including defending it from those within it who wish to dissolve it.

Notes

1. See Chapter 10 and especially Chapter 10, note 2.
2. For the growth of reformism and the diminution of radicalism in the 1980s, see Duberman, 1998.
3. This 'neo-conservative' climate was characterised by a polemical advocacy of 'smaller government', with the aim of reducing government responsibility for social services, such as health and welfare, as well as reducing government involvement in ameliorating social inequalities and discrimination. The rejection of government responsibility was commonly accompanied by a social conservatism involving a withdrawal of public compassion and support from the marginalised, including those dealing with the AIDS epidemic. See Whittle, 1996: 199–200; Duberman, 2002a; Andriote, 1999; Tolson and Ewers, 2004; Greenberg, 1992; Waldman, 1986.
4. Check Glossary for accounts of Marx and Marxism. See also Outhwaite and Bottomore, 1993; Beilharz, 1991: 168–74. For accounts of the work of Sigmund Freud and psychoanalysis, see Chapters 4 and 5 of this book.
5. For perhaps the most antagonistic feminist assessment of Libertarianism in relation to its impact in the sexual revolution of the 1960s and 1970s and its ongoing presence within Queer Theory, see Jeffreys, 1990, 1994b.

Social Constructionism: Jackson, Weeks

I spent some time in the section dealing with Feminism (Part 1) discussing Modernist thinking, including Emancipatory Humanist, Gender Difference, and Race/ethnicity/imperialism perspectives. I mentioned the Social Constructionist approach only in passing (see Chapter 1) but return to it here largely because, while it has a diminished significance in Feminism (Jackson, 1998a: 25), the approach remains very important in Sexuality (and Masculinity) Studies. Social Constructionism, on the one hand, resists any set or fixed content to identities (rejects, for example, any notion of 'woman' or 'lesbian' as having certain set qualities), but also refuses the Postmodern antagonism to identity. Gender and sexuality are not, within this framework, simply a matter of identity differences but of hierarchical social division analogous to class and founded upon concrete material oppression (Jackson, 1998b: 139). As can be seen in Chapter 10 (Figure 10.2), the Social Constructionist (SC) position sits at the borderlands of the Modernist–Postmodern continuum, even if fairly firmly on the former side of the boundary.

Figure 10.2 draws attention to the five main theoretical directions in Sexuality Studies, including (1) Emancipatory, (2) (Singular) Sexuality Difference, (3) (Multiple) Differences, (4) Social Constructionist, and (5) Postmodern approaches. In this chapter, I skip over discussion of (2) Sexuality Difference – which offers a version of an Identity politics framework – and (3) Differences. Instead, I move directly on from the discussion of emancipatory Liberationist thinking in Chapter 11 to Social Constructionist thinking within Sexuality Studies. I adopt this strategy in part because I have spent some time already in the context of Feminism considering the characteristics of Identity politics (the singular Difference framework). The particular interpretation of it in Sexuality Studies will in any case be examined in the process of considering other theoretical trajectories.

Even though I also skip over the Differences trajectory in Sexuality Studies, I nevertheless discuss it in other locations. The Differences grouping includes writers attending to 'sex radicalism', as well as those concerned with sexuality minority groupings and with Transgender theorising. I have chosen to discuss Transgender theorising under the heading of Postmodern/Queer to avoid duplication because it arises in both Differences and Postmodern/Queer frameworks and because such theorising is increasingly perceived as providing the case *par excellence* for Queer Theory. The Differences framework also includes writers dealing with race/ethnicity/imperialism. Since I have skipped this framework in Sexuality Studies, I instead mention race/ethnicity/imperialism matters as they arise in other settings. For instance, the Social

Constructionist trajectory in Sexuality Studies often pays considerable attention to historical and cultural specificity. However, these accounts of race/ethnicity/imperialism are usually more concerned with broadly cultural, anthropological or cross-cultural analysis. I draw more clearly on writers *speaking from* a position of marginalisation related to race/ethnicity/imperialism writings when considering Postmodern/Queer Theory. In other words, I briefly consider the REI Differences literature and its impact in Sexuality Studies when comparing its alternative viewpoint from that of the Postmodern/Queer framework.

Having explained how I have undertaken my examination of Sexuality Studies, I now move to examine the characteristics of the fourth main theoretical direction in this sub-field. Social Constructionism (SC) is a Modernist position in terms of its continuing engagement with identity as a basis for politics, its tendency to conceive power as oppressive (largely negative or constraining), and its focus on structural limits associated with large-scale forms of power (such as capitalism). Power is more materially specific and less fluid in SC accounts than in Postmodern analyses.[1] Nevertheless, SC writers share with Postmodernism a stress upon *social* (that is, changeable) construction and a refusal in particular of any simple recourse to biological or natural explanations, even if their constructionism is not as all-embracing as that of Postmodern thinkers.

In this chapter I want to outline certain critical features of Social Constructionism, including:

1. The critique of essentialism (especially the critique of biological explanations for social matters).
2. The strong focus on the material (economic in particular) and historical basis of social construction (specifically on variation within specific limits, which constrain fluidity).
3. The difference between this approach and that of Postmodernism, given that the latter is ironically more thoroughly social constructionist than Social Constructionism.
4. SC politics.

I will then turn briefly to debates.

Critique of Essentialism

Some writers, such as Diana Fuss (1989: 9, 18) and Gayatri Spivak (1984–85: 183–4), have noted that it may be difficult to entirely escape from or dispense with notions of identity or notions of some stable essence in considering sexuality or gender. Social Constructionist (SC) writers do, as we shall see, tend to agree with Fuss and Spivak that some usage of less simplistic and homogeneous identity categories may be strategically necessary. Nevertheless, what is specifically associated with SC is its critique of notions of 'essentialism' in Sexuality Studies.

SC writers challenge sexual essentialism, as Jeffrey Weeks (1985: 8) notes, by rejecting forms of thinking which reduce any sexual phenomena to some central core or 'inner truth'. In general, sexual essentialism amounts to universalised and often biologically based understandings of sex acts, sexual identities or sexuality *per se*. Sexual essentialism is the belief in the deep, unchanging, innate character of sexuality such that its biological basis is viewed as 'uncontaminated by cultural influences' (Jackson and Scott, 1996: 11).

What is significant about SC is that, as Carol Vance (1992: 133) points out, it challenges the eternal, universal or natural status of gender and sexuality. Why is this significant? Because for most, if not all of us, sexual essentialism was 'our first way of thinking about sexuality' and it still remains the dominant way of thinking, the taken-for-granted way of understanding sexuality in our culture. For example, it is almost entirely taken as given in our culture that men are somehow more sexual beings than women on the basis of some innate drive, such that men who do not conform to this conception are considered odd, deviant, unnatural – that is, not proper, real men.

Social Constructionist perspectives vary in degree. I have already intimated that Postmodernism offers a strong, extremely radical version of social constructionist thinking, to the point of questioning any essence to identity or any set bodily foundation to identity. There is in Postmodernism no set basis for the 'human', 'women', 'men', or to sexuality beyond perhaps a very nominal bodily set of conditions (such as, humans must eat). Social Constructionism as the proper name for the grouping of self-designated thinkers tends to offer an approach which pulls back somewhat from this complete anti-foundationalism (see Glossary for terms like foundationalism). By contrast, SC writers proceed to argue that sexuality may have varying social significance in different cultures and historical periods. The SC writers stress *specific* social variation and complexity rather than emphasising virtually unlimited elasticity or fluidity (mutability *per se*). In short, they stress specific variations/complexity rather than broad, often more abstract notions of fluidity/instability.

SC writers offer a culturalist or social nurture argument (as against a nature argument) for human relations. Rather than challenging *any* continuing basis for set identity, they focus on refusing simple or singular accounts of identity. This is their grounds for rejecting **biological reductionist** thinking, such as the simple reduction to biological explanation found in the notion that men rape because of a biological drive to spread their sperm. The inclination to reject reductionism and to pursue notions of specific historical/cultural variation means that, 'all social constructionists' will, at a minimum, assert that similar *sex acts* like sodomy do not have 'a universal social meaning' (Vance, 1992: 134). Sex acts do not always have an identical meaning in terms of sexual identities or social location. Sodomy, for example, may not always mean homosexuality or social marginalisation or any particular community belonging.

Many contemporary Social Constructionist writers would go further and also assume that *desire is not innately channelled* – that is, heterosexual/homosexual 'object choices' are not biologically written into one's genetic make-up or proscribed as drives by the imperatives of evolution (see, for example, Weeks' critique of 'Sociobiology' in Weeks, 1985: 108–20, 246–50). For these SC writers there is 'no essence of homosexuality' or heterosexuality (Ibid.: 6).

Finally, a smaller number of contemporary Social Constructionist thinkers (especially those influenced by Postmodernism) would assert that *desire/sexuality itself* is not biologically inevitable in the sense that there is 'no essential, undifferentiated sexual impulse, ... drive or lust which resides in the body due to physiological functioning and sensation' (Vance, 1992: 134). These writers offer a repudiation of the

Libertarian view of sexuality as an inherent universal drive and as necessarily subversive of social relations (Weeks, 1985: 5). In other words, they offer a refutation of the Dennis Altman position outlined in the previous chapter. Sexuality in this analysis is removed from its pedestal as the expression of the 'natural', the animal within, that which is untouched and uncontaminated by culture and necessarily rebellious in opposition to 'civilisation' and order. Such romantic conceptions are discounted in these more radical or thorough-going Social Constructionist writings. Such writings assert that sexuality itself is constructed by culture and history (Vance, 1992: 135).

Not all SC writers accept the utter renunciation of any inherent sexuality or sexual desire/impulse, but all assert that biology and bodies can explain very little and that the social constitution of Sexuality is highly variable (Weeks, 1985: 6). There are evident links here between Social Constructionism and social anthropology. However, the emergence of Social Constructionism in Sexuality Studies is commonly associated with the refutation of essentialism in the work of sociologist Mary McIntosh, the 'symbolic interactionist' approach of John Gagnon and William Simon, and Michel Foucault's Postmodern framework (Richardson, 2001: 14018; Jackson, 1996b: 62–73; Weeks, 2001: 13998–9).

Focus on a material/historical approach to Sexuality Studies

The stress on the variable social construction of sexuality in Social Constructionism leads writers like Stevi Jackson and Jeffrey Weeks, among others, to note how this trajectory rejects much that has been associated with the subfield of Sexuality Studies. They outline in a typical SC fashion a critical history of approaches in the subfield. In other words, they subject the subfield itself to a social constructionist form of appraisal, focusing upon the socio-historical formation of its several varieties. Their analysis tells us much about central features of the Social Constructionist paradigm, as well assisting us in providing a brief map of the historical terrain of the Sexuality Studies subfield (Figure 12.1).

SC writers like Jackson, Weeks and Segal point out that the 'chief guardians' of what is defined as sexual in modern Western societies were pioneer sexologists and sex reformers of the late nineteenth and early twentieth centuries, including Havelock Ellis in England, Magnus Hirschfeld in Germany, Richard von Krafft-Ebbing and, of course, Sigmund Freud. These were scientists of the 'laws of nature' (Weeks, 1985: 64). They studied sexual activity and sexuality as an aspect of studying natural phenomenon. These scientists were mostly in favour of removing laws against homosexuality and all proposed to remove ignorance by subjecting sexuality to medical scientific analysis (see Chapter 10 for discussion of these sexologists' work). They assumed at all times that sexuality was the manifestation of natural instinct, that sex was of deep significance to the self and a necessary aspect of 'health' and normality. In addition, these early sexologists believed that sex was an overpowering and unruly force kept under wraps by social constraints – a force outside and against society (Weeks, 1985: 11, 81). While some, like Freud, refused any

Figure 12.1 Social Constructionism's account of the development of Sexuality Studies

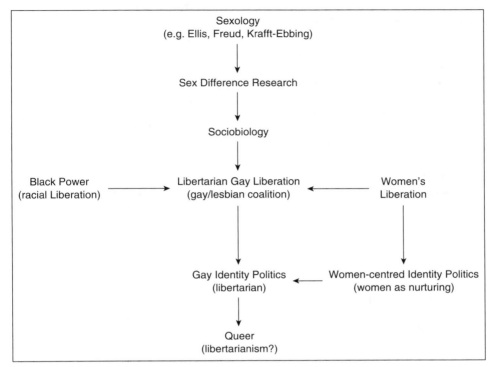

straightforward connection between bodies, sexuality and gender, most assumed that sexuality had innately gender differentiated forms. However, even if they perceived women and men as partaking of a naturalised sexuality differently and to different degrees, these sexologists offered a broadly 'hydraulic' model of sexuality. Sex in this model is like a gushing stream that may be dangerously dammed up or given full rein, or better still channelled into socially appropriate directions. Whatever the case, there was ultimately in their view no healthy way of stopping this stream. Sex was literally a force of nature.

SC writers draw attention to the essentialist construction of sexuality in these accounts. They note the ongoing salience of this sexual essentialism in later analyses. For example, they point out its continuance in the sexology of the twentieth century (for example, in Alfred Kinsey's large-scale surveys), in 'sex differences' research which is still prominent in the discipline of Psychology, and in the genetic determinism of sociobiology which still dominates popular understandings of the scientific objective study of sexuality today (Segal, 1999: 153–9; Weeks, 1985: 108–20). However, perhaps more significantly, writers like Jackson, Weeks and Segal assert that the notion of sex as an essence, a core intrinsic unchanging force outside culture, also runs through the critical Sexuality Studies that is the focus of this book. They cite the durability of this notion even in ostensibly progressive theories arising from critical analyses of heteronormativity. For example, the emergence of the mass 'Gay Liberation' movement of the 1960s and 1970s put forward a celebration of a universal libertarian polymorphous human sexuality drawing upon Marcuse, Marx and Freud, as well as the liberationist rhetoric of the Black Power movement. The aim, as Altman has noted, was to break down socially constructed divisions between sexual identities and to overthrow sexual repression and liberate 'nature'. (By contrast, Women's Liberation/Feminism displayed considerable ambiguity towards the notion of a sexual revolution and notions of sexual essentialism.)

By the 1980s, these SC writers argue, essentialist accounts of innate 'human' sexuality had been largely replaced by essentialist separatist sexual identities. Gay men and lesbians both asserted the notion of separate and deeply founded sexual identities (which were reminiscent of notions of ethnic minority identities) (Ehrenreich, 1983; see also Altman, 2001: 5896; Seidman, 1993: 117–26). Sometimes these identity-based forms of sexual essentialism claimed support from sociobiological arguments – that is, employed ideas of a genetic basis for homosexuality – or support from notions of biological sex differences – such as in the work of Mary Daly (1978; see also Chapter 4). Using such claims, homosexuality could be asserted as natural, not as sinful wilfulness but as something one could not help (Weeks, 1985: 199). Gay men departed from lesbians, however, in *also* continuing to support a strongly libertarian approach as an aspect of gay men's identity and gay community (Seidman, 1993: 123).

Feminists (including lesbian feminists) were increasingly inclined to reject notions of human or masculine (or even gay masculine) sexuality as an expression of 'nature'. Rather, sexuality within feminist approaches tended to be more likely to support accounts of sex as socially constructed and to be less essentialist about *sexuality per se* – that is, to be less Libertarian. Because they were more inclined to view sexuality as social, as embedded in contemporary power relations, feminists were decidedly uncertain about the particular forms of sexuality available to women in contemporary societies (see, for example, Leeds Revolutionary Feminists, 1981; Bunch, 1987; MacKinnon, 1982; Dworkin, 1987; Kelly, 1988). Although others were certainly less pessimistic, Sheila Jeffreys (1990) blankly asserted that 'sexual liberation' was not in women's interests. The main stance in Feminism during this period was not essentialist about sexuality but rather essentialist about women's distinct *gender* identity – as expressed in women-centred feminism. This identity was increasingly seen as distinctly at a distance from conceptions of sex as (natural) polymorphous pleasure that simply needed to be unchained and expanded. Women-centred feminism became associated with an antagonism to Libertarian conceptions of sex, a position which to some dissenting feminists appeared to be 'anti-sex'.

This debate, which centred on arguments about whether expansion of sexual choices might include feminists embracing sadomasochism (S/M) and pornography, gave rise to the so-called 'sex wars' between women-centred feminists who eschewed Libertarianism, which they saw as about men's sexuality rather than women's, and 'sex radicals' who did not.[2] At stake, according to Social Constructionist commentators, were different versions of essentialism, the former rooted in gender essentialism and the latter in sexual essentialism. The result within Sexuality Studies was that many lesbians returned to a coalition politics with gay men under the banner of

Queer. Queer Theory was precisely predicated upon the rejection of Identity politics, in particular gender Identity politics, but it is a matter of debate whether it has been as thorough in its critique of libertarian sexual essentialism.

The critiques of Identity politics that arose in the late 1980s and 1990s produced an increasing emphasis upon social construction, which fuelled both Social Constructionist and Postmodern/Queer frameworks (Vance, 1992: 132–6). Nevertheless, the SC approach itself tended to continue the divisions along sexual/gender identity lines. Gay writers like Jeffrey Weeks tend to retain a strong affiliation to a 'sex affirmative' or 'pro-sex' approach (even as he rejects the individualism of Libertarianism), while feminist writers like Stevi Jackson tend to offer more 'sex critical' perspectives (for another feminist perspective, see Kitzinger, 1994).[3] Both, however, dissent from 'the extreme constructionism' of Postmodern approaches (Weeks, 1985: 200; Jackson, 1998b: 138).

Critique of Postmodernism

Social Constructionist writers do follow aspects of the work of the Postmodern writer Michel Foucault. They follow Foucault's rejection of sexuality as simply natural, his refusal of sexuality as simply the expression of a biological drive, and his insistence on the cultural historical character of sexual identities. Like Foucault, they argue that sexualities are a matter of social sexual categories. Nevertheless, they are disinclined to reject entirely, as Foucault does, the political benefits of Identity politics (Seidman, 1993: 127). Moreover, while SC sets up biological essentialism as its nemesis, these writers do not totally refuse status to the body. For SC writers, the body is not emptied of meaning, nor is it a passive surface that is entirely socially shaped, as is the case in the works of Queer Theory writers like Judith Butler (Jackson, 1998b: 142). SC notes the limits imposed by the body and grants the body some determining input into social forms. As Diane Richardson (1993a: 78) puts it: 'clearly there are limits imposed by the body. We are for instance capable of experiencing different things depending on whether we have a vagina or a penis'. There are 'biological parameters' in this analysis, though 'biology is not destiny in any absolute sense' (Jackson, 1999: 31). This is a step back from the strong anti-foundationalist tenor of Butler's Postmodern/Queer analysis of the body.

Political stance

Social Constructionism remains on the side of Modernism with respect to maintaining a place for identity, and for bodily trajectories that are not simply reducible to culture and social construction. Moreover, they emphasise above all the material and economic nature of sexualities, offering a macro and structural institutional account of sexual politics that is often linked to capitalism (Weeks, 1985: 6; D'Emilio, 1997). Although the institutional orientation in SC is also in keeping with Foucault's Postmodern work, many contemporary Postmodernists focus on a politics against and around identity rather than, as Seidman (1993: 127–37) puts it, a politics of institutional subversion. Indeed, SC (by contrast with Postmodernism) has a strongly Marxian flavour, or at least is associated with interpretations of Marxist analyses, which highlight material economic matters in social organisation (see Glossary for the term 'Marxism'). This Marxian tinge retains the tendency of radical Left politics, which sees sexuality as only one focus of political thinking. By comparison, Postmodern/Queer Theory has an almost singular concentration on sexuality as a means to politics. In one sense Social Constructionism is a contemporary version of Gay Liberation, without its emancipatory universalism and Libertarian overtones. The Social Constructionist framework continues the practical political and Left focus of this earlier movement.

Debates

There are several common criticisms of the Social Constructionist trajectory in Sexuality Studies. For instance, it is sometimes argued that the stress on 'social construction' may lead to a voluntarist approach. It may seem as if sexuality is merely cognitive, a matter of voluntary choice, and may inadvertently de-emphasise the coercive aspects of sexuality, as well as its deep and recalcitrant investments for individual subjects. Weeks' (2001: 14000) reply to this criticism is that the social formation of sexual identities does not undermine 'the fact that they are fully lived as real' and that they cannot 'readily be sloughed off'.

Stressing social construction may also not solve the status of the body and the question of essentialism. Carol Vance looks at genital mutilation of women in North Africa as a means to consider this question. If we stress social construction of sexuality, does this mean that we cannot speak of 'mutilation' or body rights or presume that women who have had their clitorises removed have had their sexual responsiveness diminished. After all, if sexuality is socially constituted, we cannot assume any pre-existent character to sexual requirements or pleasure. And if we *do* still think that these women have in any sense been sexually mutilated, does this indicate that we are still stuck with a physiological/biological/essentialist mindset? Or does this mean that Social Constructionism has evident limits?

Finally, if sexuality is socially constructed and varies over places and times, how are we to construct an analysis of sexuality? What *is* sexuality? Is a relationship between British middle-class women in the nineteenth century, which does not involve genital contact, sexual? It was not, after all, seen in social terms as sexual at that time. Are certain Papuan rites of manhood, which involve fellatio and ingestion of semen (Herdt, 1981, 1997), homosexual or even sexual? How do we know something *is* sexual? Are we still reliant upon something that looks very like an essence, a universal foundational and naturalised understanding of sexuality that is recognisable as sexuality forever and everywhere?

Conclusion

Social Constructionism rests precisely upon its account of sexuality as socially structured rather than merely a matter of voluntary personal choice or biological mechanisms. However, as the debates outlined above indicate, Social Constructionism may not have solved the very things which it takes as central to its viewpoint. This issue is taken up in more depth in the following chapter on the work of Jeffrey Weeks.

Notes

1. For example, compare the social constructionist work of Gilbert Herdt (1981, 1997) with the postmodern approach of Judith Butler (1993a, [1991] 1993b).

2. For exemplary instances of these opposing views, see Jeffreys (1996), on the one hand, for a 'sex critical', women-centred account, and Califia (1996), on the other, for a 'sex radical or 'pro-sex' position. For overviews of this 'sex wars' debate between feminists emphasising the dangers of sexuality in contemporary society and those who would celebrate its pleasures and potential for social subversion, see Richardson, 1993a, 1993b. See also Weigman, 2001a: 370; Rubin, 1984, 1994; Califia, 1980, 1996; Wectvsler, 1981; Echols, 1983a; Jeffreys, 1990, 1994a; Barry, 1982; Raymond, 1979; Linden et al., 1982; and brief discussion in Chapter 18, as well as note 3 below.

3. This division along identity lines (gay versus feminist) over the possibilities of sexuality was marked in the 1970s and 1980s but it became less evident through the 1980s and in any case was by no means absolute. For instance, feminist writers Carol Vance (1984) and Lynne Segal (1990) were inclined to line up with the more 'sex affirmative' position of gay writer, Jeffrey Weeks.

13 | Social Constructionism: Weeks

My aim in this chapter is to focus more closely on one of the major Social Constructionist (SC) writers in the subfield of Sexuality Studies – that is, Jeffrey Weeks. Weeks is one the world's leading historians and sociologists of sexuality. He is a good example of the tendencies of contemporary Social Constructionism because he is British, Socialist and shows signs of both contributing to and retreating from Identity politics as well as Queer Theory's 'extreme constructionist' criticisms of identity (Weeks, 1985: 200).

Why mention these elements? As I noted in Chapter 12, SC offers a culture-specific, socio-historical analysis of Sexuality Studies, including of Queer.[1] It is appropriate to apply in turn this approach to SC itself, to contextualise its approach. In keeping with the SC approach, we too can consider the ways in which theories develop out of, rather than in isolation from, a cultural context. On this basis, it is useful to observe that Social Constructionism is a designated label for a particular grouping of thinkers in Sexuality Studies (as against social constructionism written in lower case, which refers to a broad anti-essentialist stance). SC is much more likely to be espoused in Britain than in the USA – in contrast to Queer Theory – and, relatedly, is strongly associated with an inclination to address class and material social and political conditions. SC is, in other words, a perspective that speaks from a more macro and sociological/historical/anthropological viewpoint, a 'social science' viewpoint, than Queer Theory generally does. Queer Theory, in contrast, has in broad terms been more thoroughly taken up in North America, and is typically more focused upon the question of individual identity and upon cultural/symbolic and literary/textual issues (Hostetler and Herdt, 1998: 249; Weeks, 1995: 115). Other English-speaking countries have different relationships to these approaches. Australia, for example, seems as usual to have developed something of a hybrid of both traditions. Weeks, in many ways, exemplifies the 'British' mode of SC.

SC represents a form of thinking that is in a number of respects an intermediate position. It offers a position somewhere between gay/lesbian identity politics and Queer Theory. Weeks, for instance, partakes of and resists sexual identities and communities. He contributes to both an identity-based politics and to Queer theorising, as well as offering a critique of both. This is a position that both reflects gay/lesbian divisions and undercuts these divisions. For those of you who see some difficulties with identities, yet remain unpersuaded by Queer, this may be the position for you.

In order to outline Weeks' contribution to SC I will first consider his critique of biological and identity-based essentialism, as well as his support for a 'constructed' account of social life and sexual identity. Secondly, I will outline his retreat from or wariness regarding the more thoroughly social constructionist position of Queer Theory, inasmuch as Queer involves a refusal of stable identity. Finally, I suggest some problems with and advantages of this position.

Anti-essentialism

Weeks has been a prolific writer in Sexuality Studies. His earliest book, *Coming Out: Homosexual Politics in Britain from the Nineteenth Century to the Present*, was published in 1977, not long after Dennis Altman's *Homosexual: Oppression and Liberation* (1971) (see Chapter 11). However, its approach is significantly different. As against Altman's support for liberation of an innate sexuality from (sexual) repression, Weeks questions the truth of sexuality in 'nature' and any identity-based essence (Weeks, 1985: ix). Weeks, like Altman, was and is involved in the gay movement but proposes in *Coming Out*:

> the historical variability and mutability of sexual identity in general and the gay identity in particular. ... the idea that there is such a *person* as a 'homosexual' (or indeed a 'heterosexual') is a relatively recent phenomenon. ... This of course, propels us into a whirlwind of deconstruction. (Ibid.: 6, emphasis added)

Weeks' approach in *Coming Out* rejects the Freudian 'sexual repression' theory pursued by Altman (following Marcuse) and other Libertarian Liberationists. In other words, Weeks rejects an innate conception of sexuality and any account that presumes a set biological core can explain human behaviour. This SC approach also uses the example of 'the homosexual' to demonstrate that the issue was not the repression of a natural asocial sexuality but the socio-historical production of sexuality and sexualities. Weeks points out that while homoerotic behaviour or 'acts' have 'most likely occurred at all times and places ... the emergence of the 'homosexual 'as a distinct category of personhood is a late-modern Western phenomenon' (Hostetler and Herdt, 1998: 249).

Weeks, in the first instance, rejects *biological essentialism*. He rejects the notion of a timeless, universal natural – that is, purely physiological – sexuality, at odds with social organisation and power. In the second instance, he rejects *identity-based essentialism* – that is, the presumption of sexual/gender categories as set eternals that are expressed in a linear unchanging stream throughout history (Weeks, 1985: 6). Such a perspective refuses the notion of power as acting to repress these essential identities and instead supports an account of social power as actually involved in the *construction* of (sexual) identities. It is a perspective which has much in common with the work of Michel Foucault, the Postmodern writer now commonly seen as the father of Queer Theory, and indeed as the predominant thinker of contemporary Sexuality Studies *per se* (an authority he would no doubt have resisted) (McRuer, 2002: 227).[2]

Holding on to identity?: Weeks's equivocal relationship with Foucault and Queer thinking

Foucault's *History of Sexuality: Volume One* has been a pervasively influential book in this subfield. It was first published in French in 1976 and was available in English translation in 1978 (Butler, 1993d: 82). Foucault's analysis was published shortly after that of Altman and was contemporaneous with that of Weeks. It shares many similar ideas with Weeks' approach. Foucault, for example, like Weeks, rejected the 'repressive hypothesis' and in the *History of Sexuality* insisted that while for most of the nineteenth century 'the sodomite had been a temporary abberation; the homosexual was now a species' (of person) (cited in Traub, 1999: 363).

As a result of the work of Social Constructionists like Weeks and the Postmodern work of Foucault, it is now widely accepted in Sexuality Studies that the notion of sexuality and sexual identities as being a matter of unchanging, untouched nature – nature 'in the raw' – is a 'modernist myth' (Hostetler and Herdt, 1998). Moreover, their work has also led to wide acceptance in Sexuality Studies of an 'axiomatic' *distinction between sex acts and identities*, such that while sex acts may occur throughout history, by contrast sexual identity is viewed as a peculiarly modern invention. The exemplary case here, for both Weeks and Foucault, is that 'there was no *category* of "homosexuality" before the nineteenth century, but only of sodomy' (Traub, 1999: 363, emphasis added). I would add however that positions regarding the rejection of biological explanation or identity based essentialism taken as axiomatic in Sexuality Studies, are not necessarily accepted by sexuality activists or sex researchers who continue to be strongly influenced by biological or fixed identity-based accounts.

Despite the contemporaneous overlaps between the approaches of Weeks and Foucault, Weeks is nevertheless regularly regarded as contributing to Queer Theory's germination (McRuer, 2002). He is often seen as offering a perspective associated with Foucault, as 'a pioneer of queer sociology', or as heavily reliant on Foucault and Queer thinking (Heath and Stacey, 2002; Ferrari, 2002). Weeks, in other words, is frequently viewed as somehow just a footnote to Foucault. Just as feminist approaches to Sexuality Studies are sometimes subsumed under the development of Queer – as either contributing to or resisting Queer – such that Foucault's centrality and Master status in Sexuality Studies is always affirmed, so too are SC perspectives frequently obscured by presenting them as merely helping in the final end-product of Foucauldian Queer Theory. Consequently, SC perspectives may be presented as 'following in [Foucault's] wake' (Traub, 1999) even if, in the case of Weeks, the work is contemporaneous with or precedes Foucault's. This is not a competition to head a team, but it is often oddly represented as if it were. Such is Queer's influence in contemporary Sexuality Studies that the diversity of approaches in the subfield, as well as overlaps between these approaches, are frequently underestimated.

Weeks' work in the 1980s remained focused particularly on two targets. First, he concentrates in this work on the question of biological reductionism and undermining the reification and consolidation of unproblematic collective sexual categories (identity categories) (see Weeks, 1985). He is preoccupied with the *critique of essentialism*. Secondly, he offers a detailed examination of the 'social organization of sexuality', in particular the *social construction of identity categories*. Specifically, this is considered along the lines of asking how shifts in social meaning and sexual labelling occur. For example, he considers the shifts from 'socially labelled "sodomite" to legally categorized homosexual to criminalized homosexual' (Ferrari, 2002), to notions of gay identity as a minority identity (like 'ethnic minority' in which gay is less a sexual classification and more a particular type of person) (Weeks, 1985: 8, 195, 1995: 110). These two themes (critique of essentialism and historical focus on sexual constructions) are extended in Weeks' publications during the 1980s. In *Sex, Politics and Society: The Regulation of Sexuality since 1800* (1981) Weeks links capitalism to the historical development of sexuality, and in *Sexuality and its Discontents* (1985) he discusses modern debates and identities.

By the 1990s and 2000s, however, Weeks' focus shifted somewhat. He becomes less interested in pointing out the problems of biological essentialism, but continues to reject any simple identity politics, while outlining the historically and socially contextual nature of sexual experiences and identities. This amounts to support for rendering visible socially constructed but marginalised identities (see Seidman, 1993: 125–7). In the co-edited book *Between the Acts: Lives of Homosexual Men 1885–1967* (first edition 1991, second edition 1998), which is devoted to the period in British law when sexual activities between men where criminalised, Weeks further outlines the development of homosexual sub-cultures and identities in Britain (see also the use of Weeks' perspective in Losey and Brewer, 2000). In two other books produced in the 1990s and 2000s (*Invented Moralities: Sexual Values in an Age of Uncertainty*, (1995) and *Same Sex Intimacies: Families of Choice and other Life Experiments* (2001)) he outlines, in a largely celebratory fashion, the ways in which non-heterosexual ethical practices and intimate relationships offer new community identities and community ideals. In the latter work (in concert with co-authors) Weeks suggests that the lesbian and gay community offers distinctive, innovative and seemingly superior patterns of reciprocity and care. 'Like most prior research', the co-authors find that gays/lesbians subscribe to egalitarianism and seek to overcome inequalities in their relationships based on race/class/gender. Relatedly, these groups 'divide emotional and household labour more flexibly and equitably' than heterosexual partners. This 'very optimistic' account (Heath and Stacey, 2002) preserves a portrait of community that clearly does *not* involve a rejection of identity along Queer Theory lines.

Indeed, the problems associated with this kind of identity-based community portrait, to which Queer Theory has drawn attention, are evident in a similar book by David Nimmons, entitled *The Soul Beneath the Skin* (2002). In this book Nimmons asserts that gay males have a different and superior set of 'personal ethics and community institutions' compared with heterosexual men. He cites the comparative absence of gay male community violence, the high rate of volunteerism among gay men, and notes gay men's consistently higher scores in studies measuring empathy and altruism. However, Nimmons does not explain this in terms of a socially constructed sexual self but rather in terms of innate differences (Nimmons, 2002; Duberman, 2002b: 42). This example indicates how Weeks' support for identity-based communities sometimes looks disconcertingly similar to the essentialist politics he disavows.

Nevertheless, Weeks' position is clearly an intermediate one. On the one hand, he criticises notions of fixed identities and clearly perceives such identities as the result of 'socio-historical transformations' rather than as 'the outgrowth of essential internal characteristics' (Weeks, 1985: 201). Yet, on the other hand, he refuses to renounce identity or entirely support conceptions of fluidity associated with Queer Theory. He notes as early as 1985 that 'coming out' as a homosexual, speaking as a homosexual and hence asserting an identity, challenges and subverts oppressive representations and suggests new possibilities. Moreover, essentialist Identity politics enables, he asserts, 'defence of minority status', consolidation of political gains and 'enhancement ... of gay community' (Ibid.: 2000–1). Extreme rejection of the value of stable identity and glorification of transgressive fluidity associated with Queer theorising, Weeks suggests (1995: 114–15), is itself no more or less than another socio-historical particular moment.

Clearly, in his view, assertions of identity such as 'coming out' are not to be dismissed as merely reaffirming normative binaries. This involves a much greater commitment to identity than Queer Theory would allow. (To consider this point it may be useful to return to Chapters 8 and 9 to examine Queer Theory in the form of Butler's interpretation of Foucault.)

Critique of Queer

Weeks' critique of Queer Theory offers a way of demonstrating his intermediate perspective. Like a number of other writers in the SC approach, Weeks proposes a viewpoint in which *identities are reclaimed*, though simultaneously subject to criticism. As compared with an emphasis on fluidity and diversity, Weeks suggests the limits of deconstructing identities, the necessity of their strategic deployment and the importance of projects and political activities which draw attention to the specific socio-historical character of LGBTI (lesbian/gay/bisexual/transgender/intersex) lives and modes of organisation. His approach has much in common with the work of Gilbert Herdt (1997) and Ken Plummer (1994) who both consider alternative terms to 'sexual identity', such as 'sexual lifeways' or 'sexual stories' respectively, in an attempt to convey historical/cultural/individual flexibility while maintaining some focus on identity continuity and coherence (Hostetler and Herdt, 1998: 249). The intention in these writings is to try to recoup the meaningfulness of identities without any essentialist or overly fixed baggage.

Weeks' contribution to a collection that is openly hostile to Queer theorising, entitled *Lesbian and Gay Studies* (Sandfort et al., 2000), is telling (Weeks, 2000). Here he refuses the 'rhetorical erasure of the gay or lesbian subject' (Hostetler and Herdt, 1998) and explicitly argues that Queer focuses too much on diversity rather than on commonalities in Lesbian and Gay Studies. His work regularly questions both the fixity of Identity politics and the fluidity of Queer Theory in terms of their narrow focus on the question of sexual identity (Weeks, 1985: 187). Instead, he walks a path between determinacy and fluidity which contextualises sexual identity categories within the ordering frameworks of socio-historical periods and material/economic shaping of class relations. In short, he attends to social location, materiality, social structure and stability in identities, to their *social fixity*, as against offering a multiperspectival, open and slippery account.

The two features of Weeks' work, reclaiming social identities and attending to their social fixity, lead in tandem to Weeks expressing doubts about Queer *politics* (Weeks, 1995: 116). While some feminists (such as Sheila Jeffries (1994b) and Elizabeth Grosz (1994b)) have raised concerns about the subordination or erasure of women and their particular relation to power within the term 'Queer', writers like Weeks point to Queer Theory's elitism: 'It speaks most obviously to … a relatively narrow social stratum, largely of the progressive middle class' (Weeks, 1995: 116; for similar concerns, see also Escoffier, 1990; Malinowitz, 1993).

Relatedly, he finds a middle ground between the assimilationist liberalism of certain Identity politics writers (like Andrew Sullivan, writer of *Virtually Normal*, 1996) and the confrontational anti-assimilation, anti-orthodoxy, transgressive politics of Queer thinking. On this middle ground Weeks contributes to debates on sexual citizenship and rights, despite the political limits of these conceptions in relation to a radical transformative politics (Weeks, 1998).[3] What is evident here once again is Weeks' engagement with material/structural matters and a willingness to consider the role of government and law in their constitutive impact on identities and politics (Goodman, 2001: 643). This appears very macro and Modernist in approach,[4] as against the local and often symbolic iconography of Queer performative models of political transgression. Weeks is disinclined to support an 'endless "queer" reactivity … a politics that valorizes and idealizes the "sexual outlaw"' (Hostetler and Herdt, 1998). Instead he offers a qualified defence of identities. 'If we deny their validity too completely', he asks, 'are we disempowering ourselves from the best means of mobilizing for radical change?' (Weeks, 1995: 37).

Debates

Yet Weeks' critical or qualified Modernism (see note 4 in this chapter), his support for macro-social, anti-capitalist analysis and a politics drawing upon social identities and related notions of community has been the subject of much debate. Does his Social Constructionist agenda still leave us with some of the problems he has himself associated with identity? Does he indeed return us to some of the problems of gay male Identity politics in particular? In this setting Weeks has been accused of ignoring feminist concerns about the relationship between sex, sexual identity and power in his tendency to celebrate sexual identity. Shane Phelan (2000) argues that Weeks, along with Queer theorist Steven Seidman, fails to 'get' feminism. She notes his tendency to be ill-informed about feminist scholarship (heterosexual and lesbian) and his limited awareness of women's gendered subordination or issues of sexual dominance. In response, it could be reasonably argued that many feminists do not 'get' sexuality writings. Moreover, some Queer theorists would resist any requirement that Sexuality writings take account of Feminism. Nevertheless, Phelan's criticism has some sting for Weeks' position. The criticism is particularly important given Weeks' very determined advocacy of a political coalition between gay men and lesbians, his focus on sexual ethics and his inclination to provide a perspective on community care and responsibility that has much in common with feminist approaches (heterosexual and lesbian) which emphasise nurturance. In other words,

Weeks offers a SC stance that is strongly linked to feminist agendas regarding egalitarian reciprocity, agendas typically associated with the position and activities of women, as against a viewpoint that valorises being on top/being a 'top', which are traditionally associated with masculinity. Phelan's critique of his work as failing the feminist test matters in this context.

Her analysis raises questions about Weeks' inclination to subsume lesbians almost entirely under the general theme of *sexual* autonomy, which may well not be adequate to their concerns regarding their positioning as women. We might also raise questions regarding his comments on the transgressive potential of macho-style gay men as a refusal of any necessary equation between homosexuality and effeminacy. The links between this mode of sexual identity and normative masculine dominance go unremarked (Weeks, 1985: 49).

Similarly Weeks' celebration of same-sex families, in *Same Sex Intimacies*, as distinctively egalitarian and caring ignores 'less inspirational elements', such as the rate of domestic violence in same-sex families, which ranks up there with heterosexual domestic violence, and other problems including substance abuse (Duberman, 2002; Heath and Stacey, 2002). Additionally, this book omits the 'marginalisation of lesbians in gay communities and movements' as well as 'lesbian critiques of gay male sexual practices and gender privileges' (Heath and Stacey, 2002).

Despite his clear concern with sexual ethics, Weeks is much less critical of sexual relations between adult men and boys than he is of relations between adult men and girls. While he argues that the latter, given the patriarchal power imbalance, is difficult to see as anything other than exploitive, he is less sure about men and boys (not described as young children) and wants to insist that it is not sex that is the problem but power. Although his view is very cautiously put, it seems curiously ahistorical, not material, strangely liberal, as an analysis of the supposed availability of 'choice' open to pubescent boys/young male teenagers in their dealing with male adults (Weeks, 1985: 225–30).

At times it appears as though Weeks could be accused of returning to a certain kind of unexamined gay man's politics. If he does offer a celebratory apology for gay men's sexuality without sufficient attention to power, this is a position that he has himself rejected explicitly.

Conclusion

Weeks' work in many ways exemplifies contemporary Social Constructionism in Sexuality Studies. He pays attention to the social and historical materiality of sexuality, and his stress on social construction rests at the juncture of Modernist Identity politics and Queer Theory. He refuses to disavow Identity politics, and yet repeatedly draws attention to the historical and hence changeable formation of identities. Relatedly, Weeks emphasises both social fixity and social contingency. He appears to offer a viewpoint that indicates potentially conflicting investments. This is particularly evident in regard to his analyses of gay identity. The problem may indeed be unacknowledged tensions, to the level of paralysing equivocation, in Social Constructionism itself. Its 'middle ground' positioning may perhaps suggest new ways of thinking through the Modernist–Postmodern divide but may also limit its usefulness.

Notes

1. Relatedly, Bob Connell (2000: 9) goes so far as to describe SC or materialist analysis as 'the ethnographic moment' in Masculinity Studies. See also Weeks, 1995: 115.

2. For one account of the links between the social constructionist approaches of Weeks and Foucault, see Turner, 2000.

3. For a Queer social constructionist account of the links between citizenship and sexuality, see Bell and Binnie, 2000.

4. Indeed, Weeks specifically asserts the promise of 'radical humanism', the latter term being strongly associated with large-scale Modernist frames of reference. Yet at the same time he declares himself on the side of the 'particularistic' rather than 'universalistic' forms of analysis. It would seem that Weeks partakes of a qualified Modernism in which macro theoretical themes and ethics are combined with the use of historical detail. (Weeks, 1995: 12 and 6 respectively).

14 | Transgender Theorising: Califia

Until the 1990s those who sought recognition for cross-identification, identity 'migrations' or ambiguous identification were viewed medically and socially as divisible into two groupings. These groupings referred, on the one hand, to those requiring recognition for a sexed identity/gender different from the anatomical sex/gender which they were assigned at birth (transvestite, transsexual, transgender) and, on the other, to those deemed ambiguous in their sex at birth or later (hermaphrodite/intersex). Transgender, transsexual and transvestite people were perceived in terms of psychology, of having a mind problem, whereas intersex people were conceived as having a body problem. This distinction is still common and to some extent shapes political activism today. Transsexual, transgender and transvestite may be also distinguished in terms of the extent and kind of identity change undertaken, for example in relation to bodily modification. Transsexuals are described in relation to seeking to change their bodily sex, hormonally or surgically – that is, as seeking 'sex change' – whereas transgender refers to people adopting a sexed identification different from their assignment at birth, which may be either ambiguous or gender-specific, without medical intervention. Transvestites are considered to undertake more temporary identity migrations and hence they, like transgender people, do not undertake bodily modification.[1]

In the 1990s, however, Trans and Intersex theorising tended to suggest some overlaps between these groupings in the sense of all occupying a position of sexed category crisis, of bodily sex and/or gender boundary crossing. Nevertheless there remain significant differences. For example, Trans and Intersex perspectives typically offer different responses to medical intervention. Trans individuals, particularly transsexuals, are more likely to embrace intervention and intersex individuals more commonly reject intervention, because in their case it is likely to have been undertaken in infancy without their consent. All the same, in recent times Trans and Intersex theorists and activists have become increasingly more likely to share uncertainties about medical intervention and increasingly speak not so much in terms of sexed category crisis as in terms of a crisis around categorisation itself. These approaches evince a growing challenge to the very existence of the categories of gender/sexuality, a growing questioning of these categories as unitary and coherent (Garber, 1992: 17; Whittle, 1996: 205). In other words, Trans and Intersex perspectives tend to invoke forms of 'transgression' which threaten to dismantle the meaning of these terms. For example, if a person deemed a man 'changes sex' through use of medical interventions and through social presentation as a woman and then engages in sexual activity with another woman, is this person a lesbian?

While contemporary debates between Liberationist, Social Constructionist and Queer Theory frameworks have revolved around the issue of the fixity of identities, in the arena of Trans/Intersex theorising the debate comes home to roost. In this arena debates about identity categories are not in the least abstract, semantic or utopian, but rather a problem of everyday life. Reclaiming a gender identity or a refusal of it may mean rather different things in this setting than it does in other feminist or sexuality writings (Whittle, 1996: 209).

Trans/Intersex theorising may be found across the Modernist–Postmodern continuum, stretching from deeply Modernist accounts of gender as essence to a refusal of identity categories associated with Queer Theory. In order to indicate the way in which the sex category transgressions of Trans and Intersex theorising offer a particular form of questioning of gender/sexuality terms and concepts, I will largely limit this chapter to developments in Trans theory. I specifically focus on the debate that emerges regarding notions of stable identity in exchanges between transsexual and transgender analyses. This debate is in certain respects an exchange about the merits of Modernist versus Postmodernist thinking.

Trans theory and the identity debate: transsexual thinking

Trans politics as an articulated position has involved the self-help orientation of the 1960s and 1970s (Whittle, 1996: 206), assimilationist transsexualism and, more recently in the late 1990s, 'transgender' queer politics. Trans theorising has shown a similar path with an increasingly explicit delegitimation of notions of fixed identity. It has, in short, become increasingly Queer (Hausman, 2001: 465). In this context, it is worth noting that the term 'Transgender' is sometimes used as a generic term to denote the whole field of Trans theorising – that is, the whole field of gender identity transgressions, including transvestism, drag, transsexualism and so on (see note 1 of this chapter). Yet it is also employed more specifically to refer to those associated with a Postmodern- inflected Queer stance opposed to stable identity, promoting outlaw or ambiguous positionings, and set against transsexualism's commitment to finding identity (see Chapter 15). I will make use of the latter, more specific usage to highlight the debate in Trans theorising regarding identity.

Margaret O'Hartigan (1993: 20) argues very vociferously that sex change is *not* gender change, let alone gender dismantling. She, along with most transsexuals (either pre or post-operative), argues that she changed her bodily sex from male to female,[2] but did this to maintain and enhance a *gender continuity* – her deeply-felt sense of femininity (O'Hartigan, 1993). As a result, she refuses the term 'transgender' outright, as she does not see herself as engaged in gender-crossing. Similarly, Jay Prosser proposes that sex (anatomical/bodily sex), is not simply a socially-constructed 'fiction' but is also not a given. For Prosser (1998: 81–3), the body is neither reducible to biology or the social. In this analysis (bodily) sex is a malleable accessory, but gender is a definitive 'home'. Prosser, like O'Hartigan, argues for surgeries and treatment to create a bodily home for those denied embodied representation of their 'true gender' (Prosser, 1998: 211; Hausman, 2001: 470). While bodily sex is flexible, Prosser urges conformity with the normative gender binary and recognises 'the value of gendered realness', as Bernice Hausman (2001: 473) puts it. This major mode of transsexual theorising is decidedly Modernist and sees gender identity as being a deep essence. Even if biological/anatomical sex is dismissed, O'Hartigan notes that the sense of a gender identity at odds with the sexed body may be biologically based or at least deeply constituted in the personality. Transsexuals experience a definitive core identity (O'Hartigan, 1995).

O'Hartigan (MTF – male to female) and Prosser (FTM – female to male) are explicitly refusing notions of transgender and relatedly Queer Theory's renunciation of stable gender identity. They are evidently employing a Modernist framework. Hence, the relevance for them of the term 'trans-sexual' (not trans-gender). They support changing sex but not undermining the binary gender distinction. Similarly, Holly Devor (1999) argues that this Modernist position is a 'corrective' to Postmodern/Queer theorising about sex and gender, which she sees as refusing to acknowledge the materiality of identity, its limits, its concrete physicality. Rather than supporting the Postmodern/Queer notion of fluidity, Devor notes that sociality is circumscribed by its embodiment, that bodily sex cannot be lived as fluid. Moreover, she supports Prosser's approach, asserting that 'gender is ultimately far more real ... and far less pliable than contemporary and queer theorists would have us believe' (Devor, 1999: 207). Prosser and Devor argue that many trans people are 'anything but queer. ... They are not, and do not aspire to be, in any way transgressive. What they want is to be authentically themselves. ... This requires that they straighten (not queer) the relationship between their sex and their gender' (Ibid.).

In this perspective transsexual represents a claim to identity (to a gender identity and to an authentic true core self). This would seem to involve a version of identity essentialism. To deny this 'essence' is indeed taken as erasing/violating/denying transsexuals (O'Hartigan, 1993). Here Postmodern/Queer Theory proposals regarding gender instability – particularly as developed in the work of Judith Butler – are viewed as decidedly unhelpful and as encouraging transsexuals' ongoing social exclusion, rather than recognising the legitimacy of their identity claims (Prosser, 1998: 59). In the setting of transsexualism, Postmodern/Queer Theory is accused of universalising its position concerning the advantages of gender destabilisation and in the process marginalising and excluding the voices of those who wish to stabilise their gender. Queer stands itself accused of replicating the practices of normative power (speaking from a universal position that silences other perspectives) which it attacks Modernists for inciting.

Yet this advocacy of Identity politics is by no means straightforward, given that another target of transsexual critique is Identity politics (women-centred) feminism. The representative figure for Transsexual theorists is in this case not Butler but Janice Raymond (another is Germaine Greer). Raymond's *The Transsexual Empire: The Making of the She-Male* argued, when first published in 1979 and in its second edition containing a new Introduction in 1994, that transsexualism is (1) not an authentic gender identity and (2) involves social conformity (1994: xxxiv–xxxv). In the first instance, Raymond asserts that transsexuals cannot claim the identity of women because women constitute a biological grouping determined by bodily female sex at the chromosomal level (Roth, 1997). In the second instance, she claims that surgical sex change involves individuals conforming to traditional patriarchal relations rather than supporting any form of political resistance to these relations – that is, transsexualism is not aligned with Feminism.[3] Transsexualism is individualist gender conformity. On these grounds, Raymond regards Transsexualism and Queer Theory as on the same side, as having much the same anti-feminist politics. Raymond's absolutism has produced an equally strong response. In many Transgender and Queer Theory writings, Raymond stands in for all of Feminism, which is assumed to be committed to gender identities and to keeping womanhood for itself (Hausman, 2001: 473, 489).[4]

Transgender and its uncertain links with Queer thinking

Both Feminist and Sexuality Studies writers who espouse Postmodern/Queer thinking are inclined to see Transsexual theorising and Modernist Feminism as largely gender essentialist and gender conformist. Postmodern/Queer theorists writing within Feminist or Sexuality Studies tend instead to support 'transgender' positions. These theorists are relatedly much less straightforwardly sympathetic to sex change surgery, but not because they reject the authenticity of the adopted gender identity undertaken by transsexuals. Rather they reject the necessity for commitment to binary gender identity *per se*. As Bornstein (1994: 114, 106, 107–8, 133), a post-operative transsexual who now supports Transgender thinking notes:

> it's the gender system itself – the idea of gender itself – that needs to be done away with. … The trap for women is the system itself: it's not men who are the foe so much as it is the bipolar gender system that keeps men in place as more privileged. … I think that male privilege is the glue that holds the system together. … Straights and gays alike demand the need for an orderly gender system … neither willing to dismantle the gender system that serves as a matrix for their (sexual) identity.

In an article originally published in 1983, Pat Califia (1994: 181–2) (at that time a self-designated lesbian pro-sex radical) adopted a similar position:

> Why does our society allow only two genders and keep them polarized? … Why do transsexuals have to become 'real women' or 'real men' instead of just being transsexual? … Aren't there some advantages to being a man with vagina or a woman with a penis? … And why can't people go back and forth if they want to?

Califia's comments arose during a period in which she had considered but decided against sex-change procedures. Until the late 1990s Califia espoused a non-operative transgender way of living out a 'female masculinity', and did not undertake any medical intervention to 'transition' towards a transsexual (transman) positioning.[5] Judith Halberstam also promotes a non-operative *female* masculinity. She sees this option as undertaking a particular gender (Halberstam, 1998: 77). Her focus is particularly on the 'butch' lesbian who continues to deploy a female embodiment, as against the FTM (female to male) transsexual. Halberstam rejects the view that only transsexuals who want to change their bodily sex can represent queer deviance and disruption of gender. Instead, she draws attention to the number of ways in which a range of people may experience their sex or gender as something to which they do not straightforwardly feel they belong (Ibid.: 153–4; Heyes, 2003). She argues that the aim is to proliferate and resignify 'alternate modes of being gendered' (Hausman, 2001: 481; Halberstam, 1998: 173).

However, the degree to which even transgendered people can be regarded as, by definition, under the umbrella of Queer thinking, in that 'they unsettle and disrupt notions of gender', is open to question. First, some writers like Pat Califia clearly dispute the political strategy of gender disruption and show many allegiances to normative gendered and transsexual identities. For example, in her playful essay, 'Dildo Envy' in the collection *Dick for a Day* (Giles, 1997), she presents an 'oddly conservative' (Hausman, 2001: 481) and somewhat nostalgic attachment to traditional masculinity. In certain respects, this analysis is sympathetic to masculinity and dismissive of heterosexual women's concerns in ways that are resistant to feminist critiques of traditional masculinity as a set of social meanings and institutions linked to dominance (Califia, 1997b: 138–43). Relatedly, in *Sex Changes* (1997a), Califia counters Bornstein's denunciation of the 'bipolar gender system' as held together by the glue of male privilege (see quote above) and instead suggests that men and women *both* have power (Califia, 1997a: 90, 252–3). Gender hierarchy is acknowledged but in some senses disavowed.

Califia asserts that masculinity can be disengaged from gender constructions (as well as bodily sex). Masculinity can be merely a marker for attraction, an 'erotic vocation'. What if, she says, gender identity were an individual voluntary choice, not an indication of social privilege, personality traits or roles (Ibid.: 277). Yet it is indeed hard to imagine what gender identity is other than these socially framed elements – unless Califia is suggesting that the seed of one's gender identity is located deep within the individual. Moreover, gender seems here to be made more palatable, even a good, in odd contrast to its presentation in Queer thinking. Califia's account of 'female masculinity' may offer some criticism of heterosexual identities and the heterosexual norm of men as authoritative, but it does not attend to feminist/lesbian/gay critiques of masculinity as a gender/sexuality norm which privileges dominance over those deemed not-masculine.

Califia renders gender identity and masculinity in particular into an issue of individual style or presentation rather than as an attribute of a social regime. Gender identity is here disengaged from its social materiality and institutional framing – an approach to some extent shared with Halberstam (see Chapter 21).[6] Califia's position may be contrasted with Bob Connell's insistence on gender identities as *only* that which is shaped by a social gender regime, not something that can be disengaged from social practices (Connell, 2002). The presentation of gender identity in terms of individual style enables Califia's investments in masculinity to be reclaimed as not to do with social inequality. She does not question her sense of belonging within the masculine as problematic, partly because of her somewhat sympathetic view of traditional masculinity and partly because she conceives female masculinity as not implicated in the existing gender hierarchy – that is, as transgressive. Similarly, Califia does not question the ways in which sex and pleasure might be implicated in power but rather tends to see power as simply repressing sex/pleasure (Cusac, 1996: 34–7). In this, her work resembles the Libertarian approach of Altman (see Chapter 11). This is particularly evident in her arguably romanticised and clearly Libertarian account of sexual freedom and pleasure in sexual minority identities like SM (sadomasochist) butch lesbianism.

In an S/M context, the uniforms and roles and dialogue become a parody of authority, a challenge to it. … If you walk into a typical S/M party, you are going to see a lot more communication about people's desires and limits, negotiation about exactly what will take place, care in the performance of sexual activity, and nurturing care afterwards than you would ever see at the typical singles or suburban cocktail party. I truly wish others would adhere to the same high standards of consent and consideration that sadomasochists uphold. (Ibid.: 36)

Califia retains investments in particular marginal but stable identities as necessarily essentially anti-conformist and as representing freedom, which is precisely a position that Queer Theory would dispute.

It would seem that transgression of some identity norms, for example to do with desire and sexuality, may not entail transgression of other social norms, such as those regarding gender identity and conceptions of the innate character of sexuality. Indeed, Califia indicates a number of ongoing investments in maintaining gender identities – that is, some form of gender conformity – and in maintaining a naturalised account of sexuality, which retreat significantly from Bornstein's queer vision of gender erasure and the socially constituted character of human relations (Califia, 1997a: 272). Califia says, with regard to sex/gender identities:

it must be possible for some of us to cling to our biological sex and the gender we were assigned at birth while others wish to adopt the body of their gender of preference, and still other others choose to question the very concept of polarized sexes. (Ibid.: 275)

Queer thinking is one among many options in this open-ended, yet individualist account. Cressida Heyes (2003), though sympathetic towards the political uses of 'gender voluntarism' in Transgender rhetoric, notes that the emphasis on 'the freedom of individual self-expression' avoids important questions about power. Self-expression can, after all, mean violence against women and homosexuals in certain forms of masculinity.[7]

Not Queer enough?

Bernice Hausman, a Queer theorist whose work follows that of Butler, is similarly critical of this tendency towards voluntarist individualism in Transsexual theorising. She also argues that current Transgender theory – that is, the writings of queer-inflected Transgender theorists, including Califia, Bornstein and Halberstam – amounts to little more than proliferating or re-doing gender by adding more identity positions to it (such as a 'third' gender or 'female masculinity'). She suggests that Transgender thinking is not strongly oriented towards displacing gender. Replacing a two gender/sex model with a multiple gender/sex model, she asserts, will not necessarily remove gender discrimination.[8] Indeed, the focus on '*being* queer', associated in her view with Transgender writings, remains individualist and misunderstands identity *as* politics (Hausman, 2001: 484). Consequently, these writings 'stay within the conventional parameters of the gender identity paradigm rather than transgressing that paradigm, as [they] claim to do' (Hausman, 1995: 197).

Hausman (2001: 486) is noting what she sees as a reassertion of Identity politics in Transgender thinking. Rather than, as Bornstein suggests, transgender being inherently radical and transgressive, Hausman argues that transgender texts retain a certain 'gender essentialism'. They may not, like traditional transsexual approaches, suggest an innate core gender identity, but they do appear to presume that 'gender as a way of organising identity is central to the human project' (Ibid.: 473). Gender is construed as necessary and even sometimes as biologically based, even if individual bodies are capable of gender modification. Califia's (1997a: 257) comments about identity hierarchies as perhaps part of 'our primate heritage' may support this assessment. On this basis, it may be that while Transsexual approaches for the most part seem to fall within the emancipatory individualist logic of Liberal Libertarianism or Liberal feminism, Transgender thinking is connected to several rather different strands of theorising. In some ways Califia's work seems close to the Libertarian impulses associated with Liberalism, but in others her work seems to hover between a multiple Differences approach and Queer Theory.[9]

Hausman, however, questions the Postmodern/Queer credentials of Transgender theorising, including Califia's approach. Hausman asserts that she is employing a Queer feminism to critique Transsexualism and Transgender thinking, not to shore up gender identities like women for Feminism, as Janice Raymond does, but to disavow them. She argues that we need to 'give up on gender' as a fundamental goal even in the guise of 'gender pluralism' (Hausman, 2001: 486). Gender identity is here perceived as irredeemable. Hence, Hausman most strongly rejects Transsexual theorising in particular. She sees sex change as promoting a gender conformity dangerously dependent upon the medical establishment. She states along with some other feminists that the medicalised construct of sex change is not equivalent in any case to becoming 'the other sex' and is sharply antagonistic to sex change surgery (Ibid.: 475; for a critical analysis of Hausman's position, see Heyes, 2003; and Hemmings, 1996).

Is Queer the way forward for Transgender?

Myra Hird agrees with Hausman that the simple aim of gender proliferation, proliferation of gender identities, is problematic and insufficient in terms of political strategy. She too links this strategy to problematic individualist and essentialist assumptions. In this context, she asks 'why use any categories at all?' Hird suggests, along with Hausman, that we call for an end to sex and gender rather than just re-combining or parodying existing gender practices. Transgender is once again not queer enough. Nevertheless, she also intimates that Queer may not be sufficient either.

Hird is not convinced by Hausman's strenuous critique of Transsexualism and sex change surgery. She argues that Hausman's approach, despite its Queer label, itself retains a certain gender identity essentialism. Where Hausman says 'since gender identity is a fiction why do surgery since it is in any case not going to result in the other sex', Hird says in reply, 'if gender identity is a fiction WHY NOT undertake surgery'. All gender identities are ongoing constructions and none are the 'real thing'. Consequently, it does not matter if sex change identity is not the same as an identity constructed on the basis of bodily sex and not 'mandated by biology'. As Hird (2000: 350) notes, bodily sex itself is not singular and neatly coherent. Fausto-Stirling (1993) suggests at least five biological sexes and Cheryl Chase of ISNA (Intersex Society of North America) estimates that one in every 100 births shows some physical 'anomaly'.

Despite some differences regarding transsexualism, Hird is just as uncertain as Hausman regarding the radical potential of transsexualism or transgenderism. In particular, the malleability of gender and bodily sex that she outlines does not, for her, guarantee any particular political subversion. Identity proliferation may be more achievable, she notes, than the goal of identity fluidity associated with Queer Theory, but neither will necessarily result in radical political change (Hird, 2000: 247, 358–60, 2002). This is a position responsive to Queer criticisms of transsexualism/transgender, but also one that raises questions about the limits of Queer thinking as a trajectory. Certainly, as Hird (2001) notes, the inclination among many commentators to conceive transsexuality/transgender as *either* 'entirely essentialist' *or* as the axiomatic epitome of Queer's focus on transgression and subversion may itself be a restrictive lens through which to consider this arena of theorising (More and Whittle, 2001; Johnson, 2002: 331).

Conclusion

Is transsexualism a form of gender conformity or a transgressive politics that makes evident the fictional base of bodily sex, gender's supposed bedrock, and thus also reveals the fictional nature of gender. Does Transgender thinking represent the epitome of gender incoherence and disruption along queer lines as Bornstein (and Butler) would suggest? Is transgender the iconic 'gender outlaw' or is transgender typically a mere proliferation of gender, more of the same, and not so far from the assimilationist aims of transsexualism as it would first appear? In short, how 'Queer' is Trans theorising and in particular Transgender theorising? Does Transgender thinking escape identity? Is it necessary to do so? Can it do so? And even if such an escape is possible, is this politically sufficient?

Notes

1. All of these terms have complex and contested histories. I will give condensed accounts in this note and also consider them within this chapter and in Chapters 15 and 21. Transvestism (sometimes spelt transvestitism) refers to 'cross-dressing' and may specifically refer to erotic pleasure derived from dressing in the clothing of the opposite gender or to a more general wish to adopt the social role of the opposite gender. It is usually linked with relatively temporary dress/gender role change, and with psychiatric discourses. Transexual or transsexual (I follow Pat Califia's usage of the latter spelling) is used to distinguish those who wish to change their sex in a more permanent and literal sense by employing hormone and/or surgical techniques. It is particularly employed to refer to those FTMs (females to males) or MTFs (males to females) who intend to or have undertaken SRS (sex reassignment surgery) and, consequently, is strongly associated with medical/psychiatric/legal discourses. It is often connected with the more general diagnostic term 'gender disphoria' or 'gender identity disorder'. Transgender is a terminology coined in the 1970s but only widely employed from the

1990s. It is used to distinguish those who wish to alter their gender in a permanent but less literal sense – that is, those who live as the opposite gender, as a third gender or as an ambiguous gender, without resort to surgical or perhaps even hormonal interventions. As is outlined in Chapter 15, this term is increasingly and controversially used in a generic manner to refer to a wide range of people who cross or transgress the conventional boundaries of gender/sex distinctions. Intersex refers to those who were once described as hermaphrodites, the latter being a medical terminology for people who have non-normative genitals. Intersex is a broader label for a range of bodily possibilities in which chromosomal sex, gonad sex, genital sex, or secondary sex characteristics are deemed to be inconsistent with one another. In place of the notion of hermaphrodites as having both sexes, as doubled individuals, contemporary medical/legal management of intersexuality has been more directed towards surgical/hormonal intervention to create at least an outward consistency. For various discussions of such terms, see Heyes, 2003; Stryker, 1994; Cromwell, 1999; Chase, 1998; Valentine and Kuick, 2001.

2. She attempted this initially herself by trying to cut off what she saw as the 'wrong genitals' but then underwent surgery (O'Hartigan, 1995: 17A).

3. Related views contemporaneous with Raymond's 1979 publication of *Transsexual Empire* include Daly, 1978 and Yudkin, 1978; related views in more recent times include Jeffreys, 1994a; Card, 1994.

4. See also Martin's (1994) related view that in many iconic Queer writings gender (and hence Feminism) is often cast as fixity in contrast to sexuality's representation as mutable.

5. Pat Califia now goes by the name Patrick Califia and, having undertaken some hormonal and surgical treatments, lives as a bisexual transman (www.suspectthoughtspress.com/califia. html; accessed September 2004). However, I use Pat Califia throughout the book since this is the name used in the sources I discuss and, in keeping with Califia's lesbian positioning at the time these sources were written, I refer to Califia as she. The term 'female masculinity' is taken from Judith Halberstam's book title, *Female Masculinity* (1998).

6. Califia shares with many Queer thinkers a rather thinned down Foucauldian analysis. There is an inclination to take up the emphasis of Michel Foucault's later work on remaking the self (see Chapter 9). Foucault's tendency to evade intersubjectivity and social solidarity while focusing on the subversive possibilities of individual self-reconstruction is highlighted in such Queer theorising. However, Foucault's social institutional analysis is downplayed or ignored. See Best and Kellner, 1991: 61–7; Konstan, 2002.

7. This critical analysis may also be relevant to Leslie Feinberg's work, which, like that of Califia, advocates gender diversity and acceptance of self-expression. Feinberg (1998: 24) says: 'Each person's expression of their gender or genders is their own and equally beautiful. To refer to anyone's gender expression as exaggerated is insulting and restricts gender freedom.' See also a similar concern with self-expression in Kanner, 2002: 27.

8. While Hird (2000: 358) disagrees with certain aspects of Hausman's assessment, she has a similar view of the political limits of multiplying genders. However, other commentators draw attention to the possibility that such an analysis of Transgender theorising as failing to transcend gender may be setting an overly high bar in which transgendered people are criticised whatever they do (Heyes, 2003).

9. Her work on sadomasochism and Feminism (Califia, 1996) is most obviously under the umbrella of a feminist (multiple) Differences perspective.

Queer Theory:
Jagose, Seidman

In this chapter I will attempt a short history of 'queer' and of 'Queer Theory' more specifically. I use the upper case Queer to distinguish 'Queer Theory' from broader uses of 'queer', a point that will be explained more fully below. In the process I will adopt a strategy recommended by Butler, the iconic Queer theorist, as a means to consider Postmodern approaches – in this case Postmodern approaches in the Sexuality Studies subfield, which are largely associated with the word 'Queer'. The strategy entails paying attention to what Queer selects and what it excludes (Cacoullos, 2001: 97).

In particular I will consider four main points. First, I will attend to Queer Theory's focus on destabilising identity, which is registered through the construction of a supposedly 'inclusive', non-normative (almost invariably non-heterosexual) sexuality and a simultaneous dismantling of gender. I will particularly examine Annamarie Jagose's account here. Following this, I will outline the possible tensions between these moves, in particular in relation to possible exclusions by briefly considering the implications of this double action regarding sexuality and gender for race/ethnicity/imperialism perspectives. The discussion raises the issue of what Queer may silence. Such concerns will lead into consideration of some issues for a queer politics. Finally, I will note certain responses to the difficulties outlined above, in particular by brief reference to the work of Steven Seidman.

However, in order to discuss Queer Theory in terms of selections and exclusions, I will try to characterise what 'queer' means by looking at a history of the use of the term, a history of theories and theorists, and a history of contributing socio-political transformations.

Three histories of queer

1. A history of terms

Like the term 'transgender', 'queer' has at least two main uses that are rather different and hence potentially confusing. These different uses do nevertheless tell us something about the meaning of 'queer'. I noted in the last chapter that the arena of 'Trans' Studies includes analyses of transvestism, transsexualism and transgenderism, among others. The meaning of the term 'transgender' in this context refers to a focus on a particular category of persons/issues within or under the coverall label 'Trans', who 'do gender' in non-normative ways. Transgender refers in this case to those who have rejected their gender of social assignment, but refuse to occupy an invisible or conformist place in the

Figure 15.1   Transgender meanings

(a) Meaning 1: Transgender as particular name (i.e. Postmodern/Queer)

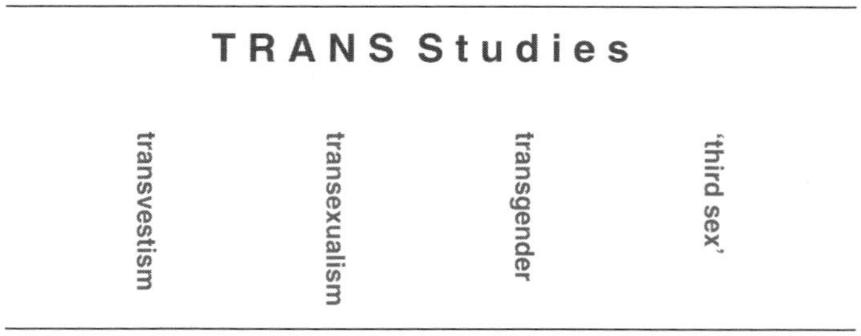

T R A N S S t u d i e s

transvestism   transexualism   transgender   'third sex'

(b) Meaning 2: Transgender as general area name

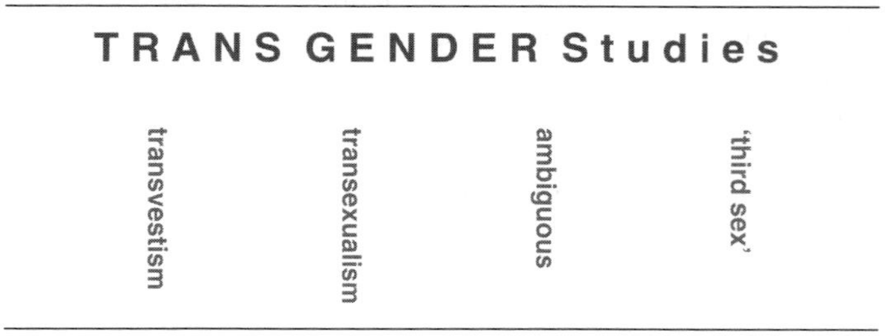

T R A N S G E N D E R S t u d i e s

transvestism   transexualism   ambiguous   'third sex'

men/women gender binary. Transgendered people remain 'in trans-it', ambiguous or 'impure' (Lugones, 1994). Transgender theorising in this setting means a Postmodern or Queer version of Trans Studies. However, sometimes Transgender is used as itself the generic term for the whole Trans Studies area. It becomes the 'master' term or 'proper name'. This slippage in meaning from particular to general and overarching may suggest a take-over bid in which all Trans Studies are seen as necessarily Postmodern or Queer (Figure 15.1). Such a claim is strongly resisted by some Trans writers.

This slippage from the particular to the general happens with the term 'queer' as well. 'Queer' or 'Queer Theory' (more precisely) is used as a particular specialised term to refer to the Postmodern turn in Sexuality Studies. In this usage it refers to a specific kind of Sexuality Studies approach (Figure 15.2).

Queer Theory offers a Postmodern critique of metanarratives of identity, a critique of universal homogeneous and fixed identity gender/sexuality categories, which are deemed essentialist (see Chapters 1, 5 and 8 for more detail regarding the Postmodern critique). Instead of affirming such identity categories, Queer Theory sees identity as thoroughly socially constructed and internally unstable and incoherent. Such an assessment necessarily also involves deconstructing mutually reinforcing neat divisions of identity binaries such as men/women and heterosexual/homosexual. This Queer trajectory has much in common with similar and sometimes strongly interconnected Postmodern turns in Gender Studies and Race/Ethnicity/Imperialism Studies. In the

Figure 15.2   Meaning 1: Queer (Queer Theory) as particular name (i.e. Postmodern)

S E X U A L I T Y S t u d i e s

Liberal	Libertarian	Social Constructionist	Queer

latter case identity binaries of East/West, Third/First World or South/North are the subject of deconstruction (Milner and Browitt, 2002: chapter 5). Queer Sexuality Studies, like Queer feminism, Post-colonial Studies and Postmodernism in general, focuses on what is excluded and devalued within these identity binaries to illustrate their socially prescriptive and fabricated character. While Queer Theory can be and sometimes is applied to heterosexuality (see Chapter 9), it focuses upon that which is excluded by the heteronormative and hence, with few exceptions, attends to sexualities other than the heterosexual (see note 5 in this chapter).

However, 'queer', as a stand-alone term, has a much broader and older usage. It does often act as the descriptive term nowadays in popular and even scholarly usage for non-normative minority sexuality and frequently as a coverall term for categories of non-normative sexual – for example, as a quicker way of saying LGBTI (lesbian, gay, bisexual, transsexual/transgender, intersexual) (Figure 15.3).

Figure 15.3   Meaning 2: queer as general area name

q u e e r s t u d i e s

Gay	Lesbian	Trans	Bisexual	Intersex

In this second usage it reworks the old pejorative, indeed abusive, employment of 'queer' as meaning homosexual and therefore abnormal. The broader utilisation of 'queer' in scholarly work can mean studies of non-normative, minority sexualities (the non-heterosexual) or even simply refer to homosexuality. In other words, queer can be used as just another new hip term for gays and lesbians. This slippage of meaning can occur in the same article. For instance, if we look at a piece like 'Attack of the Homocons: They're Here … They're Queer … They're Conservative', in *The Nation*, this bitterly chronicles the rise of out-and-proud conservative gays and lesbians who are described as 'queers' (Goldstein, 2002: 11). And yet the author, Richard Goldstein, also discusses the 'queer community' in terms of radical politics and inclusive multiplicity – that is, in terms which closely resemble the notion of Queer in Queer Theory. Goldstein's usage in his work on the homosexual Right-wing in the USA is not unique.

The term queer/Queer is used in several ways, as Jagose (1996) notes. However, I will attend in this chapter to the more precise or particular usage that is signalled by the label 'Queer Theory'. In this usage Queer Theory has a specific trajectory, which may give us some guidance about our assessment of it. However, to clarify its particularity, some further discussion of the broader term 'queer' is necessary.

The etymological (terminological) history of the broad usage of 'queer' can be viewed as representing shifts in the conceptualisation of non-heterosexual sex, especially of same-sex sex. Just as the term 'homosexual' was overtaken by 'gay' and then by 'gay and lesbian' from the 1960s and 1970s, so too 'queer' has now become the word of the day. A term like 'gay' aimed to transform the solely sexual and pathological descriptor 'homosexual' by drawing upon light-hearted notions of carefree joy and nineteenth-century slang regarding women of doubtful morals (Jagose, 1996: 73; Cranny-Francis et al., 2003: 75). By contrast, the history of the term 'queer' is far less positive. A tougher, less jokey label, it draws upon a long history of mostly abusive use from at least the early twentieth century. Indeed, this negative history means that it remains, for some, a controversial term (Cranny-Francis et al., 2003: 75). However, the term does not just signal a new use of a term on an old subject. Jeffrey Weeks (1977: 3) notes that such shifts in terms also point to changing understandings and changing socio-political conditions. 'Queer Theory' refers in this context, according to Jagose (1996: 76), to transformations in theory and politics around the late 1980s and early 1990s (see also Walters, 2001: 12659–61).

The term 'Queer Theory' entered theoretical discussion in the early 1990s. Teresa de Lauretis coined it in her introduction to the lesbian and gay issue of the journal *differences* in 1991 (Andermahr et al., 2000: 220). She refers to the 'necessary critical work of deconstructing our own discourses and [what they silence]' (de Lauretis, 1991: v). Here Queer Theory is aligned with anti-essentialism and the Postmodern turn in theorising. In particular, according to Jagose's (1996: 98) widely used characterisation, Queer 'marks a suspension of identity as something fixed, coherent and natural'. Queer Theory, she says, opts for *denaturalisation* as its primary strategy and indicates 'a critical distance from … identity politics' (Ibid.; Cranny-Francis et al., 2003: 75). Queer involves both a 'challenge to the notion of unitary identity (as in "gay" or "straight")' and 'a rejection of binary models (gay/straight, man/woman)', leading to 'a more *generic critique* of identity-based theories and politics' (Walters, 2001: 12659, emphasis added). Such identity-based agendas are seen as invariably reproducing the silencing exclusionary practices of power that they precisely arose to resist. This critique of identity is accompanied by a constructive stress on *multiplicity*, *fluidity* and *instability*. As Joseph Bristow and Angela Wilson (1993: 1–2) put it, 'an erstwhile politics of identity has largely been superseded by a politics of difference'. Differences, rather than universalised commonality within categories, become critical (Duggan, 1992: 15).

Finally, Jagose notes, Queer exemplifies the use of *Postmodern theorists* to conceptualise identity as provisional and dependent on context rather than singular and unitary (Jagose, 1996: 77). Commonly, Postmodern interpretations of psychoanalysis and language are employed to demonstrate this analysis of identity. The aim is to show that, on the one hand, the self is not stable and coherent (think of Freud's emphasis on the unconscious) and, on the other, that the social ordering of language involves a fixing of meanings, including meanings of the self. Set or fixed identity is thus conceptualised as a cultural myth – a form of social regulation that denies recurrent instability (Ibid.: 78). Differences between and within subjects/persons are taken as challenging any assumption of unified identity.

2. A history of theories and theorists

A number of theorists from several perspectives can be seen as shaping the theoretical porridge that has generated Queer Theory. These contributing perspectives include Psychoanalysis (Sigmund Freud, Jacques Lacan), Structural Linguistics (Ferdinand de Saussure), Marxism (Louis Althusser), Social Constructionism (for example, Jeffrey Weeks), Feminism (including Diana Fuss and Denise Riley), and writers on 'race' (for instance, Hazel Carby and Henry Louis Gates). Nevertheless, several names repeatedly bob up as central figures.

Michel Foucault's work is usually seen as of special significance (see also Chapter 9). Foucault explicitly reconceptualises identity in ways that have reworked Sexuality Studies along Queer lines. In particular, argues Jagose (1996: 79), his work is explicitly concerned with 'denaturalizing dominant understandings of sexual identity', such that sexual identities – including the homosexual – are seen as having a history, as being historical products of social regulation (Halperin, 1990: 46). Hence, Foucault's historical studies of the emergence of sexual categories demonstrate that marginalised sexual identities are not merely victims of power – a natural form of self repressed by power – but produced by power. These marginalised identities, no matter how socially excluded they might be, are not outside but part of the organisation of societies.

This insight has important political implications. If society makes the homosexual, then this raises doubts regarding the aim of liberating the homosexual. Certainly Foucault's approach suggests that liberating homosexuality is not a profoundly resistant strategy. Rather he indicates that this identity-based politics involves affirming a socio-historical product in terms that promote its supposedly demonstrable natural status. Such a political strategy confirms the existing dominant social organisation of sexuality as fixed for all time and beyond reassessment. As Cocks (1989: 74) puts it, Foucault exhibits 'no trust in power emergent, that seeks to replace power entrenched'. While Foucault offers a critique of the status quo, he is very wary of potential new ideological agendas presumed by political movements that advance sexual minorities. He is doubtful, in other words, of claims by marginalised groups like gays and lesbians that their advancement will necessarily revolutionise the dominant social system. Instead, Foucault suggests that we pay close attention to the forms of selection and exclusion in these identities too. For Foucault, resistance to power that promotes itself as a new sexual truth replicates the dangerous naturalised certainty of the existing order. It is precisely this certainty which requires dismantling (Jagose, 1996: 79–83).

Foucault has, however, been widely criticised as focusing on sexuality to the point of offering an analysis that is gender-blind (Cahill, 2000; Beasley, 1999; Braidotti,

1991, 1994a; McNay, 1991; Grosz, 1987, 1994c; Bartky, 1988). He is charged with concentrating upon heterosexual/homosexual hierarchies in sexuality while largely ignoring gender hierarchies, which cut across sexual divisions. It is suggested that he presents a history of the regulation of sex which largely ignores the ongoing deployment of women. Does this implicate Foucault himself in the reiteration of the existing regulatory practices of society regarding the privileging of men and sexuality associated with men? Just as Foucault's work remains crucial in Queer Theory, so too the tensions and debates his work generates remain a feature of Queer.[1]

The works of Eve Kosofsky Sedgwick, David Halperin, Michael Warner and Judith Butler are also commonly recognised as highly influential and as furthering Foucault's insights.[2] As I have already given some attention in Chapters 8 and 9 to Butler's particular elaboration of Foucault's approach, it is useful to return to her analysis as a particularly fertile source for current Queer thinking. Moreover, Jagose's characterisation of Queer Theory, which is the main subject of this chapter, is particularly sympathetic to Butler's approach. Given my earlier account I will be brief here.

Butler asserts, like Foucault, that 'marginalized identities are complicit in [the] identificatory [systems/regimes] … they seek to counter' (cited in Jagose, 1996: 83).[3] While her analysis has been critical to Queer Theory, it is specifically framed in terms of Feminism and indicates how gender is implicated in heteronormativity. Butler's focus means that, by contrast with Foucault, her critique of identity is directed towards Feminism and gender identity. She argues that Feminism works against its own aims if it 'takes women as its grounding category' (Jagose, 1996: 83). Butler suggests that the danger of identity politics (of organising politically around any category) is that it homogenises those in the category and creates a 'political closure'. This closure creates a norm that excludes everybody who does not fit, and polices those within it to ensure they continue to do so. Feminist identity politics (in this case gender identity politics) produces fixed meanings of 'women' which Feminism claims to resist.

Butler argues that gender and the category 'women' within it do not designate stable or coherent identities but rather identities tenuously constituted in particular historical and cultural contexts. There is no essential 'core' natural to women or men (Butler, 1997b: 402). Rather, human beings are constructed socially and specifically through language, which shapes and organises our social understandings and hence possibilities. This 'nominal' account of gender identity gives little credence to any intrinsic content for gender and gendered embodiment. Such a position is asserted in similar fashion by Post-colonial feminist Gayatri Spivak, who states that her 'definition as a woman' is not in terms of some essence but is provisional and subject to political context (Spivak, 1987b: 77).

Queer theorists have in general taken up this critique of *gender* categories with enthusiasm. They have largely ignored, however, the ongoing concern with links between gender and sexuality that marks the work of both Butler and Spivak. The suggestions of these two writers regarding the continuing use of gender categories such as women in certain circumstances, though cautious, are somewhat at a distance from many Queer Theory thinkers who largely focus upon simply dismantling or disavowing gender. Most understand what Whittle describes as the 'gender fuck' as the abolition of gender. Very often the stress which Queer Theory places upon a general deconstruction of categories/identities is in practice directed towards discounting gender and its categories. As a leaflet circulated in London in 1991 put it: 'Queer means to fuck with gender. There are straight queers, biqueers, tranny queers, lez queers, fag queers, SM queers, fisting queers in every single street in this apathetic country of ours' (McIntosh, 1997: 365).

Queer thinking does involve a multiplicity of sexualities and a rejection of singular gay/lesbian identities, but arguably the queer that is invoked is not simply a refusal of identity *per se*. While Jagose (1996: 76) claims that 'its non-specificity guarantees it against recent criticisms made of the exclusionist tendencies of "lesbian" and "gay" as identity categories' and Brenkman (2002) insists that Queer can 'never define an identity: it can only ever disturb one', other commentators are less convinced. Hostetler and Herdt (1998), in this context, assert that '"queer" is not the unfixed horizon of possibility it was designed to be'. For them, Queer is not a fluidity resistant to and somehow outside the boundaries of heteronormative labels, mandatory/pathologised identity distinctions, and insider/outsider moral assessments. Given that Queer theorising asserts non-specificity as the basis of its challenge to normative domination, it is worth considering the extent to which Queer itself might be deemed to produce an identity and hence remain implicated in normative exclusion.

In the first instance, the queer in question may not so much involve a non-identity but rather a multiplied and/or ambiguous *sexual* identity. Queer arises, after all, out of the history of sexuality politics and occupies an expressively activist stance (Creed, 1994).[4] Importantly, Queer Theory invokes a rebellious sexual identity but not a rebellious gender identity. Gender is 'fucked' it would seem, while ironically sexuality is not. Hence, for Turcotte (1996: 4), Queer unites those who want to deconstruct gender by sexual practices other than heterosexual and affirms a sexual identity that is different from this dominant sexuality. In this context, Butler herself can sometimes be said to re-affirm marginal sexual identities such as the lesbian, while rather more reluctantly acknowledging political space for marginal gender categories like woman (Goldstein, 2002; Webster, 2000).

The uneven attention in Queer Theory to the deconstruction of some social identities as against others may also suggest a Libertarian residue. Gender (the identity associated with the self) is typically depicted as (mere) social artifice, while sexuality (the identity associated with desire) tends to remain in place as a foundational essential categorisation (Smyth, 1997). Michael Warner's views on pornography are indicative of this broad inclination in Queer Theory to assert a somewhat lop-sided resistance to identity. Warner sees pornography as the opposite of the normal, a freedom to experiment, as 'queer'. Yet, whatever the view of pornography, it may be argued that the depiction of women and the use of actual women in most pornography is organised by social assumptions regarding heterosexual masculinity and is decidedly an aspect of the 'tyranny of the normal' – in this case, the gender 'normal' (Warner, 1999). Warner's failure to locate pornography in relation to this norm reveals a common lacuna in Queer Theory's claims regarding resistance to identity. Gender tends to be either dismantled as a requirement of resistance or ignored in accounts of resistance. In either case it is largely discounted. By contrast, sexuality remains centre stage and relatively untouched, with the result that its social construction is oddly reinforced.

These Queer manoeuvers look remarkably similar to those of many feminist writers who are inclined, in reverse fashion, to side-line sexuality rather than gender. However, the possibility that Queer Theory remains identity-oriented and foundationalist with regard to sexuality (while insisting that gender be demolished) is heightened by the tendency of most Queer theorising to propose uncoupling gender and sexuality.

Following the work of Gayle Rubin and Eve Kosofsky Sedgwick (Wiegman, 2001a), most Queer theorists assume that gender and sexuality are not reducible to each other and are analytically (if not socially) distinct. It is, in other words, possible to imagine a society organised by a heterosexual norm (desire reserved for one's designated 'opposite') without the requirement of gender identities, and similarly to imagine a society organised by gender norms of selfhood that do not require heterosexuality. In concert with Rubin and Sedgwick, Queer theorists typically assume – in sharp contrast to the majority of feminist thinkers – that gender and sexuality involve completely separable areas of analysis and tend to privilege the latter over the former (Andermahr et al., 2000: 220; Jackson, 1998b: 140–3). Given Michel Foucault's crucial status in Queer thinking, it is relevant to note that his work is 'more centrally preoccupied with heteronormativity and more rarely take[s] account of [gender hierarchy]' (Jackson, 1998b: 142). To the extent that sexuality is often separated off from and privileged above gender as the ongoing focus of Queer, there is an increased likelihood that Queer Theory can be accused of displaying commitments to sexual identity that sit awkwardly alongside its ironically universalised claims to destabilising all foundational categories. Such a differentiation in commitments could, for example, have implications for Queer's analysis of other axes of identity including race/ethnicity. I will return to this problem shortly.

3. A history of politics

Despite Queer Theory's vociferous support for subjecting all positions to a de-essentialising critique, it may itself fail to be self-reflexive about its own selections (what it privileges) and its exclusions. While Queer can be seen as an inclusive solidarity which rejects gender divisions and brings men and women together, it may also be viewed as retaining an exclusionary approach towards women, an unacknowledged masculinist privileging, and a convenient refusal to deal with gendered domination. This point regarding Queer's selections and exclusions may be examined further by considering a brief history of Queer's politics.

The 1980s produced several challenges to established notions of identity. The HIV/AIDS epidemic in the West led to a necessary acknowledgement that sexual behaviour was not as neat as it was supposed to be. The epidemic did not fit tidily with a minority sexual practice. Rather, it involved men who did not see themselves as gay but might have sex with men and heterosexuals who might engage in practices supposedly only associated with gay men. The educational materials informing the populace about the epidemic were forced to focus on sexual practices, not *sexual identities*. Identity did not appear to work at the level of significant public policy initiatives (Cranny-Francis et al., 2003: 77).

In addition, the Identity politics of gay and lesbian communities proved difficult to maintain. Both appeared to abjectly accept gender division and stereotypes (McIntosh, 1997: 366). Gay/lesbian Identity politics largely took for granted normative notions of women/lesbians as sexually romantic and monogamous rather than predatory or aggressive, and related notions of men/gays as sex machines with no emotional life who just wanted more anonymous sex. The story of these prescriptive identity positions in Queer theorising offers one perspective on the debates that followed.

Many overviews of the political beginnings of Queer from various perspectives tell us that it was women/lesbians who had to change and men/gays who were largely right all along. A common account of the history of Queer presents gay male identity politics as offering a 'thorough-going rejection of essentialism' *per se*, whereas Feminism, including lesbian feminism, supposedly offered a more limited refusal of essentialism regarding mainstream gender stereotypes concerning women (Ibid.). Moreover, in this account, Feminism is typically presented as being the 'wicked stepmother', the originator of a prescriptive identity-based morality which wags a mumsy finger at improper behaviour and against which it is important to rebel (Ibid.: 369; Hausman, 2001: 466–7, 473–4; Wilson, 1997: 369). Feminism is cast as rejecting butch-femme lesbians as heterosexist, as well as rejecting sexual objectification, pornography and S/M (sado-masochistic) lesbians. Feminism becomes the sanctimonious upholder of 'politically correct' gender identity stereotypes regarding the sexuality of progressive women activists. Queer, by contrast, is depicted as rescuing lesbian feminists in particular from vociferous disputes in Feminism – the so-called 'sex wars' – concerning what sexual behaviour Feminism should endorse or denounce (Sullivan, 1997; Duggan and Hunter, 1996; Richardson, 1993a).

Moreover, Cherry Smyth (1997) argues that for her Queer represented a means to overcome a history charged with political differences and divisions between gay men and lesbians, a means to move towards 'political inclusivity' (Turcotte, 1996). Queer in Smyth's analysis is a way of identifying with a mixed movement attending to the politics of sexuality (Tessa Baffin, cited in Smyth, 1992a: 21). Queer offers, in this version of its history, a politics of sexual identity in which lesbians are enjoined in a rebellion against prescriptive Feminism and are absorbed into a form of politics developed by the struggles of gay men. Queer politics is seen in this version as a refusal to shape its political analysis/activism in terms of gender hierarchy (in terms of gender dominants and subordinates) and instead offering a focus on social hierarchy in relation to sexuality (the social division between heterosexual and non-heterosexual) (A. Ferguson, 1997).

While this story of Queer politics undoubtedly represents an important theme in its development, it tends to underplay forms of Feminism which did not support a prescriptive and gender separatist model, such as Socialist feminism (Wilson, 1997: 369), and ignores the ways in which feminist approaches were and are critical to Queer theorising. It also tends ironically to present a homogeneous model of gay community, a form of sexual essentialism, in terms of equating gay with individualist libertarianism. This account of Queer's history cannot speak about gay family life or long-term relationships. While Queer Theory remains a positioning that questions identity affiliations, critics of its selections and exclusions have noted its tendency to refuse a location in relation to gender identity while shoring up a sexual identity positioning.

Queer Theory's positioning may be further specified. It is almost invariably associated with the non-heterosexual. For this reason, Queer Theory's analysis of heterosexuality and the extent to which heterosexuality is included within Queer thinking is the subject of continuing debate. Some Queer writers suggest that the point about Queer thinking is precisely that it is not attached to any identities and hence heterosexuality, as much as any identity, may be queered. By contrast, most other writers on this question simply assume Queer's links with sexualities other than the heterosexual, or suggest that the inclusion of the heterosexual in a Queer agenda amounts to 'gate-crashing' by already privileged heterosexuals and politically accomplishes nothing. A more critical assessment of the association between Queer and the non-heterosexual regards Queer as replete with its own insider/outsider politics, noting its inclination to fix heterosexuality as opposed to its supposedly subversive agenda. Once again there appears to be a tension between Queer's aim of resisting identity and its unresolved legitimation of particular identities.[5]

What does Queer exclude/silence?

Its seemingly uneven inclination to question identities has also produced many concerns related to race/ethnicity/imperialism. While Queer may be ambiguously masculinist and evasive in terms of confronting gender hierarchy and unambiguously focused upon non-heterosexual identities, many writers have claimed that its model of the 'in-between', the 'outlaw', the transgressor, as a non-specific identity reveals further commitments. These critics suggest that the claim to invoke a non-specific or destabilised identity involves a spurious and convenient side-stepping of race/ethnic/cultural location in bodily and geographic terms. Such side-stepping amounts, it is argued, to an erasure of those marked as racialised 'others'. The fluid, unmarked 'nomadic' subject of Postmodern/Queer Theory is viewed as actually white, Western and able to choose to travel (Jackson, 2003; Sullivan, 2003: Chapter 4; Wuthnow, 2002; Lewis, 2002: 217–18; Roen, 2001; Cohen, 1997; Namaste, 1996; Gordon, 1995: 388; Dhairyan, 1994; Anzaldúa, 1991). Queer in this perspective does not escape identity or specific social investments in the normative status quo.

In 'Queer Race', Barnard argues that to the degree Queer theorists focus solely or primarily upon sexuality, they are implicated in not only ignoring matters of race[6] but enforcing a specific ('white-washed'), rather than non-specific, conception of queer. Barnard points out that 'sexuality is always already racialised' (Sullivan, 2003: 72) and that only those who are in positions of race privilege can afford to ignore this: 'only white people can afford to see their race as unmarked, as an irrelevant or subordinate category of analysis' (Barnard, 1999: 202). Relatedly, critics of Queer's ethnocentrism note that its rhetorical polemic concerning disavowal of identity category groupings reveals a white individualism that has no need of collective group support to survive (Cohen, 1997; Outlaw, 1996: 141, 157; Mercer, 1994: 132–3; Scheman, 1992: 191).

The accusation of ethnocentrism militates against Queer's claims to be a deconstructionist strategy that moves beyond categories and resists particular location (Roen, 2001; McRuer, 2002). Indeed, the accusation links it more closely to Modernist Gender and Sexuality Difference frameworks – that is, the Identity politics it associates with women-centred feminism and ethnic model gay/lesbian Sexuality

Studies – than its strong antagonism to these frameworks might suggest.[7] While Queer is intended to signal a 'critical distance' from the singular focus of these identity-based analyses and thereby to overcome their exclusionary practices, it may be asserted that Queer Theory's inclination to prioritise sexuality invokes the same kinds of exclusions as the analyses it seeks to replace (Andermahr et al., 2000: 221).

The potential residues of masculine privilege and race/ethnicity/imperialist bias in Queer Theory not surprisingly have impacted upon assessments of its political strategy of outlaw transgression. Many commentators have asserted, as Nussbaum does (Chapter 3), its political 'quietism', its failure to attend to social, material 'non-sexual' matters, and its tendency simply to ignore the state and questions of governance (Hennessy, 1995; Edwards, 1998). In short, a crucial point raised by a number of critics is just how transgressive is Queer's transgressive politics. Elizabeth Wilson wonders about this question by considering the following extract from a US magazine: 'When I strap on a dildo and fuck my male partner, we are engaging in "heterosexual" behaviour, but I can tell you that it feels altogether queer.' Wilson notes that no matter how queer this couple feels, to the world they are just a kinky heterosexual couple. Experimentation with sexual practices and roles does not, she suggests, mean social revolution. Transgression, for Wilson, is limited in its effects. It may be:

> personally liberating and may indeed make an important ideological statement, but whether it can do anything more seems uncertain. Like those other words – dissidence, subversion, resistance – [transgression] is a word of weakness ... we can shake our fist at society or piss on it, but that is all. (Wilson, 1997: 169)

Wilson's doubts concerning the revolutionary potential of dildos constitute the caustic edge of a range of critical assessments of Queer Theory. I leave you to consider whether such criticisms undermine Queer's claims to represent a new and politically radical direction in Sexuality Studies. However, before leaving this subfield, it is useful to note that several self-defined Queer theorists have developed approaches that may be said to provide a response to such criticisms. One example of this form of Queer thinking arises in the work of Steven Seidman.

Answering the critics: Seidman and Social Postmodernism/Social Queer

Queer Theory has been the subject of sustained critique on the grounds that its rhetoric of social transgression has retreated from an engagement with the material social conditions faced by marginalised groupings and from a visionary concern with the active promotion of a society based on social justice. In particular, Queer thinking has been assessed as diminishing and scaling down its potentially far-reaching challenge to the exclusionary practices of supposedly democratic egalitarian modern Western societies in relation to domestic and international populations.

Critics argue that Queer's refusal of assimilation into the normative order of the West, Queer's rejection of the fixity and supposedly self-evident clarity of the identity definitions available in this order, has been debased into an espousal of individualist transgression (Hausman, 2001; Seidman, 1993: 132–5). In this way Queer's revolutionary agenda is seen as having made amends with the dominant organisation and values of Western Liberal capitalism in recasting the queer political programme as the promotion of individual 'choice' to be who you want to be, without excessive social regulation (at least in regard to personal presentation and sexual proclivities). When Queer becomes understood as simply another identity – albeit a fluid, provisional one that sets itself in opposition to categorisation and normalisation – then it can become domesticated into a matter of non-conformist 'style', a new 'cool' fad (Sullivan, 2003: 45–51; Martin, 1994). Ironically, this move simply sets up a new norm against which some will be found wanting. Its critics note that to the extent that Queer merely reinstates another norma-tive regime based in *being* a queer, its political challenge to the present social arrange-ments is muted.

As Weeks and others suggest, the choice of being a transgressive individual, of *being* queer, is in any case not equally available to or desired by all, and this is not just a question of submission to social conformity. To suggest that refusing to buck the sta-tus quo is merely cowardly conformity, involves a refusal to acknowledge differential economic and other material social constraints upon subjects, and their differing com-mitments to communities of identity 'belonging' (which may provide support in the face, for example, of racism). On this basis Weeks suggests that the sexual radicalism of queer identity speaks to a narrow social stratum associated with the relative privi-leges and decision-making freedoms of the 'progressive middle class' (Weeks, 1995: 116). Relatedly, other commentators have noted that this queer identity constructs a 'false unifying umbrella' which erases the different racial/cultural, class and gender positioning of subjects to produce a prototypical figure unmarked by these social dis-tinctions. White gay males thus become the prototype of queer (Anzaldúa, 1991: 250; Sullivan, 2003: 48; Walters, 2001: 12661).[8] Moreover, the emphasis upon this proto-type identity disallows discussion of the specific investments of white gay and middle-class men in power relations and puts to one side ethical questions regarding these investments. As Grosz notes, the celebration of transgression against persecution by the normative order is not sufficient. Under the rubric of transgression are placed sub-jects with very different access to and complicity in the rewards of the normative: some are more vulnerable and have more at stake than others. Moreover, she argues, the broad church of transgression erases ethical matters regarding different visions of social change – for example, it erases differences between the meaning of transgression in the case of pederasts as against its meaning in relation to other sexual minorities (Grosz, 1994a: 7, 10, 1994b: 113).

Many self-defined Queer theorists have in more recent times taken to heart criti-cisms regarding Queer's failure to maintain its social 'edge' in confronting concrete questions of social power, developing concrete political strategies to effect substantive social change, and engaging in ethical debates regarding visions of a future better world. For instance, writers like Rosemary Hennessy (1995) attempt to hold on to the insights of Queer Theory concerning the links between social domination and the enforcement of identity, yet also insist that Queer thinking must pay greater attention to 'the material social conditions (such as class) that help to determine who can or can-not have access to the brave new queer world' (Walters, 2001: 12662). Similarly, Gayle Rubin, who may be seen as crucial to the inauguration of a Queer perspective, has herself recognised the ways in which it can be disengaged from social conditions, and has lamented Queer's disregard for Marxist class analysis. Given that Marxism may be seen as an iconic Modernist framework, such a lament suggests a stepping back from the strongly Postmodern analysis that shapes Queer Theory on the part even of those who most avidly advocated the analysis (Rubin, 1994: 90; Maynard, 1998). Similarly, Fraser and Nicholson (1990: 20) propose a moderated Postmodernism in which its tendency to 'anemic' social criticism is boosted by an injection of Feminism. Queer, these contributions suggest, may more effectively queer society if it draws upon other traditions of thought concerned with structures of power – traditions which Queer has typically viewed as its antagonists.

In this context, Steven Seidman's work is particularly relevant. Seidman (in concert with Nicholson (1995)) promotes a 'Social Postmodernism' that is intended to move Queer beyond another form of Identity politics. Queer for Seidman is not just about making a new space for the non-heterosexual, for the non-conformist; it is about the reform of the social. In this usage, Queer is a verb, not an identity, and the aim is to 'queer society' by fully recognising difference to the point of declaring war on all norms, all authorities.[9] This socialised Queering strategy serves as a model for a new radical democracy (Seidman, 1997; Epstein, 1999: 270–1). Such an account is a far cry from Queer as individualised style. He also suggests that aspects of this retreat into transgressive self-formation may be laid at the door of Butler's influential Queer analysis (Seidman, 1993: 132–3).

In promoting Queer as a social theory, Seidman necessarily gives attention to two elements which have been cause for criticism of Queer. Seidman argues that Queer thinking must learn from Social theories and attend to material social practices by undertaking concrete forms of 'institutional analysis' (Seidman, 1993: 134–7, 1997). Additionally, he specifically allies Queer with a new 'ethical politics' founded in recognition of otherness/difference. This ethical politics would be brought to bear upon issues like the age of consent and same-sex sexualities, but would also remove moral assessment from a number of areas related to bodies and intimacies (such as pornography) to allow for a flowering of a society with no privileged centre of 'the normal'. Rather he proposes an interactive or communicative model of ethical assessment which is concerned with how interactions engage respect, reciprocity and consent between subjects and disavow exclusionary practices (Seidman, 1997: 226–35). However, as Shane Phelan (2000) intimates, this reworking of Queer as Social offers a social vision which raises certain concerns about its positioning and specifically could be argued to reinstitute the prototypical investments of the white gay male queer identity by the back door. His judgment that issues like the age of consent are a matter of ethical debate, whereas pornography should be removed from this arena may be said to betray these investments. Once again we might ask, how socially transformative is Queer, even in its potentially more socially attentive form.

Conclusion

In this chapter I delineate the lines of thinking associated with the term 'Queer Theory'. On the one hand, Queer is concerned with opening up the normative rules of modern Western societies and challenging their rhetoric of egalitarian democratic participation by revealing their exclusionary practices. Yet many critics have suggested that Queer itself is highly selective and hence exclusionary, and even complicit in the individualist framework of the modern West, which raises the questions regarding its socially transformative agenda. Debate about the advantages and limits of Postmodern-inflected theories like Queer rages in Sexuality Studies, but is still emergent in the next subfield of Masculinity Studies.

Notes

1. For discussion of the particular ways in which Foucault's work is interpreted in Queer thinking that may exacerbate this potential inclination towards (masculinist) individualism, abstraction from material conditions and related evasion of gendered power relations, see Chapter 9 and Chapter 14, note 6. See also Seidman, 1993: 132–7; Konstan, 2002).

2. The tendency in such listings is to include only writers who focus on sexuality, or less often on sexuality and gender, while writers like Gloria Anzaldúa (1987), who attend to race/ethnicity, gender and sexuality, are frequently not mentioned. This inclination seems telling and relates to the question of whether queer equates to whiteness, discussed later in this chapter.

3. Butler's analysis may, however, be argued to contain investments in such marginalised identities that are not perhaps entirely distant from the identity-based approaches she challenges. She argues overall that marginalised identities are part of power – that is, heterosexual and homosexual are alternate faces of the same sexual order, and lesbian is therefore not to be specifically valorised. Yet, sometimes in her assertions that homosexuality is not a mere bad copy of heterosexuality (such as occur in notions that lesbians are fundamentally masculine) she seems to invoke and reinstate lesbian specificity: 'As a young person, I suffered for a long time … from being told … that what I "am" is a copy, an imitation, a derivative example, a shadow of the real' (Butler, [1991] 1993b: 312). See also Sinfield, 2002.

4. My thanks also to Angelique Bletsas for her thinking on this point.

5. Gaines (1995), Waldby (1995) and Halperin (1995: 62) provide examples of those who envisage a queer heterosexuality, while Smyth (1992b), Brook (1996) and Hostetler and Herdt (1998) do not consider, do not accept or note the absence of such possibilities respectively.

6. He is joined in this critique of Queer as marked by its failure to attend to race by Barbara Smith (1999). Smith indeed asserts that 'for the most part queer theory and queer politics … offer neither substantial anti-racist analysis nor practice'.

7. It may also be worth considering whether Queer Theory shares something of the logic and tactics of *Postmodern* Gender Difference frameworks associated with 'sexual difference' writers like Rosi Braidotti and Elizabeth Grosz. The tendency in sexual difference writings is to employ one axis of power and difference as standing in for or representing difference *per se*, and to stress the irreducibility of that difference – that is, the irreducibility of sexual difference. Queer Theory for the most part focuses exclusively on sexuality difference. Gender is often discounted and race is largely invisible. Furthermore, it is inclined to place this form of difference as standing in for differences *per se*, to privilege its status, and in typically avoiding/disclaiming the question of Queer heterosexuality emphasises by default or design the irreducibility of sexuality difference – that is, the irreducibility of queer/hetero difference. If the discursive techniques of Queer Theory can be said to resemble Postmodern versions of Gender Difference feminism, then perhaps Queer is less queer than its rhetoric claims.

8. This problematic delimitation of Queer is also discussed in Chapter 9.

9. For a further investigation of this reconfiguration of Queer, see Chapter 21.

PART 3

Gender/Masculinity Studies

16 Gender and Masculinity Studies: an Overview

The subfield of Masculinity Studies[1] offers a particular range of ideas and debates which exist in relation to but also at some distance from masculinity *politics* (Connell, 1995: 10) or the 'men's movement'. Many feminist and pro-feminist Masculinity writers have argued that the so-called 'men's movement' is largely about shoring up masculinity and its existing social status (Adams and Savran, 2002; Nelson, 2000; Clatterbaugh, [1990] 1997; Messner, 1997: Chapter 1; Flood, 1996a, 1996b; White, 1996; Schwalbe, 1995; Kimmel and Kaufman, 1993; Wootten, 1993; Adair, 1992; Etkin, 1991; Mercer and Julien, 1988), whereas Masculinity Studies as an arena of academic scholarship has generally been concerned to offer critical analyses of masculinity. As I have noted previously (Introduction and Chapter 1), the focus of the field of gender/sexuality and its subfields, including Masculinity Studies, is upon critical analysis of gender and sexuality in social life. This entails a search for justice in relation to gender and sexuality arrangements and indeed frequently involves a concern with social justice more generally.

On these grounds, when I discuss Masculinity Studies (its terms, history, themes and particularities), I will not be discussing the whole arena of masculinity politics or the men's movement. In fact I will be examining a delimited section of masculinity politics. This point itself begins the analysis of the particularities of the Masculinity subfield. Feminist and Sexuality Studies (or Environment or Labour Studies), are characterised by connections with broad political movements that are (at least to some extent) necessarily socially critical. By contrast, Masculinity Studies is linked to an activist 'network'/movement that is largely not especially socially critical (Goldrick-Jones, 2001). Rather, the masculinity/men's movement is predominantly a site for 'apolitical' therapy and personal support or for a politically conservative reassertion of men's rights and in turn of masculinity itself. In this context Masculinity Studies represents one aspect of the more politically progressive wing of this movement.

However, this account may perhaps be further qualified. Many Feminist and Sexuality writers argue that even within Masculinity Studies, as against the broader arena of masculinity politics, there is an uncertain relationship to the typically socially critical and social justice orientation of the gender/sexuality field (see references cited above, and Justad, 2000; Kann, 2000; Dowsett, 1998; Modleski, 1991; Cannaan and Griffen, 1990). Masculinity Studies itself may not always be unequivocally socially critical in orientation.

Terms

Debates about terms indicate some parameters for these uncertainties. References to the subject of Masculinity Studies rarely mention 'males' as most of the field eschews a biological or bodily sex account in favour of discussing the social character of 'masculinity' as an aspect 'gendered' character of society. In other words, masculinity is seen as socially, historically and culturally variable and as constituted in relation to, or more accurately as against, that which is deemed non-masculine. On this basis most writers in the field refer to 'men' or to 'masculinity' as their subject of analysis. This is intended to reflect recognition that men are a social group.

Those writers who employ the term 'masculinity' do so in order to demonstrate, arguably even more definitively than references to 'men', that the subject is not a naturalised *category* of persons. Rather, the focus is upon a social construction, which may not even signal so-called 'male' bodies in that the masculine may be associated with female bodies (Connell, 2000: 16). Other writers advocate a return to the term 'men' (which is distinguished from 'male'), insisting that 'masculinity' is vague, insufficiently concrete, and may be associated with a convenient inclination to divert political attention away from actual men (Hearn, 1994: 49–52; 1996, 2004). While the vast majority of writers in the subfield I have described as Masculinity Studies nowadays refer to masculinity, this is a more recent and more theoretical term. It has only become dominant since the mid-1990s. Before this, most commentators talked about men and men's studies. Nevertheless, 'men's studies' is still widely used when discussing programmes of study rather than theoretical writings.[2] Moreover, Masculinity writers almost invariably in practice simply assume that the topic is men, those with male bodies, and indeed those who may be characterised as masculine males. They also typically focus on men who are heterosexual (see, for example, Brod and Kaufman, 1994; Franklin II, 1994; Seidler, 1991; Segal, 1990; May and Strikwerder, 1992).[3] The inclination of most writers in the field to now refer to Masculinity, rather than men or Men's Studies, indicates a growing awareness of debates concerning the problems of Identity politics which may be attached to the group term 'men'. Such debates have been described earlier in relation to Feminist and Sexuality Studies. To a much lesser extent, use of the term also reflects the influence of Postmodern antagonism to Identity politics.

History

As is the case in Feminist and Sexuality Studies there are different accounts of the history and forms of Masculinity Studies. Bob Connell (2001), an Australian academic who is perhaps the most widely known Masculinity Studies writer of our times, argued in 1995 that masculinity *politics* may be viewed in terms of four main patterns. Michael Flood (1996a) has also outlined four. By contrast, Michael Messner (1997) suggested there are eight. However, these accounts describe the broad arena of masculinity politics. We are concerned with only those analyses that are critical of existing gender/sexuality arrangements. All the same, it is useful to outline this arena briefly to contextualise Masculinity Studies more specifically.

Some writers stress that the current focus on analysing masculinity and perceptions of a crisis in masculinity is not entirely new (Hunter, 2003; Connell, 1995: 85; Messner, 1997: 8–11). Yet the notion that masculinity is 'in a very bad condition' and that it is difficult 'to be proud of being a man' has certainly picked up speed as an academic endeavour in recent times (Hunter, 2003: 171; see also Savran, 1996). As many feminist thinkers have pointed out, Western thinking has been dominated by an unexamined focus on men (Davies, 1994; Shanley and Pateman, 1991; Grimshaw, 1986: Chapter 2; Lloyd, 1984), but an explicit focus on men *as men* that is found in the form of scholarship described as Masculinity Studies began in earnest in the 1970s with the rise of 'Men's Liberation' (Messner, 1997: 36–7; Goldrick-Jones, 2001).

Men's Liberation was a response, primarily focused on the psychological and on consciousness-raising, to Women's Liberation feminist critiques of gender injustice. Some commentators also note the early influence of Gay Liberation and Black Power movements, though this is rarely a focus in overview 'histories' of Masculinity Studies (Goldrick-Jones, 2001: 323–4). The development of Men's Liberation may also be linked to increased concerns about men's powerlessness in a corporatist, globalising world and the decreasing significance of men's creative physical labour – that is, of traditional markers of 'proper' masculinity (Hunter, 2003; Connell, 2000: Chapter 3, 2003).

Importantly, though, Men's Liberation looks very different as a beginning from the putative starting points for Feminist and Sexuality Studies, which both arose in the context of large-scale and increasingly influential political movements. Men's Liberation in the 1970s could scarcely be called a 'movement'. Even now, the critical stance of Masculinity Studies is linked to a small 'network' of pro-feminist men's organisations and groups, which include NOMAS (previously NOCM) in the USA (National Organisation of Men Against Sexism), the White Ribbon Campaign in Canada, and MASA in Australia (Men against Sexual Assault), as well as having some connections with other men's groupings such as New Age spiritual ('Mythopoetic') and Christian groups.[4]

Significantly, 1970s Men's Liberation was largely more a psychological and support-oriented approach than a political one. Men's Liberation saw itself as providing support for individual change. It relied upon a notion of 'sex roles' and, consequently, its approach and residual influence is often discussed under the rubric of 'sex role theory' (see, for instance, Connell's analysis in Connell, 2000: 6–7, 2001). Men's Liberation employed a version of Liberalism in its concern with individual psychological aspects of gendered attitudes and personality. This approach may be contrasted with accounts of masculinity that take power as the centre of concern and conceive masculinity politics as about institutional and other forms of social change. The relationship between Men's Liberation and critical Masculinity Studies is therefore somewhat equivocal. Men's Liberation argued that 'sex roles' hurt both women and men. This notion of gender symmetry enabled a view of both men and women as equally oppressed by sexist society. Later critics of this 'sex role' approach employed the notion of oppression in a more politicised way to indicate that the costs and benefits of traditional male and female roles were not symmetrical and that oppression was relational. For example, writers like Messner and Connell assert that gendered oppression necessarily means there is a hierarchy of privilege in which one gender grouping gains advantages over another (Messner, 1997: 38; Connell, 2000: 202 on men's 'patriarchal dividend'). While the Men's Liberation 'sex role' approach did acknowledge difficulties faced by women, this recognition was somewhat submerged under a focus on liberating men.

The development of Warren Farrell's thinking offers an exemplary instance of the path taken by this approach. Farrell's early work *The Liberated Man* (1974) is perhaps the classic enunciation of Men's Liberation thinking and shows its associations with a weakened and rather depoliticised version of liberal feminism. Farrell was indeed an early member of the peak liberal feminist body in the USA, NOW (National Organization for Women). However, his equivocal relationship even to this somewhat cautious concern with equality for women became increasingly evident. Farrell's Men's Liberationist treatise gave equal weight to the costs of 'sex roles' for both men and women, but by 1993 Farrell wrote a definitive text for the growing 'men's rights' lobby called *The Myth of Male Power*. In this book Farrell claimed that it is women who have power and men who are powerless (see also Messner, 1997: 41, 43).

By the late 1970s and early 1980s 'Men's Liberation' was largely dead in the water, or rather had split into several main groupings: Men's Rights, Mythopoetic/Spiritual and Pro-feminist groups. The first of these was for the most part anti-feminist and represented a political backlash against efforts to overcome discrimination against women. Men's rights groupings are concerned with either men as victims or a reassertion of traditional masculinity (Messner, 1997: 47, 40; Clatterbaugh, 2000). The men's rights approach became arguably the most prominent face of masculinity politics in the 1980s and has since gathered strength in many Western countries in terms of group organisation, funding, and a place in Western public policy.[5] This approach proposes an ideology of men's victimisation and argues for a reshaping of traditional masculinity because it has produced costs for men as against benefits for women. Perhaps the most widely recognised example of men's rights thinking may be found in 'fathers' rights' groups. Such groups typically assert that the fact that women are more likely to retain custody of children following divorce is evidence of rampant judicial bias against men, and are likely to resist what they see as onerous child support. They frequently support fathers' rights to intervene in women's decisions about pregnancy, whether or not fathers are involved in an ongoing relationship with such pregnant women. Additionally, these groups are inclined to advocate the reintroduction of more restrictive divorce laws, because they see women's increasing inclination to initiate divorce proceedings as harming men in terms of custody, property and financial outcomes (Gross, 1990; Tippet et al., 2003; Shanley, 1997; Coltrane, 2001).

The reassertion of men's victim status in men's rights approaches is also linked to decidedly uncritical (and often anti-feminist and anti-gay) approaches to masculinity that reassert traditional 'masculine' characteristics and often traditional understandings of proper masculine authority over women. Men's rights thinkers argue against what they see as the feminisation of men. In this way, they show certain connections with 'Mythopoetic' and fundamentalist Christian/Islamist[6] men's groupings, which are now often identified as equivalent to a 'men's movement'. These groupings, though perhaps less blatantly misogynist than those associated with Men's Rights, also espouse what they see as the high costs to men of existing social arrangements and consider that men suffer as a result of an increasing feminisation (Clatterbaugh,

2000). Mythopoetic approaches focus on realigning men with an essential or 'deep' manhood through rituals of male-bonding and spiritual consciousness-raising. They lionise what they regard as quintessentially masculine activities such as hunting and sports, and associate ideal manhood with indigenous cultures, ancient times and the Middle Ages. For this reason Mythopoetic philosophy urges men to meet with each other in natural settings, away from the presence of women and civilisation. Examples of this way of thinking may be found in the work of mythopoet Robert Bly (1990) and in Steve Biddulph's influential *Raising Boys* (1997) (Gross, 1990; Clatterbaugh, 2000).

The Christian organisation, the Promise Keepers, and the Nation of Islam, led by African-American Muslim activist Louis Farrakhan, exemplify spiritually-oriented but fundamentalist religious groupings concerned with upholding masculinity. Such groupings have similar agendas to those enunciated within the Mythopoetic approach in terms of advocating an idealised masculinity (Messner, 1997: Chapter 2; Singleton, 2003; Carbado, 1999a: 6–7; Harris, 1999: 54–67; Grünell and Saharso, 1999: 205–7). However, these religious groupings do not advocate an essential core masculinity derived from interpretations of archetypal myth, but rather a reassertion of traditional masculine authority in the family and community. The Promise Keepers argue that men have abdicated their proper leadership role and, without negotiation with women, must take this position back. Relatedly, Farrakhan's Nation of Islam famously organised the 'One Million Men March' (1995) which explicitly excluded women and called upon African-American men to shoulder the special responsibility that God requires of them. While the Promise Keepers' agenda asserts that the (supposedly racially unmarked) community will be redeemed by the restoration of men's authority over women, Farrakhan's fundamentalist Islamist approach insists that the Black American community will be redeemed by the restoration of black men's authority over black women in particular.

These several spiritually oriented men's groupings may be distinguished from those espousing Men's Rights in that Mythopoets, Promise Keepers and Nation of Islam focus on personal/community authority rather than directly on public policy. Yet all assert forms of masculinity which differ little from traditional patriarchal conceptions of manhood, beyond a greater acknowledgement of men's emotionality and of shared (non-sexual) bonds between men. All, indeed, assert a clear categorical or Identity politics in which men and women are taken to be definitively, eternally and biologically different.[7] I will not discuss Men's Liberation, Men's Rights or the essentialist Mythopoetic/Christian/Islamist groupings at any further length, given that they are for the most part neither critical of masculinity nor interested in progressive social change. In other words, these trends in masculinity politics are only thinly linked to the field of gender/sexuality theory as I described it in the Introduction. Rather, I will focus on Masculinity Studies, which typically highlight a pro-feminist socially critical stance.[8]

I referred very early in this book (Chapter 1, Figure 1.1) to five main theoretical directions in the overall gender/sexuality (G/S) field and have so far outlined the particular versions of these directions in Feminist and Sexuality Studies (Chapters 1 and 10 respectively). These broad directions are also to be found in Masculinity Studies. It is perhaps useful to remind you of the overall map of the G/S field before outlining their specific formulations in the latter subfield (Figure 16.1).

Figure 16.1   Map of the gender/sexuality field: continuum and directions

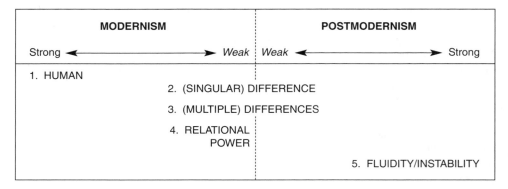

The five directions outlined above are taken up in the following ways within Masculinity Studies (Figure 16.2).

Figure 16.2   Map of Masculinity Studies: continuum and directions

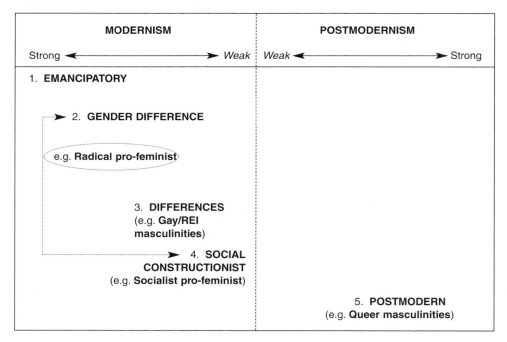

These specific formulations (in bold) within Masculinity Studies resemble those in Feminist and Masculinity Studies. For example, the somewhat ambiguous location of the Radical pro-feminist approach between Gender Difference and Social Constructionist thinking reiterates the Radical feminist position of Andrea Dworkin outlined in Chapter 4. However, these formulations are also marked by certain specific characteristics of the subfield.

Characteristic features of Masculinity Studies in brief

Masculinity Studies, as a subfield of gender/sexuality theory, differs in many ways from the two previous subfields discussed. Since this point is outlined in greater detail in the next chapter, I will only briefly touch on it here. By comparison with Feminist and Sexuality Studies, this subfield is smaller and is generally more consistent (less racked by dispute). It is a simpler matter to describe the stance of the whole subfield. This is because Masculinity Studies remains largely Modernist in approach and has only just begun to entertain the fraught debates associated with challenges to this frame of reference that are now almost 'old hat' in Feminist and Sexuality theorising. Writings in Masculinity Studies are also more likely to share a disciplinary framework. Many are sociological in approach. The subfield is dominated by Social Constructionist writings (a theoretical direction much diminished in Feminism and under serious attack in Sexuality thinking). Moreover, Masculinity theorists very often express Socialist pro-feminist commitments. Once again, this is a far less common viewpoint in the other subfields.

The greater degree of commonality in approach is perhaps related to the domination of Masculinity Studies by a smaller range of writers. Connell's contribution is, for example, acknowledged by virtually every commentator in the area. Such a degree of synergy is almost unimaginable in Feminist and Sexuality Studies. The smaller array of views and writers in the subfield leads necessarily to a more restricted range of concepts, debates and topics. For example, Connell's concept of '**hegemonic masculinity**' is very widely employed. Debates such as 'which form of feminist stance is most useful?', 'how critical of masculinity should its theorists be?', and 'how universal/homogeneous or diverse is masculinity?' reoccur. Topics such as work, health, violence, education, intimacy, ethnographic-based cross-cultural perspectives and representations are common (Hunter, 2003; Connell, 2000: 32–3). Sex continues to be less often discussed.[9]

However, perhaps the most distinct feature of Masculinity Studies arises in the attitude expressed towards its subject matter. Connell, among others, has distanced the subfield from the development or maintenance of a political 'movement' on the grounds that this subfield requires of its contributors a critical distance from its subject, masculinity (Connell, 2000: 208–10, 2001). Indeed, Masculinity Studies theorists decidedly do not take up the cause of masculinity. One way of briefly summarising their stance towards masculinity may be found in the novel, *A Hitchhiker's Guide to the Galaxy* (Adams, 1979). The positioning of Masculinity Studies writers may be seen in Ford's exasperated exchange with the macho Vogon.

'Resistance is useless!'
'Oh, give it a rest', said Ford. He twisted his head till he was looking straight up into his captor's face. A thought struck him.
'Do you really enjoy this sort of thing?' he asked suddenly.

The Vogon stopped dead and a look of immense stupidity seeped slowly over his face. 'Enjoy?' he boomed. 'What do you mean?'
'What I mean', said Ford, 'is does it give you a full satisfying life? Stomping around, shouting, pushing people out of space ships ...'
The Vogon stared up at the low ceiling. ... Finally, he said, 'Well, the hours are good ...' (Ibid.: 57)

Such a critical approach to their subject matter may be contrasted with the stance found in Feminist and Sexuality Studies. Feminist and Sexuality Studies stand as examples of political thinking that put forward and connect with the marginalised categories they are said to speak for. Although Masculinity Studies writers certainly do not have the straightforwardly 'positive' attitude to their subject matter that is associated with Feminism and Sexuality thinking, they do nevertheless appear overall to be rather more positive towards the socially privileged category of masculinity than the latter two subfields. Indeed, this measured engagement with the category is a source of some tension between Masculinity Studies and these subfields. After all, for Feminist and Sexuality Studies the heterosexual 'mainstream' masculinity that is commonly the specific subject of Masculinity Studies is precisely that which represents the solidification of power. Masculinity Studies stands somewhat apart from the other arenas of gender/sexuality because it examines power from a point of view of some relative privilege rather than starting from a perspective of marginality.

Conclusion

Masculinity Studies is a form of Gender Studies scholarship which focuses upon critical studies of masculinity. It consequently has a somewhat problematic relationship with the rest of masculinity politics, since the latter is often explicitly antagonistic to such critical scholarship. This might seem to locate Masculinity Studies in close proximity to, or even overlapping, with Feminism. However, the connections are not entirely self-evident or without tension or controversy. The characteristics of the subfield will be examined in greater depth and in concert with analysis of its main directions in the next chapter.

Notes

1. For brief discussions of the terminology employed here, see Chapter 17 and Chapter 19, note 3.
2. The usage of 'men's studies' as a generic label covering programmes/analyses concerning masculinities is, however, disputed by those who regard 'men's studies' as having a specific meaning. For these commentators, 'men's studies' refers to programmes of study or approaches that are politically conservative or at a distance from concerns about power relations (see Chapter 17).
3. Judith Newton (1998) and Gary Dowsett (1993) provide accounts of certain limitations in such analyses.
4. See Goldrick-Jones (2001) and Clatterbaugh (2000) for an analysis of these groupings; see Flood (1996a), for an Australian critical account of connections between pro-feminist and

'Mythopoetic' groups, as compared with more sympathetic versions from Schwalbe (1996) and Doty (1993).

5. For example, in Australia the current neo-conservative government, headed by Prime Minister John Howard (first elected in 1996), has reduced funding to women's organisations and cut staff in government organisations attending to the position of women, while simultaneously giving financial aid to men's rights groups. This same government is supportive of changes to child custody arrangements along lines supported by such groups. See Summers, 1997; Johnson, 2000: Chapter 3; Tippet et al., 2003.

6. I refer here to Islamist to indicate a particular religious fundamentalism, as against the much broader meaning of Islamic, which pertains to all views broadly following Islam. My thanks to Carol Johnson for this distinction.

7. See for men's rights Goldberg, 1976; for the Mythopoetic approach, see Biddulph, [1994] 1995; for the Promise Keepers approach, see Hicks, 1993; for Nation of Islam, see *Manifesto of the Million Man March on Washington* (1995) cited in Carbado, 1999a.

8. Gildrick-Jones (2001) outlines discussions about the relative merits of 'pro-feminist' versus 'profeminist' among Masculinity Studies theorists. Unlike her, I have adopted the former usage, in keeping with the arguments of Michael Flood.

9. Connell, for example, has written at a schematic level about sexuality and, in concert with co-authors, criticises analyses of men's positioning that do not attend to *sexual diversity*. However, though he has attended to sex/sexuality more than most writers in Masculinity Studies approaches, this remains an area to which he has given relatively limited attention. In particular, Connell provides very limited attention to sex/sexuality in his analyses of hetero masculinity. This is intriguing given his wide-ranging work and interest in related matters such as male bodies and sexual practices in the context of AIDS. See Connell and Dowsett, 1992; Carrigan, Connell and Lee, 1987; Connell, 2000: Part 3; Connell and Kippax, 1990.

17 Gender, Masculinity/Men's Studies and Feminism: Brod

In the preliminary outline of the parameters of Masculinity Studies presented in the last chapter, I suggested that this subfield (as against Feminist and Sexuality Studies) shows a stronger disjunction between the politics and theory associated with the subfield. There is a comparatively marked disjunction between the whole arena of masculinity politics, the 'men's movement' and the academic study of masculinity.

In discussing this point I noted that the history of masculinity politics, like that of feminist politics, began from a largely liberal agenda but, like sexuality politics, has a relatively shorter organisational and theoretically articulated history. Masculinity politics emerges around the 1970s. Like the feminist and sexuality movements, masculinity politics split into various directions. However, the crucial point here is that, by contrast with those other movements, masculinity politics largely split into conservative and inward/psychological, rather than political, directions.

Masculinity politics, Masculinity Studies

Masculinity Studies, which is a part of the progressive arm of masculinity politics, stands at odds therefore with much, if not most, of masculinity politics. In this chapter I will flesh out the preliminary comments concerning Masculinity Studies made in Chapter 16 by adding more detail on its particularities and contextualising these particularities in the gender/sexuality field by reference to a debate about its status. This debate is described by considering arguments raised in relation to the views of Harry Brod as well as more recent commentaries in the same vein.

What is immediately striking about Masculinity Studies, as compared with Feminist and Sexuality Studies, is its relationship to associated activist groupings. While elements of Feminist and Sexuality Studies may be accused of being at a distance from, or inaccessible to, activists in their associated movements, they are not in the sense of general political direction markedly at odds with these movements. Rather, the distance here (to the extent that it exists) is largely the usual one of theory versus practice, of intellectual specialisation versus broad-based political coalition.

In the case of Masculinity Studies, however, the distance is also political. Masculinity Studies is really the intellectual voice of only a distinct part of masculinity politics – most obviously the pro-feminist part. In more recent times this socially critical Masculinity Studies has also attended to pro-LGBTI (lesbian, gay, bisexual, transgender, intersexual), Queer, and race/ethnicity/imperialism issues, but its orientation remains largely a form of comparatively singular *gender* thinking and political activism. In other words, Masculinity Studies most evidently shows its political difference from the conservative agenda of mainstream masculinity politics (the men's movement) in relation to a pro-feminist commitment. Masculinity Studies is most clearly a form of Gender Studies. The activism associated with this approach is now significantly reduced. Socially critical forms of masculinity politics – that is, activist organisations which make up the pro-feminist men's movement – are few in number. I noted in the previous chapter that NOMAS in the USA (National Organization of Men Against Sexism) and MASA (Men Against Sexual Assault) groups, as well as some men's centres in Australia, provide examples of organisations that adopt a pro-feminist masculinity politics in their social development and therapeutic work.[1] Masculinity Studies often draws closely on this activist work.

The strongly pro-feminist approach of virtually all Masculinity Studies gives this subfield a particular character.[2] It is marked by a much more strongly acknowledged relationship to Feminism and feminist theorising than Sexuality Studies (Messner, 1997: 1–15; Moore, 1998; Clatterbaugh, 2000). Indeed, its disputes often arise out of the take-up of different feminist traditions, such as disputes between those adopting Radical, Socialist or Postmodern feminist approaches. While the socially critical arm of masculinity politics I linked to Masculinity Studies tends to be a men's gender politics concerned with rejecting men's social dominance over women – that is, a form of gender Identity politics – the subfield of Masculinity Studies is becoming more uncertain about employing identity categories. Masculinity Studies today, like more recent feminist work, is increasingly inclined to question homogeneous gender identity categories such as the category 'men' and hence more often refers to 'masculinity'. This is not just a question of semantics but often indicates some differences even between pro-feminist masculinity *politics* as opposed to the pro-feminist agenda of Masculinity Studies. Just as the activist politics of Feminism and Sexuality is more usually identity-based and related theoretical analyses in Feminist and Sexuality Studies are usually less categorical, so too the activism associated with pro-feminist masculinity politics is identity-based whereas Masculinity Studies theorising is less so. One example of this distinction between pro-feminist masculinity politics and theory may be seen in Connell et al.'s (2000) discussions concerning strategies in 'Men's Health'.[3]

Contextualising pro-feminist masculinity approaches, including Masculinity Studies

The development of socially critical and pro-feminist masculinity approaches (both activist and theoretical) may be seen on the right side of Figure 17.1 while ambiguous or anti-feminist approaches concerned with reasserting dominant conceptions of manhood are located on the left. Directions in Masculinity Studies are in bold and are found almost exclusively on the right side of the figure. The chapters that follow attend to these main directions.

Figure 17.1 shows the full range of masculinity politics and the several locations of Masculinity Studies within this, but does not give any indication of the proportional

Figure 17.1   Masculinity politics – the field[4]

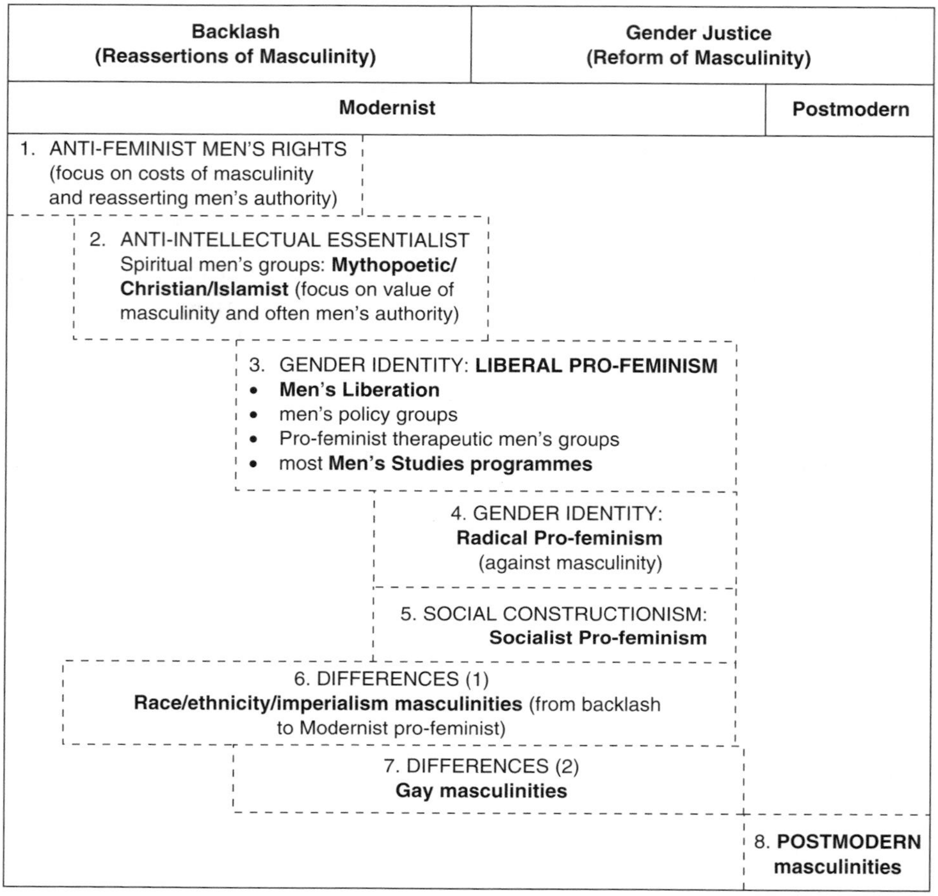

Backlash (Reassertions of Masculinity)		Gender Justice (Reform of Masculinity)	
Modernist			**Postmodern**

1. ANTI-FEMINIST MEN'S RIGHTS
(focus on costs of masculinity
and reasserting men's authority)

2. ANTI-INTELLECTUAL ESSENTIALIST
Spiritual men's groups: **Mythopoetic/
Christian/Islamist** (focus on value of
masculinity and often men's authority)

3. GENDER IDENTITY: **LIBERAL PRO-FEMINISM**
- **Men's Liberation**
- men's policy groups
- Pro-feminist therapeutic men's groups
- most **Men's Studies programmes**

4. GENDER IDENTITY:
Radical Pro-feminism
(against masculinity)

5. SOCIAL CONSTRUCTIONISM:
Socialist Pro-feminism

6. DIFFERENCES (1)
Race/ethnicity/imperialism masculinities (from backlash
to Modernist pro-feminist)

7. DIFFERENCES (2)
Gay masculinities

8. **POSTMODERN
masculinities**

significance or size of the political-theoretical positionings within masculinity politics. Figure 17.2, based on a variety of assessments, is a very approximate assessment intended to give you my broad sense of their comparative weightings at the time of this book's publication. You may arrive at a different assessment. The different positionings are designated by the numbers employed in Figure 17.1. The general span of locations in which Masculinity Studies approaches may be found is also indicated.

The purpose of Figures 17.1 and 17.2 is to indicate that Masculinity Studies has a specific and limited place in relation to masculinity politics. What is called Masculinity Studies is not, I suggest, especially representative of the features of masculinity politics. I draw attention to this point because you may miss it if you read overviews like those of Messner (1997), Flood (1996a) and Connell (2000), which are immersed in the pro-feminist versions of masculinity thinking. Messner, for example, outlines eight trajectories in masculinity politics, which gives the impression that all of them have

Figure 17.2 Masculinity politics – relative significance of contributions[5]

The field of masculinity politics							
Backlash		Gender Justice					
1. ANTI-FEMINIST MEN'S RIGHTS	2. ANTI-INTELLECTUAL ESSENTIALIST	3. GENDER IDENTITY: PRO-LIBERAL FEMINISM	4. GENDER IDENTITY	5. SOCIAL CONSTRUCTIONISM	6. DIFFERENCES	7. DIFFERENCES (2)	8. POSTMODERN

←———— MASCULINITY STUDIES ————→

equal weight. Of the eight he outlines, five are decidedly associated with Masculinity Studies and the same five are pro-feminist. It seems as though these five trajectories form a majority and are preponderant. Yet most of the viewpoints that characterise masculinity politics are not seen as part of the scholarly study of masculinity and are not pro-feminist. Messner's careful and scholarly account, not surprisingly, gives a lot of space to positions that are found in academic theorising on the subject and to socially critical and pro-feminist work. Within this orientation he also gives greater attention to approaches that offer a more subversive or radical social vision, and gives limited space to assimilationist liberal approaches that may be found in men's policy groups, pro-feminist consciousness-raising men's groups and many Men's Studies programmes. The overall impact of the analysis may be unintentionally misleading. What is also somewhat obscured in overviews like Messner's is that the particular terrain that is occupied by Masculinity Studies is not especially diverse.

Masculinity Studies: clarifying its particularities

Having contextualised Masculinity Studies within the broader setting of the gender/sexuality field (see also Figures 16.1 and 16.2) and masculinity politics, I will now return to my preliminary discussion (in Chapter 16) regarding the particularities of the academic study of masculinity.

First, as pointed out earlier, Masculinity Studies is a small and relatively new subfield in the wider arena of Gender/Sexuality Studies. As Connell (2001) notes, only since the mid-1980s has there been an upsurge of interest in this subfield. This is evident when examining the limited range of publications and journals in the area until quite recently. Around 30 years after the beginnings of contemporary second-wave

Feminism and the Sexuality movement in the 1960s we find a 1990s focus on publishing work on masculinity. In 1990 the Australian national magazine *XY: Men, Sex, Politics* came into being. While the magazine is now defunct, this material is still available online.[6] In 1992 and 1998 two international academic masculinity journals surfaced, *Journal of Men's Studies* and *Men and Masculinities* respectively (Hunter, 2003).

Similarly, there is a considerable lag between the emergence of scholarly conferences on Feminist as against Masculinity issues. Messner (1997: 6) notes that he attended one of the first National Conferences on Men and Masculinity in the USA in the early 1980s. Moreover, the first Australian National Men's Health Conference was not held until August 1995 (twenty years after the Australian Women's movement launched its first national forum on Women's health) (Connell et al., 2000). Masculinity issues are also only just beginning to find a place in international forums. For instance, in 1997 UNESCO sponsored a conference on masculinity, violence and peacemaking (Breines et al., 2000).

Perhaps largely because Masculinity Studies is still an emerging, rather than long-established academic arena, it remains a not particularly diverse field.[7] Certainly, any comparison with Feminist and Sexuality writings is instructive. As pointed out in the previous chapter, there is, despite disputes, a considerable degree of consistency in most of the Masculinity Studies texts (Gardiner, 2003, see also Gardiner, 2002). They all tend to describe gender as a hierarchical *relationship* that involves men's dominance. Gender difference is seen as 'a result of gender inequality not its cause' (Kimmel, 2000: xi). Gender is not symmetrical in this approach (as it was in 1970s Men's Liberation writings) but rather masculinity is presented as involving men's dominance of both women and other men (Cohen, 2001; Kimmel and Messner, 2001; Ferrée et al., 1999; Kimmel with Aronson, 2000). It is difficult to imagine this degree of congruence in the other subfields of the gender/sexuality field.

Such congruence is largely due to the wide acceptance of a common broad theoretical frame of reference. Masculinity Studies writings are almost invariably Modernist (Gardiner, 2003; see, for example, Mac an Ghaill, 1994; Berger et al., 1995; Williams, 1993; Barrett, 1996; Cheng, 1996; Gilbert and Gilbert, 1998; Wajcman, 1999; Lesko, 2000; O'Donnell and Sharpe 2000; Evans and Frank, 2003). They pursue large-scale macro-structural accounts and explanations of social phenomena and are predominantly sociological in orientation, although there has been a growth of work on representations of men/masculinity in the media especially – that is, a growth of media/cultural studies approaches (Gardiner, 2003; Connell, 2000: 208, 2002: 65–8; see, for example, Jeffords, 1993; Tasker, 1993; Cohan and Hark, 1993; Langer, 1996; Cohan, 1997; Leighninger, 1997; Reiser, 2001). Perhaps because of this macro social science orientation, there is an inclination to dismiss or ignore the contemporary turn in gender/sexuality theory to Postmodernism or at least pay little attention to it, despite the prevalence of this development in recent Feminist and Sexuality Studies. Connell, for example, arguably the major masculinity theorist writing today (Newton, 1998), mentions Postmodern perspectives only in passing if at all in *The Men and the Boys* (2000), and then perhaps rather dismissively. He is also inclined in this book to view such perspectives as only associated with 'symbolic practices', as if they did not have much to offer to an analysis of the other three main 'structures' he identifies as crucial in understanding masculinities and gender regimes. By 2002, in his book *Gender*, Connell is rather less dismissive and more inclined to observe the ways in which Postmodern perspectives might also inform the other structures, but such forms of theorising remain very much at the margins of his approach. This characteristic tendency to pay limited attention to the growth of Postmodern theorising may be said to give the subfield of Masculinity Studies a slightly 'old-fashioned' feel, in that the major writers tend to work from assumptions that were more common in the late 1980s and early 1990s in the other subfields. I should stress, however, that 'older' theoretical directions are not necessarily less useful, and 'newer' or more 'fashionable' does not inevitably mean better.

Masculinity writers do offer a distinct and thoroughly argued case for undertaking macro analysis and the use of identity categories like women and men as part of a political focus on oppression as dominance (men's dominance over women). We should note that this Modernist emphasis on macro oppression arises in the political/ intellectual context of much masculinity *politics* refusing to acknowledge or ignoring or embracing men's differential social advantages *vis-à-vis* women. In this setting, the focus on concrete and structural gender relations – on men's benefits/advantages relative to women (what Connell calls the 'patriarchal dividend' (2000: 202)) and their power over women (for example, in relation to domestic violence) – has a definite strategic significance.

That said, the Masculinity Studies subfield is nevertheless dominated by one theoretical trajectory – (anti-essentialist) Social Constructionism and, within this, by a Socialist pro-feminist version of it (Gardiner, 2003). This is a trajectory with which you are now likely to be familiar, at least in relation to Sexuality Studies, given the extensive account in Chapters 12 and 13.[8] Debates between this Socialist pro-feminist approach and a focus on categorical identity distinctions largely associated with the Radical pro-feminist approach still mark the Masculinity subfield. In addition, interactions between the Socialist pro-feminist approach and those highlighting gay, race/ethnicity/imperialism and Postmodern/Queer concerns are beginning to be more central. Nonetheless, the centre-stage position in Masculinity Studies remains the Socialist pro-feminist perspective.

The subfield of Masculinity Studies is not only dominated by one theoretical trajectory but relatedly, as I mentioned in the previous chapter, the field is still dominated by a small number of writers. Where Feminist and Sexuality Studies host a dizzying variety of positions, writers, concepts, debates and topics, Masculinity Studies is heavily indebted to one writer, Bob (R.W.) Connell. Connell is almost without exception quoted or cited or implicitly referenced in every masculinity publication. A limited range of concepts and understandings of them occurs in part because of the prevalent, even pervasive use of Connell's take on gender and masculinity.[9]

This is perhaps exacerbated by Connell's fairly consistent use of similar concepts over a long period of time. For example, in *Gender and Power* (1987) he proposed that the word 'gender' be discussed in terms of three structures (power, production/ labour and emotion/sexual relations), drawing upon the ground-breaking structural model developed by Juliet Mitchell in 1971. Some years later in *The Men and the Boys* (2000: 208) he adjusted this a little by adding 'symbolism' to the list, picking up to a certain extent on Postmodern discussions about language and other sign systems as organising social relations. In similar fashion, Hearn (2004) has pointed out Connell's early development and ongoing usage of the term 'hegemonic masculinity' (first proposed in Connell, [1979] 1983) – a term which is now almost ubiquitously employed in Masculinity Studies. The continuing usage of a range of concepts and terms by such a major writer in Masculinity Studies certainly contributes to its particular characteristic tone and scope.[10] In keeping with the longevity of concept use in the subfield, major debates are reiterated over time. It is in this context that I will consider one of the most common debates regarding the status of Masculinity/Men's Studies itself. This is where Harry Brod's account of 'Men's Studies' becomes relevant.

Comparing Masculinity Studies with other subfields in the G/S field

While Masculinity Studies can be viewed as another aspect of Gender Studies – much like Feminism – in the gender/sexuality field, in many ways it is rather different from the other subfields. Most obviously, both Feminist and Sexuality Studies focus on the marginalised 'other' of bipolar and hierarchically organised social binaries like men/women and heterosexual/homosexual. By contrast, Masculinity Studies privileges the privileged but typically in a critical or at least sceptical, non-accepting fashion – that is, it is almost always pro-feminist. Masculinity Studies resembles more closely critical 'Whiteness' or 'Heterosexuality' Studies (Pruett, 2002). On this basis, Connell (2000: 208–11) argues, masculinity politics cannot operate as a political movement like Feminism. It must recognise its limits. This means Masculinity writers' relation to their subject matter is usually very different.

Feminists often attempt to evaluate positively aspects of women's marginalised identities, but reject or question gender and demonstrate scepticism and distance towards femininity as the honored or normative form of womanhood. Sexuality writers are similarly quite positive about, for example, gay men's marginalised identities, as well as about the subject of sexuality itself, while demonstrating distance from the norm of heterosexuality. Masculinity writers largely invert these priorities. They are almost invariably negative about the privileges accruing to masculinity, and question gender arrangements. However, oddly enough these scholars appear to retain certain investments in masculinity (even at times honouring normative forms of it) which undercuts the degendering agenda of the subfield. Although as Jeff Hearn (1994: 48) has argued, masculinity scholars are gender 'traitors' – traitors to their gender 'class' much like middle-class anti-capitalists – many still evince an apparent 'desire to hold on to men's masculinity' as a grounding of identity, correlated with a concern that men not be rendered androgynous or feminised. According to Michael Kimmel (2000: 268), the goal is not for men and women to become the same but, rather, to embrace differences which will exist even in a gender equal society and become 'more deeply and fully themselves'.

This rather equivocal relation to masculinity as identity partly reflects widespread use of the Social Constructionist framework, which involves at least partial support for mobilising identities (even privileged ones in this instance) in strategies for social change. More particularly, it may reflect difficulties with politically 'selling' an entirely negative picture of masculinity or an entirely negative political project to a potential audience of men who may precisely be nervous about losing privileged status and/or calls to be less or not masculine. 'Castration anxiety', the fear of being feminised or somehow made 'gay' may well be a serious political barrier to Masculinity writers' departure from the normative. As Connell (1995: 221) notes, a politics whose main theme is anger towards men cannot broadly mobilise men.

Tensions between Men's/Masculinity Studies and Feminism: the Brod debate then and now

This holding on to 'manhood' (so to speak) provides the context for considering Harry Brod's work on 'Men's Studies'. Brod developed an early and influential argument for men's studies as a programme of study in the 1980s (Brod, 1987c, 1987d). (Men's Studies was then a more common generic terminology than Masculinity Studies.)[11] The debate around this argument provides a revealing means to consider further the particular features of Masculinity Studies as a theoretical project, and how it may be distinguished from the other subfields of gender/sexuality theory.

Brod writes from within the Social Constructionist framework and adopts a broadly Socialist pro-feminist position (Brod, 1987d: 12; see also Messner, 1997: 58).[12] He also is concerned to set at a distance what he calls 'the new men's studies' from earlier Men's Liberation 'sex role' approaches as well as some contemporary forms of masculinity politics, which perceive men and women as both sharing equally in the costs of the patriarchal social order (Brod, 1987d: 12–13). Brod, by contrast, is at pains to emphasise the inequality of gender arrangements while acknowledging the costs of manhood. In this vein, Brod (Ibid.: 9) says he is 'critical of masculinity' but sympathetic to men.

His focus on men conceives manhood as unitary identity (Brod, 1987c: 61). The stress here is upon the universal character of manhood as gender power, and upon the violence/coercion associated with this identity. On this basis, pornography is strongly opposed as the representation of eroticised violence by men towards women, as the eroticising of dominance (Brod, 1984). Gender is described largely in terms of identity categories. Men and women are seen as separate identity groupings in a bipolar hierarchy (Brod, 1987c).

Not surprisingly, Brod takes up certain aspects of identity or category politics when he argues for a specific 'men's studies' that is qualitatively different from the traditional unacknowledged emphasis of Western thinking on men as the generic universal. He insists on a separate Men's Studies programme. Brod argues that an integrated Gender Studies approach suggests a spurious parity between Men's and Women's Studies, an 'equal time for men' notion, which he sees as at odds with the pro-feminist motivation of the former. He also argues that Women's Studies programmes are concerned with the question of how women are socially marginalised and have not attended to men. For the 'feminist project that undergirds both [men's and women's studies programmes] to be completed', he recommends a focus on men which he sees as requiring the specific and separate development of Men's Studies (Ibid.: 60 on Gender Studies, 40 on women's studies and Feminism).

This agenda was criticised by feminist commentators during the late 1980s and early 1990s on the basis that such an account appeared to be taking ground from Women's Studies and its critique of gendered power. They were also not persuaded by Brod's account of Men's Studies as a 'complement' to, not a co-option of, Women's Studies.[13] His view that Men's Studies would place masculinities 'on a par with femininities' did not, according to Canaan and Griffen (1990), sound very far from the spurious equalising notion Brod himself had rejected. Cannaan and Griffen asserted that his proposal for Men's Studies assumes a kind of symmetry in gender Identity politics (a sense of mutual suffering) and an embrace of manhood that should be questioned. In short, they questioned the political legitimacy of Brod's account of Men's Studies. Feminist writers like Canaan and Griffen articulated early doubts about the whole project of Masculinity Studies by suggesting that perhaps under the cover of a pro-feminist mission Brod was reinstating men back at the centre of the picture, where they have always been. Men's studies ran the danger, they intimated, of being part of the conservative backlash rather than a rightful contributor to the socially critical gender/sexuality field and could also divert scarce resources away from women's programmes.[14]

Such debates about whether Men's/Masculinity Studies should be seen as an ally, or as actually more indebted to conservative masculinity politics than it was prepared to admit and hence part of the political opposition, did not go away. One ongoing response has been to mark out the 'Men's Studies' associated with Brod's argumentation, as a specific rather than generic terminology describing a doubtful political project (typically North American) which failed to develop an analysis of gendered power, pays little more than lip service to feminist critiques of gender hierarchy, uses feminist rhetoric to gain resources for men while ignoring broader questions of power, or at worst is anti-feminist (Maynard, 1990; Cornwall and Lindisfarne, 1993: 32; Hearn, 2004: 49–50). However, this delineation of the term 'Men's Studies' as signalling a position at a distance from the critical studies I have placed under the umbrella term 'Masculinity Studies', cannot be easily maintained.[15] For this reason, the challenge that Canaan and Griffen mounted in relation to Brod's account of 'Men's Studies' must also be seen as relevant to Masculinity Studies.

Two main concerns regarding the politics and institutional claims of Men's/ Masculinity Studies continue to be raised to this day.[16] The first of these – that is, doubt about the politics of Masculinity Studies and its potential (even unwitting) complicity in the resumption of men's centrality and women's marginalisation/erasure – was clearly crucial to the Brod debate but has remained a very significant issue for feminist and sexuality theorists. White (2000) has articulated in this context the hazards of a scholarly focus on men in terms of legitimating a diversion of resources away from women in relation to 'gender and development' policy. Mark Kann, who has worked with Brod to develop men's studies programmes, from a North American perspective notes the ongoing tensions that may arise from this focus on men.

In a nation where whites enslaved blacks for hundreds of years, anything called 'white studies' automatically is suspected of being a façade for white supremacy. Similarly, in a nation where men dominated women's lives for hundreds of years, anything called 'men's studies' automatically is suspected of being a front for male supremacy. (Kann, 2000: 415)

Secondly, the focus in Men's/Masculinity Studies on men *qua* men, combined with Brod's assumption that women would be dealt with by women's studies, can mean that attention to men's problems begins to resemble a 'men as victims' or 'men and women as equally victimised' scenario. Derek Nystrom (2002) links this possibility with what he sees as the continuing 'perils' of masculinity analyses and relatedly raises the problem of a persistent failure to address questions of sexuality and heterosexism sufficiently. The men-on-men analysis at the centre of Brod's account appears, on this reading, as invested in traditional conceptions of masculine identity rather than strongly concerned with re-imagining it.

The potential for Men's/Masculinity Studies to reassert a sympathetic and privileged place for men was perhaps most forcefully argued in 1991 by Tania Modleski in her book, *Feminism without Women: Culture and Criticism in a 'Postfeminist' Age*. She charged that the rise of Masculinity Studies and the authorisation of men as critics and speakers for feminist concerns indicated the victory of 'a male feminist perspective that excludes women' and thus returned social analysis of gender to a 'pre-feminist world' (Modleski, 1991: 14, 3; Wiegman, 2001a).

Such criticisms were somewhat headed off by the emergence of two bridges towards so-called Gender Studies at around the same time as the emergence of the Brod debate. On the one hand, Eve Kosofsky Sedgwick in her work *Between Men: English Literature and Male Homosocial Desire* (1985) moved to make links between feminist analysis and sexuality theorising, between the positioning of women and gay men. On the other, the publication of Connell's *Gender and Power* gave credence to analysis of the position of women *and* men under the rubric of 'gender' (1987). Both may be seen as inaugural texts in the rise of Gender Studies[17] – that is, in the rise of an approach that eschews a separate focus on men, with its potential political dangers, and moves away from a focus on dichotomous constructions of gender and identity characteristics. The theoretical turn to locating Masculinity Studies under the auspices of Gender seemed to undercut concern about Masculinity Studies reasserting a 'boys' own' club and apparently enabled men like Connell to speak about the gender order without appearing to take on the role of speaking for feminism. Certainly Modleski saw Sedgwick's work in a positive light despite her strong discomfort about the rise of Masculinity Studies and, despite warning Connell that he might be straying too close to Brod's agenda, Canaan and Griffen largely exonerate him from their criticisms.

As a final point it is necessary to consider at least briefly whether the move to Gender Studies as the home of masculinity analyses and to the language of masculinity rather than men is necessarily the answer to the Brod debate. These developments have not stilled uncertainty about the legitimacy and character of Masculinity Studies, which continues to be evident in contemporary versions of the debate.[18] Perhaps one way to examine such ongoing questions is to compare Brod's use of the term 'men', and hence men's studies, with Connell's use of Gender and masculinity.

Brod is clearly concerned about men's power over women, as is evident in his view of pornography, and on this basis argues that men should be treated as a unitary category (Brod, 1987c, 1987d; Brod and Kaufman, 1994; and note 11 in this chapter). For him, the focus on diverse masculinities misses the point, which is that 'virtually all masculinities require and justify women's subordination' (Kann, 2000: 414). Even though he is aware of the importance of recognising multiple masculinities

(Brod, 1987d/c; Messner, 1997: 58), he argues that use of the singular identity-based category 'men' is politically more effective in confronting the material and dominant forms of masculinity than accounts which substitute 'masculinities' (Brod and Kaufman, 1994). This terminological shift to 'masculinities' he suggests, though well intentioned, displaces attention away from power relations between men and women and on to the challenges of diversity between men. Jeff Hearn (1996) is also inclined to stress that the term 'masculinity' concentrates too heavily on ideological symbols and diverts attention away from 'what men do', away from 'men's material practices'. He asserts that this diminishes analysis of gendered power relations. In this context, Justad (2000: 403) argues that 'focusing on diversity among men too easily allows men's studies scholars to believe that masculinity is less than the sum of its parts and therefore not really all that bad'.

Connell, by contrast, supports the use of a masculinity perspective that stresses relationality rather than holding to identity categories. He asserts that one gender cannot be studied in isolation from another (Connell et al., 2000; see also Scott, 1986, 1999). To demonstrate this point he uses the example of 'men's health'. Connell notes that 'men's health' is problematically identity-bound, like 'Men's Studies'. An identity orientation in men's health, he says, does not show how what is supposedly particular to men may actually be particular to only some men. Similarly, a focus on men cannot indicate how men's health is highly dependent on men's construction in relation to women. It may not be that being a man or being a male – as a separate category of person – is what produces health differences between men and women, but rather the social relation between masculinity and femininity. For example, men's greater access to hazardous polluted trades and labouring occupations goes a long way to explaining so-called sex differences in occupational health (Connell et al., 2000).

Where Brod asserts an identity-based politics around men and their supposed characteristics, Connell parts company more thoroughly with these universalising tendencies. Brod's version of Social Constructionism seems to overlap much more with the identity category focus of Men's Liberation and Radical pro-feminist analyses than Connell's strongly relational conception of masculinity as an aspect of Gender. Like bell hooks (see Chapter 7), Connell insists on differences between men, within the category of men, though neither choose the Postmodern strategy of thoroughly destabilising this category. The point is, does this stress on multiplicity and relationality actually water down the potentially sharp critique of masculinity? Does it diminish the strength of the political attack on gender hierarchy if you adopt a model which complexifies the masculine? Does Brod's Men's Studies provide, after all, the greater political support to movements that aim for social change like Feminism? On the other hand, Brod's perspective has been criticised by certain feminists as precisely taking ground from Feminism and at the same time dangerously removing analysis of men away from feminist concerns.

Conclusion

This discussion raises a question crucial to the examination of Masculinity Studies as a form of critical Gender analysis: should Masculinity Studies have any independence from Feminism? To the degree that it has any independence, does Masculinity Studies risk its credentials as a politics of gender justice? And if it must be in tune with a broadly feminist perspective, then what is the reason for having a Masculinity Studies at all. In the light of such considerations how do we characterise Masculinity Studies? What *is* specific to it?

When Brod insists on sympathy for men he demonstrates a potentially different positioning from many feminist approaches. He appears to show an involvement with manhood and caution about criticising men that may be borne of different political realities, such as the strategic problems attached to speaking in an environment in which masculinity politics is largely conservative.[19] Is this complicity in masculinity by masculinity writers an important grounding for Masculinity Studies? In short, do men have particular understandings of masculinity that form at least part of the rationale for Masculinity Studies? Or does this involvement spell its most serious limitation? Certainly our next masculinity writer thinks it is most definitely Masculinity Studies' greatest limitation and that masculinity must be abandoned.

Notes

1. For example, the Dulwich Centre in South Australia is one such Australian centre. For comparisons between US, Canadian, British and Australian men's organisations and groups, see Goldrick-Jones, 2001; for material on Australia, see Flood, 1996b; see also Chapter 16, note 4.

2. Nevertheless this pro-feminist stance is not universal. For example, some accounts of race and masculinity are ambiguous about or even at odds with feminist agendas (see Chapter 19).

3. Connell et al. (2000) point out that the prevailing 'men's health' discourse frequently relies upon notions that 'being a man' produces a health disadvantage comparative to women. By contrast, Connell is inclined to question the stability of this gender/sex-based identity, for example, by indicating the ways in which socio-economic disadvantage may cut across sharp distinctions between men's and women's health, and by showing the ways in which the presumed distinctions may not be between all men and all women.

4 See Connell, 2001; Singleton, 2003; for an interesting point of comparison, see in Messner (1997: 12) his Figure 1.1 on 'The terrain of the politics of masculinities'.

5. See note 4 above and Connell, 2000: 3–36; Flood, 1996a; Clatterbaugh, 2000.

6. *The Men's Bibliography*, (11th edition, May 2003) compiled by Michael Flood, is located at http: //www.mensbiblio.xyonline.net (accessed September 2004).

7. This comparative lack of diversity may have been exacerbated in recent times by what some commentators have described as the declining state of masculinity politics (Goldrick-Jones, 2001; Clatterbaugh, 2000).

8. See also brief overviews of Social Constructionism in Chapters 1 and 8, as well as in the Glossary.

9. For instances that reveal the widespread use of Connell's approach and terminology, see for example, Messner, 1997: 7, 10–11; Beal, 1996; Goodey, 1997; Coulter, 1997; Wienke, 1998; Cheng, 1999; Sabo, 2000; Sea-ling, 2000.

10. There is one topic at least on which the inclination towards shared viewpoints falls away. Writers in the subfield express a wide range of opinions regarding the possible socio-political outcomes associated with masculinity politics and Masculinity Studies. Opinions about men's capacity for change ranges from gloomy to optimistic. See Singleton (2003) and compare, for example, Clatterbaugh (2000) with Pease (2000).

11. 'Men's Studies' is still a terminology he favours (Brod and Kaufman, 1994).

12. However, Brod's approach in some ways has a resemblance to Radical pro-feminist positions exemplified by the work of John Stoltenberg (see Chapter 18). Like Stoltenberg, Brod offers a largely unitary account of masculinity as a homogeneous category characterised by dominance over women. This is evident in Brod's analysis of pornography. Brod's position may be viewed as rather different from other Socialist pro-feminist writings. For example, Connell's work is focused precisely on the non-homogeneous character of masculinity (Connell, 2000) and Michael Kimmel's work on pornography is aligned to the pro-erotica anti-censorship stance of Socialist feminists like Lynne Segal. See Messner, 1997: 61; Kimmel, 1990.

13. Men's Studies as complement to and on a par with Women's Studies (Ibid.: 60 and 40 respectively).

14. Concerns regarding Men's Studies displacing women from scholarship, and displacing funding associated with the study of women, coalesced with related concerns from the late 1980s and 1990s regarding the displacement of women as a group category emerging from postmodern theorising. 'Women' appeared under siege on all sides. The issue did not die down but rather has developed into a continuing discussion about the future of Women's Studies programmes and/or of Feminism overall. Such a discussion clearly also has ramifications for Men's Studies/Masculinity Studies programmes and a pro-feminist masculinity politics (Canaan and Griffen, 1990). See also a slightly earlier version of this position in Griffen, 1989: 103–5; Wiegman, 2001b; Brown, 1997; Gubar, 1992.

15. For example, despite Hearn's critique of 'Men's Studies', he also acknowledges that the label has variable connotations in different settings. In particular, he cites the use of the label at NIKK, the Nordic Institute for Women's Studies and Gender Research, in ways that clearly cannot be regarded as insufficiently attuned to gendered power (Hearn, 2004: 50, 66).

16. Regarding institutional issues, see Canaan and Griffen, 1990: 210–11; Justad, 2000.

17. Schor (1992: 276) describes Sedgwick's work in this light, but I suggest there is a strong case for including Connell's work in the account of Gender Studies 'inaugural texts'. This emerging refusal to treat men and women separately is linked to the development of Queer theorising in Chapter 21.

18. One strand of this continuing uncertainty arises in feminist discontent regarding pro-feminist men's concrete contributions to social change. See Newton, 1998.

19. Connell (1995: 221) also refuses what he sees as a politics of anger towards men.

18 Radical Pro-feminism: between Gender Difference and Categorical Social Constructionism – Stoltenberg

While almost all of masculinity politics and much of contemporary Masculinity Studies is inclined to offer a critical but supportive analysis of manhood, a strand of men's politics and study programmes is decidedly not interested in this sympathetic critique.

From the 1970s a strand of masculinity activists/thinkers broke away from Men's Liberation (and its Liberal pro-feminist account of the equal costs of masculine and feminine roles). These progressive activists/theorists sharply dissented from the Men's Liberation equal treatment approach and its limited account of gendered power. As Messner (1997: 49–62) has argued, they developed a form of masculinity thinking that supported Radical feminism. Within the context of Masculinity Studies the approach is designated Radical pro-feminist and took from Radical feminism its strong emphasis on gender as a system of domination by men as a group over women as a group, and on the importance of prioritising gender subordination. In Radical feminism, power is not so much about dominance 'out there' (by bosses, white supremacists and so on) but importantly comes home to roost, and bears no necessary social distance. Power and subordination in this form of Feminism shape love, ecstasy and fun, not just cruelty, scarcity, pain and despair (MacKinnon, 1990; Echols, 1984; Rowland and Klein, 1990; Richardson, 1993a; Thompson, 2001). This means that we cannot take for granted even our most intimate enjoyments, but must consider their complicity in oppressive gender relations. Such unguarded moments may indeed be more important in maintaining our adherence to the gender status quo. For this reason, Radical feminist and Radical masculinity writers pay close attention to sexuality and pleasure.

Locating Radical pro-feminism and Radical feminism in the map of Masculinity Studies

Because Radical pro-feminist masculinity writers draw closely on a particular stream of Radical feminism (Stoltenberg, [1989] 2000a: xi), it is necessary to consider this feminist position in a little more detail. For Radical feminism, the patriarchal gender order involves fairly sharp distinctions between men as a group and women as a group. While some Radical feminists have supported a notion of largely intractable, irreducible gender differences (a notion of men and women as sharply different in nature) and others reject this essentialism,[1] most Radical feminists adopt a form of identity politics which strongly emphasises gender Identity categories as the basis of political activism. In other words, most Radical feminists may be located in the Modernist Gender Difference framework – that is, they adopt a women-centred approach. Even those Radical feminists typically associated with the Social Constructionist (SC) framework, who perceive these gender categories as the product of social relations of power and certainly not as eternal, are inclined to depict men and women as sharply divided sex 'classes'. As I have noted in Chapter 4, the stress on distinct gender categories (even if not upon conceptions of an in-built gender difference in characteristics) in some of these SC Radical feminist writings suggests an overlap or bridge between Gender Difference and Social Constructionist frameworks. The work of writers such as that of anti-porn theorist Andrea Dworkin might be seen as being at the border of these apparently different theoretical directions. Dworkin's mode of analysis might be described as either a strongly *social* account of the gender identity politics found in Gender Difference thinking, or a strongly *categorical* (identity-oriented) account of Social Constructionism.

Connell has distinguished four main ways of thinking in gender and masculinity analyses of relevance to this discussion: sex role, categorical, materialist and post-structuralist theories. He asserts that the 'categorical' approach (roughly equivalent to my account of Modernist Gender Difference thinking) perceives gender identities as pre-existing categories and gender dominance as a relationship between these pre-existent categories. Such an approach certainly attends to gendered power but, says Connell, has difficulty recognising anything outside the binary polarity of men and women. It is not well suited to analysis of power or diversity *within* each of the gender categories, such as violence by heterosexual men against gays (except as a version of the gender division). By contrast, he asserts that the 'materialist' or Social Constructionist approach focuses on the differential material 'interests' of men and women and related material practices. This approach avoids 'necessarily … [falling] back into categoricalism' by attending to the historical, cultural and institutional production of these interests, enabling a recognition that 'masculinity and femininity are not simple opposites' and contain variability (Connell, 2000: 18–21).

Andrea Dworkin's work may be seen as presenting gender in broadly social terms and as refusing a conception of gender identities as intrinsic or pre-formed prior to gendered socialisation. For her, as for colleague Catherine MacKinnon, gender is a socio-historical regime which constitutes the characteristics associated with gender identities. This places her within the Social Constructionist camp but, as Connell implies, a 'materialist' approach may slide back into categoricalism. The stress in her work is decidedly upon a binary opposition between men and women such that each category is constituted in an entirely homogeneous way. There is no cultural complexity given within this analysis (Dworkin, 1981, 1987). On this basis, I locate Dworkin as undertaking a categorical approach, which is not dissimilar to that of other Radical feminist Gender Difference writings. I have discussed Dworkin's work at some length here because this is precisely the model of analysis that is taken up in Radical pro-feminist masculinity work.

Messner (1997: 52) quotes in this setting Jack Litewka's 'The Socialized Penis', which argues in recognisably Radical feminist terms that men *learn* to see women as objects for them, to be conquered as prizes, as a means to upholding men's masculinity rather seeing women in their own right as full human beings. Messner notes that in this analysis any distinction between rape and 'normal' heterosexuality is difficult to maintain since both are constituted out of an eroticising of dominant–subordinate relations. Hetero-eroticism is tied, whether 'consensual' or not, to men's access to a sense of power via the devalued feminine, by literally entering and taking possession of the bodies of women. As we shall see, this form of analysis is also applied in Radical pro-feminism to gay men's sexuality, which is viewed as simply another variation of the construction of gendered dominant–subordinate positionings. Masculinity and masculine pleasure is tied to a practice and rhetoric of dominance, of sexualised dominance, such that effeminate gays and/or the penetrated are construed, along with women, as devalued objects.

This form of pro-feminist Masculinity Studies was and is strongly associated with the figure of John Stoltenberg (Messner, 1997: 53–4). Stoltenberg was and is particularly influenced by the Radical feminist stance of Andrea Dworkin. Interestingly, he is also held in high esteem by the highly categorical, strongly essentialist arm of Gender Difference thinking associated with the Radical feminism of Mary Daly (Douglas, 1998: 14). This, I suggest, supports my location of both Dworkin and Stoltenberg at the border between 'materialist' Social Constructionist and 'categorical' Gender Difference trajectories. Hopefully this discussion clarifies my somewhat ambiguous placement of Radical pro-feminism in the overall map of Masculinity Studies in Chapter 16 (Figure 16.2).

Stoltenberg and the rejection of manhood

Both Radical feminism and Radical pro-feminist masculinity work are now in retreat and the object of considerable criticism given their generally strong focus on a categorical universalised politics (Douglas, 1998: 14; Messner, 1997: 53–4). As I have noted before, Social Constructionist and/or Postmodern theoretical directions dominate Feminist, Sexuality and Masculinity Studies today. Both these intellectual directions emphasise a rejection of universalistic categories. In this setting, Stoltenberg's Radical pro-feminism is not the flavour of the month among masculinity theorists.

As Andrew Cornwall and Nancy Lindisfarne (1993: 40) in *Dislocating Masculinity* (a study of comparative ethnographies of masculinity) put it:

> theories which rely on notions such as … gender become problematic because they depend on ascribing essences, or essential attributes. … We have seen how oppositions like 'men' and 'women' are such essentialist categories.

The work of writers like Stoltenberg precisely discusses the essential attributes of manhood – though, like Dworkin, he does not associate men's categorical status with any biological or eternal differences. Indeed, he explicitly asserts that 'bodies are imbued with their gendered meaning through power differentials, not anatomy'. In this context Stoltenberg insists that men do not have power in-built (Stoltenberg, 1998: 18; Coulter, 2002). Instead, he links masculinity to dominance and sexual oppression, in classic Social Constructionist terms, on the basis of the social power associated with manhood:

[t]he idea of the male sex is like the idea of an Aryan race. The Nazis believed in the idea of an Ayran race – they believed that the Ayran race really exists, physically, in nature – and they put a great deal of effort into making it real. … [T]here simply is no Ayran race. There is only the idea of it – and the consequences of trying to make it seem real. The male sex is very like that. … The male sex is socially constructed. It is a political entity that flourishes only through acts of force and sexual terrorism. (Stoltenberg, 1991)

He uses the instance of all-male prisons to support the notion that while some male bodies may be subordinated, 'manhood as dominance' is 'revered' (Ibid.).

On the basis of this position, Stoltenberg develops a stance that is at a remove from most pro-feminist masculinity writers. Rather than discussing transgressing or redefining masculinity, Stoltenberg declares that 'being a man' or 'manhood' is irredeemable. Hence his work does not support the pro-feminist masculinity agenda that is the imprimatur of virtually all of Masculinity Studies (Coulter, 2002). Stoltenberg's antagonism to manhood arises because for him it is constituted *as* the subordination of the feminine. The feminine here includes men not deemed manly. Manhood is built upon social endorsement of, if not literal, everyday violence which silences women. His approach is evident in his two most famous works *Refusing to be a Man* [1989] (republished 2000) and *The End of Manhood* [1993] (2nd edition, 2000). The first of these books, in his words originated in speeches developed when he was between ages 30 and 45. He describes it in terms of an earnest, public policy-oriented and activist/theoretical approach. The second book, *The End of Manhood*, written between his 46th and 48th years, is more clearly interpersonal, informal, self-help-oriented and less academic (Stoltenberg, [1993]. 2000b: xxi).

In both books the aim is not to reform masculinity but to advocate its 'renunciation' (Messner, 1997: 53). This Radical pro-feminist call to dismantle gender emerged well before Postmodernism's similar rallying cry.[2] However, Stoltenberg's work clearly offers a Modernist Liberationist rhetoric and stresses a strongly categorical (though not biologically based) politics. As noted earlier, Radical pro-feminist Masculinity Studies is aligned with Social Constructionist Radical feminism, but it very often shares the strongly binary identity orientation of Radical feminist writings found under the umbrella of Modernist Gender Difference feminism (outlined in Chapter 4).

Radical feminism has generally supported a universalist macro-scale identity-based politics (in the 1980s especially) in which men are cast as a unitary group who oppress women as a unitary group. Radical feminism has also often strongly supported notions of women's commonality, their shared status as sisters in gender subordination, and often advocated a positive re-evaluation of womanhood or at least a positive view of their central significance in terms of claims for gender justice. Stoltenberg's Radical pro-feminism supports this largely binary account focused on gender, and on this basis utterly disavows manhood/masculinity. Interestingly, by contrast, neither Radical feminism nor Radical pro-feminism masculinity writers adopt the same utter rejection of all forms of womanhood. Radical feminist approaches, whether focused on women or men, are sharply political: women are a marginalised or subordinated sex class and men a dominant sex class. While the experience of marginalised womanhood may be crucial to creating a new world of gender justice in many versions of

Radical feminism, all variants of Radical feminism agree that manhood should be thrown into the dustbin of history.

Stoltenberg and Gender Justice

The clarity of this negative vision of manhood is evident in Stoltenberg's account of gender as an ethics – an ethical construction – by which he means that it embodies a set of values which one must disclaim if one wishes to dismantle the system of binary gender hierarchy. For Stoltenberg this is a profoundly moral (ethical) as well as polit-ical decision. We must abandon manhood because it is about injustice. His stress is upon the systematic power and privileges of masculinity and hence the moral/political reasons for renouncing it in favour of gender justice. He does pay attention to the costs of masculinity for men – that is, to men's pain and suffering in trying to locate them-selves as manly – but this does not make him any more sympathetic to manhood, indeed rather less. Manhood is like a terminal disease. It may hurt to cast it out but he clearly regards support for manhood as almost suicidal for men, even as he notes far more strongly the sinister impact of this support on women.

This is a masculinity politics which is always most strongly identified by its vocif-erous rejection of women's disempowerment. The gender order, which rests upon women's subordination, is clearly viewed as the crucial system of power upon which to focus. Like Radical feminist, Catherine MacKinnon (1982: 516, 533), Stoltenberg (1991) sees sexuality as the process which 'creates gender'. Nevertheless, MacKinnon suggests that 'sexuality is so gender marked that it carries dominance and submission with it, no matter the gender of its participants', and on this basis argues that gay men's sexuality remains constructed under conditions of male supremacy (MacKinnon, 1990: 224). Similarly, Stoltenberg's analysis of gay men's sexuality issues is organised by his view of gendered power (Messner, 1997: 54–5). In other words, both stress the cate-gorical association of manhood with oppression of women to the point that discus-sion of gay men in any other way than through the lens of manhood/gender (and hence women's subordination) is disallowed. The destructive homogeneity of mascu-line gender identity overrides any potential analysis of different men's variable posi-tionings, in this case in relation to other axes of power such as heteronormativity. What is intriguing about this strongly cast rejection of gender and manhood is that, ironically, it represents a much more thorough-going rejection of manhood, a kind of negative identity politics, than the critique of gender categories which is associated with the now more pervasive of Socialist pro-feminist masculinity work. Though Socialist pro-feminist work is influenced by Feminism, Post-colonialism, Postmodernism, and Queer Theory, it is comparatively far more committed to (merely) reforming masculinity.

Stoltenberg's categorical politics and the return of the universal Human

In this light, Radical pro-feminist approaches like Stoltenberg's may in some senses seem more 'Postmodern and Queer' in their thorough dismantling of manhood and the gender order than Socialist pro-feminism. Socialist pro-feminism is certainly less confrontational and revolutionary in approach. Its seemingly rather defensive refusal of 'guilt' on the part of men, rejection of the political aim of abandoning masculinity, and repeated espousal of the view that men really 'aren't all the same' and cannot be seen as a unified homogeneous category, may appear in certain lights as evidence of a weakening commitment to social change. Harry Brod, himself a Socialist pro-feminist, has certainly expressed this fear in relation to the focus in much Socialist pro-feminist writing on diverse masculinities (Brod and Kaufman, 1994). Undoubtedly, for Stoltenberg this agenda looks awfully close to going along for the ride and a failure of political will. He notes that his politics is certainly a far 'less popular and placating' approach, and far less 'fun' than the merely transgressive pleasures of Postmodern or Queer Theory (Stoltenberg, [1993] 2000b: xiv–xi).

For Stoltenberg, gender politics is not 'fun', nor does it matter if it is not cool. Rather, it is righteous hard work. He is, unlike the 'mainstream' of pro-feminist Masculinity Studies, not particularly 'sympathetic towards men', as Brod explicitly is (see Chapter 17). Stoltenberg is not even especially sympathetic to progressive men. Rather, his approach is characterised by its routine emphasis upon manhood's inevitable associations with sexual domination over and violence towards women, and its wholeheartedly sympathetic attitude towards the women's movement, particularly towards its Radical feminist wing. Socialist pro-feminist writers are inclined to argue that this steadfast antagonism to manhood is unproductively guilt-provoking and amounts to an antagonism to *men*, related to an obeisant attitude towards male-negative versions of Feminism (Connell, 1995: 140; Kimmel, 1996: 334). However, Stoltenberg's stance, unlike the Socialist pro-feminist viewpoint, is not a masculinity approach that assumes that the terms of the subfield can be determined at a distance from Feminism. Masculinity Studies is not a territory that men can 'own' as theirs without fear of rebuke, according to Stoltenberg. It is not and should not be 'theirs'. It cannot be a 'man's country' in any sense (Newton, 1998).

This unflinching and now rather marginalised perspective advocates a politics which stresses attention to identity. It offers another set of arguments for employing a critically informed identity politics, similar to those adopted by bell hooks and Dennis Altman (in Chapters 7 and 11 respectively). Simultaneously, the approach also reveals odd connections between this Radical pro-feminist emphasis upon identity/category politics – in this case in order to renounce manhood – and Postmodern/Queer visions regarding dismantling gender and sexuality categories (see note 2 of this chapter). It provides, in short, another instance of Lorber's (2000: 79) project of *using* gender categories 'to undo gender'.

Yet Radical pro-feminism, like other Modernist projects in the gender/sexuality field, is inclined to maintain the purity and innocence of the marginalised category term (in this case women), an innocence which is questioned by Postmodern/Queer Theory. Power is not so simple and one-way in the latter approach. And yet this focus on power in simple one-way terms does precisely suggest a strength in Radical pro-feminism. The emphasis is upon unity, unity in struggle, rather than upon differences among the oppressed and their supporters. Although this unity is grounded in women's experience of subordination, it is also available to 'men of conscience' who renounce their power seemingly as an act of will or because for some reason they do not find themselves engaged by dominance (Stoltenberg, [1993] 2000b: xxxiii). The degree to which men find themselves invested in dominance is clear, but it must be said it is hard to see from his analysis why men would renounce it. The inclination to talk in terms of clear-cut binary oppositions and unitary categories – that is, in terms of manhood as a social evil and women as its victims – gives passionate force to Stoltenberg's call for personal transformation and political activism. Nonetheless, such an inclination may also produce some difficulty in explaining the emergence of an anti-manhood agenda in men. If manhood is so infected by dominance and violence, what is it in men to which Stoltenberg can appeal? In 'How men have (a) sex' (1991), Stoltenberg appears to fall back on some intrinsic self that lies beneath the gendered self, an intrinsic humanity shared by all:

> I think somewhere inside us all, we have always known something about the relativity of gender. Somewhere inside us all, we know that our bodies harbour deep resemblances, that we are wired inside to respond in a profound harmony. ... Physiologically, we are far more alike than different. The tissue structures that have become labial and clitoral or scrotal and penile have not forgotten their common ancestry. (1991)

This return to the essential Human not only marks Stoltenberg's work as decidedly Modernist, but also undercuts his claims to a Social Constructionist positioning. The self is not driven by a biologically based *gendered essence* since this is socially constructed, but at heart there is an authentic self, a humanity, which appears beyond the social and indeed rather biologically based after all.

Stoltenberg and the erotics of gender/power

In *Refusing to be a Man* ([1989] 2000a: 112), Stoltenberg outlines the embodied deeply intimate nature of gender dominance, its visceral links to pleasure, joy, fun, 'love' and so on. Indeed, his analysis offers a fascinating account of how, far from gender being founded upon biology (anatomical or bodily sex), the social framing of gender creates the meanings and pleasures of the body: 'male sexual identity produces sensation, produces the meaning of sensation, becomes the meaning of how one's body feels'. This male sexual identity is verified by identification with the sex class 'men' and repudiation of the sex class 'women', for example by engaging in sex which constitutes men as powerful and important and women as submissive and unimportant (Stoltenberg, 1991). In particular, he associates penetrative sex (intercourse) with the enactment of male dominance.[3]

Stoltenberg ([1989] 2000a: 112) describes the socially constituted pleasures of male dominance as 'culturally eroticized'. He claims (in common with Radical feminist antipornography activists Andrea Dworkin and Catherine MacKinnon) that pornography 'institutionalizes' this eroticised dominance, that pornography exemplifies and actively shapes that dominance and does not merely reflect it. While Socialist pro-feminist writers like Michael Kimmel (1990) asserts that pornography teaches men how to have sex, how to enjoy gay sex, and is not an unalloyed evil, Stoltenberg ([1989] 2000a: 117) follows Dworkin's view that it perpetuates harm against women and naturalises and endorses male dominance by making male supremacy sexy. Dworkin similarly argues that pornography enacts women's object status – that is, it shows that women are to be used as things – and indeed is meant to show that they enjoy pain, humiliation and dominance (Dworkin, 1988: 204). In a similar vein Catherine MacKinnon (1987b: 173) declares that pornography 'institutionalizes the sexuality of male supremacy, fusing the eroticism of dominance and submission with the social construction of male and female. To the extent that gender is sexual, pornography is part of constituting the meaning of that sexuality' (see also, Stark, 1997).

Stoltenberg extends this position, however, to gay male pornography. Gay male pornography has been strongly endorsed by many gay activists and writers within Sexuality Studies as liberating and anti-normative. By contrast, Stoltenberg argues that this form of pornography silences and enacts effeminate and ethnic minority men's object status, turns them into things and is intended to show that they enjoy pain, humiliation and dominance (McCulloch, 2000: 21). He states that: 'the values in the sex that is depicted in gay male sex films are very much the values in the sex that straight men tend to have – because they are very much the values that male supremacists tend to have: taking, using, estranging, dominating' (Stoltenberg, 1990: 249).

Chris Kendall supports this analysis: 'What one sees in gay male pornography', according to Kendall (1993),

> is an almost pervasive glorification of the idealized masculine/male icon. Cops, truckers, cowboys, bikers and Nazis are eroticized. Racial stereotypes are sexualized and perpetuated. Muscle, 'good-looks', and youth are glorified. Ostensibly straight or at least 'straight-acting' men rape and/or humiliate descriptively (frequently stereotypical) gay men.

'What's so liberating about this?', the Radical pro-feminist masculinity writers argue.

You can see that in aligning himself with such views of masculinity and of pornography, Stoltenberg contributes to debates with Socialist pro-feminist, Postmodern and other masculinity commentators who are uninclined to stress a politics based on gender identities/categories. He also contributes to the so-called 'sex wars' debate about pleasure and power, which has divided Feminist and Sexuality writers in that he insists upon the links between sexual pleasure and male dominance.[4] Stoltenberg's views on sexuality and sexual liberation are not dissimilar to those of 'sex-critical' Radical feminist commentator, Sheila Jeffreys (1990). Such views may be contrasted with those of Pat Califia, for example (see Chapter 14). Califia writes on transgender/ transsexual issues among others and is a 'pro-sex' or 'sex affirmative' activist who strongly supports what she describes as consensual and ethical forms of eroticised dominance in sex. For this reason she strongly supports pornography, including pornography which eroticises dominance (for example, S/M porn) (Cusac, 1996).

Stoltenberg insists that eroticised dominance must be resisted in individual and collective struggle by engaging with a truer sense of 'self'. In the revised edition of *The End of Manhood* he differentiates between a 'manhood act', which he presents as like a mask, and a deeper 'selfhood', a 'best self' (2000b: 305). Here we have a clear statement of the Modernist paradigm of throwing off power to reveal an essential and free self unmarked by social power. Once again, as in his earlier 1991 paper, Stoltenberg appears closer to the essentialist identity politics of Modernist Gender Difference frameworks than to Social Constructionist accounts of the thoroughly socially formed character of the self. Indeed, Stoltenberg's marshalling of a negative identity politics, of a sloughing off of existing identities, is just as powerful a call to activism as the stirring incitements to positively recognise and embrace women's identity associated with Gender Difference Feminism: 'Manhood is *the* paradigm of injustice. Refusing to believe in manhood is the personal and ethical stance of resistance to all injustice done in its name' (Ibid.: 304, emphasis added).

Debates

Many criticisms have been raised regarding Stoltenberg's Radical pro-feminist position. Commonly, it is suggested that the slogan 'refusing to be men' cannot be effective as a means to political mobilisation of men. Yet, on the other hand, Stoltenberg's perspective has been taken up by masculinity activists in relation to violence, rape, domestic violence and pornography (Messner, 1997: 53–4). Perhaps this perspective works best in relation to particular issues that are especially illustrative of a clear gender polarity, like violence.

Whether or not Stoltenberg's work is politically effective, it certainly offers an unremitting analysis. He stresses a categorical view of men as oppressors and women as the oppressed, as well as a characterisation of male sexuality in terms of sexual violence such that men's domination in the sexual arena apparently becomes the singular locus of women's oppression. Stoltenberg seems to assume that masculinity is *equivalent* to violence, rape/domestic violence and violent pornography. While the approach has polemical power, it is frequently viewed as absolutist and reductionist. Socialist pro-feminists in particular wish to assert that masculinity and male sexuality is not all of a piece. The Socialist pro-feminist stress on multiple masculinities is far less absolutist, universalistic, categorical, and gives greater recognition to the unequal benefits different groups of men gain from patriarchal societies in the West.

It may be asserted, by contrast, that Stoltenberg is not unaware of diversity among men and their differential access to power. For example, he resigned his long-standing position as Chair of the Ending Men's Violence task group within the US men's organisation NOMAS (National Organization of Men Against Sexism) in 1991 in response to what he saw as its racism, and pays considerable attention to gay as well as heterosexual masculinity (Stoltenberg, 1997, cited in Goldrick-Jones, 2001).

Even if it is accepted that Stoltenberg's analysis is not entirely unresponsive to diversity within masculinity, his absolutism offers a singular and, it may be argued, reductive focus on gender. Despite his evident awareness of racism, no other axes of power apart from gender are considered in any depth in his writings, and gender itself is seen through the narrow lens of sexuality and violence. While this lens does enable Stoltenberg to concentrate on dominance/power, it leads to a highly restricted account. He fails, for example, to attend to 'wider' social institutions of masculinity.[5] In focusing on those sexual issues which most lend themselves to accounts of social life in terms of polarity and violence and depicting such polarity and violence as somehow exemplary, Stoltenberg may be attending to issues which unite a large number of women. In the process, nevertheless, he tends to ignore much of what occurs in the everyday lives of women. His analysis is more like an object lesson or morality play than indicative of the full range of gender practices and forms of power. Stoltenberg does, however, suggest that complexifying the analysis of gender is often just an excuse for watering it down.

This stance is particularly evident in his opposition to pornography. Stoltenberg refuses to resile from outright opposition to pornography as the manifest instance of what he sees as a culture of eroticised male dominance. His critics assert that pornography is not necessarily harmful and that an anti-pornography politics plays into the hands of homophobic and gender conservatives. The development of an anti-pornography legislation by Stoltenberg's feminist counterparts, Dworkin and MacKinnon, raised many concerns on these grounds. Radical feminist and Radical pro-feminist masculinity approaches were viewed as engaged in an alliance with the moral Right-wing, an alliance which amounted to a new push to limit socially acceptable sexual choices for women and new opportunities for censorship of gay/lesbian materials (Snitow, 1986; Gutmann, 1993; Dinelli, 1994; Segal, 1994). Yet, it is not entirely clear that Radical opposition to pornography can be dismissed as a ridiculously censorious and ultimately anti-sexual positioning. Stoltenberg is not alone in suggesting that the normalisation and 'mainstreaming' of pornography may be problematic in terms of challenging gender (Sorensen, 2003). The question is whether Stoltenberg's analysis of this problem is persuasive.

Conclusion

The most hotly debated aspect of Stoltenberg's controversial approach is that it relies upon a categorical account of men and women. Radical pro-feminism reasserts gender divisions even as these are criticised and Stoltenberg's own emphasis on the monolithic authority of masculinity makes it difficult to have faith in change or to see where it might come from. At the same time, Stoltenberg's work represents a serious challenge to reformist masculinity approaches and demands much more substantive transformations of social relations. The analysis connects structural and public aspects of gender organisation with the most intimate of sexual practices and bodily sensations. This is an analysis which is in every sense 'radical'. In an increasingly conservative political climate, perhaps it is more important than ever to have writers in the gender/sexuality field who simply do not accept the status quo and hence raise questions about the supposedly self-evident.

All the same, Stoltenberg's 'I am the vanguard' stance appears as moralistic and 'holier than thou', which may not appeal to a great many men. Moreover, his work is regarded by many writers in the gender/sexuality field as reinstating gender stereotypes of men as sexual beasts and women as innocent victims, as well as demonising sexuality in ways that are viewed as strangely socially conservative. His perception that his own position represents political toughness (a firm revolutionary agenda), and that others are going soft, is rather at odds with his call to reject manly authority. Once again there may be a strange resurgence of gender identity in Stoltenberg's work at the very point of its disavowal.

Notes

1. For example, Mary Daly's approach may be compared with that of Stevi Jackson and Catherine MacKinnon (see Chapter 4).

2. Stoltenberg's confronting stress on renouncing manhood (gender identity) may be viewed as demonstrating Stevi Jackson's assessment regarding overlaps between Radical feminist approaches and Postmodernism. Jackson links 'materialist' Radical feminist writing (associated with Andrea Dworkin, Catherine MacKinnon and Christine Delphy) with Postmodern feminism (for example, Judith Butler). Given Stoltenberg's close alignment with the former grouping, Jackson's argument remains relevant to Stoltenberg as well. See Jackson, 1998b: 134–9.

3. For this reason he urges men to reconfigure desire by engaging in non-penetrative sexual play (ibid.). He develops such a viewpoint by explicitly drawing upon Andrea Dworkin's portrayal of intercourse as the performance of male dominance (see Chapter 4).

4. See Chapter 12, notes 2 and 3, and Chapter 14.

5. For an alternative broader *social* account of masculinity and gender, see Segal, 1990, 1999.

19 Differences: Race/Ethnicity/Imperialism and Gay Masculinities – Dowsett, Carbado

In this chapter I discuss the third main direction in Masculinity Studies concerned with multiple Differences – that is, differences *within* the category of the masculinity and typically *between* men. This direction is in sharp contrast to the almost exclusive focus on the hierarchical distinction between men and women which characterises the Radical pro-feminism associated with John Stoltenberg (Chapter 18). Radical masculinity approaches like Stoltenberg's are inclined to subsume multiple differences between men and between women which complicate gender hierarchy under an overarching singular focus on men's power over women, the Gender divide. The central concern with multiple identity Differences *between* men is, however, the subject of masculinity writings attending to gay men and to race/ethnicity/imperialism (REI).

I will first briefly place gay and REI-focused Masculinity Studies in relation to other major strands in Masculinity Studies. Following this, I will outline some gay and REI themes in the 'mainstream' of Masculinity Studies, discussing writings that are not focused on these themes but do attend to them, and then finally consider a selection of writings which are centrally occupied with these themes.

Gay and REI masculinities in context

In order to analyse the features of those masculinity writings that are specifically attentive to gay and REI matters, it is worth returning quickly to the array of theoretical trajectories in the subfield. Figure 19.1 is a slightly abbreviated version of that found in Chapter 16 (Figure 16.2).

The emphasis on multiple differences within masculinity, in particular between men, in the work on gay/REI masculinities is not entirely distinct from the approach of writings under the umbrella of Social Constructionism. There are, as will become increasingly evident, many overlaps. However, it seems to me that there are also distinguishing elements. Both (multiple) Differences and Social Constructionist frameworks in Masculinity Studies highlight the complex nature of masculinity and the differential positionings of different groups of men. Moreover, theorists focusing on gay men and those men marginalised by REI, frequently make use of the work of Socialist Constructionist writers, especially Connell. Indeed, Connell's contribution to the disaggregation of masculinity is crucial here and might seem to locate him in the Differences camp.

Figure 19.1   Map of Masculinity Studies: continuum and directions

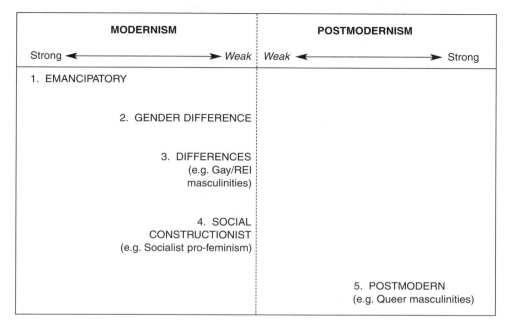

MODERNISM	POSTMODERNISM
Strong ← → Weak	Weak ← → Strong
1. EMANCIPATORY	
2. GENDER DIFFERENCE	
3. DIFFERENCES (e.g. Gay/REI masculinities)	
4. SOCIAL CONSTRUCTIONIST (e.g. Socialist pro-feminism)	
	5. POSTMODERN (e.g. Queer masculinities)

Yet there is a distinguishing tenor to the Differences framework. Gay and black male writers, for example, write as if from a distance, with a sense of speaking from the margins. They speak with an overwhelming sense of their awkward relationship to masculinity and/or to Masculinity Studies. This cannot be said of Connell. While gay and black male writers write *of* their dislocation, Connell writes *about* it. Such speaking positions alter what is discussed and why. Although Postmodern accounts of masculinity also register a discomfort with masculine gender identity, and Queer versions of this approach have links with gay Differences writers, once again there is typically a different tone. Those writing within the Differences framework usually remain strongly connected to conceptions of minority identities and communities. Indeed, this framework provides clear instances, for example, of race and sexual identity politics. In other words, unlike the equivalent Differences trajectories in Feminist and Sexuality Studies, this framework in Masculinity Studies is more clearly identified with a Modernist frame of reference. A Postmodern, for example, distinctly Post-colonial REI approach focusing on 'Third World' men as men is as yet undeveloped.[1]

To explore the 'tone' I have described as associated with gay/REI accounts in Masculinity Studies it is necessary not just to compare different directions in the subfield but to locate the Differences trajectory in relation to the whole subfield. Judith Newton (1998) argues that most of the writing in Masculinity Studies focuses on white, middle-class heterosexual men. The accounts of masculinity undertaken in these studies rest upon notions of men's dominant social position as against that of women in a gender hierarchy. Masculinity is seen as having pay-offs for men in general as against costs for women. Nevertheless, she points out that women remain relatively unseen in these analyses. Men seem to create history and culture on their own – to be overly central to the creation of an unjust gendered society.[2] While this tendency to focus on men's involvement in patriarchal social arrangements is undoubtedly related to concerns about fending off the women-blaming that occurs in masculinity politics, as elsewhere, there is perhaps some problem in this centre-stage positioning for men. The focus has been associated with suspicious, wary or even antagonistic assessments regarding the nature of Masculinity/Men's Studies from both feminists and masculinity writers (for a detailed analysis of these concerns, see Chapter 17). Such assessments revolved around the concern that Masculinity/Men's Studies might represent another means of supporting the dominance of men in thinking about society and in educational institutions.

Something of the same difficulty arises in relation to subordinated men – that is, in relation to gay men and men marginalised by REI, including 'black' and some non-Western men. In this context, most masculinity writers today make a point of indicating the ways in which the notion of Masculinity creates its own 'abject' outsiders or marginals (see, for example, Franklin II, 1994; Maynard, 1998). This concern to show what is diminished or excluded in the constitution of dominant Masculinity is part of an effort to question the naturalness of the gender order and gender categories like masculinity. It enables masculinity writers to redefine Masculinity as non-unitary, as multiple, rather than as a biological or even social given. The 'abject' aspects of the construction of Masculinity – its 'underside' – include groupings such as gay and black/Third World men. These marginalised/subordinate groupings delimit (mark the boundaries of) and yet destabilise Masculinity, even while these groups are specifically constituted by a relationship to Masculinity (Newton, 1998).

Attention to the complexity and diversity of masculinity, and hence to 'masculinities', has been increasingly emphasised in recent writings.[3] Even masculinity writers like Stoltenberg, who are more inclined to stress what men share – that is, to focus upon the unitary character of masculinity – acknowledge to some extent that masculinity has differential claims upon or rewards for different men. However, the great majority of Masculinity writers today follow a broadly Social Constructionist and Socialist pro-feminist 'line'. They are inclined to make use of Connell's conception of masculinity as a hierarchical construct built upon the 'honouring' of a certain form of manhood associated with white, heterosexual, class-privileged men in Western societies, a model which is increasingly exported globally. In this analysis of hierarchically organised multiple masculinities, the 'hegemonic' or dominant masculinity of the West is constructed *against* gay masculinities, as well as against those masculinities marginalised by race/ethnicity and/or imperialism.

In this setting, virtually all Masculinity authors today strongly assert that 'a central, if not the central dynamic in hegemonic masculinity is the subordination of gay masculinity, and the latter's construction as a repository for everything Euro-American heterosexual masculinity expels – weakness, feminisation, and the like' (Newton, 1998; Connell, 1995: 78–9). However, the rhetoric of significance, even centrality, to the study of Masculinity in the case of masculinities subordinated as gay or marginalised by REI, just as in the case of women, is not matched by their *presence* in Masculinity writings (Alsop et al., 2002; Flood, 1996b).

Gay and REI masculinities remain largely missing from Masculinity Studies and to the extent that they appear in the work of major writers in the subfield tend to be presented as not particularly active in shaping hegemonic masculinity but rather as 'negatively circumscribing dominant masculinity's borders' (Newton, 1998). As I suggested in relation to the absence of women, it may be that Masculinity writers who are themselves largely white, middle-class, Western and 'straight' are being careful not to speak too much for 'others'. Once again these writers may be attempting to avoid making gay and REI men seem complicit in a hierarchically organised gender order which deems them lesser.

Nevertheless, once again there is a default effect that in giving white, straight, Western men centre stage they are given 'too much credit (or discredit)' – that is, too much agency in creating society and history. Marginalised and subordinated masculinities are largely relegated to the sidelines and are not presented as co-constructors of social life. As we shall see from gay and REI contributors to the subfield, this does not go unrecognised.

However, before we move to writings that focus on gay and REI masculinities, I will briefly turn to the 'mainstream' Masculinity writers' approach. What I mean by 'mainstream' is those writers who do not share the awkward location in relation to Masculinity Studies I associated with the Differences framework. Typically, they discuss but do not have a *central* focus on gay/REI matters. I will use Connell's work as a major example here.

'Mainstream' accounts of multiple masculinities, 'other' masculinities

Connell combines 'meta theorising' about 'hegemonic masculinity' (an exemplary model or cultural ideal of manhood associated with white heterosexual and class-privileged men) with case histories of white heterosexual and gay men and boys from both middle- and working-class backgrounds (Connell, 1995, 2000). He also considers men in political movements like the environment movement (Connell, 1995: 120–42). Unlike many, if not most, in the 'mainstream' of Masculinity Studies he does pay considerable attention to axes of gender, class and sexuality, in presenting masculinity as multiple and non-homogeneous. Despite this attention, what is interesting is that only gender and class are thoroughly integrated into the large-scale aspects of the analysis. Though Connell is very serious about considering sexuality, in contrast to the great majority in the Masculinity subfield, sexuality and gay men still tend to operate as negative border markers rather than as active *contributors* to the shaping of masculinity, hegemonic masculinity and the gender order.

Race/ethnicity is strangely absent in his work. Connell is an Australian academic mostly located in Australia. Perhaps the lack of attention to 'black' masculinities in the Australian context is explained by the generally weak impact of gender/sexuality analyses in theorising from Indigenous Australian activists/scholars.[4] Indigenous men in Australia tend to be presented by such activists/scholars as having a subordinated, indeed victimised, status. As Carbado (1999a: 4–8) notes in the US context, this is not a position particularly inclined to consider black masculinity as the beneficiary of any (patriarchal) advantages (see also hooks, 1992b; Spraggins, 1999: 45). In other words, racial oppression is stressed over and against any stress on gender/sexuality. Gender is frequently viewed as markedly less significant than race and as threatening Indigenous identity and collectivity, a collectivity crucial to resisting/surviving the violence of racism (Moreton-Robinson, 1992, 2002; Behrehdt, 1993; Huggins, 1987). Homosexuality among Indigenous men remains a very difficult topic that is almost never the subject of discussion (Holmes, 1995; Hodge, 1993). This privileging of race is very much like the emphasis of much black writing in the USA and the UK (hooks, 1992b; Carbado, 1999a; Gilroy, 1993a: 7; Mirza, 1999: 137), but perhaps is even more antagonistic to gender/sexuality. While black feminist writers who are concerned with gender/sexuality are well established in all three countries and have commented on 'black masculinity', it is undoubtedly politically difficult for white men like Connell to offer contributions to this topic.

As Newton (1998) notes, a Masculinity Studies which focuses on whiteness involves an arena which white men can legitimately 'own' without their claims to speak being immediately constituted as colonising. Additionally, it should be noted that other forms of masculinity politics have shown no such compunction about appropriating versions of indigenous masculinities. Much popularist celebrating and reclaiming of masculinity, for example by men's groups and writers influenced by the Mythopoetic approach (see Chapter 16), involves reclaiming supposed aspects of indigenous manhood. Rituals said to derive from North American Indian and Indigenous Australian sources (sources often understood in homogeneous terms) are popular (Kimmel and Kaufman, 1994). Perhaps in this context, Connell is particularly concerned to avoid being lumped together with this usage of Indigenous Australian masculinities to enhance white masculinities.

Despite certain limitations in his account of multiple masculinities (and surely no one can do everything), Connell does attend to links between race/ethnicity/imperialism and masculinity at a broadly schematic level in terms of discussing what he calls the 'globalization of gender' and 'the world gender order' (Connell, 2000: 40–1). He links imperialism (the economic and political expansion of European States) in its various stages – conquest, colonial and post-colonial – with gender relations. Gender is here cast as intertwined with expanding capitalist/class relations. North Atlantic countries are hegemonic in this world gender order such that the 'hegemonic masculinities of neo-colonial societies are connected and poised between local and global cultures' (Ibid.: 43, 42). As North Atlantic institutions (like armies, states, corporations, capital and labour markets, schools) 'become dominant in world society, patterns of masculinity embedded in these Western institutions become world standards' (Ibid.: 45). He notes (drawing on fellow Australian Dennis Altman's book *Global Sex* (2001a)) that this is also evident in the export of Western models of gay masculinities as the 'alternative' (Ibid.: 43; see Chapter 11 for more discussion of Altman's work).

Thus, Connell says, conditions now exist for 'production of a hegemonic masculinity on a world scale'. He refers to a 'dominant form that embodies, organizes and legitimates, men's domination in the world gender order as a whole' (Ibid.: 46). The hegemonic form in the current world order, in his view, takes the pattern of 'transnational business masculinity'. It is marked by egocentrism, conditional commitments, declining ethical concerns, and is focused on accumulation and commodification, including of people and sexuality. This globalising business masculinity is not dependent on individual physicality but often commands considerable means of control, including violent control. Those who partake of such a masculinity may employ the physicality of other men to represent their interests in advertising and 'security' matters. The global hegemonic form is also increasingly libertarian – sex and pleasure as conceived as an unalloyed good. It is possible that Connell is suggesting here a lessening emphasis in conceptions of dominant masculinity upon whiteness and heterosexuality.

It is important to acknowledge at this point that the study of connections between masculinity and globalisation, and of Third World masculinities, is still in its early stages.[5] Connell's contribution to this literature is, in this sense, noteworthy. All the same, although his global analysis does refer to Western imperialism and to other countries/cultures than the West, it pays little attention to gay or race/ethnicity matters or even to the differential impact of imperialist hegemonic masculinity within non-Western cultures. The analysis is schematic and from the vantage point of considering the spread of the hegemonic. North Atlantic, white, class-privileged, straight guys necessarily remain centre stage in this global analysis. Those cast as peripheral tend to remain in the shadows.

Critical contributions to Masculinity Studies

On that note, I now turn to writings which particularly focus on the subordinated – in particular gay men and men marginalised by race/ethnicity/imperialism, including black, ethnic minority and Third World men who are not part of local elites.

What is evident straight away is the limited space occupied by these writings in Masculinity Studies. They are first of all comparatively scarce in terms of the number of writings, but also have had a restricted impact in the subfield. As Louise Archer (2001: 79) argues from a British perspective, 'issues around black masculinity remain largely undertheorized'. Race and gender are predominately addressed as distinct issues – black meaning men, gender meaning white. In the same vein, Mirza (1999: 137) notes, 'black masculinity is not something we consciously talk about much in academic study'. Gay masculinities have not been given a great deal of attention either. Carrigan, Connell and Lee (1987) point out that a remarkable silence on gay matters existed in the early Masculinity Studies literature – that is, in Men's Liberation literature. Unfortunately, such inattention has not disappeared. While, as I noted earlier, there is a rhetorical acknowledgement of the significance of homosexuality in the framing of masculinity, a failure to acknowledge and include gay scholarship remains characteristic of many contemporary areas of writing on masculinity (such as writing on the history of masculinity) (Maynard, 1998). A classic instance of the general rhetoric of inclusion accompanied by a failure to follow through with regard to gay writings is evident in the book *Manful Assertion: Masculinities in Britain since 1800*, edited by Michael Roper and John Tosh (1991).[6] They argue that among the 'preconditions for a history of masculinity' (cited in Maynard, 1998: 4) is gay history as 'first in the field and still the most productive'. The 'decisive contribution' offered by gay history is, however, not found in the book. In this context, even though Connell and his collaborators have been the most consistent writers in Masculinity Studies in insisting on the significance of gay men to Masculinity Studies, it is interesting to note how sexuality tends to drop away when Connell turns to macro-level analysis of the historical development of masculinity (see Chapter 20) and the contemporary constitution of a global hegemonic masculinity.

It would seem that while there are relatively few analyses available on black masculinity, there are many more on gay men, including those which attend to their gender identities (their masculinity), but these are generally not acknowledged within the subfield. Gay, it would appear, equates to sexuality and has little to say about masculinity, while Heterosexual unaccountably means gender/masculinity and is not about sexuality.

Gay Masculinities

Gary Dowsett (1998) has provided an outline of what adding analysis of gay masculinity might contribute to the Masculinity subfield, and in the process gives some useful guidance concerning the somewhat awkward relationship between gay and implicitly heterosexual 'mainstream' accounts of masculinity.

Dowsett notes that considering gay masculinity enables a thorough appreciation of the hierarchical character of masculinity (its non-unitary nature and its differential rewards) as well as its contingency and instability. The inclusion of gay masculinity gives weight to questioning views of masculinity as a pre-destined biology or a simple set of rules to be learned. Gay masculinity highlights failure to achieve hegemonic masculinity and specifically draws attention to the non-natural, non-inevitable status of masculinity as an achievement – indeed, as 'a performance'. His exemplar, Ian Roberts, a famous Australian professional Rugby Union player, exemplifies the complexity of masculinity in displaying a hyper-masculine yet gay body. I would add that the figures of Don Dunstan and Bob Brown, two remarkably successful Australian politicians, also demonstrate the ways in which publicly visible and 'successful' gay men challenge the assumed connections between proper manhood and heterosexuality, rendering hegemonic masculinity more indefinite and less evidently secure (Baird, 2001). In using such exemplars, Dowsett undertakes a mode of analysis that is rarely evident in Masculinity writings. He shows the ways in which gay masculinity is not merely the passive boundary marker of hegemonic (heterosexual) masculinity, but also actively contributes to the construction of masculinities especially in relation to constructions of desirability and body image. Witness, for example, the rise of television programmes like 'Queer Eye for the Straight Guy', which tell heterosexual men to take gay men's advice on such issues (see also Rohlinger, 2002; Selinger-Morris, 2004).

Dowsett, like most writers on gay masculinity, nevertheless also points out the ambiguity of the relationship between gay analyses and Masculinity Studies. The relationship is not so much an 'unhappy marriage', as based on an occasional meeting.[7] He notes that gay men are little interested in masculinity politics because it is primarily focused on heterosexual men (Dowsett, 1998: 20). Although he is sympathetic to Feminism (and therefore the pro-feminist orientation of Masculinity Studies), he notes that gay men and feminists do not always agree and is much more willing to be critical of women/Feminism than most masculinity writers. He notes, for example, that women are complicit in homophobic constructions of masculinity (Ibid.: 12, 16). In these ways Dowsett is representative of most writers on gay masculinity issues.

Increasingly, as I have noted in previous chapters on Sexuality Studies, writers attending to LGBTI (lesbian, gay, bisexual, transgender, intersexual) and queer sexualities are inclined to declare that gender rests upon a heterosexual focus of relations between the sexes and assert that gender categories should not to be prioritised over those of sexuality.[8] Whether or not this should be accepted, with the growth of Postmodern/Queer Theory approaches in Sexuality Studies, the inclination to separate gender from sexuality and regard gender as tainted by heterosexual privilege has become common. This inevitably creates a climate in which masculinity (as a gender category) becomes less of a concern within gay analyses. To the extent that Feminism is associated with Gender Studies, it too is seen as increasingly at a distance from gay concerns. The heterosexual focus of most Masculinity Studies fuels this inclination towards disengagement.

The outcome is two-fold. The forms of gay studies that explicitly speak to the field of Masculinity Studies are generally linked to the Social Constructionist framework. However, gay analyses that in some ways consider masculinity, spread as far afield as Liberal Modernist to Postmodern positions. Secondly, there is a strong tendency in the gay Masculinity Studies writings to ignore, delimit or even reject any conception of gay masculinity as complicit in gender injustice – that is, there is a certain level of disavowal of the usefulness of feminist or pro-feminist (Masculinity Studies) agendas in relation to gay men, even if such agendas are accepted in relation to heterosexual men. This occurs despite evident links between constructions of gay masculinity and those associated with heterosexuality (Nardi, 2000; Halkitis, 2001).

Masculinity tends to be seen in gay masculinity writings as something that produces costs but not benefits for gay men. Such is the strength of the oppression related to homophobia and coercive heteronormativity that gay men are more often cast as victims rather than as complicit in gendered power and male dominance. Because their masculinity is in question in heterosexist society, these writings tend not to conceive gay men as party to men's 'patriarchal dividend' (Connell, 2000: 202). Dowsett (1998: 20) notes that gay men do not see themselves as implicated in gendered power relations and hence are not much interested in gender politics/justice unless related to sexuality politics.

Dowsett himself appears implicitly to support this conception of gay men as largely in the position of victims, despite his explicit support for Feminism, when he says, 'there is little doubt that the gains made by women in many spheres of social and economic life in this country [Australia] have greatly outstripped gains made by oppressed minority groups' (1998: 12). In formal politico-legal terms this point is important since homosexuals, for instance, lag well behind heterosexual women with regard to civil rights. In most jurisdictions in the West, legal recognition of same-sex relationships, with all the attendant benefits attached to this right, remain out of reach, as do some biomedical procedures.[9] Nonetheless, the inclination to line up the problems faced by homosexual minorities *against* those faced by women tends to ignore gay men's comparative and gendered material economic benefits as against those of women. Moreover, though lesbians must confront both gender and sexuality discrimination, they seem to drop out of this analysis.

Most gay Masculinity writings do not readily accept gay men's connections to 'male supremacy' or their 'patriarchal pay-off', as described by Stoltenberg (Chapter 18) and Connell (Chapter 20) respectively. Hence, they often do operate from a rather different perspective from the overall Masculinity Studies subfield. Gay analyses of masculine privilege have been less strongly pursued than in hetero masculinity or feminist approaches (Tomsen and Mason, 2001; Carrigan, Lee and Connell, 1985;

Johnston, 1999). By contrast, these analyses typically prioritise sexuality over gender to the point where gender is largely subsumed (Tomsen and Mason, 2001: 257). On the other hand, some Masculinity writings that are focused on gay men point out that the issue of gay male domestic violence and of gender differentials in homophobic assaults upon gays and lesbians both signal a need to link analyses of gay men to the question of masculinity as a matter of urgency (Cruz, 2003; Tomsen and Mason, 2001).

REI Masculinities

It should be noted that writings on race/ethnicity/imperialism and masculinity remain very largely dominated by writings on African-American men.[10] By contrast, John Holmes has noted in a rare research study the extraordinary silence around gay Indigenous Australian men. This silence is largely the case in relation to Indigenous Australian men *per se*. This occurs in part because black Australians, like African Carribeans in the UK (Benson, 1996), have primarily been understood in a homogeneous fashion and subsumed under the singular question of 'race'. Hence, it is difficult to find scholarly research on Indigenous Australian men in terms of analyses of masculinity, of Indigenous men *as* men. It is even more difficult to find analyses of masculinity undertaken *by* Indigenous men.[11] Archer (2001: 80–1) notes that a number of other marginal racial/ethnic minority masculinities also fail to attract much attention or analysis. Having recognised the somewhat narrow range of REI masculinity work, it is evident that the main body of these writings – on African-American masculinity – bear some similarities with those on gay masculinity.

Devon Carbado outlines certain tendencies in the much smaller field of REI masculinity studies which are similar to those I have described in relation to gay writings. 'Black' men (especially heterosexual black men), he says, frequently remain silent about gender (Carbado, 1999a; hooks, 1992b; Zook, 1995). While power relations between genders in African-American families may be more egalitarian than white equivalents, perhaps reflecting the greater likelihood of earning equality, African-American men tend generally to support hegemonic conceptions of masculinity. Such support is registered in a defensive embrace of masculine authority over women – in part a response to the denial in a white male-dominated society of the usual gender confirmations and privileges to black men – and in homophobia (Shelton and John, 1993; Sties and Tierda, 1993; hooks, 1992b; Segal, 1990: 187; Battle and Lemelle, Jr., 2002; Lewis, 2003; Brandt, 1999). Solidarity in the black community is frequently conflated with solidarity between black men and, in turn, this is conflated with affirming black men's masculinity.[12] The shoring up of what hooks calls 'phallocentric black masculinity' is evident in the Black Power writings of the 1960s, but continues in misogynist versions of Black Nationalism, as well as in fundamentalist Islamist groupings such as Louis Farrakhan's Nation of Islam (see Chapter 16) (Lewis, 2003; Spraggins, 1999; Grünell and Saharso, 1999: 205–7). African-American men writing on masculinity have also often echoed support for, rather than offering critical analyses of, masculinity. The work of Robert Staples (1982) is commonly cited in this context, but more recently, as Clarence Walker (2003) notes, a number of writers on black American masculinity have adopted the therapeutic mode typically associated with the Mythopoetic men's movement (see Chapter 16), reasserting a masculinist ethos by reference to mythical heroes who rescue the black community (see hooks, 1992b: 96–8; Spraggins, 1999; Byrd and Guy-Sheftall, 2001).

REI masculinity studies, like many gay studies of masculinity, indicate significant difficulties with the notion of benefits rather than costs arising from their masculine positioning. In this case gender is subsumed into race rather than sexuality. Aileen Moreton-Robinson (1992: 5), in an Australian context, describes this imperative as 'masking gender and exalting race'. Indeed, paying attention to gender rather than prioritising race is commonly viewed in terms of disloyalty to racially marginalised communities, in this case to the black community (Carbado, 1999a: 117; Moraga, 1983: 105; Tessman, 1998). Criticism of relations between black men and women is construed in terms of betrayal and, importantly, what is highlighted in this account is betrayal of black men (equated with the black community) rather than the evident betrayal of black women in ignoring their concerns. The paucity of writing on black masculinity and its tendency to be distanced from Feminism tends also to explain its somewhat uncertain relationship to the pro-feminist agenda of Masculinity Studies. Some black masculinity approaches, for example, are decidedly anti-feminist. Carbado, in common with bell hooks, sees the One Million Men March in the USA in October 1995 as a telling instance of the continuing distance between pro-feminist agendas and many black men. This march was organised by the Nation of Islam under the leadership of Black Muslim separatist Louis Farrakhan and urged black men to take their proper place as the head of families and wrest control from black women (see Chapter 16). The march mobilised large numbers of African-American men and many significant black male activists attended, including those who had been sympathetic to black feminist endeavours and associated with reassessing black masculinity (Carbado, 1999a: 6–7; bell hooks in Grünell and Saharso, 1999: 205–7).[13]

Unlike those gay analyses distanced from Feminism, African-American men's ambiguous (or sometimes even antithetical) relationship with Feminism is more inclined to be associated with reassertions of traditional masculinity. Hence, American black men's theorising and activism may even be aligned with conservative men's groups like those on the 'backlash' side of Figure 17.1, illustrating the field of Masculinity politics in Chapter 17. In this setting, black feminist writers like Michelle Wallace and, later, bell hooks asserted in their work on black masculinity that, 'collectively black men have never critiqued the dominant culture's norms of masculine identity' (hooks, 1992b: 96; Wallace, 1979). Relatedly, important scholarly work on black masculinity has often been concerned to discuss black men's positioning as racially victimised rather than bearing any investments in gender injustice.[14] For example, Robert Staples' work is regularly and often uncritically cited (Staples, 1982; Mercer and Julien, 1988: 110–21), despite a gender analysis which assumes that black men are 'crippled' because they cannot fully partake of the hegemonic masculine ideal and asserts that black feminists are conspiring with white feminists to 'emasculate' black men (Staples, 1979). It is indicative that the essays in Carbado's edited collection, titled *Black Men on Race, Gender and Sexuality* (1999d), do 'not all … reflect feminist ideological commitments'. He notes ruefully that '[a] Black male feminist collection remains to be published' (Carbado, 1999d: 417).

Yet black masculinity writings have been able to contribute to, develop and critique Masculinity Studies. First, these writings contribute to the subfield by indicating alternate 'styles' of masculinity. These demonstrate the limits of any homogeneous and overly unified picture of masculinity and further the notion of multiple masculinities. Secondly, black masculinity writings draw attention to the frequently white and Eurocentric assumptions of the subfield. Carbado's enthusiastic support for a pro-feminist masculinity politics and scholarship faces the difficulty of the still overwhelming whiteness of Masculinity Studies (Ibid.: 423). Writers who attempt to deal with *both* gay and black masculinity issues may find themselves even more marginalised.

Conclusion

Analyses of Masculinity Studies that focus on gay men and men marginalised by REI offer some possibilities and close down some too. As yet they remain poorly integrated into the field. Sometimes this is because they express forms of politics at odds with the broadly pro-feminist approach of the subfield, but more commonly this reveals continuing heterosexual and racist/ethocentric elements in Masculinity Studies (Mercer and Julien, 1988: 122). While such elements are undoubtedly evident in the other Gender Studies subfield, Feminism, it would also seem that sexuality and REI theorising has more thoroughly reshaped feminist thinking. Possibly the, as yet, limited integration of such theorising in Masculinity Studies is a reflection of its shorter history and narrower 'pool' of contributors.

Carbado's advocacy of a pro-feminist black Masculinity politics thus faces the difficulty of the prevailing whiteness of Masculinity Studies. In similar fashion it may take time for gay theorists to find their contributions infuse the field of analysis. In addition, it is not entirely evident that women contributors to gender theorising will welcome even these additions to Masculinity Studies. For example, some black feminists remain very wary of even pro-feminist black masculinity studies (Carbado, 1999d: 423). As for writers who attempt to deal with both gay and black masculinity issues, their attempts at bringing together a combination of still peripheral concerns in Masculinity Studies remain unusual and barely acknowledged, let alone integrated into its established parameters.

Notes

1. Writings on men as men in Third World countries often follow Bob Connell's version of Socialist Social Constructionism (see Chapters 16 and 20).

2. Discussion of this potentially problematic feature of Masculinity Studies will be spelled out in greater depth in Chapter 20, and is extended in Chapter 21 when considering writers who attempt to disengage Masculinity Studies from a singular focus on men.

3. Indeed, I term the subfield Masculinity Studies, rather than Men's Studies or Studies of Masculinities, as a compromise, enabling recognition of the recent general (though not unanimous) move to the word 'masculinity' over 'men' but still acknowledging the force of debate between unified/singular and complexified (multiple) notions of masculinity.

4. The inclusive term 'Indigenous' in the Australian context is relatively recent. It is the successor term to 'Aboriginal and Torres Strait Islander' (Bourke and Bourke, 2002: 181).

5. For example, Ouzgane (2002) points out that although there has been a boom in Masculinity Studies in North America, Europe and Australia, 'scholarship on gender in Africa continues to operate ... as though African men had no gender'.

6. The example outlined is taken from Maynard (1998).

7. The notion of an 'unhappy marriage' between two forms of potentially linked modes of thinking was coined by Heidi Hartmann (1981), in relation to the uncertain relationship between Marxism and Feminism.

8. Such views follow on from the work of Gayle Rubin (see Jackson, 1998b) and Eve Kosofsky Sedgwick (see Maynard, 1998).

9. Access to reproductive technologies is typically not available to homosexuals.

10. I have noted the same strong presence of writings from the African diaspora and from North America in discussion of work by black feminists (see Chapter 6).

11. Most socially critical research on Indigenous Australians concentrates upon the drastic impact of racism in terms of dispossession, poverty and ill-treatment by the majority white community. Those critical gender studies which exist generally treat gender as about women's position, or more narrowly as about violence against women. Men are oddly sidelined. Moreover, many Indigenous women are uncertain about a focus on gender and masculinity as potentially undermining Indigenous solidarity in the face of ongoing racism. While some Indigenous male activists have raised concerns about conceptions of masculinity in Indigenous communities (notably Mick Dodson, 11 June 2003, at the Australian National Press Club), most extended analyses of Indigenous Australian men *as* men have been undertaken by women (Huggins et al., 1991; Seymour, 2001; Bhandari, 2003; Smallacombe, 2004).

12. Relatedly, many 'women of color' note that 'racial loyalty' is understood as loyalty towards men in their communities (Tessman, 1998).

13. Cornel West was one of those who attended the march, even though he has expressed support for feminist analyses of masculinity such as arise in the work of bell hooks. See West, 1999a, 1999b: 386, and in conversation with hooks, 1999d: 541–8.

14. See Carbado's detailed analysis of this (1999a: 4–11). For other contributions to the notion of black male victimhood, see also Dalton, 1999b; Brown, 1999; and Carbado, 1999b; Briggs and Davis, 1994; Potter, 1995.

20 Socialist Pro-feminism and Relational Social Constructionism – Connell

In this chapter I will outline the particularity of Socialist pro-feminist Masculinity writings, the most prevalent academic position in Masculinity Studies. It is worth noting that this distinguishes the Masculinity subfield from contemporary Feminist and Sexuality Studies. Arguably the latter subfields have been dominated by Postmodern thinking positions since at least the mid-1990s. By contrast, Masculinity Studies has only very recently shown any acquaintance with Postmodern influences and to this point has few Postmodern adherents (Pfiel, 1995; Petersen, 1998; Pease, 2000; Martino, 2000).

Socialist pro-feminism, Connell and 'relational' Social Constructionism

In outlining the particularity of Socialist pro-feminism I will draw upon the work of Bob (R.W.) Connell. Connell may now be seen as the most influential theorist in Masculinity Studies (Newton, 1998), but he initially wrote on class and capitalism. He is a Socialist and was at one point a Marxist scholar. For example, he wrote a still influential book called *Ruling Class, Ruling Culture* (1977). He continued this interest in cultural (not simply economic) accounts of class structure in the 1980s in works like *Class Structure in Australian History* with Terry Irving (2nd edition, 1992) (see also Hollier, 2003). Broadly culturalist accounts of class also show up in his work on masculinity. Class came first as a scholarly direction in his work but gender and masculinity swiftly followed. This Socialist orientation remains crucial to his writings on gender and masculinity, shaping the kind of Masculinity Studies he writes and his placement in debates in the subfield.

Connell's strong alignment with the Socialist tradition goes some way to explaining why Connell's version of Social Constructionism (SC) is much closer to that of Stevi Jackson, Lynne Segal and Jeffrey Weeks (see Chapters 12 and 13) than that of Harry Brod (Chapter 17) and is quite distant from the Radical feminist Social Constructionism of Stoltenberg (Chapter 18). Connell's version of SC is attentive to differentiation within social categories, in particular to class differentiation, while also drawing attention to macro structural hierarchies in power. In other words, he pays attention to diversity within masculinity, to multiple masculinities, while remaining strongly focused upon the overall hierarchical positioning of men as a group in relation to women as a group. This nuanced reading of macro power relations refuses sharply oppositional conceptions of binary gender power and unitary notions of gender identities. Men, in Connell's analysis, are not all in exactly the same social position, even in their relation to women.

Such a complex approach, which resists any simple identity politics in favour of focusing on the multiform yet broadly hierarchical *relations of power*, shares much with the analyses of Jackson, Segal and Weeks. It is, however, somewhat distant from Brod's version of Socialist Social Constructionism, which is inclined to retain a unitary account of masculinity in order to stress the question of gender power rather than diversity within Masculinity Studies. Brod's more categorical analysis moves towards the comparatively absolutist approach of Radical pro-feminist Social Constructionism associated with John Stoltenberg. On the basis of these comparisons, I have termed Connell's model 'relational Social Constructionism'.

Connell is an Australian academic and most definitely draws upon this background in all his work. Australia is strongly associated with the Socialist pro-feminist variant of Social Constructionism in Masculinity Studies. Like the UK and Europe, Australia has a long-standing cultural attachment to, or at least lack of horror, concerning Marxism, **Socialism** and anti-capitalist agendas among intellectuals as well as in popular culture. As Messner (1997: 60) notes, this has always been a less comfortable position in the USA, which by comparison has never had a strong Socialist or Social Democratic (welfare state-oriented) movement and is dominated by forms of Liberalism.

Connell is a sociologist who has mostly taught and lived in Australia, apart from a brief sojourn in California. He has published prodigiously over many years, initially in relation to class, but also on education, AIDS, men's health, sexuality, men's bodies, sport and psychoanalysis. His most important contribution from the point of view of this book lies in his articulation of crucial perspectives on gender and masculinity. He is one of the main writers in the English-speaking world on the term 'gender' and his work undoubtedly provides the 'central reference point for many, if not most, writers on men and masculinity' (Wetherell and Edley, 1998: 156). He started writing in the field of Masculinity Studies well before the rush in the 1990s, well before it was fashionable or established. He is certainly no fly-by-night, recent contributor to this subject. His most crucial publications on gender and masculinity are *Gender and Power: Society, the Person and Sexual Politics* (1987), *Masculinities* (1995), *The Men and the Boys* (2000) and *Gender* (2002). Connell is also (like Stoltenberg) an activist and writes accessibly with the aim of a broad audience. He is particularly interested in issue-based solidarity work.

In this chapter I will first offer some introductory remarks on the relationship between Socialist pro-feminisms and other pro-feminist positions in Masculinity Studies. I will follow this with a discussion of Connell's account of gender and masculinity as socially constructed, rather than based in sex roles or pre-formed identity categories. In order to illustrate his Socialist pro-feminist *and* Social Constructionist perspective I will consider his account of the terms 'gender' and 'masculinity' and how he conceives them by attending to historical detail and to class/capitalism. This historical and material/economic orientation produces a macro relational account of gender (of relations between men and women in particular) and a focus on multiplicity with regard to masculinity (within which the relational analysis of gender tends to drop away). I will then look more closely at Connell's approach to masculinity. In particular, this chapter examines his concern with a multiple rather than monolithic model in which men do not benefit equally, a direction that leads him towards a consideration of dominant or 'hegemonic masculinity' as well as 'other' masculinities. Finally, I will discuss Connell's account of politics/strategy in the light of his understanding of masculinity. I will point out issues and debates as I go along.

Socialist pro-feminism and the critique of identity/categorical politics

Masculinity Studies, as I have noted before, is almost entirely pro-feminist. Though these writing do not dismiss the pain and costs of masculinity to men, as well as women, they always to a lesser or greater degree also emphasise power relations and men's dominance over women (Messner, 1997: 55–62). They acknowledge and typically focus, in other words, on gender hierarchy and gender injustice.

While Men's Liberation (a form of Liberal pro-feminism) was more inclined to stress men's costs rather than their advantages and did not strongly focus on gendered power, Radical (Stoltenberg) and Socialist (Connell) pro-feminisms both concentrate upon power and the unequal benefits of gender. However, while Radical and Socialist pro-feminists often work hand in hand in men's organisations, and have a similarly strong relation to Feminism, they do employ different approaches and have somewhat different histories.

Radical pro-feminism has rather diminished over time along with other revolutionary and categorical approaches. Its strong rejection of masculinity and tendency to concentrate on the problematic character of men's sexuality was never particularly widely accepted in masculinity *politics* beyond its association with work on men's violence and on men's consumption of pornography. Moreover, it is now largely out of favour in Masculinity Studies as insufficiently nuanced and overly absolutist about men. Established Socialist and emerging Postmodern doubts about homogeneous and absolute accounts of identities have had a part to play in this loss of favour. Radical pro-feminists' antagonism to the social category of masculinity – on the grounds that it is a positioning steeped in violence and injustice and is therefore irredeemable – has frequently been viewed as inducing a politics of guilt, antagonism to men and as kowtowing to Feminism. Socialist pro-feminism represents a firm rejection of much of this (Newton, 1998).

While supporting the view that 'men's dominant position in the gender order has a ... pay-off' – that is, a definite *material* as well as symbolic pay-off – for men, Socialist pro-feminists like Connell argue that this pay-off, or 'patriarchal dividend', is not spread equally. (Take note here of the class-oriented language deployed to describe gender relations.) According to Connell, specific groups of men gain very little of this dividend. Some groups 'pay part of the price, alongside women', for the unequal gender order (Connell, 2000: 202, 203).

This insight regarding the unequal rewards of Masculinity is strongly related to Socialist pro-feminism's awareness of class in particular. Writers developing this framework, unlike Radical pro-feminists, are not likely to see class-privileged and working-class men as sharing equally in the social rewards of gender. Socialist pro-feminists most particularly break up the category of 'men' and men's power by declaring that there are 'divisions of interest [between] among men on gender issues' (Ibid.: 203). They also indicate that there are interests that some men share with at least some women (for example, the requirement for childcare provisions) and by implication at least they also suggest differences in women's positioning.

All of this results in a refusal to cast masculinity as an absolute unity, as utterly distinct from and always privileged over all women, as only productive of and responsible for violence and injustice. Socialist pro-feminists reject such a thoroughly antagonistic account of masculinity and the self-hatred they see as associated with it. Socialist pro-feminists reject 'guilt and "refusing to be a man" as a place from which to speak', while insistently foregrounding the social reality of unequal gendered power relations.[1] Though critical of masculinities that are at the top of the heap, they are not antagonistic to men or manhood *per se* and are supportive of (progressive) men. They are also willing to be critical of Feminism (rather than kowtowing to it) (Newton, 1998).

Socialist pro-feminist writings indicate a discomfort with wholesale critiques of manhood (Ibid.). Socialist pro-feminist views are usually interpreted on this account as displaying a 'healthy' distance from Feminism. However, there might be other factors at play here. This discomfort could also be considered in terms of a response within the context of Masculinity writings. It might be a response to the absolutism of Radical pro-feminism in particular and to Masculinity writings from other categorical perspectives in masculinity politics like the Mythopoetic approach. In similar fashion, gay and REI commentaries tend to provide wholesale undifferentiated accounts of heterosexual white masculinity. Socialist pro-feminism represents a theoretical direction in Masculinity Studies which attempts to complicate all these accounts to some degree.

Having placed Socialist pro-feminist approaches in context, it is now possible to look at some more specific features of this framework and concentrate on Connell's work a little more.

Relational Social Constructionism

1. Gender as relational

Connell offers an account of gender that illustrates the difference between Socialist pro-feminism and other Masculinity Studies approaches. He describes gender as 'a social practice', which refers to bodies (that is, sex), but is not reducible to bodily sex or reproduction (Connell, 2000: 27).[2] Gender, in this analysis, is an organisation of social patterns or structures that can be impersonal or personal in orientation. Gender is a social structure, or socially organised set of practices forming relationships between people, rather than a matter of *kinds* of people (Ibid.: 24).

This is a very different framework from the one offered by Men's Liberation (Liberal Pro-feminism), with its focus on different sex roles. It is also different from Radical pro-feminism's focus on gender as a strictly binary or dichotomous arrangement, which produces sharply distinct kinds of people (the gender categories of men and women). Connell asserts that these gender category-based approaches cannot grasp the 'complexities of gender' and thus promote universalising and ethnocentric generalisations about men and women (Ibid.: 19). In this account Connell shows how Socialist pro-feminism offers a Social Constructionist perspective, in that his analysis rejects biological and identity/category-based essentialism. He rejects, in short, any view of a homogeneous, singular and fixed (essential) core to gender categories.

This stance enables Connell to perceive some links between his approach and the more thorough-going social constructionism associated with the Postmodern framework. Nevertheless, he perhaps rather dismissively suggests that writers like Foucault and Butler have little to offer to analysis of gender. Foucault's approach is rejected on the grounds that he 'had no gender theory at all' and Butler's work is discarded on the basis that it is 'strikingly unable' to account for 'material' social aspects of gender such as childcare, institutional life and work (Ibid.: 20). In this context, Connell specifically characterises his work as a 'structural' approach in contrast to the 'discursive' orientation of Postmodern masculinity theorising. Such Postmodern analyses, he states, 'have significant limits' because they 'give no grip' on vitally significant elements of gender, such as 'economic equality and the state' or 'poverty and global change'. These analyses are poorly integrated with 'more general theories of social change', which examine neo-liberalism, market society and the question of violence throughout the contemporary world. Additionally, Postmodern analyses, in Connell's view, are too abstract and cannot adequately attend to the 'situationally specific production of gender', including 'the development of gender identities through the life cycle', because they largely fail to consider the full range of evidence and rarely consider quantitative research. In short, Connell distinguishes his own Social Constructionist approach from Postmodern work largely on the basis of the former's concern with, on the one hand, macro-level class analysis and, on the other, the detail of empirical study (Connell, 2003).

Connell makes here a case for a 'materialist' analysis of gender (meaning a Socialist-inflected analysis concerned with the concrete specificity of the socio-historical shaping of bodies and forms of labour for subsistence, reproduction and nurture) (Andermahr et al., 2000: 158–60). Such an approach focuses on macro, institutional 'interests' or benefits associated with a particular gender order and men's variable placements in this gender order. On this basis he focuses on life histories, on detailed research about actual men's lives, as studies of 'social structures' (Drummond, 2002: 129–30).

2. The social production of Gender and Masculinity

According to Connell, the Socialist pro-feminist or 'materialist' approach promotes a social relational account of gender and masculinity, and avoids a category/identity-based essentialism, in a number of ways.

1. This approach discusses 'masculinity' not 'men', which avoids a strict dichotomy of men versus women (Connell, 2000: 16). Masculinity may or may not be taken up by both sexes and is not firmly aligned to a male body in the same way as it is in the term 'men'.
2. The approach stresses the historical, fluid and non-static character of masculinity.
3. Socialist pro-feminism also emphasises the relational processual nature of gender rather than focusing on dichotomous groups of people. It attends to diversity within gender groupings and in gendered practices rather than to the one truth of masculinity.
4. In particular, it pays attention to multiple masculinities.

With regard to the first point, it is evident that Connell avoids strictly dichotomous accounts of gender and masculinity without sacrificing a concern with gender power. Connell does make Modernist macro statements about masculinity, men and power, which – like those from Brod and Stoltenberg – reflect a fundamental sense of the overarching significance of a dichotomous gender order organised around two sexes. He says in this context, 'Men *in general* gain a patriarchal dividend' (Ibid.: 209, emphasis added). However, while this overarching gender binary largely offers greater rewards to men, it contains within it a pyramid-like arrangement of these rewards. Certain masculinities operate as 'ideal types' (hegemonic or socially dominant forms) which function to produce wide support from men for men's position of dominance. Men who approximate these ideal types are especially rewarded as 'real men'. In other words, he says, while men mostly do better than women in the gender order, some men do significantly better than others. These general categorical-type statements do refer to gender identities. While such identity categories are not entirely dismantled or refused, they are also not taken as given. They are also critiqued, de-naturalised and, importantly, de-massified. This amounts to an archetypal Social Constructionist 'in-between' stance of critical engagement with identities alongside a concern with placing these identities in material social structures (see also Chapter 13).

In relation to the second point, Connell's concern to see gender as historical (as fluid over time) enables him to present the non-static character of masculinity and hence refute categorical and/or essentialist (including biologically based) conceptions of it. All the same, this historical orientation arguably leads him to present masculinity in a delimited fashion. I suggest that Connell, in his macro and historical moments, presumes that masculinity (a gender category) is to be understood by its constitution through class relations. Connell asserts, for instance, that the very concept of masculinity is linked to early capitalism. He proposes that we are witnessing a struggle between a masculinity developed in 'imperialist ventures' (in relation to empire-building) – based on racialised group status and violent domination – and a more recent modern ideal of masculinity based on competitive individualism and technical unemotional expertise (Connell, 1995: 80–6, 185–203, 2000: 40–56; Newton, 1998). In this account it can be argued that there is a tendency to conceive history and social change through the lens of, as equivalent to, changing class relations. Though Kate Hughes's analysis of Connell's perspective is not intended to make this point, her summary of it supports my interpretation. She says Connell 'provides an interesting analysis of the ways in which globalisation has exported a version of patriarchy … to cultures whose economies have come to be vulnerable to such [multinational executives] and to such corporations' (Hughes, 2001: 46).

This slippage into a primarily class-based reading of gender (and race/ethnicity) appears related to a failure to imagine any specific historical periodisation for *gender* relations. Connell's 'structural' theorising is inclined to conceive class *as* Structure (with a capital 'S'), to position class as *the* formative active force in history and social change. While gender certainly gives particular characteristics to globalising capitalism, it seems to be carried along by and within host class relations, a comparatively passive and responsive sub-structure.[3]

Nevertheless, masculinity is here linked to institutions, economics and everyday life. It is part of domestic *and* public history. It is a *socially constructed* account.

Masculinity is not biologically fixed or monolithic, and it is linked to Socialist concerns regarding class structures. Perhaps because of Connell's concern not to fall into making women equally responsible for this historically shaped gender order, women seem to disappear from empire and capitalism. It seems as if men and class structures (which are also seemingly predominantly made up of men) make history (Newton, 1998). Moreover, men's sexuality appears to drop away from this macro analysis (see Chapter 19). On this basis, it is a partial account of social formation. This issue is of some consequence when considering the third point concerning Connell's relational emphasis.

Connell presents gender and masculinity as *relational*, rather than as about gender identity differences. To understand gendered power, argues Connell, we must move beyond men and women, beyond identity categories characterised as discrete and dichotomous which encourage a notion of their separation as distinct classes of person. Focusing on difference between groups and locating gender in the supposed characteristics of these groups, he suggests, assumes that these group categories have an inherent and set meaning and that these supposed differences in characteristics *cause* power differentials. Rather, Connell says, we should shift to a focus on 'social relations' (Connell, 2002: 9). Our concern should be to consider macro relations *between* groups of people, while avoiding simple dichotomies. This enables us also to see differences among women and among men, and connections between men and women, as well as gender hierarchy.

This relational approach means that Connell sees distinct problems with studying one gender in isolation from other gender categories (Moore, 1998: 1–2). 'Men's Studies' programmes that exclusively focus on men would not gain his support. Similarly, Connell disputes with 'men's health' discourses that discuss their health as entirely distinct from women's health (Schofield et al., 2000). With his co-authors, he notes that these kinds of discourse exclude any conception of men and women as groups connected through specific social mechanisms that may be significant in terms of considering health issues. For example, the over-representation of men in industrial injuries does not necessarily say anything about 'being a man' *per se*, but says a great deal about men's historical over-representation in the most hazardous industries and occupations. For Connell, the relation between the genders in the division of labour is an aspect of this health issue. In the case of women, the point remains the same. Women's higher rates of depression and mental illness disappear when married men and women both share paid and domestic duties. Once again gender relations rather than something specific to women shape health (Ibid.).

This relational approach is very different from the dichotomous categorical emphasis of Radical pro-feminists like Stoltenberg (Chapter 18), even if Connell's relational approach seems to sometimes drop away. As I have noted earlier, in his historical analyses, women's contributions seems to disappear (Newton, 1998).

With regard to the fourth point, Connell stresses that gender positions such as masculinity are multiple and not fixed identities. Masculinity is not an homogeneous or unified category. I have said that Connell explores this by noting class/race/sexuality differences and differential rewards associated with these sub-groupings. However, Connell is most famous for undermining fixity in identities and stressing multiplicity by focusing upon ideal types of masculinity which support hierarchy among men.

Postmodern discussions of masculinity stress the fluidity, internal instability and performative quality of identities, including gender identities (see Chapter 21). Social Constructionists in Masculinity Studies with an anthropological focus, like Gilbert Herdt, show masculinity's cross-cultural variability. For example, among the Sambia of the New Guinea highlands boys achieve adult masculinity through fellatio and ingesting semen (Herdt, 1981; Moore, 1998; Connell, 2001; for other related work, see Hogg, 2002). However, Connell's account of multiple masculinities is most strongly associated with the term 'hegemonic masculinity'. The term derives from Italian Marxist Antonio Gramsci's usage of 'hegemony', meaning a cultural/moral leadership role assumed by ruling elites to ensure popular or mass consent to their coercive rule and thus the continuance of the status quo (Milner and Browitt, 2002: 231; Ashcroft et al., 1998: 116–17). In Connell's usage the 'ideal type' of hegemonic masculinity is not particularly tied to a ruling identifiable group with specific interests but rather involves a socially dominant ideal of manhood which consolidates solidarity among men for the maintenance of masculine authority. This dominant ideal of manhood encourages men in particular to identify with this idealisation as the natural, proper and best masculinity and to be constituted in relation to its protocols. The characteristics of this leading ideal differ over time, in cultures, and even within social sub-cultures.

Hegemonic masculinity in Western cultures equates to male domination and oppression of women/femininities as well as subordinated/marginalised masculinities. Its tenets, according to Connell, are heterosexuality, homophobia and misogyny.[4] It offers 'cultural authority and leadership' and is 'highly visible' (Connell, 2001: 8). This term is sometimes used simply to refer to the common or main form of masculinity, but Connell is actually concerned with its 'top' or honoured positioning rather than with prevalence. Indeed, he notes that hegemonic masculinity may actually describe the position of a minority of men (Connell, 2000: 30). Elite sportsmen epitomise this iconic form in Australia (Ibid.: 69–85, 2001; Drummond, 2002). Gay men are subordinated in this idealisation, while 'black' men (for example, in Australia and the USA) are marginalised.

The question is, 'does this terminology and focus on multiple masculinities amount to a neat way of evading responsibility?', as Brod suggests. Certainly it does enable many, perhaps even most men to be configured – along with women – as victims too, victims of a socially structured and enforced false image. If most men are not the bad guys, and the problem lies in a largely unlocatable, amorphous bad ideal upheld by a powerful minority, this raises the issue of whether this more complex and nuanced account lets men off the hook.

Politics and strategy

Connell is not particularly focused on personal self-analysis. For him, transformation occurs through collective and public politics. He is suspicious of men's groups that focus on self-help and therapy and suggests that the best strategic mode should not be a men's movement which parallels Feminism (Newton, 1998; Connell, 2000: 208–11). Rather, he says, any decent masculinity politics worth its salt will more likely divide than unite men (Connell, 2001). The best approach is short-term coalitions around issues that unite men and women and are not centrally around gender division (Newton, 1998). Despite his belief that gender disparities could get worse, he remains optimistic, as optimistic now as much as he was in the 1980s.

Conclusion

Connell's approach appears generous, inclusive and supportive and yet it remains (like most of Masculinity Studies) an approach written by a man about others similar to himself – that is, white, middle-class, straight guys. Women are mentioned but ironically in rather homogeneous terms and only in passing, and gays and black men are mentioned largely in terms of 'negatively [defining] what straight (white) masculinities can mean' (Ibid.). Perhaps the very things which make it an attractive point of view for Connell's male audience are precisely what makes it a still circumscribed perspective that may replicate the centre-stage privileging of dominant masculinity that it endeavours so strongly to resist.

Notes

1. See Socialist pro-feminists, Kimmel (1996: 334), Brod (1987b: 9) and Seidler (1990) for a rejection of antagonism to manhood and Radical pro-feminist, Stoltenberg ([1989] 2000a), for the strategy of refusing manhood. See also Newton, 1998.

2. Hawksworth (1997b) has provided a rare critical assessment of his account of gender. She asserts that, as he goes about defining the term gender, he unthinkingly affirms a narrow reproductive meaning for the term – defining gender as a set of social structures concerned with fixing men and women as categories organised by their reproductive role. Hawkesworth suggests that his diminished definition of the term may be contrasted with a broader, more nuanced understanding of it in his discussions of gender as social practices.

3. This assessment of Connell's approach draws attention to a tendency that is widely evident in Socialist analyses generally and can be seen in other Socialist pro-feminist writings, but is not at all accepted in Socialist feminism. Socialist feminists have argued lengthily that class cannot be privileged as the active shaping force in history and social change, and gender cannot be seen as primarily responsive. See Andermahr et al., 2000: 253–4; Beasley, 1999: 62–3; Bryson, 1992: 232–60.

4. In Connell's definition of hegemonic masculinity, race/ethnicity appears for the most part to drop away. Race/ethnicity reappears in his discussion of hegemonic masculinity and globalisation.

21 Queer(ing) Masculinity Studies: Female Masculinity – Halberstam

In this last chapter on specific frameworks, I examine a theoretical trajectory that in many ways provides highly appropriate subject matter. This trajectory offers a fitting end point because it is a perspective in which Gender and Sexuality Studies within the overall gender/sexuality field both meet and perhaps collide. Postmodern/Queer approaches in Masculinity Studies include writings which draw upon and show the possible limitations of both gender and sexuality.

I have noted previously that the subfield of Masculinity Studies is largely not particularly Postmodern, although its writers show an increasing awareness of this framework. Nevertheless, an as yet relatively small body of such postmodern contributions is emerging: they focus on the non-natural aspects of masculinity and question the naturalness of masculinity by indicating the constructed nature of the normative. For some this involves a focus on masculinity as performative, following Butler – for example, Mark Simpson's *Male Impersonators* (1994). For others it leads to a concern with the cultural representations of masculinity (Pfiel, 1995). It may also produce an increasing unwillingness to always conceive masculinity in terms of men's dominance over women, such that dependence on feminist analysis and the stability of gender categories in terms of their position in relation to power is placed in doubt (Newton, 1998).

What I have decided to focus on is one form of Postmodern/Queer theorising that concentrates on avoiding any reduction of masculinity to the male body, and to men. This form of analysis therefore radically brings to bear Postmodern and Queer attention to both gender and sexuality. My intention here is to use this work as the final exemplary case, if you like, of present debates on Gender and Sexuality Studies. This work is Postmodern *and* Queer in that it refuses macro and universal conceptions of truth, power, society and the self as well as specifically applying this insight within the framework of non-essentialist, non-naturalist accounts of gender/sexuality. In suggesting a Masculinity Studies without men, without male-born bodies, this approach is radically at variance with almost all writings in the subfield. If Postmodern/Queer approaches are not particularly common, then those which do not interpret '"masculinity" as a synonym for men or maleness' are indeed few and far between (Halberstam, 1998: 12; see also Rubin, 1992).

What Halberstam has named 'female masculinity' offers 'gender variance' and sexual dissidence. We have touched on this area before in looking at the work of Trans theorists, such as Stephen Whittle and Pat Califia, whose analyses from the point of view of female-to-male (FTM) positioning are outlined in Chapters 9 and 14 respectively. These writers attend to Gender and Sexuality Studies and provide useful ways in which to consider their interconnections. In the context of this Chapter, I will focus on the specific question of a masculinity analysis without men, not because it is an uncommon focus but precisely because Judith Halberstam claims that masculinity 'becomes legible', understandable when it leaves the domain of 'dominant masculinity'. She asserts that we may learn a great deal more about masculinity if we look at masculinities which undermine any straightforward wedding of masculinity 'to maleness and to power and domination' (Halberstam, 1998: 2). Indeed, Halberstam suggests that the focus of Masculinity Studies upon masculinity as men/male bodies tends to sustain this connection. A focus on subordinate or marginalised masculinities offers a corrective, in her view.

Halberstam's concern with 'female masculinity' therefore represents a different direction from most Masculinity writings, but at the same time her work offers support for the criticisms raised by gay and REI masculinity writers. In other words, like most writing considering Trans issues, Halberstam's analysis may be placed at the cross-roads of multiple Differences and Postmodern/Queer theoretical trajectories. As I noted in Chapter 19, both the predominant stream of Masculinity writers who deal with 'hegemonic masculinity' and gay/REI masculinity writers insist that marginalised and subordinated masculinities are central to the construction of 'masculinity' (as the social valued gender identity). The 'abject' (ignored, disavowed or tokenistically exoticised) versions of masculinity highlight, it is argued, what 'proper', idealised manhood *is*. However, as I have indicated, in practice the predominant stream of Masculinity Studies concentrates upon 'hegemonic masculinity', and pays rather limited attention to alternate masculinities that destabilise masculinity's claims to power and reveal the differential rewards and costs accruing to manhood for different groups. Female masculinity, a masculinity without men or male bodies, clearly undermines the myth of masculinity as the promise of social privilege and authority, and extends even further the critique of Masculinity Studies offered by gay and REI masculinity writers by refusing to accept any naturalised basis for manhood or indeed, more controversially, any necessary connection between masculinity and power.

I will now briefly indicate how this perspective has come into being – its relationship to Queer Theory – and then suggest how it nevertheless is not simply Queer in terms of dismantling gender or in terms of sexuality. Following these preliminary comments, I will point out the particularities of the framework, its challenge to Masculinity Studies, and debates related to this challenge.

Female masculinity and Queer Theory

The fracturing of monolithic understandings of men/masculinity along Postmodern/Queer lines is often associated in the gender/sexuality field with Eve Kosofky Sedgwick's work on the historical character of masculinity in her book, *Between Men* (1985). It is also linked to the Gayle Rubin's (1984) essay on sexuality, 'Thinking sex' (see also Wiegman, 2001a).[1] Both of these analyses suggested in different ways the beginnings of a self-consciously Queer approach. Within their formulations of Queer thinking, masculinity is seen as partaking of both gender and sexuality,[2] but these elements are disarticulated and do not always work hand in hand. For example, in Sedgwick's book she notes that in some cultures masculinity involves power over women, and at the same time sex between men along class-based lines is expected. In other cultures like our own, sex between men is violently rejected. Masculinity is thus not always the same: nor is it the same for all men (Wiegman, 2001a). Men's power over women, notes Sedgwick, does not necessarily tell you much about their sexual relations with men. In similar fashion Rubin (1984: 33) suggests that gender and sexuality amount to 'two distinct areas of social practice'.

These analyses together suggested the incoherence of masculinity; its non-unitary historically variable character, its framing as both relationship between men and between men and women, and, most particularly, its social framing rather than natural foundation. Such analyses also coincided with movements in Masculinity Studies to differentiate hierarchally organised forms of masculinity as social practices rather than viewing masculinity as an expression of biology (Connell, 1987; Segal, 1990). This anti-biological, largely Social Constructionist account (Chapters 12 and 20) was developed still further in Judith Butler's *Gender Trouble* in 1990 (Chapters 8 and 9).

Butler's analysis not only rejected the view that gender identities, including masculinity, were founded on some essential location in bodily sex, but additionally asserted that notions of bodily sex difference were themselves effects of socially organised gender. Butler used both gay male drag and the figure of the intersexed hermaphrodite to question the fixity of gender and the self-evidence of the body as showing the essential truth of gender. This form of scholarship, primarily located under the term Queer Theory, made possible the line of enquiry that is associated with Halberstam's work on 'female masculinity'. As Wiegman (2001a: 357, 377) puts it, here the Postmodern critique 'is taken to its critical extreme, as masculinity and men are severed altogether' in order to relocate the question of masculinity away from the male body 'to the realm of identification'.

Halberstam's approach disarticulates male from masculine and indeed masculine from men. And since masculine in her analysis no longer speaks of men, the gender hierarchy and sexualities that cluster around *men* are no longer necessarily part of this masculine. In a Masculinity Studies that abandons men there can be no pre-given assumption that the social-historical features that have attached to male masculinity will also be found in female masculinity. Here masculinity is merely an 'identification'. It is not tied to a sexed body and apparently escapes the biological. It also appears to escape the social, since it is no longer conceived in historical terms and aspects of masculinity's social production, as a positionality whose definition rests upon the subordinated status of women, seem to disappear. By contrast with Social Constructionist accounts, for example, masculinity in Halberstam's reading is not viewed as a relational institutional form firmly tied into gender and sexuality regimes. Halberstam posits the emergence of a masculinity, shorn of its history of being about dominance.

Female masculinity, she says, is a specific subordinate masculinity, and not just a copy. It cannot be a copy, since this assumes that there is a 'real' masculine. Female masculinity is a powerful 'style', not *social* dominance. This specific form of masculinity is not the same as male masculinity. It escapes the associations between male masculinity and dominance. Where male masculinity is constituted through its embedded location in social institutions and practices like the state, the military and so on, female masculinity seems to be rather more small-scale, an individual mode of being (Halberstam, 2001: 15). It escapes the social engagements of male masculinity and makes new, more individualised ones.

Distance from Queer

Is this analysis to be identified with Queer? For all its intellectual linkages to Postmodern and Queer theorising about masculinity, Halberstam's approach also stands at an interesting remove from Queer. Halberstam explicitly deploys what she calls a 'queer methodology', referring here to 'a certain disloyalty to conventional disciplinary methods' that enable her to draw upon textual analysis, historical research and ethnography in her discussion of female masculinity (Halberstam, 1998: 10; Antoniou, 2000: 381). Nevertheless, inasmuch as Halberstam's analysis considers the tough/strong woman, the tomboy, the butch lesbian, the drag king, the stone butch,[3] and FTMs (female-to-male transsexuals), she enables a discussion of ambiguous, possibly dissident gender identifications which does not disallow the transsexual desire for a gender 'home'. This open framing[4] of the analysis includes identifications that sit at a distance from the emphasis in Queer theorising upon destablising gender/sexuality identities (see Chapters 8, 9 and 15). Instead, female masculinity for Halberstam 'overlaps' with Transgender, 'an umbrella term (coined in the late 1980s) ... for cross-identifying subjects' (Halberstam, 2001: 15, 14). In this respect Halberstam's work should be seen in the light of Trans theories, which typically speak for those who do not necessarily wish to reside outside of identity categories altogether, but rather want to claim particular categories in the face of normative policing (Ibid.: 15).

Indeed, she says (following Jay Prosser (1998))[5] that Judith Butler's highly influential Queer analysis of gender and sexuality identities as 'performative' precisely threatens the desire of some transgendered persons to enact a 'realness' of gender locations, even as they may or may not be especially committed to maintaining the reality of particular body parts associated with men and women. Female masculinity may not require or indeed be able to achieve a functional penis and yet decidedly claim manliness. Halberstam notes Prosser's point that so long as this positioning involves transgender ambiguity it is lauded in Queer Theory as transgression, but as soon as it shifts to transsexual gender transition (from female to male), the positioning is ignominiously cast out as gender/sexuality conformity (Prosser, 1998: 14–17). Halberstam (2000: 313) is persuaded that the transsexual in Butler's work is placed in opposition to Queer. Halberstam's concern with the entire gamut of female masculinity leads her to critique what she sees as Butler's exclusionary tactics (Halberstam, 1994: 220). Queer thinking is, in this context, depicted as ironically upholding a particular norm of Queer identity, which runs counter to its own rhetoric of destablising identity and refusing identity's exclusions.

Halberstam (2001: 16–17) also notes Prosser's point that Butler's insistence on instability, on not attaining a gender identity, precisely stresses that which is the most unsettling and unsafe option for transgenders. Halberstam and Prosser argue that transgenders 'become real' by 'inhabiting categories of their own making' (Ibid.: 18). This may or may not involve body modification of various kinds, social presentation/display, and legal recognition. As a 'cultivated' gender/sexuality position, 'female masculinity' is a term that recognises the whole history of transgendered persons rather than a final outcome, unlike transsexual histories which often render invisible early parts of the story (their sex/gender designation at birth) to become 'real' men or women (Ibid.: 20).

In Halberstam's Transgender theorising, masculinity becomes a project (a gender process) in a very strong and intimate sense. While in some ways her account is very distant from the materialist and macro *Social* Constructionist analysis of masculinity associated with Connell, it does extend Connell's analysis of gender as a material socially (rather than biologically) shaped process in a very practical sense. Female masculinity is precisely not biologically based, though materially constituted and socially 'cultivated'. Indeed, in certain respects Halberstam's work might be said to be more definitively historical than that of Connell and most other Masculinity Studies writers. She demonstrates the historical relationship between the 'normal' (male) masculinity – which such writers take as their subject (typically rendering the historical specificity of its normality invisible) – and 'other' masculinities deemed perverted or 'hyper-real', such as female masculinity (Raffo, 1998: 28). Almost without exception Masculinity Studies writers start, and usually end, with the normal. Even if they perhaps (though rarely) mention 'alternative' masculinities that are not constituted by a male body, this observation 'seems remarkably difficult to follow through on' (Halberstam, 1998: 14).[6] The result is that, no matter how historically and empirically detailed the analysis of most Masculinity writing, the grounding of this analysis is not historically/socially specified, to the extent that 'an essential relation between masculinity and men' is reinforced (Ibid.).

The subject matter of almost all of Masculinity Studies is masculinity as it is usually understood – that is, male masculinity. From this starting point such studies move into investigations of the particularity of masculinity (in time and across cultures). By contrast, Halberstam considers a prior question – the historical particularity of this usual understanding. In so doing, she examines the historical constructedness, 'the strangeness of all gendered bodies', not only the transgender, 'alternative' ones (a point to which I will return) (Halberstam, 1994: 226).

Halberstam's approach also offers concrete social specificity to Queer thinking. Although Halberstam differs from Butler's proposals regarding gender performativity, she does engage with Butler's account of the non-natural unstable basis of identities in a decidedly material way. In many ways Halberstam's 'female masculinity' provides a remarkably embodied (material) and practical exemplar of gender ambiguity, which avoids the inclination to abstraction in a good deal of Queer theorising (Halberstam, 2000: 313, 2001: 16). Yet, despite Halberstam's assertion that female masculinity describes not simply an identity but a social relationality between people, both intimate and communal, her understanding of this figure as residing in 'the realm of identification' and as distanced from the social associations of masculinity (such as masculinity's association with the subordination of women) suggests that it somehow stands in isolation. In these respects, female masculinity appears as disembodied from the historical/social formation of masculinity.

Characteristic features and relation
to Masculinity Studies

Halberstam (and other Transgender writers like Califia) offers significant reconfigu-
rations of gender and sexuality that are not simply identifiable with positions in
Masculinity Studies or Queer. The notion of female masculinity rejects conservative,
biologistic notions of female masculinity as about 'real men', but also rejects femi-
nist/gender-oriented and lesbian/sexuality-oriented critiques of this positioning as disloyal to women or to same-sex identities. These critiques of Transgender theorising
suggest that writers like Halberstam are merely reasserting the normative. For example, Molly, a character in Rita Mae Brown's famous novel *Rubyfruit Jungle* (1973)
exclaims upon entering a butch-femme bar:

> That's the craziest dumbass thing I ever heard tell off. What's the point of being a les-
> bian if a woman is going to look and act like an imitation man? Hell, if I want a man, I'll
> get the real thing, not one of these chippies. (Cited in Sinfield, 2002)

Similarly, in Leslie Fienberg's more recent novel, *Stone Butch Blues* (1993: 151), the
character Theresa protests when her lover Jess begins to take hormones to pass as a man:

> I'm a woman, Jess. I love you because you're a woman too. ... I'm a femme ... If I'm
> not with a butch everyone just assumes I'm straight. ... I've worked hard to be dis-
> criminated against as a lesbian'. (Cited in Sinfield, 2002)

Halberstam's female masculinity refuses the notion of a copy and suggests instead
its dissidence is just another way of life like any other. Rather than stressing the non-
natural and indeed political character of social identities by focusing on what is excluded
from them (Hale, 1996: 94), Halberstam notes their constructed, political nature by
concentrating positively on their permeability. In the process she gives attention to a
range of 'types' of gender variance. She is, however, particularly drawn to stories of lesbian female masculinity rather than heterosexual female masculinities (Halberstam,
1998: 28). In particular, she pays attention to a female masculinity which asserts itself
as not woman, but also at a distance from the category man – that is, the butch (Ibid.:
19, 21, and photographs on 34, 36–7, see also 1999). However, her inclusive understanding of butch is not limited only to those whom Queer thinkers like Butler have
taken under their wing (Butler, 1990: 123).[7] Her understanding is not restricted to
those presenting ambiguity – those alluding to masculinity (or even masquerading as
men) but whose 'purpose is to pursue particular ways of being women'. Halberstam's
butch asserts other possible alternatives, including cross-identifying subjects whose aim
may not be ambiguity but a form of manhood (Halberstam, 1994: 220; Sinfield, 2002).

This expansive perspective leads her to consider, among other possibilities, the work
of drag-kings like Mo B. Dick who 'celebrates butch culture', yet offers the opportunity
'to purge conflicting love/hate feelings' about men and men's authority (Che, 2001:
67; Joiner, 2002). Halberstam's commentary in *The Drag King Book* (with Volcano,
1999) provides an extended study of such issues. She has also spent some time considering cases of gender/sexuality variance like that of Brandon Teena (whose story

was outlined in the 1999 feature film *Boys Don't Cry*) and Billy Tipton. Brandon Teena was born female but later successfully passed as a young man in a small North American town. Teena was then raped and murdered in 1993 when this dissidence between a female body and social masculinity was discovered. Billy Tipton was a jazz musician who was found to have a female body after his death in 1993, though he had married a number of times. These examples do not fit comfortably into transsexual or gay/lesbian identities. They indicate instead what she calls a 'complex personhood' under the sign of the masculine. (Halberstam, 2001: 13, 28, 35).

The analysis Halberstam elaborates not only puts into question many of the traditionally cherished (or discredited) aspects of masculinity, but also the framing of Masculinity Studies. Halberstam not only rejects any assumption that masculinity = gender dominance along the lines proposed by Stoltenberg (Chapter 18), but explicitly accuses the bulk of Masculinity writers of re-centring 'the white male body' (Halberstam, 1998: 4, 2). She is quite scathing about approaches which obscure other masculinities even when their intention (in focusing upon hegemonic masculinities) is to attend to men's shared patriarchal dividend (shared rewards) (Ibid.: 16–17). The suggestion here is that this reiteration of a traditional focus on dominant masculinities amounts to the continuation of this distribution of power. A good deal of Connell's work on this basis is clearly subjected to serious criticism. In the context of Masculinity Studies, female masculinity represents the opportunity to escape from and/or reconfigure gender and sexuality power arrangements, rather than being merely a minority version of masculinity. Its importance as a commentary on masculinity outweighs its numeric significance within the masculine.

Whereas Masculinity Studies writings almost invariably stress the non-natural and non-determinate character of masculinity by focusing on what is excluded from it as marginal (non-white, non-Western), subordinate (gay) or opposite (women), Halberstam's analysis attends to the incoherence at its 'heart'. Halberstam finds that even 'normal' masculinity is 'impure' (Lugones, 1994) because female masculinity reveals this category can be inhabited by women. Masculinity is impure at the supposed foundation of masculinity, at the foundation of 'normal' and indeed 'proper' gender identity, not just in its marginalised and subordinated variations or in its dependence on placement against the feminine 'other'. Such a lens unsettles gender (and sexuality) identity fixity rather more than Connell's focus on socially variable, multiple but always male masculinities. As I noted earlier, Halberstam brings to light in this attention to the incoherence at the centre of the 'normal', 'the strangeness of all gendered bodies', not just the excluded or transgendered ('deviant') ones (Halberstam, 1994: 226).

Such an approach places her work not only at something of a remove from most Masculinity theorising, but also from many Queer and Trans thinkers. In this context, it is relevant that she employs 'queer' as a verb, and sees queer as 'about doing rather than being' a noun/identity (Halberstam, 1997: 1030; on this distinction, see Sullivan, 2003: 37–56; Corber and Valocchi, 2003). In other words, she *makes queer* all gender/sexuality positionings, rather than upholding gender/sexuality crossings like transgender as *being* Queer. Gender/sexuality transgressions are democratised and recognised within the 'normal', rather than regarded as the exclusive province of the marginalised. This way of thinking sets Halberstam at odds with Queer *and* Trans theorists who assign gender deviance/rebellion only to cross-identifying subjects and consign all other bodies to gender conformity (Halberstam, 1998: 153–4). Female masculinity in Halberstam's work both draws upon and disturbs contemporary gender and sexuality scholarship as a kind of critical case.

Debates

Is this account of Halberstam's female masculinity as the apothesis of the gender/sexuality field justified? There are several possible criticisms that might be raised against this viewpoint.

The non-essentialist, non-natural perspective Halberstam shares with Butler supposedly escapes from a biological body-based account of gender and masculinity. However, her account of 'female masculinity' is 'haunted' – in much the same way as is Rubin's earlier account of 'butch' – by linguistic (Wiegman, 2001a: 376) and perhaps analytical difficulties. While her analysis might be said to disconnect masculinity successfully from men/male bodies, it does not and indeed cannot fully disconnect the subject of female masculinity from female bodies. Without the presence of such bodies, the approach loses its political imprimatur. On the one hand, gender identity is discussed as simply a form of 'identification' rather than as requiring a particular body or traditional social location, on the other hand, female masculinity is crucially linked to a particular body in order precisely to demonstrate its disconnection from the biological (male) and from the traditional social context of masculinity.

Halberstam's approach claims to banish from view the specific material implications of actually living in a body defined as male/man. If a 'woman' can be a 'man', these material and specific implications may disappear and with them the gender justice project associated with both Feminism and Masculinity Studies pro-feminist agendas. These agendas are organised along lines which distinguish these groups and see them as differently located with regard to power. If they are interchangeable, indistinguishable, then where does this analysis of power go? This possibility does seem potentially imminent in Halberstam's reconception of the masculine merely as an 'identification', a mere identity, rather than as a set of institutional processes or techniques. Here Connell's dismissive response to Butler's account of gender as too narrowly focused on individualised identity seems potentially relevant (Chapter 20). Halberstam's disengagement of masculinity from its social construction suggests, along the lines of Connell's critique, that 'female masculinity' like Butler's 'performative gender' is a distinctly individualised strategy.

Halberstam's disarticulation of masculinity from dominance and gender hierarchy also makes it very unclear what this 'identification' means. What is masculinity but a complex of patterns of dominance and hierarchally organised privilege?[8] Halberstam seems to revert to some essence of masculinity that is beyond its social/historical frame. Moreover, even if the claim that female masculinity offers a very specific version of masculinity that is not a copy of hegemonic masculinity is accepted, how does it manage to *do* 'masculinity' and at the same time escape issues of dominance and power without stretching the term to pointlessness. In what sense is it a masculinity if, unlike other masculinities, it is not compliant with hegemonic masculinity's investments in power? This is a particularly telling difficulty given that the historically specific, 'cultural characteristics that constitute the masculine and feminine remain unchallenged' in Halberstam's analysis (Zicklin, 2002).

Cheshire Calhoun argues that to adopt masculinity (or femininity) 'is to make use of a set of meanings produced through and sustained by men's oppression of women'. The deployment of masculinity in this social context cannot be rendered 'politically harmless' from the point of view of a feminist/pro-feminist concern with gender justice (Calhoun, 1997: 207–9). While female masculinity may undermine the organisation of heteronormative sexuality and thereby promote the agenda of Sexuality Studies, it leaves in place the traditional gender hierarchical equation of masculinity with power, aggression, toughness and stoicism without attending to how these can be disengaged from their entrenched practice as social dominance. Halberstam's account of the social may be further diminished by its relative inattention to the ways in which race/ethnicity, class and other axes of power inform constructions of the masculine. If Masculinity Studies writers like Connell can be assessed as recentring 'the white male body', as Halberstam charges, then it could be suggested, for example, that she recentres the white masculine.

The above discussion might suggest that Halberstam's approach to gender analysis remains rather more committed to traditional gender categories than her concern with 'queering' masculinity, and with the transgressive possibilities of all identities, might suggest. However, it can also be argued that her work offers a rather less than 'queer' look at sexuality categories. Halberstam's approach to female masculinity is apparently inclusive. She refuses to exclude either tomboy heterosexuals or female-to-male transmen as either disloyal women or as gender conformists, (Rosario, 2000) and, relatedly, explicitly refuses to limit socially transgressive possibilities to only those deemed ambiguous. Queer thinking for her does not mean the reassertion of just another normative insider/outsider regime, this time lauding a queer (ambiguous) identity as the subversive 'ideal type'. All the same, her work does rest upon a revalorisation of the lesbian butch and there is no acknowledgement of the 'revolutionary potential of "alternative femininities"'. On this basis, Anoniou (2000: 382) fears that Halberstam 'implies that the female female is always a "victim" of the binary system of gender, whereas the masculine female poses a radical challenge to it'.

Conclusion

Halberstam's work directly challenges many of the typical features of Masculinity Studies in that it disengages masculinity from men and their social positioning. Halberstam examines the suppression of gender variance in women and claims masculinity in ways which also challenge aspects of Feminism. Yet her work cannot be simply viewed as another Queer assault on Gender Studies, since it raises questions about Queer thinking and Queer's iconic figure of the transgender. On the other hand, in certain respects Halberstam perhaps has not gone so far afield from the assumptions of these bodies of thought as might be imagined. She has been criticised for reiterating identities (masculine and queer – that is, non-heterosexual) rather than destabilising them.

Halberstam herself seems to suggest that female masculinity alone is a limited strategy in terms of reconfiguring social relations and power. She has commented generally that 'the relation between sex and transgression ... is far from clear' and is cautious about notions of queer 'outlaws' (Halberstam, 1997). Additionally, she notes that an 'emphasis on alternative masculinities is not, in and of itself, enough to guarantee its political effectivity' (see Wiegman, 2001a: 378, note 22):

> I suggest that we think carefully ... about the kinds of men or masculine beings that we become. ... [A]lternative masculinities ultimately will fail to change existing gender hierarchies to the extent to which they fail to be feminist, antiracist, and queer. (Halberstam, 1998: 173)

While one could argue that this suggests feminine masculinity amounts to little more than a plea for some legitimacy to be granted to identities that are transparently constructed, on the other hand, perhaps that is not so small a point. Female masculinity reveals, in a material fleshly sense, the constructed political character of gender and sexuality. The gender/sexuality field, if it asserts anything at all, says we must think critically about ourselves in the world and Halberstam's analysis certainly enables that.

Notes

1 The ironic links between new formulations of *Gender* Studies in ways which refused separate disengaged analysis of women and men, and the emergence of new Queer understandings of Sexuality Studies, which disengaged gender and sexuality are intriguing. Almost in a reversal of theorising associated with the 1960s, 1970s and early 1980s, in the late 1980s, 1990s and 2000s some connections were taken up and others discouraged (see also Chapter 17, note 17).

2 Rubin's position has often been interpreted among Queer writers as indicating the complete disjunction of Gender and Sexuality Studies, but in an interview some ten years after the essay 'Thinking Sex' Rubin explained that she was *not* claiming gender and sexuality 'should have no analytic traffic' (Rubin, 1994).

3 Stone butch refers to self-designated, non-feminine, sexually untouchable females (Halberstam, 1998: 21).

4 The analysis is also open-ended in the sense that it does not equate female masculinity with a study of lesbianism – that is, Halberstam does not construe female masculinity as identical with a particular (gendered) sexual identity and as merely a subset of lesbianism. Such a framing simultaneously enables her to claim an irreducible specificity for female masculinity.

5 See Chapter 14 for a more detailed account of these disputes between Trans and Queer theorists.

6 Connell's passing mention of masculinities without male bodies is illustrative (Connell, 2000: 16).

7 See also the use of butch to refer to ambiguity, a masculine performance chafing against an embodiment deemed female, in Munt, 1997: 1, 41; also Plymire, 2000; Kanner, 2002.

8 The same question may be asked of femininity.

Conclusion

In this 'epilogue' I will attempt to pull together succinctly some significant features of what we have examined in the book. This book has been arranged in the style of an analytical survey or smorgasbord. I have tried to present a compendium (or reasonably comprehensive summary and analysis) which would give a fair sense of the whole field of gender/sexuality theory. You have been invited to sample a wide range of theories and theorists, and see if any of them take your fancy. Perhaps several have been of interest, perhaps none. Indeed, given this invitation to sample, the analogy to bring to mind might not be so much about consumption – the tasting of various theory dishes – but rather, seduction. In this sense you have been invited to try out the 'text appeal' of theories and theorists. The life of the mind has its seductive charms after all.

Theory can indeed be sexy. When Michel Foucault lectured in the 1970s it was not unusual to see him surrounded by a troop of admirers. In the USA students started a fanzine devoted to fantasies about feminist academic, Judith Butler. You don't need to go this far to see that sometimes theories cause a stir in the frontal lobes which is distinctly seductive (Ffytche, 1994: 30). On this basis a compendium like this one might be better considered not in terms of smorgasbord but rather a dance club. The question then is, will you pick anyone up and give them a whirl on the dance floor or even consider taking them home? Will you choose more than one, or none? And if you do, what will your friends or parents think about your new companion? Will you 'come out', for example, as 'Liberal Feminist and Proud!' or will your choice be a guilty and solitary pleasure? Of course what you may now consider attractive doesn't necessarily mean a permanent affiliation. Stoltenberg may take your eye today but soon be forgotten. What you say today, like this book, is a snapshot of what is on offer at the moment and probably will change as theories and theorists change too. That said, let us investigate the possibilities on the dance floor.

In discussing the gender/sexuality field I covered five main theoretical trajectories in Feminist, Sexuality and Masculinity Studies (Figure C.1).

In terms of theories and theorists this meant a list in three parts.

1. Liberal feminism: Wolf, Nussbaum
2. Gender Difference feminisms: Rich, Daly, and Flax, Grosz
3. REI feminism: hooks and Spivak
4. Postmodern/Queer(ing) feminism: Butler, Whittle

5. Liberationist sexuality: Altman
6. Social Constructionist (SC) sexuality: Jackson, Weeks
7. Transgender: Califia
8. Queer Theory: Jagose, Seidman

9. Gender Difference (GD) masculinity: Stoltenberg
10. Gay/REI masculinities: Dowsett, Carbado
11. Social Constructionist (SC) masculinity: Connell
12. Queer(ing) masculinity: Halberstam

Figure C.1   Map of the gender/sexuality field: continuum and directions[1]

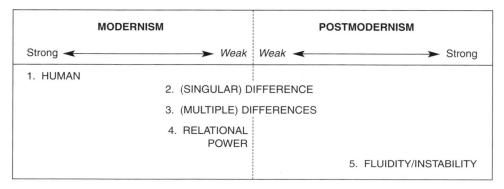

These possibilities may be laid out on the grid of gender/sexuality directions (outlined in Figure C. 2) to better illustrate the spread of the perspectives that have been discussed, always remembering that these frameworks are not as distinct as such an image may suggest. Moreover, certain theorists and theories are decidedly ambiguously located (for example, Stoltenberg's Radical pro-feminism and Califia's Transgender sexuality theorising).

There are, necessarily, weaknesses in the selection presented to you in this book. I did not and, indeed, could not (given constraints of one volume) invite everyone of interest to this dance club. In my view some of the most important missing or barely discussed themes are disability, class, environment, and international relations/globalisation. Every dance club is a partial selection. We must remember the other possibilities outside the door queuing up. If you didn't find your Ms/Mr/Trans Right-for-the-Moment, maybe they are waiting elsewhere and you'll have to read yet another book.

Nevertheless, even if this book could not invite all the possible contenders for your attention, there are, I think, a number of benefits in attending this dance party. First of all, if we look at the theorists/theories in terms of 'text appeal', after reading this book hopefully you too can now engage in 'textual healing' and offer it to others. Hopefully, you too can 'talk the talk'. One commentator has noted that the gender/sexuality field offers the pleasures of being able to debate with all sorts of people you broadly agree with. While there are undoubtedly many benefits attached to debating with people who believe women and/or queers are inferior folk; for myself the intellect and heart

Figure C.2   The gender/sexuality field: detailed directions

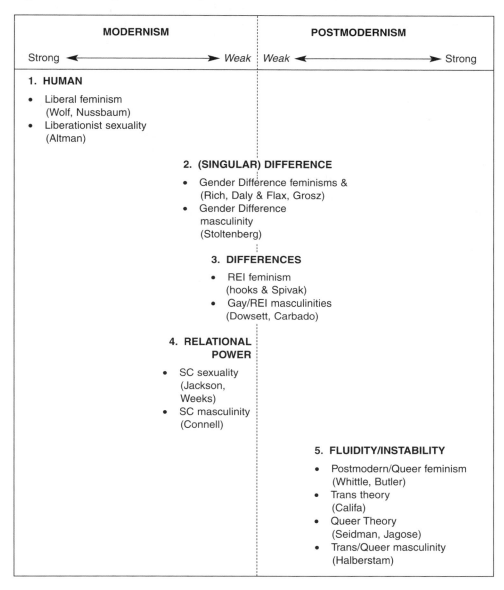

flutters when we start from justice for all and the notion of social life as a shared endeavour, when we try to re-imagine and even practise a new way of life. This compendium offers that rare opportunity of prioritising, of focusing on discussions that presume justice and equality but argue passionately about how to achieve it.

In reading the book you gain entry to, if you weren't already a signed-up member, a slightly masochistic (given the sometimes treacly prose) but nevertheless excitable and vigorous dance club. But what do you get for the entry fee? The chance, as I said, of a stranger who surprises perhaps, or even an old mate who looks better now you've seen the others. To those of you who now feel less sure than ever of what theoretical choice(s) you do fancy, I suggest playing the field a while longer. Uncertainty has its uses. And finally what you get is not just potentially new ways to discuss issues, consider political alternatives, and even have intellectual fun but, perhaps most of all, another way of looking at the world. This book is intended to enable, or further develop, your ability to look at ordinary everyday matters and think of several ways of understanding them. In other words, the aim is to assist you in developing at least double vision – that is, both a normative vision and at least one critical perspective of the everyday and the unusual. And once you've got this multiple vision, it doesn't really go away. It's yours for life. As those various theoretical dance partners approach you, I suspect, if you ever did, you'll never see straight again.

Note

1. This figure was initially presented in Chapter 1 (Figure 1.1).

Appendix: Methodological Issues

I stated in the Introduction that the intention of this book is to provide a reasonably comprehensive account of gender/sexuality theory through an analytical survey. I also noted that the main methodological tools used in the book are a theoretical continuum, major directions, and an interrogatory accessible style. The continuum and directions are contextualised by reference to specific approaches, thinkers and debates, sometimes involving a closer focus on individual texts and/or particular issues.

With regard to the methodological device of a continuum within gender/sexuality theory, ranging from strongly Modernist to strongly Postmodern thinking, the intention is to demonstrate flows and interactions along the continuum. Weaker Modernist approaches may overlap with weaker Postmodern ones, and even those apparently most far apart may share more than is initially evident. References to the 'borderlands' of the continuum, positioned on the cusp between Modernist and Postmodern thinking, are meant to convey the potentially permeable division between these frames of reference.[1]

The thematic use of the Modernist/Postmodern continuum as an overview map is, however, by no means regarded as the ultimate methodological technique to reveal the array of gender/sexuality approaches. Instead, it is viewed as a pragmatic means of capturing in time – after the fashion of a snapshot – the contemporary state of the sub-fields and debates. This method of highlighting broad frames of reference will no doubt in time be viewed as itself a function of theoretical preoccupations at a particular historical moment.

The 'directions' methodology employed in the book shares much in common with the metaphor of 'lenses' employed by Jaggar and Rothenberg (1993: xvii), as well as supporting a notion of the gender/sexuality field as a many hued tapestry (Anzaldúa, 1990: xxv). It refuses any account of the field as a singular unity or as a set of incommensurable types of framework between which one must decide (Young, 1997a: 17). Rather, my concern in using this methodology is to present a 'perspectivism' in which different problems and historical periods may produce a number of theoretical trajectories, all of which are open to debate and question.

Nevertheless, this methodology does not escape the many criticisms of overview books with a typological or key authors and/or key texts orientation. Overview books that outline 'types' of theory are frequently accused of not being closely enough tied to specific practical political problems, setting in concrete a static canon, imposing too neat an order upon the content of different approaches in a theoretical field, and underestimating cross-overs between approaches. Overview books attending to key writers and/or key texts are similarly viewed as promulgating a canon of 'classics', which inevitably produces exclusions and polices theoretical boundaries with the added disadvantage of promoting an individualist orientation and ignoring collective effort (Kensinger, 1997; Stacey, 1993: 49–73; Kemp and Squires, 1997: 9; Maynard, 1995). While the methodology I have adopted is not strictly focused on 'type', 'character' or 'major text', its concern with 'directions' in or ways of seeing the gender/sexuality field does retain an explanatory, systemic agenda that has a typological orientation.

There is no doubt that use of the typological methodology in overview books is not problem-free. I remain persuaded, however, that the typological method is one important technique for clarifying the gender/sexuality field. In the first instance, it allows readers to make comparisons and connections between this book and existing overviews of the subfields since it is the most common technique employed in such texts. Secondly, the criticism that a typological method insufficiently links theory to practical, concrete political issues may be somewhat offset in this book by attention to particular writers and/or texts and issues. For instance, discussion of transgender theorising in Sexuality Studies leads to an analysis of the work of Pat Califia and to the question of sexual reassignment surgery. The more abstract and broadly typological mode gives way to example and illustration.

Thirdly, the most frequent and most telling criticism of the typological method – that it amounts to asserting a static eternal canon of Great Ideas and assuming that a field of thought like gender/sexuality is made up of discrete fixed types of thinking – should be weighed against the issue of accessibility. While this criticism is certainly powerful, I am less certain that typological categorisation methods should be entirely abandoned because I suspect that only those with very specialised knowledge can afford the luxury of discussing gender/sexuality theory without reference to some typological labels. In this context, I suggest that genuine concerns regarding the potential of a typological (or key writers and/or texts) orientation to diminish the contingency and complexity of the gender/sexuality field must be balanced against the danger of reducing its availability to a broader readership. The typological mode allows underlying assumptions to be made explicit and hence accessible to the widest possible audience. Like a great number of other writers of overview books, the issue of broadening participatory engagement with ideas in the field of gender/sexuality matters to me sufficiently to risk some loss of subtlety or fluidity.

For the uninitiated reader, the field of gender/sexuality theory can seem extremely confusing at first. In my experience with tertiary students, some guidelines about general patterns are seen as a considerable help. Once new learners have a grasp of these situating patterns they can then begin to recognise legitimate concerns about the limits of categorisation raised by commentators (Stacey, 1993). Similarly, readers new to the field will need to know what might be regarded as 'classics', if only to reject them later. If these readers are not aware of approaches, writers and works which are usually seen as influential, they may well find it difficult to understand debates which almost invariably rest on such assumed knowledge. Indeed, it can be argued that issues raised by established scholars, regarding the ways in which overview texts may promote a canon, rest heavily upon their own existing 'cultural capital', upon their own specialised knowledge. Such scholars have no need of a typological/author 'canon' – a map of major directions in the field – and see its limits, precisely because they already have a sufficient knowledge of influential approaches, writers and works in the field and are aware of how maps simplify the terrain.

Commentators who emphasise the dangers associated with typological approaches sometimes suggest that there are alternative methodologies that involve no losses or that the problems of categorisation can be entirely avoided. In this context, some writers have indicated a preference for discussions of theory to be undertaken by using topics or debates, but these alternatives are not necessarily any less prescriptive. Such methods also involve a 'canon' of topics or debates, references to favoured individuals and/or texts, an account of general patterns and labels, and must exclude something. Indeed, all forms of characterisation of a field involve some categorisation. The point is not whether to categorise but *how* to do so in ways that are explicit and that enable readers both to enter into debate with the approaches discussed and consider alternative choices. This book attempts to encourage such critical readings. While the book does contain an incremental aspect[2] – intended to outline a broad map of gender/sexuality theory which can indicate continuities, overlapping connections and echoes that currently exist in the field – it can also be read discontinuously and its stress on the variety of theoretical positions undercuts authorial omnipotence.[3] Furthermore, though I provide an overview account of the gender/sexuality field, I also continually direct readers to examine a range of perspectives. For instance, in relation to accounts of Sexuality Studies I refer readers to different approaches outlined by Stephen Whittle, Stevi Jackson and Steven Seidman.

Critics of typological overview books may, in any case, overstate the dangers of any form of systemic characterisation of a field since they tend to equate characterisation with pinning a field down, with the closure of debate and diversity. In alerting us to the dangers of writings which insist there is a fixed canon in the gender/sexuality field, some commentators may well have overly presumed the fixing effects of such commentaries. In my view, this underestimates the processual aspect of these texts in terms of how they are written and read. As McDermott (1998: 403) notes, overview texts 'are often analysed as though they were static documents, but … [these] texts are more usefully approached as products of a long-term dynamic process'. Moreover, the equation of characterisation of a field with closure rather prejudges the task of characterisation. This task is not always conceived as concerned with revealing the central essence of the field (finding its truth or core identity). Instead, characterisation may be viewed as a relatively modest enterprise, as a clarifying device.[4] Rather than producing an outcome or answer which captures an already existent meaning, the characterisation undertaken in an overview text like this one might be better seen in terms of an activity generating a range of possible meanings for different readers.

Certainly, the aim of this book is to balance 'informative' and overview/systemic with 'interrogative' and perspectival elements (Parker, 2001). In other words, I wish to draw attention to the usefulness of developing and maintaining a critical unease towards rather than a ready acceptance of all views, including my own characterisation of the field. Even if I had not adopted such an approach, I am sure that you, the reader, will interpret and use the content of the book in myriad ways that I cannot prescribe or foresee.

Notes

1. What I am drawing attention to here is work at the 'borderlands' which operates at the intersections of Modernist and Postmodern assumptions and perhaps engages with both. For instance, psychoanalytic feminist work influenced by Jacques Lacan clearly owes a debt to the Modernist universal explanatory claims of psychoanalysis and yet employs a stress on meaning and language associated with Postmodernism. Jeffrey Weeks' writings are Socialist and pro-feminist, by no means uncritical of Foucault and yet show the influence of Postmodern agendas. Similarly, bell hooks moves between Modernist and Postmodern engagements with identity politics. (For other points concerning the continuum, see Chapter 1 notes 9 and 11, and Chapter 2 note 6.)

2. For example, the characterisation of Postmodernism is gradually built up over several chapters in Part 1 in particular, and then expanded in Part 2 and to a lesser extent in Part 3. This incremental aspect of the book does not, however, prevent readers from employing the index to dip into the book at several points, or from reading individual chapters or parts in any order.

3. I am attracted here to Foucault's concern with outlining both connections between different viewpoints and his rejection of any all-encompassing theoretical vantage point in his consideration of discursive fields, as well as his interest in mixing methodologies. See Best and Kellner, 1991: 39–40, 43–4.

4. For a lengthier analysis of the task of characterising or defining fields of thinking, see Beasley, 2001: 203–5, or, for an earlier assessment (though published later), see Beasley, 2005.

Glossary of Key Terms

(Compiled by Angelique Bletsas, with assistance from Chris Beasley)

Androcentric   A view or theory that is male-centred.

Assimilation   Usually intended as a critical, even pejorative, term; a policy or political stance that is assimilationist and advocates an excluded group becoming integrated into the social whole without actually questioning or challenging the nature of social organisation itself. The politics of assimilation are generally identified with broader liberal agendas.

Binary pair   Considered to be a central organisational principle within much Western intellectual thought, which involves depicting social phenomena in matched pairs. Generally, the phenomena paired in this way are attributed different values, even being construed as oppositional. The two categories of a binary pair, such as men and women, are not merely regarded as distinct and opposed; they are also put into a hierarchy in which one is typically cast as positive and the other negative.

Biological reductionism   Arguments that seek to explain unequal and unjust social arrangements by reference to biological 'facts'.

Collectivism   The focus on group resistance as a political strategy.

Cosmopolitan   The view that political citizenship should not be viewed narrowly in terms of the nation state but should be considered in global terms.

Cultural relativism   The view that ideas about what it means to be human are culturally, rather than biologically, determined. Ideas of the human are conceived in such a view as specific to, or relative to, their cultural and historical context, rather than as eternal or self-evident. In this way cultural relativism stands in opposition to universal accounts of humanity (Humanism), of which it is often critical. (*See also* **Universalism, Humanism**)

Deconstruction   A central concept in the work of Postmodern thinker, Jacques Derrida, it is concerned with a critique of foundationalism (that is, notions of founding or underlying 'truths' which have large-scale, usually universal explanatory scope). Deconstruction is a technique of dismantling foundationalist systems of thought in order to reveal their assumptions about what is important and what is not. Deconstruction questions the ability of foundationalist thinking to make large-scale or universal claims on behalf of objectively eternal truths by delineating its connections with specific relations of power. More loosely, the term deconstruction may simply refer to the critical analysis of 'texts' in order to uncover messages and meanings that may not at first seem apparent. (*See also* **Foundationalism**)

(Singular) Difference   In Gender and Sexuality Studies, this refers to the way in which particular marginalised and oppressed social groups are conceptualised as against dominant social groups. Singular understandings of Difference involve focusing solely on one axis of power between social groups (for example, gender difference – in particular women's gendered difference from men) such that other axes of power (like race) recede. Notions of (singular) Difference are usually strongly linked to Modernist identity politics. Attention to (singular) Difference in this case produces a concern with the common subordination of those marginalised by one form of power relations, which is seen as creating a shared identity and political agenda. Differences *among* those identified with such a shared identity and political positioning are de-emphasised or suppressed.

For this reason, a focus on (singular) Difference associated with Modernist identity politics may be expressed in terms of an 'ethnic minority' model. For example, the marginalised social category of homosexuality may be seen as marked by particular, easily identifiable, characteristics and a distinct community. This conception of identity politics understands power relations as being about the separation of already clearly distinguishable groups. Power relations between groups arise when what is already different is placed in a social hierarchy and thereby rendered both different and differently valued.

By contrast, the (multiple) Differences approach disputes this focus on a singular axis of power relations and at the very least complicates distinctions between social groups. The (multiple) Differences approach questions notions of a singular common subordination creating a discrete marginalised community by referring to at least two axes of power. Postmodern-influenced analyses go further and reject any notion of already existent and clearly separable social groups. For example, such analyses may represent homosexuality as a diffuse possibility available to all.

While the terms Difference and Differences are used in this book to register recognisably distinctive approaches, the former is widely used in the gender/sexuality field to cover both singular Difference and multiple Differences approaches. (*See also* **(Multiple) Differences, Identity politics**)

(Multiple) Differences   In Gender and Sexuality Studies, this refers to the way in which marginalised and oppressed social groups are conceptualised as against dominant social groups. A (multiple) Difference(s) framework raises doubts concerning singular identity models, focusing on plural identities as well as differences *within* identity categories. For example, the category 'women' is considered in terms of class, sexuality, 'race' and ethnic differences. (*See also* **(Singular) Difference**)

Emancipatory politics   *See* **Liberationist politics**

Enlightenment   The seventeenth- and eighteenth-century European movement where science and reason were positioned as superior to religion and culture in intellectual thinking. Within the intellectual traditions of the Enlightenment project the ideas of individualism and universalism were established as fundamental to political claims. Science and reason were positioned as necessarily representing the route to social progress, an idea which was itself conceived as inevitable. (*See also* **Individualism, Universalism**)

Essentialism   Largely intended as a critical, even pejorative term, essentialism constitutes a particular way of understanding the Human Self as having a timeless, universal and often natural/biological inner core or foundation. This account can be considered against Postmodern or Social Constructionist theories, for example, which argue that there is no such thing as a self that exists beyond the bounds of socially constructed life. (*See also* **Foundationalism**)

Foundationalism   Usually identified with Modernist social theories, which are concerned to explain all of social life by revealing some account of its basic foundation. Foundationalism often refers to the idea, for example, that there are certain constant features of what constitutes a human being that govern or underlie all of human existence. (*See also* **Deconstruction, Essentialism, Humanism, Modernist**)

Gay Liberation   A social movement emerging in the 1960s and 1970s as a response to the restricted rights and opportunities available to gay men and lesbians. Gay Liberation as a movement advanced the ideal of a liberated sexuality for all people and homosexuals in particular. It aimed to overthrow established social attitudes towards sexuality, which were considered repressive of natural feelings of desire and as such damaging to individuals. As a theoretical viewpoint, Gay Liberation may be summarised as sexual freedom providing the means to overthrowing power.

Grand Theory   *See* **Macro theories**

Gynocentrism   A view or theory that is female-centred.

Hegemonic masculinity   From the work of Bob Connell, hegemonic masculinity refers to the most valued and most rewarded form of masculinity, which provides a widely accepted model legitimating masculine social dominance. (*See also* **Hegemony**)

Hegemony   From the work of Marxist scholar Antonio Gramsci, hegemony refers to the establishment, through gaining the consent of the masses, of the values and beliefs of an elite as a compulsory norm for all. (*See also* **Hegemonic masculinity**)

Heteronormativity   Expresses the view that within social life heterosexuality is constructed as a compulsory norm and non-heterosexualities are constructed as deviant.

Humanism   A key idea, as well as outcome, of Enlightenment thinking in which humans rather than God or the divine became the central fact against which social life was explained and understood. This repositioning of the explanatory basis of social life away from the religious to the secular was an expressly political investment in the liberationist potential of rationalism. Humanism is a term describing those theories that hold the human subject as foundational in explanations of social life and usually propose a fundamental core essence to the human in their definitions of the human subject. Humanism frequently describes the core of what is specifically human as rationality. (*See also* **Enlightenment, Essentialism, Universalism**)

Identity politics   Emerges from social movements which mobilise around a particular 'identity' as marking the basis of inclusion into the movement. Identity politics reflect the idea that certain characteristics (for example, characteristics derived from one's gender, 'race', sexuality and so on) produce a shared experience and a related commonality. In contemporary societies marked by social hierarchy, these supposedly pre-existent characteristics may also be the basis upon which one is categorised as belonging to a subordinate social group. Individuals, then, not only share characteristics, but additionally develop a common worldview and political positioning derived from their socially marginalised identity. Identity produces insight into society's oppressive structures and, by this means, marginalised social groups develop resistance to its dominant ideas. In some analyses (for example, standpoint theory) marginalised identity is seen as producing greater insight than other social positionings and hence is constituted as having a central, even unquestionably knowledgeable, role in progressive political struggle for social change. (*See also* **Difference, Essentialism, Standpoint theory**)

Individualism   Emerging with the rise of Enlightenment thinking, individualism involves the privileging of the individual as an autonomous, rational subject in considering political claims and social explanations. In social theories and politics which take an individualist stance, individuals – rather than social groups, processes or structures – are privileged as the ultimate unit in explanations of social life.

Liberalism   The political philosophy of Liberalism emerged during the Enlightenment and is the dominant political philosophy in the West today. Liberalism, at least in principle, asserts the rights of the individual against the intervention of the state. However, Liberalism has, in practice, also been associated with the subjugation of such rights in relation to those deemed, at various historical moments, to not be fully human and hence not capable of full human individuality. (*See also* **Individualism**)

Liberationist politics   Identified with several Modernist political projects, liberation involves overthrowing power to reveal a 'true' shared and universal humanity that is free of repressive power. This can be achieved through group or collective struggle, which usually takes the form of an identity politics. (*See also* **Power, Identity politics**)

Libertarianism   A political philosophy which holds that all people have certain inalienable rights which can never be taken away in the name or interests of the collective. Libertarianism involves a zealous attachment to individualism and maintains a deep distrust and opposition to social or government intervention. (*See also* **Individualism**)

Macro theories   Are often associated with Modernist theories which forward accounts of social life presuming to explain all of its variations by reference to one aspect of human existence which is posited as foundational or fundamental. Macro theories can be considered against Postmodern arguments that social theories should be fluid, context-specific and localised. (*See also* **Universalism, Modernist**)

Marxism   Broadly refers to the works of theorists who are explicitly influenced by the works of Karl Marx and to the privileging of concern about economic systems in analyses of social organisation. Marxist analyses commonly maintain a focus on criticisms of capitalism and class distinction as an organising mode of society and social relations.

Metanarrative   *See* **Macro theories**

Modernist   Describes social and political theories, which are based upon key Enlightenment principles. Modernist theories assert knowledge systems based on principles of universalism and scientific reason. However, following the seminal work of Michel Foucault, Modernist theories are typically the subject of criticism in Postmodern theories. Postmodern criticisms of Modernist thinking arise on the grounds that the latter – far from delineating universally applicable and rational (objectively neutral and valid) explanations of the human and social – in fact represents the dominant views of a particular historical period in European thought. Critiques of Modernism forwarded by Post-colonial and Postmodern scholars have been keen to draw attention to the way in which Modernist theories implicitly ascribe value judgements that often reproduce systems of dominance and subordination. (*See also* **Enlightenment**)

Multiculturalism   Advocates a cultural pluralism, which establishes ethnicity and 'race' as significant in rethinking progressive forms of social organisation. Such a viewpoint may ironically tend towards the institutionalisation of set notions of 'race'/ethnicity – that is, it may institutionalise set notions of distinct difference. (*See also* **Difference, Other**)

Other   In psychoanalytic theory 'the other' and otherness are central to the development of the self. The self requires 'difference' – the other – to become a formed presence, indeed to become a (social) human being. The other (that which is not-self) must be differentiated and cast out from the self for the infant to become a distinct person. In psychoanalysis, the other (not-self) is suppressed in the unconscious and represents the continuing uncertain boundaries of the self. The other is both not entirely separate from the self and rejected by the self. This psychoanalytic theory of the individual self is strongly linked in Gender and Sexuality Studies with the individual's incorporation into the hierarchically organised social realm. 'Others' (those supposedly different from oneself or one's social group) in social life are once again not entirely separate (they shape one's social self-definition) and at the same time are often demonised and rejected. The other represents ambiguity and anxiety in the self and society, at least in current social contexts. Gender and Sexuality Studies consider ways in which the self/other distinction may be unsettled and re-imagined within the individual and within society. (*See also* **Difference, Othering**)

Othering   In Post-colonial theory the process, central to the imperialist political enterprise, whereby the colonising cultural group is privileged as the norm whereas the oppressed cultural group is constructed as aberrant, as less than human. (*See also* **Other, Liberalism**)

Patriarchy   In Feminism, systemic and trans-historical male domination over women.

Performativity   Deriving in large part from the work of Judith Butler, in Queer Theory and in Feminism, performativity refers to the profoundly socially constructed character of gender and sexuality. Gender and sexuality are conceived as the product of endless citation and reiteration of certain normative categories (such as man or heterosexual), rather than as formed out of an already existent biological basis. Subordinated categories (including woman, lesbian, homosexual) are no less socially framed and hence do not inevitably amount to resistance to normative categories or categorisation. There is no 'real' underlying source or essence of gender and sexuality in notions of performativity. (*See also* **Queer theory, Essentialism**)

Post-colonial   In Feminism and more broadly, theories which engage and critique imperialist practices. This includes writings which directly address the experiences of colonial oppression, as well as those which speak about imperialism more generally as the political project of Othering specific cultural groups while privileging Whiteness in particular. (*See also* **Other, Othering**)

Postmodern   Theories and theorists expressly positioned as rejecting and critiquing the fundamental premises and ideas of Modernist theories of social life. Postmodern theories argue in common that there is no special, objective vantage point outside the social context from which social life can be accessed or explained. They focus instead on local, fragmented ideas of social life. Postmodern theories of the self, for example, stress the fluidity, internal instability and performative quality of identity as a creative process of signification. In Postmodern work social life is inflected by power, which itself is understood as a creative, constituting force. (*See also* **Foundationalism, Modernist, Power**)

Power   The concept of power has a series of competing interpretations within contemporary social theory. Traditionally, power has been understood as a negative force, as functioning in a hierarchical, top-down model to repress behaviours and individuals. Following the work of Michel Foucault, in Postmodern theory, power is understood as a creative, constituting force, which functions in a diffuse way across the social whole. For example, Foucault's historical studies of the emergence of sexual categories demonstrate that marginalised sexual identities are not merely victims of power – a natural form of self repressed by power – but produced by power. These marginalised identities, no matter how socially excluded they might be, are not outside, but are part of, the organisation of societies. (*See also* **Identity politics, Liberationist politics, Postmodern**)

Psychoanalytic theories   Following the prototypical work of Sigmund Freud, these are concerned with explaining the unconscious psychic processes involved in the development of the self.

Queer Theory   Is typically focused upon the question of individual identity, and upon cultural/symbolic and literary/textual issues. Queer Theory aims to destabilise identity through the construction of a supposedly 'inclusive', non-normative (almost invariably non-heterosexual) sexuality and a simultaneous dismantling of gender roles. Queer Theory sees identity as thoroughly socially constructed and as internally unstable and incoherent. (*See also* **Identity politics, Liberationist politics, Postmodern, Social Constructionism**)

Reason   A central precept of Enlightenment politics and thought, where the ability of individuals to reason came to be regarded as a defining characteristic of human beings. In this way, reason was deployed as a fundamental premise in arguments for universal suffrage. Reason was strongly identified with the secular, rational project of progress as opposed to 'traditional' religious and cultural views. (*See also* **Enlightenment**)

Reformism   Political interventions that seek to improve conditions for a particular marginalised group in contrast to radical political interventions which seek to transform social organisation itself.

Second-wave feminism   The popular designation for the feminist movement in the West during the 1960s, 1970s and even 1980s, to distinguish it from feminist thinking and politics developed in earlier times (first-wave feminism). Popular renderings of 'Feminism' often presuppose the politics of Liberal feminism during this second wave. However, in feminist writings the second wave refers to at least four main directions: Liberal, Radical, Marxist and Socialist feminisms. (*See also* **Third-wave feminism**)

Social Constructionism   The rejection of universalist, biological accounts of human being in favour of cultural or social accounts. Social Constructionist theories resist the idea of any set or fixed content (essence) to identities, but also refuse the Postmodern antagonism to identity. Social constructionists stress culturally and historically specific variations and complexity in relation to identity rather than broad, often more abstract notions of fluidity/instability. For example, gender and sexuality are not, within this framework, a matter of in-built, pre-existent identity differences but of particular forms of identity constituted through hierarchical social relations analogous to class relations and founded upon concrete material oppression in social life. (*See also* **Essentialism, Postmodern**)

Social hierarchy The view that social identities are constructed along a continuum of power and privilege.

Social transformation In radical politics, social transformation is the pursuit of significant structural change to existing unjust social institutions.

Socialism A political ideology emerging in the nineteenth century which advocates collectivism, the redistribution of unequal wealth, and frequently collective ownership of the technological means of production, in order to eradicate poverty and establish norms of altruism and co-operation in society. In more recent times, democratic socialism represents a more politically reformist agenda marked by a concern to ameliorate the worst effects of capitalism and class distinction through the development of an extensive welfare state. (*See also* **Reformism**)

Standpoint theory Arising from Marx's concern with the positive political possibilities associated with the marginal class category, the working class. Standpoint theory holds that political resistance arises from those groups most exploited within the existing social structure. In Marx's work, as in broader examples of standpoint theories, social transformation is itself tied to the actions of the most subordinated groups in society who thus become privileged in political analysis. In this way standpoint theories assume that identity locations, for example 'woman', equate to generalised understandings of the social world and that those groups that experience subordination and oppression are able to better gauge the 'true reality' of social organisation due to their subordinate location within it. Political analyses that are informed by standpoint theory focus upon the shared characteristics of subordinated groupings, their shared subversive political potentiality, and the greater access their marginal status affords them to a true/better understanding of reality. (*See also* **Difference, Identity politics, Marxism**)

Third-wave feminism The popular designation for the largely liberal but sometimes Postmodern-inflected feminist movement in the West during the 1990s. This movement frequently promotes the idea that Western societies have reached an era of 'post Feminism', suggesting that the goals of second-wave feminism have been achieved and/or that this older form of feminism is now outmoded because it is overly focused on women's victimised status. In this way, third-wave feminism often positions itself in antagonism to more established feminist projects and displays doubts about the concept of women as a broad social grouping, arguing that this category is unhelpful. Sometimes, however, the term third-wave feminism merely refers to recent feminist thinkers who are attuned to differences between women and are dubious about collective political action.

Trans politics As an articulated position Trans politics has involved the self-help orientation of the 1960s and 1970s, assimilationist transsexualism and, more recently in the late 1990s, 'transgender' Queer politics. Trans theorising has shown a similar path to Queer Theory, increasingly critiquing and rejecting notions of fixed identity. The term 'Transgender' is sometimes substituted as the coverall term to denote the whole field of Trans theorising. However, Transgender is perhaps more usefully employed as a particular direction in the latter, closely associated with Queer Theory, which represents the specific avowal of gender and sexual ambiguity (the avowal of a positioning as, for example, neither man nor woman).

Trans theory *See* **Trans politics**

Tyranny In political philosophy any form of rule which is not recognised as legitimate constitutes a tyranny over those ruled.

Women's Liberation Liberationist feminists in the 1960s and 1970s developed a critique of patriarchal societies and heterosexuality. In the process of examining men's power over women, they drew attention to power within sexuality, conceiving sexuality as reflecting existing unequal social relations rather than having an innocent or 'natural' beneficent status. Unlike Gay Liberation thinkers, these feminists perceived sexuality as intimately tied to normative power. (*See also* **Patriarchy**)

Universalism Central to Enlightenment thinking, and crucial to Modernist social theories, universalism can refer generally to any theory that asserts a single underlying explanation for large-scale social phenomena. It often appears in the idea that there exists a fixed basis for the Human shared by all people across all time. (*See also* **Enlightenment, Foundationalism, Macro theories, Modernist**)

Bibliography

Abelove, H. et al. eds, *The Lesbian and Gay Studies Reader*, Routledge, London, 1993

Ackerly, B.A. 'Feminist Theory: Liberal', *International Encyclopedia of the Social & Behavioural Sciences*, N. Smelser and P. Baltes editors-in-chief, Elsevier, New York and Oxford, 2001 (www.iesbs.com)

Adair, M. 'Will the real men's movement please stand up?', in K. Hagan ed., *Women Respond to the Men's Movement*, Pandora, San Francisco, 1992

Adam, B. *The Rise of a Gay and Lesbian Movement*, 2nd edition, Twayne, New York, 1995

Adam, B. et al. eds, *The Global Emergence of Gay and Lesbian Politics: National Imprints of a Worldwide Movement*, Temple University Press, Philadelphia, 1999

Adams, D. *The Hitchhiker's Guide to the Galaxy*, Pan Books, London, 1979

Adams R. and Savran, D. 'Introduction', in R. Adams and D. Savran eds, *The Masculinity Studies Reader*, Blackwell, Malden, MA, 2002

Adamson, W. 'Interview: Gayatri Spivak', *Thesis Eleven*, 15, 1986

Advertiser, Saturday, 6 February 1993, p.17

Ahmad, A. *In Theory: Classes, Nations, Literatures*, Verso, London, 1992

Ahmed, S. 'Beyond humanism and postmodernism: theorizing a feminist practice', *Hypatia*, 11: 2, Spring 1996

Alcoff, L. 'Philosophy matters: a review of recent work in feminist philosophy', *Signs*, 25: 3, Spring 2000

———— 'Cultural feminism versus post-structuralism: the identity crisis in feminist theory', *Signs*, 13: 3, 1988

Alice, L. 'Whose interests? Decolonising "race" and "ethnicity"', *Race, Gender, Class*, 11: 12, 1991

Alsop, R. et al., *Theorizing Gender*, Polity Press, Cambridge, 2002

Altman, D. 'Internationalising queer identities', paper given at a one-day conference titled, 'Sex and Society: History, Politics, Intimacy', University of Sydney, 1 March 2002

———— *Global Sex*, University of Chicago Press, Chicago, 2001a

———— 'Global Sex/Global Gays', in M. Blasius ed., *Sexual Identities, Queer Politics*, Princeton University Press, Princeton, NJ, 2001b

———— 'Case to the contrary' (Review of *Bowling Alone: The Collapse and Revival of American Community*), *The Gay & Lesbian Review Worldwide*, 8: 2, March 2001c

———— 'On not speaking', *Arena Magazine*, February 2001d

———— 'Gay/Lesbian movements', *International Encyclopedia of the Social & Behavioural Sciences*, N. Smelser and P. Baltes editors-in-chief, Elsevier, New York and Oxford, 2001e (www.iesbs.com)

Altman, D. 'From Gay Power to Gay Mardi Gras', *The Harvard Gay & Lesbian Review*, 6: 3, Summer 1999

—— *Defying Gravity: A Political Life*, Allen & Unwin, Sydney, 1997

—— *Homosexual: Oppression and Liberation* [1971], 2nd edition, New York University Press, New York, 1996

—— 'Political sexualities: meanings and identities in the time of AIDS', in R. Parker and J. Gagnon eds, *Conceiving Sexuality: Approaches to Sex Research in a Postmodern World*, Routledge, New York, 1995

—— *Power and Community*, Taylor & Francis, London, 1994

—— 'The Gay Movement ten years later', *The Nation*, 13 November 1982a

—— *The Homosexualization of America*, St Martin's Press, New York, 1982b

—— *Coming Out in the Seventies*, Wild and Woolley, Sydney, 1979

—— *Homosexual: Oppression and Liberation*, Outerbridge and Dienstfrey, New York, 1971

Ambercrombie, N. et al., *The Penguin Dictionary of Sociology*, 2nd edition, Penguin, Harmondsworth, 1988

Andermahr, S. et al., *A Glossary of Feminist Theory*, Arnold, London, 2000

Andolsen, B. *'Daughters of Jefferson, Daughters of Bootblacks': Racism and American Feminism*, Mercer University Press, Macon, GA, 1986

Andriote, J.M. *Victory Deferred: How AIDS Changed Gay Life in America*, University of Chicago Press, Chicago, 1999

Antoniou, M. 'Review of *Female Masculinity*', *Feminist Theory*, 1: 3, December 2000

Anzaldúa, G. 'La conciencia de la mestiza: towards a new consciousness', in L. Kaufmann ed., *American Feminist Thought at Century's End: A Reader*, Blackwell, Oxford, 1993

—— 'To(o) queer the writer: loca, escrita y chicana', in B. Warland ed., *InVersions: Writing by Dykes, Queers and Lesbians*, Press Gang, Vancouver, 1991

—— ed., *Making Face, Making Soul/Haciendo Caras: Creative and Critical Perspectives by Feminists of Colour*, Aunt Lute Foundation Books, San Francisco, 1990

—— *Borderlands/La Frontera: The New Mestiza*, Aunt Lute Foundation Books, San Francisco, 1987

Archer, L. '"Muslim brothers, black lads, traditional Asians": British Muslim young men's constructions of race, religion and masculinity', *Feminism and Psychology*, 11: 1, 2001

Ashbolt, A. Review of *Defying Gravity: A Political Life, Arena Magazine*, 34, April–May 1998

Ashcroft, B. et al., *Key Concepts in Post-Colonial Studies*, Routledge, London and New York, 1998

Ashe, F. et al., *Contemporary Social & Political Theory: An Introduction*, Open University Press, Buckingham and Philadelphia, 1999

Baird, B. 'The death of a great Australian', *Journal of Australian Studies*, 71, 15 December 2001

Banton, M. *The International Politics of Race*, Polity, Cambridge, 2002

Barnard, I. 'Queer Race', *Social Semiotics*, 9: 2, 1999

Barrett, F. 'The organizational construction of hegemonic masculinity: the case of the US Navy', *Gender, Work and Organization*, 3: 3, 1996

Barrett, M. 'Words and things: materialism and method in contemporary feminist analysis' in M. Barrett and A. Phillips eds, *Destabilizing Theory: Contemporary Feminist Debates*, Polity, Cambridge, 1992

—— *The Politics of Truth: From Marx to Foucault*, Stanford University Press, Stanford, CA, 1991

Barry, K. 'Sadomasochism: the new backlash to feminism', *Trivia*, 1, Fall 1982

Bartky, S. 'Foucault, femininity, and the modernization of patriarchal power', in I. Diamond and L. Quinby eds, *Feminism and Foucault: Reflections on Resistance*, Northeastern University Press, Boston, MA, 1988

Battle, J. and Lemelle Jr., A. 'Gender differences in African American attitudes toward gay males', *The Western Journal of Black Studies*, 26: 3, Fall 2002

Beal, B. 'Alternative masculinity and its effects on gender relations in the subculture of skate-boarding', *Journal of Sport Behaviour*, 19: 3, August 1996

Beasley, C. *What is Feminism?: An Introduction to Feminist Theory*, Sage, London, 1999

——— 'Negotiating difference: debatable feminism', in P. Nursey-Bray and C. Bacchi eds, *Left Directions: Is There a Third Way?*, University of Western Australia Press, Perth, 2001

——— 'Speaking of feminism … What are we arguing about? An essay in the politics of meaning', in L. Burns ed., *Feminist Alliances*, Rudopi, Amsterdam and London, 2005

Beasley, C. and Bacchi, C. 'Citizen bodies: embodying citizens – a feminist analysis', *International Feminist Journal of Politics*, 2: 3, 2000

Becker, D. et al. eds, *Postimperialism: International Capitalism and Development in the Late Twentieth Century*, Westview Press, Boulder, CO, 1987

Behrehdt, L. 'Black women and the feminist movement: implications for Aboriginal women in rights discourse', *Australian Feminist Law Journal*, 1: 27, 1993

Beilharz, P. ed., *The Bauman Reader*, Blackwell, Oxford, 2001

——— *Postmodern Socialism: Romanticism, City and State*, Melbourne University Press, Melbourne, 1994

——— 'Karl Marx', in P. Beilharz ed., *Social Theory: A Guide to Central Thinkers*, Allen & Unwin, Sydney, 1991

Bell, D. and Binnie, J. *The Sexual Citizen: Queer Politics and Beyond*, Polity Press, Cambridge, 2000

Benhabib, S. 'Subjectivity, historiography, and politics: reflections on the "feminism/post-modernism exchange"', in S. Benhabib et al. eds, *Feminist Contentions: A Philosophical Exchange*, Routledge, New York, 1995

——— 'Feminism and the question of postmodernism', in *The Polity Reader in Gender Studies'*, Polity, Cambridge, 1994

——— *Situating the Self*, Polity Press, Cambridge, 1992a

——— 'Feminism and postmodernism: an uneasy alliance', in J. Butler and J. Scott eds, *Feminists Theorize The Political*, Routledge, New York, 1992b

——— 'Subjectivity, historiography, and politics: Reflections on the feminism/postmodernism exchange', in J. Butler and J. Scott eds, *Feminists Theorize The Political*, Routledge, New York, 1992c

Benson, S. 'Asians have culture, West Indians have problems: discourses on race inside and outside anthropology', in T. Ranger et al. eds, *Culture, Identity and Politics*, Avebury Press, Aldershot, 1996

Berger, M. et al. eds, *Constituting Masculinities*, Routledge, New York, 1995

Berlant, L. and Warner, M. 'What does Queer Theory teach us about X?', *PMLA*, 110: 3, 1995

Best, S. and Kellner, D. *The Postmodern Turn*, Guilford Press & Routledge, New York and London, 1997

——— *Postmodern Theory: Critical Interrogations*, Palgrave Macmillan, London, 1991

Bhandari, N. 'Aboriginal violence against women', *Contemporary Review*, 283: 1655, December 2003

Biddulph, S. *Raising Boys*, Finch Sydney 1997

——— *Manhood: An Action Plan for Changing Men's Lives* [1994], 2nd edition, Finch, Sydney 1995

Bjerklie, D. 'Academic action figure: the life of the mind', *Time*, 158: 26, 17 December 2001

Blasius, M. *Gay and Lesbian Politics: Sexuality and the Emergence of a New Ethic*, Temple University Press, Philadelphia, 1994

Blasius, M. and Phelan, S. eds, *We Are Everywhere: A Historical Sourcebook of Gay and Lesbian Politics*, Routledge, New York, 1997

Bly, R. *Iron John: A Book about Men*, Addison-Wesley, New York, 1990

Bordo, S. 'Feminism, postmodernism, and gender-scepticism', in L. Nicholson ed., *Feminism/Postmodernism*, Routledge, London, 1990

Bornstein, K. *Gender Outlaw: On Men, Women and the Rest of Us*, Routledge, New York and London, 1994

Bourke, C. and Bourke, E. 'Indigenous studies: new pathways to development', *Journal of Australian Studies*, June 2002

Boyce Davies, C. *Black Women, Writing and Identity*, Routledge, London, 1994

Brah, A. 'Feminist theory and women of color', *International Encyclopedia of the Social & Behavioural Sciences*, N. Smelser and P. Baltes editors-in-chief, Elsevier, New York and Oxford, 2001 (www.iesbs.com)

―――― *Cartographies of Diaspora, Contesting Identities*, Routledge, London and New York, 1996

Braidotti, R. *Nomadic Subjects: Embodiment and Sexual Difference in Contemporary Feminist Theory*, Columbia University Press, New York, 1994a

―――― 'Feminism by any other name' (interview), *differences: A Journal of Feminist Cultural Studies*, 6: 2/3, 1994b

―――― *Patterns of Dissonance*, Blackwell, Oxford, 1991

Brandt, E. ed., *Dangerous Liaisons: Blacks, Gays and the Struggle for Equality*, New Press, New York, 1999

Bray, A. 'Not woman enough: Irigaray's culture of difference', *Feminist Theory*, 2: 3, December 2001

Bray, A. and Colebrook, C. 'The haunted flesh: corporeal feminism and the politics of (dis)embodiment', *Signs*, 24: 1, Autumn 1998

Breines, I., Connell, R. and Eide, I. eds, *Male Roles, Masculinities and Violence: A Culture of Peace Perspective*, UNESCO Paris, 2000

Brenkman, J. 'Queer post-politics', *Narrative*, 10: 2, May 2002

Brennan, T. 'An impasse in psychoanalysis and feminism', in H. Crowley and S. Himmelweit eds, *Knowing Women: Feminism and Knowledge*, Polity Press/Open University, Cambridge, 1992

Briggs J. and Davis, M. 'The brutal truth: putting domestic abuse on the black agenda', *Emerge*, September 1994

Bristow, J. and Wilson, A. eds, *Activating Theory: Lesbian, Gay and Bisexual Politics*, Lawrence and Wishart, London, 1993

Brod, H. 'The new Men's Studies: from feminist theory to gender scholarship', *Hypatia*, 2: 1, Winter, 1987a

―――― ed., *The Making of Masculinities: The New Men's Studies*, Allen & Unwin, Boston, MA, 1987b

―――― 'The case for men's studies', in H. Brod ed., *The Making of Masculinities: The New Men's Studies*, Allen & Unwin, Boston, MA, 1987c

―――― 'Themes and theses of men's studies', in H. Brod ed., *The Making of Masculinities: The New Men's Studies*, Allen & Unwin, Boston, MA, 1987d

―――― 'Eros thanatized: pornography and male sexuality', *Humanities in Society*, 7, 1984

Brod, H. and Kaufman, M. eds, *Theorizing Masculinities*, Sage, Thousand Oaks, CA, 1994

Bronski, M. *The Pleasure Principle: Sex, Backlash, and the Struggle for Gay Freedom*, St Martin's Press, New York, 1998

Brook, H. 'Queer football: feminism, sexuality, corporeality', *Critical inQueeries*, 1: 2, 1996

Broom, D. 'Gendering health, sexing illness', in J. Davis et al. eds, *Changing Society for Women's Health*, Proceedings of the 3rd (Australian) National Women's Health Conference, 17–19 November 1995, AGPS, Canberra, 1996

Brown, K. 'The social construction of a rape victim', in D. Carbado ed., *Black Men on Race, Gender, and Sexuality: A Critical Reader*, New York University Press, New York and London, 1999

Brown, R. *Rubyfruit Jungle*, Daughters Plainfield, VT, 1973

Brown, W. 'The impossibility of women's studies', *differences: A Journal of Feminist Cultural Studies*, 9, Fall 1997

Bryson, V. *Feminist Political Thought: An Introduction*, Palgrave Macmillan, Basingstoke and New York, 2003

—— *Feminist Political Theory: An Introduction*, Macmillan, Basingstoke and London, 1992

Buenor Hadjor, K. *Dictionary of Third World Terms*, 2nd edition, Penguin, London, 1993

Bunch, C. *Passionate Politics: Feminist Theory in Action, Essays 1968–86*, St Martin's Press, New York, 1987

Burr, V. *An Introduction to Social Constructionism*, Routledge, London and New York, 1995

Butler, J. 'Restaging the universal: hegemony and the limits of formalism', in J. Butler et al., *Contingency, Hegemony, Universality: Contemporary Debates on the Left*, Verso, London, 2000

—— 'Critically queer', in S. Phelan ed., *Playing with Fire: Queer Politics, Queer Theories*, Routledge, London, 1997a

—— 'Performative acts and gender constitution', in K. Conboy et al. eds, *Writing on the Body: Feminist Embodiment and Feminist Theory*, Columbia Univeristy Press, New York, 1997b

—— Excerpt from *Gender Trouble* [1990], in D. Meyers ed., *Feminist Social Thought*, Routledge, New York and London, 1997c

—— 'Contingent foundations: feminism and the question of "postmodernism"', in S. Benhabib et al. eds, *Feminist Contentions: A Philosophical Exchange*, Routledge, New York, 1995a

—— 'For a careful reading', in S. Benhabib et al. eds, *Feminist Contentions: A Philosophical Exchange*, Routledge, New York, 1995b

—— *Bodies That Matter*, Routledge, New York, 1993a

—— 'Imitation and gender insubordination' [1991], in H. Abelove et al. eds, *The Lesbian and Gay Studies Reader*, Routledge, New York and London, 1993b

—— 'Critically queer', *GLQ: A Journal of Lesbian and Gay Studies*, 1, 1993c

—— 'Sexual inversions', in J. Caputo and M. Yount eds, *Foucault and the Critique of Institutions*, Pennsylvania State University Press, University Park, PA, 1993d

—— *Gender Trouble: Feminism and the Subversion of Identity*, Routledge, New York and London, 1990

Byrd, R. and Guy-Sheftall, B. eds, *Traps: African American Men on Gender and Sexuality*, Indiana University Press, Bloomington and Indianapolis, IN, 2001

Cacoullos, A. 'American feminist theory', *American Studies International*, 39: 1, February 2001

Cahill, A. 'Foucault, rape and the construction of the feminine body', *Hypatia*, 15: 1, Winter 2000

Calhoun, C. 'Separating lesbian theory from feminist theory', in D. Meyers ed., *Feminist Social Thought: A Reader*, Routledge, New York and London, 1997

Califia, P. *Sex Changes: The Politics of Transgenderism*, Cleis Press, San Francisco, 1997a

———— 'Dildo envy and other phallic adventures', in F. Giles ed., *Dick for a Day: What Would You Do If You Had One?* Random House, Sydney, 1997b

———— 'Feminism and sadomasochism', in S. Jackson and S. Scott eds, *Feminism and Sexuality: A Reader*, Edinburgh University Press, Edinburgh, 1996

———— 'Gender bending: playing with roles and reversals' [1983], in P. Califia, *Public Sex: The Culture of Radical Sex*, Cleis Press, Pittsburgh and San Francisco, 1994

———— 'Gender blending', *Advocate*, 15 September 1983a

———— 'Doing it together: gay men, lesbians and sex', *Advocate*, 7 July 1983b

———— 'Feminism vs sex: a new conservative wave', *Advocate*, 21 February 1980

Canaan, J. and Griffen, C. 'The new men's studies: part of the problem or part of the solution?', in J. Hearn and D. Morgan eds, *Men, Masculinities and Social Theory*, Unwin Hyman, London, 1990

Carbado, D. 'Introduction', in D. Carbado ed., *Black Men on Race, Gender, and Sexuality: A Critical Reader*, New York University Press, New York and London, 1999a

———— 'The construction of O.J. Simpson', in D. Carbado ed., *Black Men on Race, Gender, and Sexuality: A Critical Reader*, New York University Press, New York and London, 1999b

———— 'Epilogue', in D. Carbado ed., *Black Men on Race, Gender, and Sexuality: A Critical Reader*, New York University Press, New York and London, 1999c

———— *Black Men on Race, Gender, and Sexuality: A Critical Reader*, New York University Press, New York, 1999d

Carby, H. 'White women listen! Black feminism and the boundaries of sisterhood', Centre for Contemporary Cultural Studies eds, *The Empire Strikes Back: Race and Racism in 70s Britain*, Hutchinson, London, 1982

Card, C. 'What is Lesbian Philosophy? A new introduction, in C. Card, *Adventures in Lesbian Philosophy*, Indiana University Press, Bloomington, IN, 1994

Carmen et al., 'Becoming visible: black lesbian discussions', *Feminist Review*, 17, Autumn 1984

Carrigan, T., Connell, R. and Lee, J. 'Hard and heavy: toward a sociology of masculinity', in M. Kaufman ed., *Beyond Patriarchy: Essays by Men on Pleasure, Power and Change*, Oxford University Press, Toronto, 1987

Carrigan, T., Lee, J. and Connell, R. 'Towards a new sociology of masculinity', *Theory and Society*, 14, 1985

Carver, T. 'A political theory of gender: perspectives on the "universal subject"', in V. Randall and G. Waylen eds, *Gender, Politics and the State*, Routledge, London and New York, 1998

———— *Gender Is Not a Synonym for Women*, Lynne Rienne, Boulder, CO, 1996

Charlesworth, H. 'Martha Nussbaum's Feminist Internationalism', *Ethics*, 111: 1, October 2000

Chase, C. 'Hermaphrodites with attitude: mapping the emergence of intersex political activism, *GLQ: A Journal of Gay and Lesbian Studies*, 4, 1998

Che, C. 'She's king of the road', *The Advocate*, 5 September 2001

Cheng, C. 'Marginalized masculinities and hegemonic masculinity: an introduction', *The Journal of Men's Studies*, 7: 3, Spring 1999

———— ed., *Masculinities in Organizations*, Sage, Thousand Oaks, CA, 1996

Chodorow, N. 'Gender, relation, and difference in psychoanalytic perspective', in D. Meyers ed., *Feminist Social Thought: A Reader*, Routledge, New York and London, 1997

———— 'The psychodynamics of the family', in H. Crowley and S. Himmelweit eds, *Knowing Women: Feminism and Knowledge*, Polity Press/Open University, Oxford, 1992

Chodorow, N. *The Reproduction of Mothering: Psychoanalysis and the Sociology of Gender*, 1978

Clark, M. 'Profeminist men's studies and gay ethics', *Journal of Men's Studies*, 3: 3, February 1995

Clarke, C. 'The failure to transform: homophobia in the black community', in B. Smith ed., *Home Girls: A Black Feminist Anthology*, Kitchen Table/Women of Color Press, New York, 1983

—— 'Lesbianism: an act of resistance', in C. Moraga and G. Anzaldúa eds, *This Bridge Called My Back*, Kitchen Table/Women of Color Press, New York, 1981

Clatterbaugh, K. 'Literature of the US men's movements', *Signs*, 25: 3, Spring 2000

—— *Contemporary Perspectives on Masculinity: Men, Women, and Politics in Modern Society* [1990], 2nd edition, Westview, Boulder, CO, 1997

Cocks, J. *The Oppositional Imagination: Feminism, Critique, and Political Theory*, Routledge, New York, 1989

Cohan, S. *Masked Men: Masculinity and the Movies in the Fifties*, Indiana University Press, Bloomington and Indianapolis, IN, 1997

Cohan, S. and Hark, I. *Screening the Male: Exploring Masculinities in the Hollywood Cinema*, Routledge, London, 1993

Cohen, C. 'Punks, bulldaggers, and welfare queens', *GLQ: A Journal of Lesbian and Gay Studies*, 3, 1997

Cohen, T. ed., *Men and Masculinity: A Text-Reader*, Wadsworth, Belmont CA, 2001

Colebrook, C. 'From radical representation to corporeal becomings: the feminist philosophy of Lloyd, Grosz, and Gatens', *Hypatia*, 15: 2, Spring 2000

Collins, P. *Black Feminist Thought*, Unwin Hyman, Boston, MA, 1990

—— 'The social construction of black feminist thought', *Signs*, 14: 4, 1989

—— 'Learning from the outsider within: the sociological significance of black feminist thought', *Social Problems*, 33: 6, 1986

Coltrane, S. 'Marketing the marriage "solution": misplaced simplicity in the politics of fatherhood (2001 Presidential address to the Pacific Sociological Association)', *Sociological Perspectives*, 44: 4, Winter 2001

Combahee River Collective, 'A Black feminist statement' [1977], in G. Hull et al. eds, *All the Women are White, All the Blacks are Men, But Some of Us are Brave*, The Feminist Press, Old Westbury, NY, 1982

Connell, R. 'Masculinities, change, and conflict in global society: thinking about the future of men's studies', *The Journal of Men's Studies*, 11: 3, Spring 2003

—— *Gender*, Polity Press, Cambridge, 2002

—— 'Studying men and masculinity', *Resources for Feminist Research*, Fall–Winter 2001

—— *The Men and the Boys*, Polity Press, Cambridge, 2000

—— *Masculinities*, Polity Press, Cambridge, 1995

—— 'Psychoanalysis on masculinity', in H. Brod and M. Kaufman eds, *Theorizing Masculinities*, Sage, Thousand Oaks, CA, 1994

—— *Gender and Power: Society, the Person and Sexual Politics*, Polity Press, Cambridge, 1987

—— 'Men's bodies' [1979], in *Which Way is Up?* Allen & Unwin, London and Boston, MA, 1983

—— *Ruling Class, Ruling Culture: Studies of Conflict, Power and Hegemony in Australian Life*, Cambridge University Press, Cambridge, 1977

Connell, R. and Dowsett, G. '"The unclean motion of the generative parts": frameworks in western thought on sexuality', in R. Connell and G. Dowsett eds, *Rethinking Sex: Social Theory and Sexuality Research*, Melbourne University Press, Melbourne, 1992

Connell, R. and Irving, T. *Class Structure in Australian History*, 2nd edition, Longman Cheshire, Melbourne, 1992

Connell, R. and Kippax, S. 'Sexuality and the AIDS crisis: patterns of pleasure and practice in an Australian sample of gay and bisexual men', *The Journal of Sex Research*, 27: 2, 1990

Connell, R. et al., 'Understanding men's health and illness: a gender-relations approach to policy, research, and practice', *Journal of American College Health*, 48: 6, May 2000

Corber, R. and Valocchi, S. eds, *Queer Studies: An Interdisciplinary Reader*, Blackwell, New York, 2003

Cornwall, A. and Lindisfarne, N. 'Dislocating masculinity: gender, power and anthropology', in A. Cornwall and N. Lindisfarne eds, *Dislocating Masculinity: Comparative Ethnographies*, Routledge, London and New York, 1993

Corrin, C. *Feminist Perspectives on Politics*, Longman, London and New York, 1999

Cranny-Francis, A. et al., *Gender Studies: Terms and Debates*, Palgrave Macmillan, Basingstoke, 2003

Creed, B. 'Queer Theory and its discontents: queer desires, queer cinema', in N. Grieve and A. Burns eds, *Australian Women: Contemporary Feminist Thought*, Oxford University Press, Melbourne, 1994

Cromwell, J. *Transmen and FTMS: Identities, Bodies, Genders, and Sexualities*, University of Illinois Press, Urbana, IL, 1999

Coulter, G. Review of *Men and Power*, *The Canadian Review of Sociology and Anthropology*, 39: 2, May 2002

Coulter, N. 'Boys: masculinities in contemporary culture', *Sex Roles: A Journal of Research*, 36: 5–6, March 1997

Crowley, H. and Himmelweit, S. eds, *Knowing Women: Feminism and Knowledge*, Polity Press/Open University, Cambridge, 1992

Crozier, M. 'The Frankfurt School', in P. Beilharz ed., *Social Theory: A Guide to Central Thinkers*, Allen & Unwin, Sydney, 1991

Cruz, J.M. '"Why doesn't he just leave?": gay male domestic violence and the reasons victims stay', *The Journal of Men's Studies*, 11: 3, Spring 2003

Cusac, A. 'Portrait of a sex radical' (interview with Pat Califia), *The Progressive*, October 1996

Dalton, H. 'AIDS in Blackface', in D. Carbado ed., *Black Men on Race, Gender, and Sexuality: A Critical Reader*, New York University Press, New York and London, 1999a

——— 'Pull together as the community', in D. Carbado ed., *Black Men on Race, Gender, and Sexuality: A Critical Reader*, New York University Press, New York and London, 1999b

Daly, M. *Gyn/Ecology: The Metaethics of Radical Feminism*, Beacon Press, Boston, MA, 1978

Darius, S. and Jonsson, S. Interview with Gayatri Spivak, *Boundary 2*, 20: 2, 1993

Dauphin, G. 'What's love got to do with it? A conversation with writer/painter/cultural critic bell hooks about her love books', *Black Issues Book Review*, 4: 2, March–April 2002

Davies, M. *Asking the Law Question*, Law Book Co., Sydney, 1994

Davis, A. *Women, Race and Class*, Random House, New York, 1981

de Kock, L. 'New Nation Writers Conference in South Africa' (Interview with Gayatri Spivak), *Ariel: A Review of International English Literature*, 23: 3, July 1992

de Lauretis, T. 'Queer Theory: lesbian and gay sexualities: an introduction', *differences: A Journal of Feminist Cultural Studies*, 3: 2, 1991

Deleuze, G. and Guattari, F. *A Thousand Plateaus*, University of Minnesota Press, Minneapolis, MN, 1987

Delphy, C. *Close to Home: A Materialist Analysis of Women's Oppression*, Hutchinson, London, 1984

D'Emilio, J. 'Capitalism and gay identity', in R. Lancaster and M. di Leonardo eds, *The Gender/Sexuality Reader: Culture, History, Political Economy*, Routledge, New York and London, 1997

—— *Sexual Politics. Sexual Communities*, University of Chicago Press, Chicago, 1983

Denfeld, R. *The New Victorians: A Young Woman's Challenge to the Old Feminist Order*, Warner Books, New York, 1995

Deveaux, M. 'Political morality and culture: what difference do differences make?', *Social Theory and Practice*, 28: 3, July 2002

Devor, H. Review of *Second Skins: The Body Narratives of Transsexuality*, *The Journal of Sex Research*, 36: 2, May 1999

Dhairyam, S. 'Racing the lesbian, dodging white critics', in L. Doan ed., *The Lesbian Postmodern*, Columbia University Press, New York, 1994

di Leonardo, M. and Lancaster, R. eds, *The Gender/Sexuality Reader*, Routledge, New York & London, 1997

Dinelli, D. Review of Catherine MacKinnon's *Only Words*, *Michigan Law Review*, 92: 6, May 1994

Dinnerstein, D. *The Mermaid and the Minotaur: Sexual Arrangements and Human Malaise*, Other Press, New York [1976], 1999

Diprose, R. *The Bodies of Women: Ethics, Embodiment and Sexual Difference*, Routledge, London, 1994

Donovan, J. *Feminist Theory: The Intellectual Traditions*, Continuum, New York, 2000

Doty, W. *Myths of Masculinity*, Crossroad, New York, 1993

Douglas, C. Review of *Quintessence: A Radical Elemental Feminist Manifesto*, *off our backs*, 28: 11, December 1998

Dowsett, G. 'Wusses and willies: masculinity and contemporary sexual politics', *Journal of Interdisciplinary Gender Studies*, 3: 2, 2 December 1998

—— I'll show you mine, if you'll show me yours: gay men, masculinity research, men's studies and sex', *Theory and Society*, 22, 1993

Drummond, M. 'Sport and images of masculinity: the meaning of relationships in the life course of "elite" male athletes', *The Journal of Men's Studies*, 10: 2, Winter 2002

Duberman, M. *Left Out: The Politics of Exclusion 1964–2002*, South End Press, Cambridge, MA, 2002a

—— 'Gayness becomes you', *The Nation*, 274: 19, 20 May 2002b

—— *Midlife Queer: Autobiography of a Decade 1971–1981*, University of Wisconsin Press, Madison, WI, 1998

Duggan, L. 'Making it perfectly queer', *Socialist Review*, 22, 1992

Duggan, L. and Hunter, N. *Sex Wars: Sexual Dissent and Political Culture*, Routledge, New York, 1996

Dworkin, A. *Letters From a War Zone*, Secker & Warburg, London, 1988

—— *Intercourse*, Secker & Warburg, London, 1987

—— *Pornography: Men Possessing Women*, Perigee, New York, 1981

Eagleton, T. 'Capitalism, modernism and postmodernism', *New Left Review*, 152, 1985

Echols, A. 'The taming of the Id: feminist sexual politics 1968–83', in C. Vance ed., *Pleasure and Danger: Exploring Female Sexuality*, Routledge, London, 1984

—— 'Cultural feminism: feminist capitalism and the anti-pornography movement, *Social Text*, 7, Spring/Summer 1983a

—— 'The new feminism of yin and yang', in A. Snitow et al. eds, *Powers of Desire: The Politics of Sexuality*, Monthly Review Press, New York, 1983b

Edwards, A. 'The sex/gender distinction: has it outlived its usefulness?', *Australian Feminist Studies*, 10, Summer 1989

Edwards, T. 'Queer fears: against the cultural turn', *Sexualities*, 1: 4, November 1998

Ehrenreich, B. *The Hearts of Men: American Dreams and the Flight from Commitment*, Doubleday, New York, 1983

Ekins, R. and King, D. eds, *Blending Genders: Social Aspects of Cross-Dressing and Sex Changing*, Routledge, London, 1996

Epstein, J. 'Either/or – neither both: Sexual Ambiguity and the Ideology of Gender', *Genders*, 7, 1990

Epstein, S. Review of *Difference Troubles*, *Sexualities*, 2: 2, May 1999

Escoffier, J. 'Inside the ivory closet: the challenges facing lesbian and gay studies, *Out/Look: National Lesbian and Gay Quarterly*, 10, 1990

Etkin, M. 'The men's movement', *Canadian Dimension*, 25: 1, January–February 1991

Evans, J. and Frank, B. 'Contradictions and tensions: exploring relations of masculinities in the numerically female-dominated nursing profession', *The Journal of Men's Studies*, 11: 3, Spring 2003

Evans, M. 'The problem of gender for women's studies', *Women's Studies International Forum*, 13: 5, 1990

Farrell, W. *The Myth of Male Power: Why Men are the Disposable Sex*, Simon & Schuster, New York, 1993

———— *The Liberated Man*, Random House, New York, 1974

Faust, B. 'Australian-style feminism: what a gift to the world!', *The Australian*, 22 February 1994

Fausto-Sterling, A. 'The five sexes', *The Sciences*, March–April 1993

Feinberg, L. *Trans Liberation: Beyond Pink or Blue*, Beacon Press, Boston, MA, 1998

———— *Stone Butch Blues*, Firebrand Books, Ithaca, NY, 1993

Felksi, R. 'American and British Feminisms', in P. Beilharz ed., *Social Theory: A Guide to Central Thinkers*, Allen & Unwin, Sydney, 1992

Ferguson, A. 'Moral responsibility and social change: a new theory of self' (Special Issue: Third Wave Feminisms), *Hypatia*, 12: 3, Summer 1997

———— 'Twenty years of feminist philosophy', *Hypatia*, 9: 3, Summer 1994

Ferguson, K. *The Man Question: Visions of Subjectivity in Feminist Theory*, University of California Press, Berkeley, CA, 1993

Ferrari, R. Review of *Mapping Male Sexuality: Nineteenth Century England, English Literature in Transition 1880–1920*, 45: 1, Winter 2002

Ferrée, M. et al. eds, *Revisioning Gender*, Sage, Thousand Oaks, CA, and London, 1999

Ffytche, M. 'Text appeal', *Not Only Black and White*, 6, April 1994

Firestone, S. *The Dialectic of Sex: The Case for Feminist Revolution*, Bantam, New York, 1970

Flax, J. 'Monster's Ball: representations of race and gender in the contemporary United States', *Black Renaissance/Renaissance Noire*, 5: 1, Spring 2003

———— 'Reentering the labyrinth: revisiting Dorothy Dinnerstein's *The Mermaid and the Minotaur*', *Signs*, 27: 4, Summer 2002

———— *The American Dream in Black & White*, Cornell University Press, Ithaca, NY, and London, 1998

———— Keynote address, Australasian Political Studies Association Annual Conference 1995, cited in C. Johnson, 'Visiting the margins', *Theory & Event*, 1: 3, 1997

———— 'The end of innocence', in J. Butler and J. Scott eds, *Feminists Theorize The Political*, Routledge, New York, 1992

———— 'Postmodernism and gender relations in feminist theory', *Signs*, 12: 4, 1987

———— 'Political philosophy and the patriarchal unconscious: a psychoanalytic perspective on epistemology and metaphysics', in S. Harding and M. Hintikka eds, *Discovering Reality:*

Feminist Perspectives on Epistemology, Metaphysics, Methodology, and Philosophy of Science, D. Reidel, Dordrecht, Holland, 1983

Fleming, R. 'Feminist revolutionary comes down to earth' (*PW* talks with bell hooks), *Publishers Weekly*, 249: 47, 25 November 2002

Flood, M. (comp.) *The Men's Bibliography*, 11th edition, May 2003 (http://www.mensbiblio.xyonline.net)

——— 'Four strands', *XY: men, sex, politics*, 6: 3, 1996a

——— 'State of the movement', *XY: men, sex, politics*, 6: 3, 1996b

Foucault, M. *The Use of Pleasure*, trans. R. Hurley, Vintage Books, New York, 1990

——— 'On the genealogy of ethics', in P. Rabinow ed., *The Foucault Reader*, Penguin, Harmondsworth, 1986

——— 'What is Enlightenment?', in P. Rabinow ed., *The Foucault Reader*, Pantheon, New York, 1984

——— 'The subject and power', in H. Dreyfus and P. Rabinow eds, *Michel Foucault: Beyond Structuralism and Hermeneutics*, University of Chicago Press, Chicago, 1982

——— 'Two lectures', in C. Gordon ed., *Michel Foucault: Power/Knowledge*, Harvester, Brighton, 1980

——— *The History of Sexuality: Vol. 1*, trans. R. Hurley, Penguin, Harmondsworth, 1978

——— *Discipline and Punish: The Birth of the Prison*, trans. A. Sheridan, Allen Lane, London, 1977

——— *The Archaeology of Knowledge*, Pantheon Books, New York, 1972

Franklin II, C. '"Ain't I a man?" The efficacy of black masculinities for men's studies in the 1990s?', in R. Majors and J. Gordon eds, *The American Black Male: His Present Status and His Future*, Nelson-Hall, Chicago, 1994

Fraser, N. 'Pragmatism, feminism, and the linguistic turn', in S. Benhabib et al. eds, *Feminist Contentions: A Philosophical Exchange*, Routledge, New York, 1995

Fraser, N. and Nicholson, L. 'Social criticism without philosophy: an encounter between feminism and postmodernism', in L. Nicholson ed., *Feminism/Postmodernism*, Routledge, New York, 1990

Freud, S. 'Femininity' [1933], in *New Introductory Lectures on Psychoanalysis*, ed., J. Stachey, Penguin Harmondsworth, 1973

Friedan, B. *The Feminine Mystique*, Penguin, Harmondsworth, 1965

Fuss, D. *Essentially Speaking: Feminism, Nature and Difference*, Routledge, New York and London, 1989

Gaines, J. 'Feminist heterosexuality and its politically incorrect pleasures', *Critical Inquiry*, 21, Winter 1995

Gamble, S. ed., *The Routledge Critical Dictionary of Feminism and Postfeminism*, Routledge, New York, 2000a

——— 'Postfeminism', in S. Gamble ed., *The Routledge Critical Dictionary of Feminism and Postfeminism*, Routledge, New York, 2000b

Gamson, J. 'Messages of exclusion: gender, movements, and symbolic boundaries', *Gender & Society*, 11: 2, April–May 1997

Garber, M. *Vested Interests: Cross-Dressing and Cultural Anxiety*, Routledge, New York, 1992

Gardiner, J. 'Gender and masculinity texts: consensus and concerns for feminist classrooms', *NWSA Journal*, 15: 1, Spring 2003

——— ed., *Masculinity Studies and Feminism: New Directions*, Columbia University Press, New York, 2002

Gatens, M. 'The dangers of a woman-centred philosophy', in *The Polity Reader in Gender Studies*, Polity Press, Oxford, 1994

Gatens, M. *Feminism and Philosophy: Perspectives on Difference and Equality*, Polity Press, Cambridge, 1991

Gibbins, J. and Reimer, B. *The Politics of Postmodernity: An Introduction to Contemporary Politics and Culture*, Sage, Thousand Oaks, CA, and London, 1999

Gilbert, R. and Gilbert, P. *Masculinity Goes To School*, Allen & Unwin, Sydney, 1998

Giles, F. ed., *Dick for a day: What Would you Do If you Had One?* Random House, Sydney, 1997

Gilligan, C. *In a Different Voice*, Harvard University Press, Cambridge, MA, 1982

Gilroy, P. *Small Acts*, Serpent's Tail, London, 1993a

—— *The Black Atlantic: Modernity and Double Consciousness*, Harvard University Press, Cambridge, MA, 1993b

—— *There Ain't No Black in the Union Jack*, Routledge, London, 1992

Gilroy, P. et al. eds, *Without Guarantees: In Honour of Stuart Hall*, Verso, London, 2000

Glass, J. *Shattered Selves: Multiple Personality in a Postmodern World*, Cornell University Press, Ithaca, NY, 1993

Goldberg, H. *The Hazards of Being Male: Surviving the Myth of Masculine Privilege*, Nash, New York, 1976

Goldman, R. 'Who is that queer queer? Exploring norms around sexuality, race, and class in queer theory', in B. Beemyn and M. Eliason eds, *Queer Studies: A Lesbian, and Gay, Bisexual, and Transgender Anthology*, New York University Press, New York and London, 1996

Goldrick-Jones, A. 'Pessimism, paralysis, and possibility: crisis-points in profeminism', *The Journal of Men's Studies*, 9: 3, Spring 2001

Goldstein, R. 'Attack of the homocons: they're here … they're queer … they're conservative', *The Nation*, 275: 1, 1 July 2002

Gomez, J. 'Representations of black lesbians', *The Harvard Gay & Lesbian Review*, 6: 3, Summer 1999

Goodey, J. 'Boy's don't cry: masculinities, fear of crime and fearlessness', *British Journal of Criminology*, 37: 3, Summer 1997

Goodman, R. 'Beyond the enforcement principle: sodomy laws, social laws, and social panoptics', *California Law Review*, 89: 3, May 2001

Gordon, L. 'Critical "mixed race"?', *Social Identities*, 1: 2, 1995

Gray, J. *Men are from Mars, Women are from Venus*, Thorsons, London, 1993

Greenberg, D. 'Washington perspective: the new politics of AIDS', *The Lancet*, 340: 8811, 11 July 1992

Griffen, C. Review of books by Harry Brod, Michael Kimmel and Bob Connell, *Feminist Review*, 33, Autumn 1989

Griffen, S. *Rape: The Power of Consciousness*, Harper & Row, San Francisco, 1979

Grimshaw, J. *Feminist Philosophers: Women's Perspectives on Philosophical Traditions*, Harvester Wheatsheaf, London and New York, 1986

Gross, D. 'The gender rap: "toxic masculinity" and other male troubles', *The New Republic*, 202: 1, 16 April 1990

Gross, E. (now publishes as Grosz), 'Conclusion: what is Feminist Theory?', in C. Pateman and E. Gross eds, *Feminist Challenges: Social and Political Theory*, Allen & Unwin, Sydney, 1986

Grosz, E. 'Psychoanalysis and the imaginary body', in S. Kemp and J. Squires eds, *Feminisms*, Oxford University Press, Oxford and New York, 1997

—— *Space, Time and Perversion: Essays on the Politics of the Body*, Routledge, New York, 1996

—— 'Lesbian fetishism?', in *Space, Time and Perversion: The Politics of Bodies*, Allen & Unwin, Sydney, 1995

Grosz, E. 'Theorising corporeality: bodies, sexuality and the feminist academy' (interview), *Melbourne Journal of Politics*, 22, 1994a

—— 'Experimental desire: rethinking queer subjectivity', in J. Copcec ed., *Supposing the Subject*, Verso, London, 1994b

—— *Volatile Bodies: Toward a Corporeal Feminism*, Allen & Unwin, Sydney, 1994c

—— 'Identity and difference: a response', in P. James ed., *Critical Political*, Arena, Melbourne 1994d

—— *Jacques Lacan: A Feminist Introduction*, Routledge, New York, 1990

—— *Sexual Subversions: Three French Feminists*, Allen & Unwin, Sydney, 1989

—— 'The in(ter)vention of feminist knowledges', in B. Caine et al. eds, *Crossing Boundaries: Feminisms and the Critique of Knowledges*, Allen & Unwin, Sydney, 1988

—— 'Notes towards a corporeal feminism', *Australian Feminist Studies*, 5, Summer 1987

Grünell, M. and Saharso, S. 'bell hooks and Nira Yuval-Davis on race, ethnicity, class and gender', *European Journal of Women's Studies*, 6, 1999

Gubar, S. 'What ails Feminist criticism?' *Critical Inquiry*, 24, Summer 1998

Gunew, S. 'Feminist knowledge: critique and construct', in S. Gunew ed., *Feminist Knowledge: Critique and Construct*, Routledge, London and New York, 1990

Gunew, S. and Spivak, G. 'Questions of multi-culturalism: Sneja Gunew and Gayatri Spivak', in G. Spivak, *The Post-Colonial Critic: Interviews, Strategies, Dialogues*, ed., S. Harasym, Routledge, London, 1990

Gutmann, S. 'Waging war on sex crimes and videotape', *Insight on the News*, 9: 18, 3 May 1993

Halberstam, J. 'Telling tales: Brandon Teena, Billy Tipton, and transgender biography', in M. Sánchez and L. Schlossberg eds, *Passing: Identity and Interpretation in Sexuality, Race and Religion*, New York University Press, New York and London, 2001

—— Review of *Trans Liberation: Beyond Pink or Blue*, *Signs*, 26: 1, Autumn 2000

—— 'Oh bondage up yours', in M. Rottnek ed., *Sissies and Tomboys: Gender Nonconformity and Homosexual Childhood*, New York University Press, New York, 1999

—— *Female Masculinity*, Duke Universtiy Press, Durham, NC, and London, 1998

—— Review of *Sexy Bodies* and *Lesbian Erotics*, *Signs*, 22: 4, Summer 1997

—— 'F2M: the making of female masculinity', in L. Doan ed., *The Lesbian Postmodern*, Columbia University Press, New York, 1944

Halberstam, J. and Volcano, D.L. *The Drag King Book*, Serpent's Tail, London, 1999

Hale, J. 'Are lesbians women?', *Hypatia*, 11: 2, Spring 1996

Halkitis, P. 'An exploration of perceptions of masculinity among gay men living with HIV', *The Journal of Men's Studies*, 9: 3, Spring 2001

Hall, S. 'Conclusion: the multi-cultural question', in B. Hesse ed., *Un/Settled Multiculturalisms: Diasporas, Entanglements, Transruptions,* Zed Books, London, 2000

Halperin, D. *Saint Foucault: Towards a Gay Hagiography*, Oxford University Press, Oxford, 1995

—— 'Homosexuality: a cultural construct: an exchange with Richard Schneider', in *One Hundred Years of Homosexuality and Other Essays on Greek Love*, Routledge, New York, 1990

Hammonds, E. 'Black (w)holes and the geometry of black female sexuality', *differences: A Journal of Feminist Cultural Studies*, 6: 2–3, Summer–Fall 1994

Harding, S. *Whose Science? Whose Knowledge? Thinking from Women's Lives*, Cornell University Press, Ithaca, NY, 1991

Harris, L. 'My two mothers, America, and the Million Man March', in D. Carbado ed., *Black Men on Race, Gender, and Sexuality: A Critical Reader*, New York University Press, New York and London, 1999

Hartmann, H. 'The unhappy marriage of Marxism and Feminism: towards a more progressive union', in L. Sargent ed., *Women and Revolution: A Discussion of the Unhappy Marriage of Marxism and Feminism*, South End Press, Boston, MA, 1981

Hartsock, N. *The Feminist Standpoint Revisited & Other Essays*, Westview Press, Boulder, CO, 1998a

—————— 'The feminist standpoint revisited', in *The Feminist Standpoint Revisited & Other Essays*, Westview Press, Boulder, CO, 1998b

—————— 'Standpoint theories for the next century', *Women and Politics*, 18: 3, Fall 1997

—————— 'Foucault on power: a theory for women', in L. Nicholson ed., *Feminism/Postmodernism*, Routledge, New York, 1990

—————— 'Rethinking modernism: minority vs majority theories', *Cultural Critique*, 7, 1987

—————— 'The feminist standpoint: developing the ground for a specifically feminist historical materialism', in S. Harding and M. Hintikka eds, *Discovering Reality*, D. Reidel, Dordrecht, Boston and London, 1983

Hausman, B. 'Recent transgender theory', *Feminist Studies*, 27: 2, 2001

—————— *Changing Sex: Transsexualism, Technology, and the idea of Gender*, Duke University Press, Durham, NC, 1995

Hawkesworth, M. 'Confounding gender', *Signs*, 22: 3, 1997a

—————— 'Reply to McKenna and Kessler, Smith, Scott, and Connell: interrogating gender', *Signs*, 22: 3, 1997b

Hearn, J. 'From hegemonic masculinity to the hegemony of men', *Feminist Theory*, 5: 1, April 2004

—————— '"Is masculinity dead?" A critical account of the concept of masculinity/masculinities', in M. Mac an Ghaill ed., *Understanding Masculinities – Social Relations and Cultural Arenas*, Open University Press, Milton Keynes, 1996

—————— 'Research in men and masculinities: some sociological issues and possibilities', *Australia and New Zealand Journal of Sociology*, 30: 1, April 1994

Heath, M. and Stacey, J. Review Essay: transatlantic family travail (1), *The American Journal of Sociology*, 108: 3, November 2002

Hekman, S. 'Beyond identity: feminism, identity and identity politics', *Feminist Theory*, 1: 3, December 2000

—————— 'Truth and method: feminist standpoint revisited', *Signs*, 22: 2, Winter 1997

—————— Review of *Unbearable Weight: Feminism, Culture and the Body* and *Bodies That Matter*, *Hypatia*, 10: 4, 1995

—————— 'The feminist critique of rationality', *The Polity Reader in Gender Studies*, Polity Press, Cambridge, 1994

Held, D. *Introduction to Critical Theory: Horkheimer to Habermas*, University of California Press, Berkeley and Los Angeles, CA, 1980

Held, V. 'Caring relations and principles of justice', in J. Sterba ed., *Controversies in Feminism*, Rowman & Littlefield, Lanham, MD, 2001

—————— 'Feminism and moral theory', in E. Kittay and D. Meyers eds, *Women and Moral Theory*, Rowman & Littlefield, Totowa, NJ, 1987

Helliwell C. and Hindess, B. 'The "Empire of Uniformity" and the government of subject peoples', *Cultural Values*, 6: 1, 2002

Hemmings, C. 'Hausman's horror', *Radical Deviance: A Journal of Transgendered Politics*, 2: 2, 1996

Hennessy, R. 'Queer visibility in commodity culture', in L. Nicholson and S. Seidman eds, *Social Postmodernism: Beyond Identity Politics*, Cambridge University Press, Cambridge and New York, 1995

Hennessy, R. *Materialist Feminism and the Politics of Discourse*, Routledge, New York and London, 1993

Herdt, G. *Same Sex, Different Cultures: Gays and Lesbians across Cultures*, Westview Press, Boulder, CO, 1997

—— ed., *Third Sex, Third Gender: Beyond Sexual Dimorphism in Culture and History*, Zone Books, New York, 1994

—— *Guardians of the Flutes: Idioms of Masculinity*, McGraw-Hill, New York, 1981

Heyes, C. 'Feminist solidarity after Queer Theory: the case of transgender (intersex and transgender)', *Signs*, 28: 4, Summer 2003

Heywood, L. *Bodymakers: A Cultural Anatomy of Women's Body Building*, Rutgers University Press, New Brunswick, NJ, and London, 1998

Hicks, R. *The Masculine Journey: Understanding the Six Stages of Manhood*, NavPress, Colorado Springs, CO, 1993

Hindess, B. 'The liberal government of unfreedom', *Alternatives*, 26: 2, 2001

Hird, M. 'For a sociology of transsexualism', *Sociology*, 36: 3, August 2002

—— Review of *Reclaiming Genders: Transsexual Gramars at the Fin de Siecle*, *Sociology*, 35: 2, May 2001

—— 'Gender's nature: intersexuality, transsexualism and the "sex"/"gender" binary', *Feminist Theory*, 1: 3, 2000

Hocquenghem, G. *Homosexual Desire*, Alison and Busby, London, 1978

Hodge, D. *Did You Meet Any Mulagas? A Homosexual History of Australia's Tropical Capital*, Little Gem, Nightcliff, Northern Terrritory, Australia, 1993

Hogg, R. Review of *Making the Australian Male: Middle Class Masculinity 1870–1920*, *The Australian Journal of Politics and History*, 48: 3, 2002

Hollier, N. 'Scrutiny of wealth-rule', *Australian*, Wednesday 3 September 2003

Hollinsworth, D. *Race and Racism in Australia*, Social Science Press, Melbourne, 1998

Holmes, J. 'Race and sexuality: What does it mean to be Aboriginal and gay?', Master's Thesis, University of South Australia, Adelaide, South Australia, 1995

hooks, b. *Rock My Soul: Black People and Self Esteem*, Atria Books, New York, 2003a

—— 'Tearing out the root of self-hatred: racism plays upon the low self-esteem within the Black community. Our continued survival demands that we care for our own souls', *The Other Side*, 39: 3, May–June 2003b (excerpt from *Rock My Soul: Black People and Self Esteem*, Atria Books, New York, 2003a)

—— *We Real Cool: Black Men and Masculinity*, Routledge, London and New York, 2003c

—— *Communion: The Female Search for Love*, Morrow, New York, 2002

—— *Salvation: Black People and Love*, Morrow, New York, 2001

—— *Feminism is for Everyone: Passionate Politics*, South End Press, Boston, MA, 2000a

—— *All about Love: New Visions*, Morrow, New York, 2000b

—— 'Black women and feminism, in S. Kemp and J. Squires eds, *Feminisms*, Oxford University Press, Oxford and New York, 1997a

—— 'Sisterhood: political solidarity between women', in D. Meyers ed., *Feminist Social Thought: A Reader*, Routledge, New York and London, 1997b

—— *Black Looks: Race and Representation*, South End Press, Boston, MA, 1992a

—— 'Reconstructing black masculinity', in *Black Looks: Race and Representation*, South End Press, Boston, MA, 1992b

—— 'Sisterhood: political solidarity between women', in S. Gunew ed., *A Reader in Feminist Knowledge*, Routledge, London and New York, 1991

—— *Yearning: Race, Gender and Cultural Politics*, South End Press, Boston, MA, 1990a

—— 'Third World Divas', in *Yearning: Race, Gender and Cultural Politics*, South End Press, Boston, MA, 1990b

———— 'Postmodern blackness', in *Yearning: Race, Gender and Cultural Politics*, South End Press, Boston, MA, 1990c

———— 'Black women: shaping feminist theory' (excerpt from *Feminist Theory* [1984]), in S. Ruth ed., *Issues in Feminism: An Introduction to Women's Studies*, 2nd edition, Mayfield, Mountain View CA, London and Toronto, 1990d

———— *Talking Back: Thinking Feminist, Thinking Black*, Sheba, London, 1989

———— *Feminist Theory: From Margin to Center*, South End Press, Boston, MA, 1984a

———— 'Sisterhood: political solidarity between women', in *Feminist Theory: From Margin to Center*, South End Press, Boston, MA, 1984b

———— *Ain't I A Woman: Black Women and Feminism*, South End Press, Boston, MA, 1981a

———— 'Black women and feminism', in *Ain't I A Woman: Black Women and Feminism*, South End Press, Boston, MA, 1981b

hooks, b. et al. (panel discussion) 'Let's get real about feminism: the backlash, the myths, the movements', *MS*, iv: 2, September–October 1993

Hostetler, A. and Herdt, G. 'Culture, sexual lifeways, and developmental subjectivities: rethinking sexual taxonomies', *Social Research*, 65: 2, Summer 1998

Howe, S. *Afrocentrism: Mythical Pasts and Imagined Homes*, Verso, London, 1998

Huggins, J. 'Black women and women's liberation', *Hecate*, xiii: 1, 1987

Huggins, J. et al., 'Letter to the editors', *Women's Studies International Forum*, 14: 5, 1991

Hughes, K. Review of *The Men and the Boys*, *Arena Magazine*, April 2001

———— 'Feminism for beginners', in K. Hughes ed., *Contemporary Australian Feminism 2*, 2nd edition, Longman, Melbourne, 1997

Hunter, L. 'The celluloid cubicle: regressive constructions of masculinity in 1990s office movies', *Journal of American Culture* (Malden, MA), 26: 1, March 2003

Ifekwunigwe, J. *Scattered Belongings: Cultural Paradoxes of 'Race', Nation, and Gender*, Routledge, London and New York, 1999

Irigaray, L. *Speculum of the Other Woman*, trans. G. Gill, Cornell University Press, Ithaca, NY, 1985

Jackson, P. 'Mapping poststructuralism's borders: the case for poststructuralist area studies', *Sojourn: Journal of Social Issues in Southeast Asia*, 18: 1, April 2003

Jackson, S. *Heterosexuality in Question*, Sage, London, 1999

———— 'Feminist social theory', in S. Jackson and J. Jones eds, *Contemporary Feminist Theories*, New York University Press, New York, 1998a

———— 'Theorising gender and sexuality', in S. Jackson and J. Jones eds, *Contemporary Feminist Theories*, New York University Press, New York, 1998b

———— 'Sexual politics: feminist politics, gay politics and the problem of heterosexuality', in T. Carver and V. Mottier eds, *Politics of Sexuality: Identity, Gender, Citizenship*, Routledge, London and New York, 1998c

———— 'Heterosexuality and feminist theory', in D. Richardson ed., *Theorising Heterosexuality*, Open University Press, Buckingham, 1996a

———— 'The social construction of female sexuality', in S. Jackson and S. Scott eds, *Feminism and Sexuality: A Reader*, Edinburgh University Press, Edinburgh, 1996b.

———— 'Gender and heterosexuality: a materialist feminist analysis', in M. Maynard and J. Purvis eds, *(Hetero)sexual Politics*, Taylor & Francis, London, 1995

Jackson, S. and Scott, S. 'Sexual skirmishes and feminist factions: twenty-five years of debate on women and sexuality', in S. Jackson and S. Scott eds, *Feminism and Sexuality: A Reader*, Edinburgh University Press, Edinburgh, 1996

Jaggar, A. and Rothenberg, P. 'Introduction', in A. Jaggar and P. Rothenberg eds, *Feminist Frameworks*, 3rd edition, McGraw-Hill, New York, 1993

Jagodzinski, J. 'Women's bodies of performative excess' (women's bodybuilding), *Journal for the Psychoanalysis of Culture & Society*, 8: 1, Spring 2003

Jagose, A. *Queer Theory: An Introduction*, New York University Press, New York, 1996

Jeffords, S. *Hard Bodies: Hollywood Masculinity in the Reagan Era*, Rutgers University Press, New Brunswick, NJ, 1993

Jeffreys, S. 'Sadomasochism', in S. Jackson and S. Scott eds, *Feminism and Sexuality: A Reader*, Edinburgh University Press, Edinburgh, 1996

────── *The Lesbian Heresy: A Feminist Perspective on the Lesbian Sexual Revolution*, Women's Press, London, 1994a

────── 'The queer disappearance of lesbians: sexuality in the academy', *Women's Studies International Forum*, 17: 5, 1994b

────── *Anticlimax: A Feminist Critique of the Sexual Revolution*, Women's Press, London, 1990

Johnson, C. 'Heteronormative citizenship and the politics of passing', *Sexualities*, 5: 3, 2002

────── *Governing Change: From Keating to Howard*, University of Queensland Press, St Lucia, 2000

Johnston, C. *A Sydney Gaze: The Making of Gay Liberation*, Schiltron Press, Sydney, 1999

Joiner, W. 'Move over RuPaul, there's a new king in town', *Folio: The Magazine for Magazine Management*, 31: 3, March 2002

Justad, M. 'Women's studies and men's studies: friends or foes?', *The Journal of Men's Studies*, 8: 3, Spring 2000

Kamtekar, R. 'Martha Nussbaum: *Sex and Social Justice* and *Women and Human Development*: the capabilities approach', *The Philosophical Review*, 111: 2, April 2002

Kann, M. 'Ongoing tensions between men's studies and women's studies', *The Journal of Men's Studies*, 8: 3, Spring 2000

Kanneh, K. 'Black feminisms', in S. Jackson and J. Jones eds, *Contemporary Feminist Theories*, New York University Press, New York, 1998

Kanner, M. 'Towards a semiotics of butch', *The Gay & Lesbian Review Worldwide*, 9: 2, March 2002

Kaplan, C. and Glover, D. *Genders*, Routledge, London, 1998

Kapur, R. 'Imperial parody', *Feminist Theory*, 2: 1, 2001

Katz, J. *Gay/Lesbian Almanac*, Harper & Row, New York, 1983

Keller, E. 'Holding the center of feminist theory', *Women's Studies International Forum*, 12: 3, 1989

Kelly, L. *Surviving Sexual Violence*, Polity Press, Cambridge, 1988

Kemp, S. and Squires, J. eds, *Feminisms*, Oxford University Press, Oxford and New York, 1997

Kendall, C. 'Gay male pornography: an issue of sexism', presented at 'Speech, Equality and Harm: Feminist Perspectives on Pornography and Hate Propaganda' Conference, University of Chicago Law School, March 1993 (www.nostatusquo.com/ACLU/Porn/kendall2.html)

Kensinger, L. '(In)Quest of liberal feminism', *Hypatia*, 12: 4, Fall 1997

Khan, S. Review of *The Global Emergence of Gay and Lesbian Politics: National Imprints of a Worldwide Movement*, *Lambda Book Report*, 7: 11, June 1999

Kimmel, M. *The Gendered Society*, Oxford University Press, New York, 2000

────── *Manhood in America: A Cultural History*, Free Press, New York, 1996

────── '"Insult" or "injury": sex, pornography and sexism', in M. Kimmel ed., *Men Confront Pornography*, Crown, New York, 1990

Kimmel, M. ed., with Aronson, A. *The Gendered Society Reader*, Oxford University Press, New York, 2000

Kimmel, M. and Kaufman, M. 'Weekend warriors: the new men's movement', in H. Brod and M. Kaufman eds, *Theorizing Masculinities*, Sage, Thousand Oaks, CA, 1994

——— 'The new men's movement: retreat and regression with America's weekend warriors', *Feminist Issues*, 13: 3, 1993

Kimmel, M. and Messner, M. eds, *Men's Lives*, 5th edition, Allyn & Bacon, Boston, MA, 2001

King, D. 'Multiple jeopardy, multiple consciousness: the context of a black feminist ideology', *Signs*, 14: 1, 1988

Kitzinger, C. 'Problematizing pleasure: radical feminist deconstructions of sexuality and power', in H. Radtke and H. Stam eds, *Power/Gender: Social Relations in Theory and Practice*, Sage, London, 1994

Klor de Alva, J. 'Aztlán, Borinquen, and Hispanic Nationalism in the United States', in F. Aparicio and S. Chávez-Silverman eds, *Tropicalizations*, University Press of New England, Hanover, NH, 1997

Koedt, A. 'The myth of the vaginal orgasm', in A. Koedt ed., *Radical Feminism*, Quadrangle, New York, 1972

Konstan, D. 'The prehistory of sexuality: Foucault's route to classical antiquity', *Intertexts*, 6: 1, 2002

Lacan, J. *The Four Fundamental Concepts of Psychoanalysis*, trans. A. Sheridan, Hogarth Press, London, 1977

Landry, D. and MacLean, G. eds, *The Spivak Reader: Selected Works of Gayatri Chakravorty Spivak*, Routledge, New York and London, 1996

Langer, B. 'Hard-boiled and soft-boiled: masculinity and nation in Canadian and American crime fiction', *Meridian*, Special Issue: Masculinities, 15: 2, October 1996

Layton, L. *Who's That Girl? Who's That Boy? Clinical Practice Meets Postmodern Gender Theory*, Jason Aronson, Northvale, NJ, 1998

Lazreg, M. 'Feminism and difference: the perils of writing as a woman in Algeria', *Feminist Studies*, 14: 1, 1988

Leeds Revolutionary Feminists, 'Political lesbianism: the case against heterosexuality', in Onlywomen Press eds, *Love Your Enemy: The Debate between Heterosexual Feminism and Political Lesbianism*, Onlywomen Press, London, 1981

Lehrman, K. Review of *Fire with Fire: The New Female Power and How it will Change the 21st Century*, *The New Republic*, 210: 11, 14 March 1994

Leighninger, R. 'The Western as male soap opera', *Journal of Men's Studies*, 6: 2, Winter 1997

Lesko, N. ed., *Masculinities at School*, Sage, London, 2000

Lewis, G. 'Black–white differences in attitudes toward homosexuality and gay rights', *Public Opinion Quarterly*, 67: 1, Spring 2003

Lewis, R. 'Feminism and Orientalism', *Feminist Theory*, 3: 2, 2002

Libertin, M. 'The politics of women's studies and men's studies', *Hypatia*, 2: 2, Summer 1987

Linden, R. et al. eds, *Against Sadomasochism*, Frog in the Wall, East Palo Alto, CA, 1982

Litson, J. 'The personal is political', *Weekend Australian*, 12–13 June 2004, Review section, p. 16

Lloyd, G. *The Man of Reason: 'Male' and 'Female' in Western Philosophy*, Methuen, London, 1984

Lloyd, M. 'Sexual politics, performativity, parody: Judith Butler', in T. Carver and V. Mottier eds, *Politics of Sexuality: Identity, Gender, Citizenship*, Routledge, London and New York, 1998

Lodge, D. 'Goodbye to all that', *New York Review of Books*, 27 May 2004

Losey, J. and Brewer, W. eds, *Mapping Male Sexuality: Nineteenth Century England*, Fairleigh Dickinson University Press, Madison, WI, 2000

Lorber, J. 'Using gender to undo gender', *Feminist Theory*, 1: 1, 2000

Lorde, A. *Sister Outsider: Essays and Speeches*, Crossing Press, Freedom, CA, 1984

———— 'An interview: Audre Lorde and Adrienne Rich, *Signs*, 6: 4, 1981a

———— 'An open letter to Mary Daly', in C. Moraga and G. Anzaldúa eds, *This Bridge Called My Back: Writings by Radical Women of Color*, Persephone Press, Watertown, MA, 1981b

Lugones, M. 'Purity, impurity, and separation', *Signs*, 19: 21, 1994

Lyotard, J.F. *The Postmodern Condition: A Report on Knowledge*, trans. G. Bennington and B. Massumi, University of Minnesota Press, Minneapolis, MN, 1984

Mac an Ghaill, M. *The Making of Men: Masculinities, Sexualities and Schooling*, Open University Press, Buckingham, 1994

MacKinnon, C. 'Sexuality, pornography, and method: "pleasure under patriarchy"', in C. Sunstein ed., *Feminism and Political Theory*, University of Chicago Press, Chicago and London, 1990

———— *Feminism Unmodified*, Harvard Universtiy Press, Cambridge, MA, 1987a

———— 'Francis Biddle's sister: pornography, civil rights and speech', in *Feminism Unmodified*, Harvard University Press, Cambridge, MA, 1987b

———— 'Feminism, Marxism, method and the state: an agenda for theory', *Signs*, 7: 3, 1982

MacMillan, J. *On Liberal Peace, Democracy, War and the International Order*, I.B. Tauris, London and New York, 1998

Major, W. 'Audre Lorde's *The Cancer Journals: Autopathography as Resistance*', *Mosaic* (Winnipeg) 35: 2, June 2002

Malinowitz, H. 'Queer theory: whose theory?', *Frontiers*, 13, 1993

Malone, K. Review of *Who's That Girl? Who's That Boy? Clinical Practice Meets Postmodern Gender Theory*, *Signs*, 27: 1, Autumn 2001

Marcuse, H. *An Essay on Liberation*, Beacon Press, Boston, MA, 1969

———— *Eros and Civilization*, Beacon Press, Boston, MA, 1955

Marks, E. and de Courtivron, I. eds, *New French Feminisms*, Harvester Press, Brighton, 1981

Marotta, T. *The Politics of Homosexuality*, Houghton Miffin, Boston, MA, 1980

Martin, B. *Femininity Played Straight: The Significance of Being Lesbian*, Routledge, New York, 1996

———— 'Sexualities without genders and other queer Utopias and gay and lesbian studies', *Diacritics*, 24: 2–3, 1994

Martin, D. and Lyon, P. *Lesbian/Woman*, Bantam, New York, 1972

Martin, J. 'The social and the political', in F. Ashe et al., *Contemporary Social & Political Theory: An Introduction*, Open University Press, Buckingham and Philadelphia, 1999

Martino, W. 'Policing masculinities: investigating the role of homophobia and heteronormativity in the lives of adolescent school boys', *The Journal of Men's Studies*, 8: 2, Winter 2000

Mason-Grant, J. Review of *Volatile Bodies*, *Hypatia*, 12: 4, Fall 1997

May, L. and Strikwerder, R. eds, *Rethinking Masculinity: Philosophical Explorations in Light of Feminism*, Littlefield, Adams, Lanham, MD, 1992

Maynard, M. 'Beyond the "Big Three": the development of feminist theory in the 1990s', *Women's History Review*, 4: 3, 1995.

———— 'The re-shaping of sociology? Trends in the sociology of gender', *Sociology*, 24: 2, 1990

Maynard, S. 'Queer musings on masculinity and history', *Labour/Le Travail*, 42, Fall 1998

McCulloch, M. 'Gay Male Pornography: Is it a Problem?', Honours Thesis, Politics Department, University of Adelaide, 2000

McDermott, P. 'The meaning and uses of feminism in introductory women's studies textbooks', *Feminist Studies*, 24: 2, Summer 1998

McIntosh, M. 'Queer theory and the war of the sexes', in S. Kemp and J. Squires eds, *Feminisms*, Oxford University Press, Oxford and New York, 1997

McLemee, S. 'A roller-coaster ride of emotion', *The Australian*, Higher Education Supplement, Wednesday, 21 November, 2001

McNay, L. 'The Foucauldian body and the exclusion of experience', *Hypatia*, 6: 2, 1991

McRuer, R. Review of *A Genealogy of Queer Theory*, *NWSA Journal*, 14: 2, Summer 2002

Meijer, I. and Prins, B. 'How bodies come to matter': an interview with Judith Butler', *Signs*, 23: 2, 1998

Mercer, K. *Welcome to the Jungle: New Positions in Black Cultural Studies*, Routledge, New York, 1994

Mercer, K. and Julien, I. 'Race, sexual politics and black masculinity: a dossier', in R. Chapman and J. Rutherford eds, *Male Order*, Lawrence & Wishart, London, 1988

Messner, M. *Politics of Masculinities: Men in Movements*, Sage, Thousand Oaks, CA, 1997

Mieli, M. *Homosexuality and Liberation*, trans. D. Fernbach, Gay Men's Press, London, 1977

Millett, K. *Sexual Politics,* Rupert Hart-Davis, London, 1971

Mills, S. 'Post-colonial Feminist Theory', in S. Jackson and J. Jones eds, *Contemporary Feminist Theories*, New York University Press, New York, 1998

Milner, A. *Contemporary Cultural Theory: An Introduction*, Allen & Unwin, Sydney, 1991

Milner, A. and Browitt, J. *Contemporary Cultural Theory*, 3rd edition, Allen & Unwin, Sydney, 2002

Minow, M. and Shanley, M. 'Relational rights and responsibilities: revisioning the family in liberal political theory and law', *Hypatia*, 11: 1, Winter 1996

Minsky, R. 'Lacan', in H. Crowley and S. Himmelweit eds, *Knowing Women: Feminism and Knowledge*, Polity Press/Open University, Cambridge, 1992

Mirza, H. 'Black masculinities and schooling: a black feminist response', *British Journal of Sociology of Education*, 20: 1, 1999

—— *Black British Feminism: A Reader*, Routledge, London, 1997

Mitchell, J. 'Introduction I', in J. Mitchell and J. Rose eds, *Feminine Sexuality: Jacques Lacan and the école freudienne*, Macmillan, London, 1982

—— *Woman's Estate*, Penguin, Harmondsworth, 1971

Modleski, T. *Feminism without Women: Culture and Criticism in a 'Post-feminist' Age*, Routledge, New York, 1991

Mohanram, R. *Black Body: Women, Colonialism, and Space*, University of Minnesota Press, Minneapolis, MN, 1999

Mohanty, C. '"Under Western Eyes" revisited: feminist solidarity through anticapitalist struggles', *Signs*, 28: 2, Winter 2003a

—— *Feminism without Borders: Decolonizing Theory, Practicing Solidarity*, Duke University Press, Durham, NC, and London, 2003b

—— 'Introduction', in C. Mohanty et al. eds, *Third World Women and the Politics of Feminism*, Indiana University Press, Bloomington and Indianapolis, IN, 1991a

—— 'Under Western Eyes', in C. Mohanty et al. eds, *Third World Women and the Politics of Feminism*, Indiana University Press, Bloomington and Indianapolis, IN, 1991b

Moi, T. 'What is a Woman?', in *What is a Woman and other Essays*, Oxford University Press, Oxford, 2001

—— ed., *The Kristeva Reader*, Basil Blackwell, Oxford, 1986

Moore, C. 'Guest editorial: Australian masculinities', *Journal of Australian Studies*, 56, March 1998

Moraga, C. *Loving in the War Years*, South End Press, Boston, MA, 1983

More, K. and Whittle, S. eds, *Reclaiming Genders: Transsexual Grammars at the Fin de Siecle*, British Sociological Association, London and New York, 2001

Moreton-Robinson, A. *Talkin' Up to the White Woman: Indigenous Women and Feminism*, University of Queensland Press, St Lucia, 2002
—— 'Masking gender and exalting race: indigenous women and Commonwealth employment policies', *Australian Feminist Studies*, 15, Autumn 1992
Morris, M. 'Things to do with shopping centres', in S. During ed., *The Cultural Studies Reader*, Routledge, New York, 1993
Munt, S. ed., *Butch/Femme: Inside Lesbian Gender*, Cassell, London, 1997
Namaste, K. 'Tragic misreadings: queer theory's erasure of transgender subjectivity', in B. Beemyn and M. Eliason eds, *Queer Studies: A Lesbian, and Gay, Bisexual, and Transgender Anthology*, New York Universtiy Press, New York and London, 1996
Nardi P. ed., *Gay Masculinities*, Sage, Thousand Oaks, CA, 2000
Natoli, J. and Hutcheon, L. eds, *A Postmodern Reader*, State University of New York Press, Albany, NY, 1993
Nelson, J. Review of *Politics of Masculinities: Men in Movements*, *The Canadian Review of Sociology and Anthropology*, 37: 1, February 2000
Nemeth, M. 'Who's afraid of Naomi Wolf; an author criticises "victim feminism" and pushes for more women to pursue power', *Maclean's*, 106: 49, 6 December 1993
New, C. 'Women's oppression in the world and in ourselves: a fresh look at feminism and psychoanalysis', in P. Abbott and C. Wallace eds, *Gender, Power & Sexuality*, Macmillan, British Sociological Association, 1991
Newton, J. 'White guys', *Feminist Studies*, 24: 3, Fall 1998
Nicholson, L. ed., *Feminism/Postmodernism*, Routledge, London, 1990
Nicholson, L. and Seidman, S. eds, *Social Postmodernism: Beyond Identity Politics*, Cambridge University Press, Cambridge and New York, 1995
Nielsen, J. et al. 'Gendered heteronormativity: empirical illustrations in everyday life', *The Sociological Quarterly*, 41: 2, Spring 2000
Nimmons, D. *The Soul Beneath the Skin: The Unseen Hearts and Habits of Gay Men*, St Martin's Press, New York, 2002
Nussbaum, M. 'Comment on Quillen's "Feminist Theory, Justice and the Lure of the Human"', *Signs*, 27: 1, and Autumn 2001
—— *Women and Human Development*, Cambridge University Press, Cambridge and New York, 2000
—— 'The professor of parody', *The New Republic*, 22 February 1999a
—— *Sex and Social Justice*, Oxford University Press, Oxford, 1999b
—— 'Feminists and philosophy', *The New York Review of Books*, 41: 17, 20 October 1994
Nystrom, D. 'The perils of masculinity studies', *Iris: A Journal about Women*, Spring 2002
Oakley, A. *Sex, Gender and Society*, Temple-Smith, London, 1972
O'Donnell, M. and Sharpe, S. *Uncertain Masculinities: Youth, Ethnicity and Class in Contemporary Britain*, Routledge, London, 2000
Offen, K. 'Defining feminism: a comparative historical approach', *Signs*, 14: 1, Autumn 1988
O'Hartigan, M. 'In the long run my sex-change surgery saves tax dollars', *Minneapolis Star/Tribune*, 4 February 1995
—— 'Changing sex is not changing gender', *Sound Out*, May 1993
Omolade, B. 'Black women and feminism', in H. Eisenstein and A. Jardine eds, *The Future of Difference*, Rutgers Universtiy Press, New Brunswick, NJ, 1980
O'Neill, S. 'Rationality', in F. Ashe et al. eds, *Contemporary Social & Political Theory: An Introduction*, Open University Press, Buckingham and Philadelphia, 1999
Osborne, R. *Megawords*, Allen & Unwin, Sydney, 2001

Ouzgane, L. 'Guest Editorial: an introduction', *The Journal of Men's Studies*, 10: 3, Spring 2002

Outhwaite, W. and Bottomore, T. eds, *The Blackwell Dictionary of Twentieth-Century Social Thought*, Blackwell, Oxford, 1993

Outlaw, L. *On Race and Philosophy*, Routledge, New York, 1996

Parameswaran, U. *Feminism is for Everyone* (book review), *Horizons*, 16: 1, Summer 2002

Parker, D. 'Good comparisons: decorative, informative or interogative? The role of social theory textbooks', *Sociology*, 35: 1, February 2001

Parmar, P. 'Other kinds of dreams', *Feminist Review*, 31, Spring 1989

Pease, B. *Recreating Men: Postmodern Masculinity Politics*, Sage, London, 2000

Petersen, A. *Unmasking the Masculine: 'Men' and 'Identity' in a Sceptical Age*, Sage, London, 1998

Pfiel, F. *White Guys: Studies in Postmodern Domination and Difference*, Verso, London, 1995

Phelan, S. *Sexual Strangers: Gays, Lesbians and Dilemmas of Citizenship*, Temple University Press, Philadelphia, 2001

———— 'Queer Liberalism?', *American Political Science Review*, 94: 2, June 2000

———— *Identity Politics: Lesbian Feminism and the Limits of Community*, Temple University Press, Philadelphia, 1989

Phillips, A. 'Universal pretensions in political thought', in M. Barrett and A. Phillips eds, *Destabilizing Theory: Contemporary Feminist Debates*, Polity Press, Cambridge, 1992

Phoca, S. 'Feminism and gender', in S. Gamble ed., *The Routledge Critical Dictionary of Feminism and Postfeminism*, Routledge, New York, 2000

Plummer, K. *Telling Sexual Stories: Power, Change and Social Worlds*, Routledge, London and New York, 1994

Plymire, D. Review of *Butch/Femme*, *NWSA Journal*, 12: 1, Spring 2000

Pringle, R. 'Absolute sex? Unpacking the sexuality/gender relationship', in R. Connell and G. Dowsett eds, *Rethinking Sex: Social Theory and Sexuality Research*, Melbourne University Press, Melbourne, 1992

Probyn, E. 'Queer belongings: the politics of departure', in E. Grosz and E. Probyn eds, *Sexy Bodies: The Strange Carnalities of Feminism*, Routledge, New York, 1995

Prosser, J. *Second Skins: The Body Narratives of Transsexuality*, Columbia University Press, New York, 1998

Pruett, C. 'The complexions of "race" and the rise of "whiteness" studies', *CLIO*, 32: 1, Fall 2002

Potter, D. 'Tyson is not a hero; Rally was disgusting', *Orlando Sentinel*, 22 June 1995

Quillen, C. 'Feminist theory, justice, and the lure of the human', *Signs*, 27: 1, Autumn 2001

Radicallesbians, 'The woman identified woman', in S. Hoagland and J. Penelope eds, *For Lesbians Only: A Separatist Anthology*, Onlywomen, London, 1988

Raffo, S. Review of *Female Masculinity*, *Lambda Book Report*, 7: 3, October 1998

Ragland, E. 'Jacques Lacan: feminism and the problem of gender identity', in S. Gunew ed., *A Reader in Feminist Knowledge*, Routledge, London, 1991

Ramsey, D. 'Feminism and psychoanalysis', in S. Gamble ed., *The Routledge Critical Dictionary of Feminism and Postfeminism*, Routledge, New York, 2000

Raymond, J. *The Transsexual Empire: The Making of the She-Male* [1979], 2nd edition, Teachers College Press, New York, 1994

———— *A Passion for Friends*, The Women's Press, London, 1986

———— *The Transsexual Empire*, Beacon, Boston, MA, 1979

Reiser, K. 'Masculinity and monstrosity: characterization and identification in the slasher film', *Men and Masculinities*, 3: 4, April 2001

Rich, A. 'Disloyal to civilisation: feminism, racism, gynephobia' [1978], in *On Lies, Secrets and Silence: Selected Prose 1966–78*, Virago, London, 1980a

—— 'Compulsory heterosexuality and lesbian existence', *Signs*, 5: 4, 1980b

Richardson, D. 'Sexuality and gender', *International Encyclopedia of the Social & Behavioural Sciences*, N. Smelser and P. Baltes editors-in-chief, Elsevier, New York and Oxford, 2001 (www.iesbs.com)

—— 'Sexuality and male dominance', in D. Richardson and V. Robinson eds, *Introducing Women's Studies: Feminist Theory and Practice*, Macmillan, Basingstoke, 1993a

—— 'Constructing lesbian sexualities', in K. Plummer ed., *Modern Homosexualities*, Routledge, London, 1993b

Richardson, D. and Robinson, V. 'Theorizing women's studies, gender studies, and masculinity: the politics of naming', *European Journal of Women's Studies*, 1: 1, Spring 1994

Robertson, D. *The Penguin Dictionary of Politics*, 2nd edition, Penguin, London, 1993

Roen, K. 'Transgender theory and embodiment: the risk of racial marginalisation', *Journal of Gender Studies*, 10: 3, 2001

Rohlinger, D. 'Eroticizing men: cultural influences on advertising and male objectification', *Sex Roles: A Journal of Research*, February 2002

Roiphe, K. *The Morning After: Sex, Fear and Feminism*, Hamish Hamilton, London, 1994

Roper, M. and Tosh, J. eds, *Manful Assertions: Masculinities in Britain since 1800*, Routledge, London, 1991

Rorty, R. *Contingency, Irony and Solidarity*, Cambridge University Press, Cambridge, 1989

Rosario, V. 'Transgenderism comes of age', *The Gay & Lesbian Review*, 7: 4, Fall 2000

Rose, M. *The Post-Modern and the Post-Industrial*, Cambridge University Press, Cambridge, 1991

Roth, N. Review of *The Transsexual Empire*, *Women and Language*, 20: 2, Fall 1997

Rowland R. and Klein, R. 'Radical feminism: critique and construct', in S. Gunew ed., *Feminist Knowledge: Critique and Construct*, Routledge, London and New York, 1990

Rubin G. 'Sexual traffic' (interview by Judith Butler), *differences: A Journal of Feminist Cultural Studies*, 6: 2–3, 1994

—— 'Of catamites and kings: reflections on butch, gender and boundaries', in J. Nestle ed., *The Persistent Desire: A Femme–Butch Reader*, Alyson, Boston, MA, 1992

—— 'Thinking sex: notes for a radical theory of the politics of sexuality', in C. Vance ed., *Pleasure and Danger: Exploring Female Sexuality*, Routledge, London, 1984

Ruddick, S. *Maternal Thinking*, The Women's Press, London, 1990

Rudel, T. and Gerson, J. 'Postmodernism, institutional change, and academic workers: a sociology of knowledge', *Social Science Quarterly*, 80: 2, June 1999

Rust, P. *Bisexuality and the Challenge to Lesbian Politics*, New York University Press, New York, 1995

Ryan, J. 'Psychoanalysis and women loving women', in H. Crowley and S. Himmelweit eds, *Knowing Women: Feminism and Knowledge*, Polity Press/Open University, Cambridge, 1992

Sabbioni, J. et al. eds, *Indigenous Australian Voices: A Reader*, Rutgers University Press, New Brunswick, NJ and London, 1998

Sabo, D. 'Men's health studies: origins and trends, *Journal of American College Health*, 49: 3, November 2000

Saharso, S. 'Feminist ethics, autonomy and the politics of multiculturalism', *Feminist Theory*, 4: 2, 2003

Said, E. *Culture and Imperialism*, Chatto & Windus, London, 1993

—— *Orientalism*, Penguin, Harmondsworth, 1978

Sandfort, T., Schuyf, J., Duyvendak, J. and Weeks, J. eds. *Lesbian and Gay Studies: An Introductory, Interdisciplinary Approach*, Sage, London and Thousand Oaks, CA, 2000

Sandoval, C. 'US third world feminism: the theory and method of oppositional consciousness in the postmodern world', *Genders*, 10, Spring 1991

Sangari, K. 'The politics of the possible', in A. JanMohamed and D. Lloyd eds, *The Nature and Context of Minority Discourse*, Oxford University Press, New York, 1990

Savran, D. 'The sadomasochist in the closet: white masculinity and the culture of victimization', *differences: A Journal of Feminist Cultural Studies*, 8: 2, Summer 1996

Scheman, N. 'Jewish lesbian writing: A review essay', *Hypatia*, 7: 4, 1992

Schneider Jr., R. 'Summer 1999: "Stonewall hits the big 3-0"', *The Harvard Gay & Lesbian Review*, 6: 3, Summer 1999

Schofield, T., Connell, R., Wood, J. and Butland, D. 'Understanding men's health and illness: a gender-relations approach to policy, research, and practice', *Journal of American College Health*, 48: 6, May 2000

Schor, N. 'Feminist and gender studies', in J. Gibaldi ed., *Introduction to Scholarship in Modern Languages and Literatures*, Modern Language Association of America, New York, 1992

Schwalbe, M. *Unlocking the Iron Cage: The Men's Movement, Gender Politics, and American Culture*, Oxford University Press, New York and Oxford, 1996

——— 'Why mythopoetic men don't flock to NOMAS', in M. Kimmel ed., *The Politics of Manhood: Profeminist Men Respond to the Mythopoetic Men's Movement (and the Mythopoetic Leaders Answer)*, Temple University Press, Philadelphia, 1995

Scott, J. 'Some reflections on gender and politics', in M. Ferree et al. eds, *Revisioning Gender*, Sage, Thousand Oaks, CA and London, 1999

——— 'Gender: a useful category of historical analysis', *American Historical Review*, 91: 5, 1986

Sea-ling, C. 'Assuming manhood: prostitution and patriotic passions in Korea', *East Asia: An International Quarterly*, 18: 4, Winter 2000

Sedgwick, E. *Tendencies*, Duke UP, Durham, NC, 1993

——— *Between Men: English Literature and Male Homosocial Desire*, Columbia University Press, New York, 1985

Segal, L. *Why Feminism?: Gender, Psychology, Politics*, Polity Press, Cambridge, 1999

——— ed., *New Sexual Agendas*, British Sociological Association/Macmillan, Basingstoke, 1997

——— *Straight Sex: The Politics of Pleasure*, Virago, London, 1994

——— *Slow Motion: Changing Masculinities, Changing Men*, Virago, London, 1990

——— *Is the Future Female?: Troubled Thoughts on Contemporary Feminism*, Virago, London, 1987

Seidler, V. ed., *Recreating Sexual Politics: Men, Feminism and Politics*, Routledge, London, 1991

——— 'Men, feminism and power', in J. Hearn ed., *Men, Masculinities and Social Theory: Problems of Modern European Thought*, Allen & Unwin, Boston, MA, 1990

Seidman, S. *Contested Knowledge: Social Theory in the Postmodern Era*, 2nd edition, Blackwell, Oxford, 1998

——— *Difference Troubles: Queering Social Theory and Sexual Politics*, Cambridge University Press, Cambridge, 1997

——— 'Identity and politics in a "postmodern" gay culture: some historical and conceptual notes', in M. Warner ed., *Fear of a Queer Planet: Queer Politics and Social Theory*, University of Minnesota Press, Minneapolis and London, 1993

Selinger-Morris, S. 'Who's sexy now?', *Weekend Australian Magazine*, 28–9 February 2004

Serematakis, C. 'Gender studies or women's studies: theoretical and pedagogical issues, research agendas and directions', *Australian Feminist Studies*, 20, Summer 1994

Seymour, W. 'Strong men, straw men and body-less bodies: revisiting Australian manhood', *Journal of Australian Studies*, 15 December 2001

Shanley, M. 'Fathers' rights, mothers' wrongs? Reflections on unwed fathers rights and sex equality', in P. DiQuinzio and I. Young eds, *Feminist Ethics and Social Policy*, Indiana University Press, Bloomington, IN, 1997

Shanley, M. and Pateman, C. eds, *Feminist Interpretations and Political Theory*, Polity Press, Cambridge, 1991

Shelton, B. and John, D. 'White, black, and hispanic men's household labor', in J. Hood ed., *Men, Work, Family*, Sage, Newbury Park, CA, 1993

Shepard, B. 'The queer/gay assimilationist split: the suits vs the sluts', *Monthly Review*, 53: 1, May 2001

—— *White Nights and Ascending Shadows: An Oral History of the San Franciso AIDS Epidemic*, Continuum, New York and London, 1997

Showalter, E. 'Feminist criticism in the wilderness', in E. Showalter ed., *The New Feminist Criticism: Essays on Women, Literature, and Theory*, Pantheon, New York, 1985

Simpson, M. *Male Impersonators: Men Performing Masculinity*, Routledge, New York, 1994

Sinfield, A. 'Lesbian and gay taxonomies', *Critical Inquiry*, 29: 1, Autumn 2002

Singleton, A. 'Men getting real? A study of relationship change in two men's groups', *Journal of Sociology*, 39: 2, June 2003

Slemon, S. 'The scramble for post-colonialism', in C. Tiffin and A. Lawson, eds, *De-scribing Empire: Postcolonialism and Textuality*, Routledge, London, 1994

Smallacombe, S. 'Speaking positions on indigenous violence', *Hecate*, 30: 1, May 2004

Smith, B. 'Blacks and gays healing the divide', in E. Brandt ed., *Dangerous Liasons: Blacks, Gays and the Struggle for Equality*, New Press, New York, 1999

—— 'Towards a black feminist criticism' [1977], in E. Showalter ed., *The New Feminist Criticism: Essays on Women, Literature and Theory*, Pantheon, New York, 1985

Smith, M. and Petrarca, J. 'An interview with bell hooks: The Ripple talks with one of America's leading feminists', *Washington Ripple*, 9: 2, March 1995

Smyth, C. 'Queer notions', in S. Kemp and J. Squires eds, *Feminisms*, Oxford University Press, Oxford and New York, 1997

—— *Lesbians Talk Queer Notions*, Scarlet Press, London, 1992a

—— 'Queer notions' (interview), *Off Our Backs*, October 1992b

Snitow, A. 'Retrenchment vs transformation: the politics of the antipornography movement', in K. Ellis ed., *Caught Looking: Feminism, Pornography and Censorship*, Caught Looking, Inc., New York, 1986

Sorensen, A. 'Pornography and gender in mass culture', *NIKK* (Nordic Institute for Women's Studies and Gender Research) *Magasin*, 3, 2003

Spelman, E. 'Theories of race and gender: the erasure of black women', *Quest*, 5: 4, 1980–81

Spender, D. *Man Made Language*, Routledge Kegan Paul, London, 1985

Spivak, G. *The Post-Colonial Critic: Interviews, Strategies, Dialogues*, ed. S. Harasym, Routledge, London, 1990

—— *In Other Worlds: Essays in Cultural Politics*, Methuen, London and New York, 1987a

—— 'Feminism and Critical Theory', in G. Spivak, *In Other Worlds: Essays in Cultural Politics*, Methuen, London and New York, 1987b

—— 'Three women's texts and a critique of imperialism', *Critical Inquiry*, 12, Autumn 1985

—— 'Criticism, feminism and the institution' (interview with E. Grosz), *Thesis Eleven*, 10/11, November–March 1984–85

Spraggins, J.D. 'African American masculinity: power and expression', *Journal of African American Men*, 4: 3, Winter 1999

Springer, K. 'Third Wave Black Feminism?', *Signs*, 27: 4, Summer 2002

Squires, J. 'Representing groups, deconstructing identities', *Feminist Theory*, 2: 1, 2001

Stacey, J. 'Untangling feminist theory', in D. Richardson and V. Robinson eds, *Introducing Women's Studies: Feminist Theory and Practice*, Macmillan, London, 1993

Stapler, R. *Black Masculinity: The Black Male's Role in American Society*, Black Scholar's Press, San Francisco, 1982

———— 'The myth of black macho: a response to angry black feminists', in *The Black Scholar: Journal of Black Studies and Research*, 6, March/April 1979

Stark, C. 'Is pornography an action?: the causal vs the conceptual view of pornography's harm', *Social Theory and Practice*, 23: 2, Summer 1997

Stier, H. and Tienda, M. 'Are men marginal to the family? Insights from Chicago's inner city', in J. Hood ed., *Men, Work, Family*, Sage, Newbury Park, CA, 1993

Stoller, R. *Sex and Gender*, The Hogarth Press, London, 1968

Stoltenberg, J. *Refusing to be a Man: Essays on Sex and Justice* [1989], 2nd edition, UCL Press, London, 2000a

———— *The End of Manhood: Parables on Sex and Selfhood* [1993], 2nd edition, UCL Press, London, 2000b

———— Review of *Men in Pens*, *Lambda Book Report*, 8: 4, November 1999

———— 'Re: [profem]male supremacy and the men's pro-feminist movement', located at: www.igc.apc.org/nemesis/ACLU/oh!Brother, 1997 (cited in Goldrick-Jones, 2001)

———— 'How men have (a) sex', *Canadian Dimension*, 25: 1, January–February 1991

———— 'Gays and the propornography movement: having the hots for sex discrimination', in M. Kimmel ed., *Men Confront Pornography*, Crown, New York, 1990

Stryker, S. 'My words to Victor Frankenstein above the village of Charmounix: performing transgender rage', *GLQ: A Journal of Gay and Lesbian Studies*, 1: 3, 1994

Sturgis, S. 'Bisexual feminism: challenging the splits, in S. Rose et al. eds, *Bisexual Horizons: Politics, Histories, Lives*, Lawrence & Wishart, London, 1996

Suleri, S. 'Woman skin deep: feminism and the postcolonial condition', *Critical Inquiry*, Summer 1992

Sullivan, A. *Virtually Normal: An Argument about Homosexuality*, Vantage, New York, 1996

Sullivan, N. *A Critical Introduction to Queer Theory*, Circa Books, Melbourne, 2003

———— 'Fleshing out pleasure: canonisation or crucifixion?', *Australian Feminist Studies*, 12: 26, 1997

Summers, A. 'It's a very hot kitchen, Pru', *The Sydney Morning Herald*, 17 April 1997, Opinion, p. 15

Tapper, M. 'Can a feminist be a liberal?', *Australasian Journal of Philisophy*, Supplement to vol. 64, June 1986

Tasker, Y. *Spectacular Bodies: Gender, Genre and Action Cinema*, Routledge, London and New York, 1993

Teal, D. *The Gay Militants: How Gay Liberation Began in America, 1969–1971*, St Martin's Press, New York, 1971

The Men's Bibliography (11th edition, May 2003), compiled by Michael Flood, located at: http://www.mensbiblio.xyonline.net

Tessman, L. 'Dangerous loyalties and liberatory politics', *Hypatia*, 13: 4, Fall 1998

Thompson, D. *Radical Feminism Today*, Sage, London and Thousand Oaks, CA, 2001

———— 'The sex/gender distinction: a reconsideration', *Australian Feminist Studies*, 10, 1989

Tickner, A. *Gendering World Politics: Issues and Approaches in the Post-Cold War Era*, Columbia University Press, New York, 2001

Tippet, G. et al., 'Degrees of separation', *The Age*, Saturday, 28 June 2003

Tolson, J. and Ewers, J. 'The Reagan legacy', *US News & World Report*, 136: 22, 21 June 2004

Tomsen, S. and Mason, G. 'Engendering homophobia: violence, sexuality and gender conformity', *Journal of Sociology*, 37: 3, September 2001

Tong, R. *Feminist Thought: A More Comprehensive Introduction*, 2nd edition, Allen & Unwin, Sydney, 1998

Traub, V. 'The rewards of lesbian history', *Feminist Studies*, 25: 2, Summer 1999

Trin, Minh-ha T. *Women Native Other: Writing Postcoloniality and Feminism*, Indiana University Press, Indianapolis and Bloomington, IN, 1989

Turcotte, L. 'Queer theory: transgression and/or regression?', *Canadian Woman Studies*, 16: 2, Spring 1996

Turner, B. 'Understanding change: modernity and postmodernity', in R. Jureidini et al. eds, *Sociology: Australian Connections*, Allen & Unwin, Sydney, 1997

Turner, W. *A Genealogy of Queer Theory*, Temple University Press, Philadelphia, 2000

Tuttle, L. *Encyclopedia of Feminism*, Arrow Books, London, 1986

Vaid, U. *Virtual Inequality: The Mainstreaming of Gay & Lesbian Liberation*, Anchor Books, Doubleday, New York, 1995

Valentine, D. and Kulick, D. 'Transsexuality, transvestism, and transgender', *International Encyclopedia of the Social & Behavioural Sciences*, *International Encyclopedia of the Social & Behavioural Sciences*, N. Smelser and P. Baltes editors-in-chief, Elsevier, New York and Oxford, 2001 (www.iesbs.com)

Vance, C. 'Social construction theory: problems in the history of sexuality', in H. Crowley and S. Himmelweit eds, *Knowing Women: Feminism and Knowledge*, Polity Press/Open University, Oxford, 1992

———— 'Pleasure and danger: towards a politics of sexuality', in C. Vance ed., *Pleasure and Danger: Exploring Female Sexuality*, Routledge, London, 1984

Vice, S. 'Psychoanalytic Feminist Theory', in S. Jackson and J. Jones eds, *Contemporary Feminist Theories*, New York University Press, New York, 1998

Wajcman, J. *Managing Like a Man: Women and Men in Corporate Management*, Polity Press/Allen & Unwin, Cambridge and Sydney, 1999

Waldby, C. 'Destruction: boundary erotics and refigurations of the heterosexual male body', in E. Grosz and E. Probyn eds, *Sexy Bodies: The Strange Carnalities of Feminism*, Routledge, New York, 1995

Waldman, S. 'The other AIDS crisis; who pays for the treatment?', *Washington Monthly*, 17, January 1986

Walker, C. Review of *Traps: African American Men on Gender and Sexuality*, *Journal of Southern History*, 69: 2, May 2003

Wallace, M. *Black Macho and the Myth of the Superwoman*, Dial Press, New York, 1979

Walters, S.D. 'Queer Theory', *International Encyclopedia of the Social & Behavioural Sciences*, N. Smelser and P. Baltes editors-in-chief, Elsevier, New York and Oxford, 2001 (www.iesbs.com)

Warner, M. *The Trouble with Normal: Sex, Politics, and the Ethics of Queer Life*, Free Press, New York, 1999

———— ed., *Fear of a Queer Planet: Queer Politics and Social Theory*, University of Minnesota Press, Minneapolis, MN, and London 1993a

———— 'Introduction', in M. Warner ed., *Fear of a Queer Planet: Queer Politics and Social Theory*, University of Minnesota Press, Minneapolis, MN, and London, 1993b

Waugh, P. 'Postmodernism and feminism', in S. Jackson and J. Jones eds, *Contemporary Feminist Theories*, New York University Press, New York, 1998.

Webster, F. 'The politics of sex and gender: Benhabib and Butler debate subjectivity', *Hypatia*, 15: 1, Winter 2000

Wechsler, N. 'Interview with Pat Califia and Gayle Rubin', Part 1 and Part II, *Gay Community News*, July 18 and August 15 respectively, 1981

Weekend Australian, 8–9, September 2001, p. 21

Weeks, J. 'Sexual orientation: historical and social construction', *International Encyclopedia of the Social & Behavioural Sciences*, *International Encyclopedia of the Social & Behavioural Sciences*, N. Smelser and P. Baltes editors-in-chief, Elsevier, New York and Oxford, 2001 (www.iesbs.com)

——— 'The challenge of lesbian and gay studies', in T. Sandfort, J. Schuyf, J. Duyvendak and J. Weeks eds, *Lesbian and Gay Studies: An Introductory, Interdisciplinary Approach*, Sage, London and Thousand Oaks, CA, 2000

——— 'The sexual citizen', *Theory, Culture and Society*, 15, August/November 1998

——— *Invented Moralities: Sexual Values in an Age of Uncertainty*, Polity Press, Cambridge, 1995

——— *Coming Out: Homosexual Politics in Britain from the Nineteenth Century to the Present* [1977], 2nd edition, Quartet, London, 1990

——— *Sexuality and its Discontents: Meanings, Myths & Modern Sexualities*, Routledge Kegan Paul, London, 1985

——— *Sex, Politics and Society: The Regulation of Sexuality since 1800*, Longman, London, 1981

——— *Coming Out: Homosexual Politics in Britain from the Nineteenth Century to the Present*, Quartet Books, London, 1977

Weeks, J. and Porter, K. eds, *Between the Acts: Lives of Homosexual Men 1885–1967*, 2nd edition, Rivers Oram Press, London, 1998

Weeks, J. et al., *Same Sex Intimacies: Families of Choice and Other Life Experiments*, Routledge, London, 2001

West, C. 'Why I'm marching in Washington', in D. Carbado ed., *Black Men on Race, Gender, and Sexuality: A Critical Reader*, New York University Press, New York and London, 1999a

——— *The Cornel West Reader*, Basic Civitas Books, New York, 1999b

——— 'On Black-Brown relations', in C. West ed., *The Cornel West Reader*, Basic Civitas Books, New York, 1999c

——— 'Conversation with bell hooks', in *The Cornel West Reader*, Basic Civitas Books, New York, 1999d

Wetherell, M. and Edley, N. 'Gender practices: steps in the analysis of men and masculinities', in K. Henwood et al. eds, *Standpoints and Differences: Essays in the Practice of Feminist Psychology*, Sage, London, 1998

White, E.F. 'The price of success', *The Women's Review of Books*, 21: 1, October 2003

——— *Dark Continent of Our Bodies: Black Feminism and the Politics of Respectability*, Temple University Press, Philadelphia, 2001

White, M. 'Men's culture, the men's movement, and the constitution of men's lives', in C. McLean et al. eds, *Men's Ways of Being*, Westview Press, Boulder, CO, 1996

White, S. '"Did the earth move?" The hazards of bringing men and masculinities into gender and development', *IDS Bulletin*, 31: 2, 2000

Whittle, S. 'Gender fucking or fucking gender?', in R. Ekins and D. King eds, *Blending Genders: Social Aspects of Cross-Dressing and Sex Changing*, Routledge, London, 1996

Wiegman, R. 'Object lessons: men, masculinity and the sign women', *Signs*, 26: 2, Winter 2001a

——— 'Women's studies: interdisciplinary imperatives', *Feminist Studies*, 27: 2, Summer 2001b

Wienke, C. 'Negotiating the male body: men, masculinity, and cultural ideals', *The Journal of Men's Studies*, 6: 3, Spring 1998

Willett, G. Review of *A Sydney Gaze: The Making of Gay Liberation*, *Arena Magazine*, August 1999

Williams, C. 'Feminist Theory: Psychoanalytic', *International Encyclopedia of the Social & Behavioural Sciences*, N. Smelser and P. Baltes editors-in-chief, Elsevier, New York and Oxford, 2001 (www.iesbs.com)

Williams, C. ed., *Doing 'Women's Work': Men in Nontraditional Occupations*, Sage, London, 1993

Willis, E. *The Sociological Quest: An Introduction to the Study of Social Life*, 4th edition, Allen & Unwin, Sydney, 2004

Wilson, E. 'Is transgression transgressive?', in S. Kemp and J. Squires eds, *Feminisms*, Oxford University Press, Oxford and New York, 1997

Wilton, T. 'Which one's the man? The heterosexualisation of lesbian sex', in D. Richardson ed., *Theorising Heterosexuality*, Open University Press, Buckingham, 1996

Winant, H. 'Gayatri Spivak on the politics of the Subaltern' (Interview), *Socialist Review*, 20: 3, July–September 1990

Wolf, N. *Misconceptions: Truth, Lies and the Unexpected on the Journey to Motherhood*, Doubleday, New York, 2001

—— *'Fire with Fire: The New Female Power and How it Will Change the 21st Century*, Chatto & Windus, London, 1994

—— 'Let's get real about feminism: the backlash, the myths, the movement', *MS*, iv: 2, September–October 1993

—— *The Beauty Myth*, Vintage, London, 1990

Wollstonecraft, M. *Vindication of the Rights of Women* [1792], Penguin, Harmondsworth, 1978

Wootten, N. 'The men's movement and men's studies: a study of the literature', *RQ*, 33: 2, Winter 1993

Wuthnow, J. 'Deleuze in the postcolonial: on nomads and indigenous politics', *Feminist Theory*, 3: 2, 2002

Wylie, G. 'Women's rights and "righteous war": an argument for women's autonomy in Afghanistan', *Feminist Theory*, 4: 2, 2003

Yorke, L. *Adrienne Rich: Passion, Politics and the Body*, Sage, London, Thousand Oaks, CA, and New Delhi, 1997

Young, I. 'Lived body vs gender: reflections on social structure and subjectivity', *Ratio*, 15: 4, December 2002

—— *Intersecting Voices: Dilemmas of Gender, Political Philosophy and Policy*, Princeton University Press, Princeton, NJ, 1997a

—— 'Gender as seriality', in *Intersecting Voices: Dilemmas of Gender, Political Philosophy and Policy*, Princeton University Press, Princeton, NJ, 1997b

—— 'Is male gender identity the cause of male domination?', in D. Meyers ed., *Feminist Social Thought: A Reader*, Routledge, New York and London, 1997c

Yudkin, M. 'Transsexualism and women: a critical perspective', *Feminist Studies*, 4: 3, 1978

Zastoupil, L. *John Stuart Mill and India*, Stanford University Press, Stanford, CA, 1994

Zaleswski, M. et al. (contributors) 'Beyond sex and gender: the future of women's studies', in *Feminist Theory*, 4: 3, 2003

Zicklin, G. Review of *Sissies and Tomboys*, *Signs*, 27: 4, Summer 2002

Zook, K. 'A manifesto of sorts for a Black Feminist Movement', *New York Times*, 12 November, 1995

Index

Page numbers followed by an asterisk (*) refer to items in the glossary

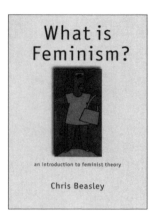